The Epistemological Spectrum

The Epistemological Spectrum

At the Interface of Cognitive Science and Conceptual Analysis

David Henderson and Terence Horgan

OXFORD
UNIVERSITY PRESS

OXFORD
UNIVERSITY PRESS

Great Clarendon Street, Oxford OX2 6DP

Oxford University Press is a department of the University of Oxford.
It furthers the University's objective of excellence in research, scholarship,
and education by publishing worldwide in

Oxford New York

Auckland Cape Town Dar es Salaam Hong Kong Karachi
Kuala Lumpur Madrid Melbourne Mexico City Nairobi
New Delhi Shanghai Taipei Toronto

With offices in

Argentina Austria Brazil Chile Czech Republic France Greece
Guatemala Hungary Italy Japan Poland Portugal Singapore
South Korea Switzerland Thailand Turkey Ukraine Vietnam

Oxford is a registered trade mark of Oxford University Press
in the UK and in certain other countries

Published in the United States
by Oxford University Press Inc., New York

© David Henderson and Terence Horgan 2011

The moral rights of the author have been asserted
Database right Oxford University Press (maker)

First published 2011

All rights reserved. No part of this publication may be reproduced,
stored in a retrieval system, or transmitted, in any form or by any means,
without the prior permission in writing of Oxford University Press,
or as expressly permitted by law, or under terms agreed with the appropriate
reprographics rights organization. Enquiries concerning reproduction
outside the scope of the above should be sent to the Rights Department,
Oxford University Press, at the address above

You must not circulate this book in any other binding or cover
and you must impose the same condition on any acquirer

British Library Cataloguing in Publication Data
Data available

Library of Congress Cataloging in Publication Data
Data available

Typeset by SPI Publisher Services, Pondicherry, India
Printed in Great Britain
on acid-free paper by
MPG Books Group, Bodmin and King's Lynn

ISBN 978-0-19-960854-6

10 9 8 7 6 5 4 3 2 1

To our wives, Marianne McHann and Dianne Horgan.

Acknowledgements

Portions of this book draw on earlier work, typically significantly revised and edited here. We thank the publishers of the following work for their permission to draw on these earlier presentations:

David Henderson and Terry Horgan, 'The Ins and Outs of Transglobal Reliabilism,' in Sanford Goldberg (ed.), *Internalism and Externalism in Semantics and Epistemology*, New York: Oxford University Press (2007), pp. 100–130.

David Henderson and Terry Horgan, 'What Does It Take to Be a True Believer? Against the Opulent Ideology of Eliminative Materialism,' in C. Erneling and D. Johnson, (eds), *Mind as a Scientific Object: Between Brain and Culture*, Oxford: Oxford University Press (2003), pp. 211–224.

David Henderson and Terry Horgan, 'The A Priori Isn't All It Is Cracked Up To Be, But It Is Something,' *Philosophical Topics* (2001), pp. 219–50.

David Henderson and Terry Horgan, 'Practicing Safe Epistemology,' *Philosophical Studies* 102 (2001), pp. 227–58.

David Henderson and Terry Horgan, 'What is A Priori, and What is it Good For?' *Southern Journal of Philosophy: The Role of the A Priori (and of the A Posteriori) in Epistemology*, Spindel Conference Supplement, 38 (2000), pp. 51–86.

David Henderson and Terry Horgan, 'Iceberg Epistemology.' *Philosophy and Phenomenological Research* 61 (2000), pp. 497–535.

David Henderson, Terry Horgan, and Matjaž Potrč, 'Transglobal Evidentialism-Reliablism,' *Acta Analytica* 22 (2007), pp. 281–300.

David Henderson and Terry Horgan, 'Would You Really Rather Be Lucky Than Good? On the Normative Status of Naturalizing Epistemology,' in Chase Wrenn (ed.), *Naturalism, Reference and Ontology: Essays in Honor of Roger F. Gibson*, New York: Peter Lang Publishing (2008) pp. 47–76.

Contents

1. An Overview — 1
2. Grades of A Priori Justification — 11
3. Neoclassical Reliabilism — 61
4. Transglobal Reliabilism — 95
5. Defending Transglobal Reliabilism — 134
6. Epistemic Competence and the Call to Naturalize Epistemology — 163
7. An Expanded Conception of Epistemically Relevant Cognitive Processes: the Role of Morphological Content — 195
8. Iceberg Epistemology: Vindicating and Transforming Some Traditional Accounts of Justification — 239

Bibliography — 281
Index — 289

Detailed Contents

1. An Overview	1
1. A retentive revisionary account	1
2. Assembling the pieces	6
2. Grades of A Priori Justification	11
1. The high-grade a priori: the full package	12
2. Rationalist and empiricist variations	15
3. Some common ground and an orientation for the investigation	21
4. Toward the low-grade a priori	24
5. The reciprocal two-stage model of philosophical reflection	32
6. Conclusion	59
3. Neoclassical Reliabilism	61
1. The agenda	61
2. A fake-barn scenario: Athena and Fortuna	63
3. Local reliability versus global reliability	64
4. Local reliability, global reliability, and the fake-barn scenarios	66
5. Global reliability as a robust disposition	68
6. Safety: a constitutive requirement for justification	70
7. Modulation	73
8. Safety as constituted by global reliability under suitable modulational control	78
9. Applying the account to the cases	79
10. Local reliability as a constitutive desideratum for justification	81
11. Brain lesions and clairvoyants	83
12. The generality problem	89
13. Summary: the neoclassical version of standard reliabilism	94
4. Transglobal Reliabilism	95
1. Epistemic safety without neoclassical reliability: the new evil demon problem	95
2. Neoclassical reliability without epistemic safety: Ashley the 'Valley girl'	100
3. Analogues of the Athena/Fortuna contrast	103
4. Experiential safety versus de facto safety	107
5. Transglobal reliabilism characterized	108
6. Transglobal reliabilism elaborated	109
7. Applying the central idea to the cases	127

8. Knowledge	131
9. Summary: replacing neoclassical reliabilism by transglobal reliabilism	132

5. Defending Transglobal Reliabilism — 134

1. Overview	134
2. The problem of infinities	135
3. Epistemic safety, postclassical reliability, and the truth connection	139
4. Key purposes served by the concept of epistemic justification	141
5. Knowledge and the dual pull	150
6. Comparative theoretical advantages	152
7. Summary: the case for transglobal reliabilism	160

6. Epistemic Competence and the Call to Naturalize Epistemology — 163

1. Engineering for truth-seeking	164
2. Systematizing epistemic normativity: a priori aspects and richly empirical aspects	168
3. Tractability: ought implies can	171
4. Idealization and epistemic competence	173
5. Epistemic competence and the meliorative dimension of epistemology	177
6. Epistemic competence and the E-spectrum	180
7. Toward a theory of epistemic competence	183
8. Some relevant work in cognitive science	189
9. Conclusion	194

7. An Expanded Conception of Epistemically Relevant Cognitive Processes: The Role of Morphological Content — 195

1. Overview	195
2. Transglobal reliabilism and evidence-sensitivity: a bridge	196
3. Reliabilism, evidential support and the being/having distinction	200
4. A proto-theory of human belief-generating and belief-sustaining processes	203
5. Examples of commitment to PT	205
6. Variants on PT	210
7. The frame problem and its morals for human belief-fixation	214
8. PT rejected	221
9. Dynamical cognition and morphological content	223
10. The causal role of morphological content: epistemically appropriate mirroring	227
11. Traditional epistemology, informational demands, and real cognitive competence	236
12. Summary	237

8. Iceberg Epistemology: Vindicating and Transforming Some Traditional
   Accounts of Justification   239
   1. Two complementary foci in epistemology   239
   2. Traditional accounts of the structure of justification   240
   3. Iceberg epistemology and its revisionary consequences   258
   4. Summary   279

Bibliography   281
Index   289

List of Abbreviations

AI	Aritificial Intelligence, first mentioned on p. 211
CGR	Conceptually grounded reflection, p. 22
DC	Dynamical cognition, p. 225
EPS	Epistemic psychological system, p. 259
JTB	Justified true belief, p. 41
PT	Proto theory, p. 204
PT-oi	Proto theory-occurrent isomorphism, p. 210
PT-p	Proto theory-proceduralization, p. 212

1
An Overview

1 A retentive revisionary account

This book argues for several dramatic breaks with the epistemological tradition, while also arguing for significant continuity with epistemology as it has come to be practiced. The result is a resounding 'yes-and-no' to several elements of both the epistemological tradition and recent trends in the discipline—as we seek to draw from various traditions and trends, while 'going between' the commonly conceived epistemological alternatives at important junctures. Our position is not merely some convenient compromise; we do not merely fold together moderate elements of competing positions into some 'reasonable' hybrid. Ours is not the basis for a 'negotiated settlement,' as if philosophy were subject to diplomatic trade-offs between parties to a dispute. Instead, we advance principled arguments that open up certain hitherto unacknowledged alternatives. Then, when reflecting on traditionally competing positions with these new alternatives in view, we argue that a 'yes-and-no' response to various familiar positions is called for. The result is both a retentive and a revisionary account of various matters: (i) of the character of a priori reflective inquiry, (ii) of conceptual analysis as a form of a priori inquiry and as a cornerstone of philosophical methodology, (iii) of reliabilism, (iv) of epistemological internalism and epistemological externalism, (v) of epistemically relevant, evidence-sensitive, cognitive processes, (vi) of both epistemic foundationalism and coherentism, and (vii) of the role of a priori, a posteriori, and empirical elements within epistemological theorizing itself.

1.1 A priori reflective inquiry

Traditionally it has been supposed that there is a distinctive route to epistemic justification: a priori reflection, which supposedly yields a kind of justification untainted by empirical considerations. Recently, some in philosophy have denied outright that there is any such thing as the a priori (often parading this denial under the banner of 'naturalized epistemology'). We will argue, to the contrary, that there is indeed a priori inquiry, justification, and knowledge. But we will also provide a revisionary account: although a priori inquiry has many of the key features traditionally associated with it—features that are central to and distinctive of the a priori as traditionally conceived—nevertheless such inquiry also has a subtle but essential empirical dimension. Contrary to the full-fledged traditional conception, a priori inquiry in philosophy is tainted by empirical considerations. We call this kind of reflective inquiry *low-grade* a priori, thereby acknowledging that it does not fully conform to the traditional understanding (which we then call high-grade a priori). We will not argue that all a priori knowledge is low-grade a priori—rather, we maintain that much of it is, particularly that which characteristically arises from philosophical reflection.

1.2 Conceptual analysis and its role in philosophy

Conceptual analysis traditionally has been regarded both as a central component of philosophical method, and as a priori. Recently, however, some philosophers have insisted either (following Quine) that there are no conceptually grounded necessary truths at all (and hence nothing for conceptual analysis to deliver), or that the semantics of concepts is not susceptible to reflective analysis (because semantics is external). Repudiations of conceptual analysis often have been advanced under the banner of naturalized epistemology, as have repudiations of the a priori. Our position, on the contrary, is that conceptual analysis is central to philosophy. There is a form of reflective inquiry into the workings of philosophically interesting concepts and terms that has many of the key features central to and distinctive of conceptual analysis as traditionally conceived—including the feature of being a priori in a certain way, and the feature of yielding (when successful) conceptually grounded necessary truths. But, contrary to traditional ways of conceiving conceptual analysis within philosophy, this kind of inquiry is not free of empirical considerations; i.e. since it possesses a subtle empirical dimension, it is low-grade a priori.

1.3 Reliabilism, as a general approach to objective epistemic justification

Some espouse the reliability of belief-forming processes as the key feature of objective epistemic justification, while others deny this. We will argue that one can only understand the significance of reliability for epistemic evaluation when one distinguishes multiple kinds of reliability and manages to identify the place of each in evaluative epistemic concepts such as the concept of knowledge and the concept of epistemic justification. Reliability in the production of true belief is relative to a reference class of an environment or environments. Distinct forms of reliability turn on different reference classes of environments. A particularly narrow reference class might be the actual local environment which a given agent happens to inhabit for a time. (Think of discussions of fake-barn scenarios as specifying such a local environment.) This sort of reliability, which we term *local* reliability, is not the concern in most epistemological discussions of objective epistemic justification. Commonly, talk of reliability is best understood as concerning reliability relative not just to the local environment that the agent encounters in a single episode, but generally the set of environments that an agent might readily encounter in the wider environment inhabited—the agent's global environment. We term this *global* reliability.[1] We will discuss considerations that have led philosophers to think that objective epistemic justification turns on global reliability. However, we will ultimately argue instead for the epistemological significance of yet another kind of reliability: reliability relative to experientially relevant possible global environments. These are the environments that are compatible with one's having experiences of roughly the character of those actually had by typical human epistemic agents—for example, an environment in which beings who are experientially much like humans are all envatted brains. The significance of this highly robust form of reliability, which we term *transglobal* reliability, has been largely overlooked.

The epistemological attraction of global reliability, and the ultimate place for transglobal reliability in an understanding of epistemically justified belief, turn on the kind of epistemic *safety* that is afforded by processes with a robust form of reliability. Global reliability is more robust than local, and transglobal reliability is more robust than global. We will elucidate the roles of epistemic safety and robustness in the concept of epistemic justification.[2]

1.4 Externalism versus internalism in epistemology

Associated with debates concerning reliabilism are more general debates about externalism vs. internalism in epistemology. Roughly and generically, internalists about some epistemic characteristic (for example, epistemic justification) hold that the characteristic at issue turns wholly on matters that are 'internally accessible' to the epistemic agent having or lacking that characteristic. That is, the reflective agent can accurately gauge it purely by introspection. Thus, an internalist holds that whether one is objectively epistemically justified in one's beliefs turns on matters that are accessible. Insofar as being justified requires that one not only have adequate contentful support for the belief in question, but also that one fixes the belief on that basis and in 'the right way,' internalism about being objectively justified has always been implausible. The character of one's own epistemic processes (at the level of causal detail that can be epistemically relevant) is not a matter that is relevantly accessible. A less ambitious

---

[1] Our use of the expressions 'local reliability' and 'global reliability' is different from that of Goldman (1986). Goldman's 'local reliability' is the tendency of a process to produce true beliefs with just a single content—for example, that yonder is a barn—while his 'global reliability' is the tendency of a process to produce true beliefs generally—for example, beliefs regarding the color of salient objects.

[2] We should note at the outset that the form of epistemic safety that emerges from our reflections, the one associated with transglobal reliability and that we argue is necessary for objectively justificatory cognitive processes, is different from what is called 'epistemic safety' by writers such as Sosa (1999, 2000, 2007) and Pritchard (2005). The epistemic safety that concerns these writers is a matter of how easily a particular belief—one with just that content, produced as it is, in just that situation—could have been false. Ours is a matter of the general reliability of cognitive processes in a wide range of experientially possible global environments. It turns out that epistemological evaluations are sensitive to both forms of safety, although in different ways—a matter we return to in section 6.3 of Chapter 5.

internalist might settle for internalism about one's grounds of justification, holding that at least the grounds themselves (and typically also the fact that they *are* grounds for the given belief), are (and must be) accessible. Beliefs and perceptual experiences—states of the agent commonly taken to constitute the evidential basis for other beliefs—are often thought to be relatively clear cases of internally accessible states.

On the other hand, externalists about an epistemic characteristic hold that it turns at least in part on matters that are not internally accessible. Thus, externalists hold that being justified in a belief turns, at least in part, on matters that are not internally accessible. The reliability of a process in the actual global environment is a paradigmatic externalist virtue. The agent may have evidence for the global reliability of a given process, but this feature is not internally accessible. Even which processes are in play in the production of a belief is not always accessible.

We will repudiate internalism both about being objectively justified and about the grounds or support for one's belief—that is, we will deny that the information on which an epistemic agent relies in a stretch of epistemically justificatory cognition need all be internally accessible. We nonetheless will respect and accommodate a judgment on which many internalists have relied in arguing against externalists: the persistent judgment that one could possess objectively justified beliefs even were one unlucky enough to be in a Cartesian situation (e.g. a lifelong brain-in-vat situation) in which one's belief-forming processes are not globally reliable. On our account, in such cases, objective justification would derive largely from transglobal reliability—a feature that belief-forming processes can possess even in the absence of global reliability (i.e. reliability within the agent's actual global environment).

1.5 The range and character of epistemically relevant, evidence-sensitive, cognitive processes

One can have justification for a belief without being justified in holding that belief. (In other words, one can have propositional justification for a belief without having doxastic justification for it.) To be justified, a belief must arise or be sustained in an appropriate way, a way commonly characterized by saying that the belief must be held because of the reasons that provide evidential support for it. This way of drawing the distinction between being justified and having justification suggests several fairly traditional epistemological questions: what kinds of information are possessed by agents in a manner that makes for evidential support (and propositional justification), and what is it for belief-forming processes to be sensitive to items in this range of information (and their support relations) in a way that makes for doxastic justification? (While such questions may seem rather foreign to the reliabilist approach just advertized, we will argue that they are not; on the contrary, the demand for transglobal reliability can only be met by cognitive processes featuring certain forms of sensitivity to evidential-support relations.) In the debates over the structure of doxastic justification, we will argue, there are certain commonly made assumptions concerning the psychological features that belief-forming processes must exhibit in order for an epistemic agent to count as being justified. They are roughly these: (1) the evidential support for a given belief-state must be explicitly represented by occurrent psychological states, (2) these states must be consciously accessible, and (3) they also must causally generate and sustain the belief-state. We will call these common assumptions into question, largely on the basis of considerations drawn from recent cognitive science and associated with the so-called 'frame problem.' Then, we will use this insight to argue that there are two important and complementary foci in epistemology: (1) consciously accessible aspects of belief-fixing processes, and (2) aspects of belief-fixing processes that (i) are not consciously accessible and (ii) implicitly accommodate much epistemically relevant information without explicitly representing it (even unconsciously) during belief fixation. We call this dual-perspective orientation *iceberg epistemology*, in view of the important differences between epistemic processes that are psychologically 'exposed' and those that are not.[3]

1.6 Foundationalism and coherentism in epistemology

Standardly, foundationalism and coherentism are seen as directly competing accounts of the structure of justification for empirical beliefs. A very different picture emerges within iceberg epistemology. We will argue that this dual-focus approach to epistemology can and should accommodate key themes from both foundationalism and coherentism; the apparent tension between them largely dissolves. Roughly, foundationalist themes apply to aspects of justification involving consciously accessible psychological states that figure as *articulable* reasons for belief (the exposed tip of the iceberg), whereas coherentist themes apply to the epistemic iceberg as a whole.

1.7 The role of a priori, a posteriori, and empirical elements in epistemological theorizing

The preceding paragraphs characterize some of the more unorthodox elements of the position to be developed in this book. They all take root in a very general approach to epistemology that structures the book as a whole, an approach that is simultaneously moderate and revisionary. The moderate aspect is the view that epistemology (along with philosophy generally) is a mixed discipline, having both a priori and a posteriori elements. This is intermediate between two extreme positions: on one hand, the historically dominant view that epistemology is wholly a priori, and on the other hand the view of some naturalizing epistemologists that epistemology is wholly a posteriori. We develop an understanding of epistemology as oriented by a low-grade a priori understanding of central evaluative concepts. Our reflection on the concept of epistemic justification leads to the conclusion that which cognitive processes are objectively justificatory depends upon contingent facts about humans as cognitive systems. That the epistemically fitting cognitive processes are those that are transglobally reliable is a low-grade a priori discovery. On the other hand, exactly which

---

[3] An 'exposed process' is the analog of being roughly at or above the water line. The analogy is apt in that to be exposed is not to be accessed, but to be accessible. To be above the water line is to be readily visible, not necessarily to be glimpsed.

processes are suitable for humans depends on facts about human cognitive architecture, and clearly this cannot be known a priori. From this spectrum of inquiry should emerge an a priori oriented, empirically informed account of how humans ought to fix belief. Thus, we will argue, low-grade a priori reflection on the character of evaluative epistemic concepts such as objective justification leads to the conclusion that any concrete epistemological standards for objectively justificatory processes (at least significant standards beyond the most abstract and unhelpful) will need to draw on a posteriori information about the kinds of cognitive creatures that humans are, and about the kinds of cognitive capacities they possess or can come to possess with training.

2 Assembling the pieces

2.1 Four stages in developing this position

Our argument for a mixed epistemology—a naturalized epistemology in which (low-grade) a priori conceptual analysis of key epistemological concepts reveals a role for the a posteriori—proceeds in four stages.

In the first stage, our second chapter, we develop a revisionary account of one specific sort of a priori reflection that we believe to be central to much philosophy—namely conceptual analysis. This kind of a priori inquiry has subtle empirical elements rather than being a wholly non-empirical enterprise; it is low-grade a priori. We explain how the empirical element enters, and we mark this break with more traditional conceptions of the a priori by insisting that much justification and knowledge that traditionally has been considered a priori is aptly termed low-grade a priori. (We leave open the question whether a high-grade, non-empirical form of a priori inquiry might be operative in other domains of inquiry, such as pure mathematics.)

In outline, we begin with the observation that philosophical reflection commonly commences with intuitive judgments having to do with concrete scenarios. This is as it should be, we argue, for one's conceptual competence typically is much better at applying concepts to concrete cases than it is at directly yielding highly abstract, highly general, conceptually grounded necessary truths. To arrive at the sorts of general conceptually grounded necessary truths to which philosophers typically aspire, one must go beyond the direct and reasonably reliable deliverances of one's conceptual competence: one must engage in what is essentially an abductive inference—an inference to the best explanatory account of the workings of the relevant concepts *and* of one's conceptual competence. We argue that the needed abductive inference has an ineliminable empirical component.

In the second stage, Chapters 3 through 5, we engage in conceptual analysis vis-a-vis the evaluative epistemic concept of justification. This brings to light the hitherto underappreciated virtue of transglobal reliability; i.e. as conceptual analysis reveals, it is a conceptually grounded necessary truth that such robust reliability is an epistemic requirement for justification. The epistemic safety afforded by transglobal reliability figures centrally in the concept of justification. We also show that the tractability of processes for the class of epistemic agents in question must be considered when describing concretely what forms of cognition constitute epistemically justificatory competence. Such results provide low-grade a priori grounds for naturalizing epistemology—that is, for introducing a posteriori elements into it. Just which kinds of belief-forming processes exhibit these epistemic virtues is a partially a posteriori matter that depends on certain a posteriori facts about human cognitive capacities and cognitive limitations.

The respective Chapters 3 through 5 contribute to the second stage in the following ways. In our third chapter, we consider scenarios that have pointed in the direction of a reliabilist account of *being objectively justified in believing*. Here we indicate how a concern for some form of epistemic safety plausibly features in this concept, although we do not yet seek to give a final account of the relevant sort of safety. From this chapter we emerge with a plausible refined version of classical reliabilist thinking—according to which, in order to be objectively justified in holding a belief, one must have fixed that belief by way of processes that are globally reliable under what we call suitable 'modulational control.' We call this *neoclassical* reliabilism.

In the fourth chapter, we find neoclassical reliabilism to be flawed, and push beyond it to a position that we claim better captures the concern for epistemic safety associated with objective epistemic justification. The inadequacy of neoclassical reliabilism is strongly suggested by variants of the so-called 'new evil demon problem.' Discussion of such scenarios, and the general association of epistemic safety with robust reliability, leads us to settle on transglobal reliability—reliability relative to the wide reference class made up of experientially relevant possible global environments. Further scenarios reinforce the idea that modulational control remains important. Thus we conclude that, for an agent to be objectively justified in holding a belief, that belief must arise or be maintained by way of processes that are transglobally reliable under suitable modulational control. We call this *transglobal* reliabilism.

In the fifth chapter, we provide a sustained defense of the form of reliabilism just suggested. Here we bring to bear a wider set of considerations illustrating the full range of data that we argue is characteristic of low-grade a priori philosophical reflection. For example, we discuss the points and purposes of the evaluative concept of epistemic justification. We discuss certain judgment tendencies that initially seem to point in directions incompatible with transglobal reliabilism, and show how these tendencies can be accounted for by transglobal reliabilists. The overall goal is two-fold—first, to illustrate how philosophical reflection leading to transglobal reliabilism fully conforms to the model of low-grade a priori reflection advanced in Chapter 2, drawing on the range of data there indicated and involving the kind of abductive inference there discussed; second, to further elaborate the overall case for transglobal reliabilism.

The third stage in our overall argument for a mixed epistemology is the sixth chapter, where we focus on the idea that justificatory cognitive processes must be tractable. That one ought to produce and sustain beliefs in certain ways, that one ought to think in certain ways, entails that one can. Fitting epistemic standards for human epistemic agents must be sensitive to which potential belief-forming processes humans are capable of employing, at least with training. In this way we arrive, by largely low-grade a priori reflection, at a demand for naturalized epistemology. The sixth chapter clarifies this demand by elaborating upon the kind of idealized normative standards one can expect from a naturalized epistemology, and on the range of disciplines that can contribute to normative epistemology.

The sixth chapter also advances a way of thinking about naturalized epistemology as a broad spectrum of inquiry ranging from low-grade reflection about central evaluative concepts to richly empirical inquiry revealing the character of actual human cognitive processes and the possibilities for variation. The organizing principle that holds the spectrum together, as a single discipline, is the concern for a kind of engineering for truth seeking. Just as various kinds of inquiry find a place within common engineering disciplines—from reflective clarification of evaluative dimensions to empirical work on materials, systems, and resources—so likewise a wide range of inquiries can find a place within naturalized epistemology. We call the spectrum of inquiry falling within naturalized epistemology (as we conceive of it) the E-spectrum (the 'E' standing both for epistemology and for engineering).

In the fourth stage (Chapters 7 and 8), we appeal to emerging results in cognitive science to provide some far-reaching consequences concerning the cognitive processes that make for doxastic justification. Epistemologists commonly suppose that epistemological tasks can be, and are, managed by cognitive processes in which all the information bearing on a stretch of belief fixation is occurrently represented in the course of these processes. Drawing on recent work in cognitive science, we will argue that this common assumption, along with several tempting, weakened versions of it, are misguided. Taking inspiration from developments in cognitive science associated with 'the frame problem,' we will argue that an epistemologically crucial aspect of effective belief-formation involves cognitive processing that accommodates a wide range of information in an implicit way—without the information being explicitly represented in the course of processing, either consciously or unconsciously. In the seventh chapter, we will make this case.

In the eighth chapter, we will explore some of the epistemological implications of recognizing this wider set of epistemically relevant processes and states. These results make connections with traditional epistemological doctrines such as foundationalism and coherentism, salvaging certain of their themes while transforming and limiting these doctrines in important ways.

As reflected in this overview, much of our discussion in this book revolves around the concept of epistemic justification. Before proceeding to that discussion, let us remark on the distinction between objective and subjective justification—a distinction that does inform our discussion. It is commonly claimed that there are two concepts of epistemic justification: a concept of subjective justification, often said to be associated with deontological appraisals, and a concept of objective justification, often said to be associated with teleological appraisals. This is something of an oversimplification. The subjective concept does seem motivated by what appears to be a deontological concern—with whether the agent in question has 'dutifully' and conscientiously conformed to the agent's own reflective epistemological standards (or those of a social group to which the agent belongs). However, it is not at all clear that there is a determinate notion of duty in view in such evaluations. Rather, 'dutiful' performance here is understood as a matter of conformity with the individual agent's (or the community's) understanding of what ought to be done. It is not as though there is some duty, which (in the fashion of deontological ethical theory) is derivative from what is good, such that the agent conforms to this (nonteleological) duty. Rather, it is a question of whether the agent conforms to that agent's own understanding of what epistemically ought to be done—however the agent understands this. The term 'subjective justification' is clearly fitting here.

In contrast, the concept of *objective* epistemic justification turns on the idea of certain ways of reasoning being objectively appropriate—rather than merely conforming to the agent's own standards. Thus, one can judge an agent to be objectively unjustified— to be using processes that are not epistemically appropriate—even when that agent is conforming to his or her own reflective epistemic standards.

So in summary, one can think of the present book as a whole as containing two 'methods' chapters, each followed by some implementation of the methods characterized. Chapter 2 (stage one of the book) provides an account of philosophical reflection that yields low-grade a priori justification. Chapters 3 through 5 (stage two of the book) then constitute an extended case study—reflection on the concept of (objective) epistemic justification. Chapter 6 (the third stage) then constitutes the second methodological moment—characterizing naturalized epistemology in terms of the E-spectrum and a representative product, a rich theory of epistemic competence. The idea of epistemic competence is to be informed by the desiderata identified in Chapters 3 through 5. Chapters 7 and 8 (the fourth stage of the book) then provide some naturalized epistemological work—work with an intermediate focus drawing on some general ideas we find by looking over the shoulders of those doing cognitive science.

Although we ourselves regard the discussion in the second stage as implementing the low-grade a priori methodology described in the first stage, we acknowledge that those with more traditional understandings of philosophical reflection will find Chapters 3–5 approachable. Our armchair-reflective arguments in support of transglobal reliabilism could be embraced even by someone who is dubious about our own construal of philosophical reflection. On the other hand, stages two through four are logically more tightly interconnected with one another. The armchair-reflective argumentation in Chapters 3–5 yields an analysis of the concept of objective epistemic justification that includes an element (namely the notion of suitable modulational control) whose detailed elaboration is largely a matter for empirical cognitive science. This leads directly to the mixed methodology for epistemology described in the third stage (Chapter 6), which in turn sets the stage for the fourth stage (Chapters 7–8) in which ideas drawn from recent cognitive science figure heavily.

The concept of objective epistemic justification does derive significant motivation from teleological concerns—notably, from a concern for a form of goodness of beliefs, and of belief-forming processes, that is constitutively linked to systematic true belief as the desideratum, the *telos*. Because our focus in this work is largely on the concept of objective justification, we will not say much more about the subjective concept.[4]

---

[4] We do find various discussions by others helpful. Foley's (1993) treatment of egocentric rationality is one very interesting development. The discussion in the early sections of Plantinga (1993a) also provides some useful historical reconstruction.

2

Grades of A Priori Justification

All philosophers are familiar with the idea that certain claims can be justified a priori, or that certain claims express bits of a priori knowledge. Some contemporary philosophers would deny that there are any such claims, insisting that the received conception of what it would be to be a priori justifiable is not satisfied by any claim. Still, philosophers all know what it supposedly would be for a claim to be a priori justifiable. In a sentence, it is for the claim to be justifiable on the basis of reflection alone (independent of experience) by anyone who has acquired the concepts featuring in that claim. Coming on the basis of reflection alone, this would constitute a distinct form of justification, one that could be had only for select claims. It is putatively made possible simply by acquiring the relevant concepts. Such, in its rudiments, is the classical conception of the a priori. We begin with this conception, unpacked and elaborated somewhat. But we do not remain straight-jacketed by it. Instead, we argue that the associated idea that reflection is devoid of empirical dimensions is mistaken. Perhaps there are domains where the full traditional conception has some application. But it is not quite right even as an account of reflective philosophical investigation concerning the workings of philosophically important concepts, and such investigation has traditionally been thought to be a prime example of the a priori. One might, as many have, conclude that there is no a priori justification to be had, or at least that there is no such justification to be had for philosophically interesting claims. However, philosophical reflection has struck thinkers through history as distinct from empirical inquiry, and for good reason. While it may not be as wholly discontinuous from other forms of inquiry as some have thought, it has tended to turn characteristically on inquiry aimed at uncovering, essentially just via reflection, certain conceptually grounded necessary truths featuring philosophically important concepts. We believe that the relevant philosophical investigation is distinct enough (distinct in important enough ways that we will highlight here) to warrant a place in an epistemological taxonomy—a priori *after a fashion*. We ourselves maintain that the demands of the classical conception are somewhat inflated by an epistemological tradition that was nevertheless on to something of importance. Accordingly, we will recommend reconceiving the a priori somewhat—accommodating some of the classical demands within a 'retentive analysis.' Ultimately, we will urge a place for both the classical conception and a complementary, revisionary but retentive conception as well.

1 The high-grade a priori: the full package

The central idea in the classical conception is that there are certain truths that are subject to a rather distinct form of epistemic justification. Their justification can come via a special epistemic route—one that is 'not dependent on experience,' but turns on 'reflection' about the claim that is understood. This central idea—of a distinct form of justification had by reflecting on the claim being considered, reflection that turns on an understanding of the claim—has called forth repeated attempts at clarification. What is this process of reflection? How does it draw upon conceptual mastery? In what way can it be independent of experience?

Typically, those who have posited a priori truths have quickly acknowledged that understanding claims, including putatively a priori claims, commonly requires a certain characteristic background of experience. However, they draw a distinction between, on the one hand, experience playing a role in an individual's coming to be able to understand or entertain a claim, and, on the other hand, experience playing a role in an individual's justification for an understood claim. They insist that experience can play a role in an individual's acquiring the capacity to understand or entertain a claim, without being involved in that individual's justification for believing that claim. Talk of 'concepts' has traditionally entered to account for this difference in the role of experience. Experience of a certain kind is acknowledged to be necessary for acquiring certain concepts. But it is said that, having acquired these concepts, the agent can understand a claim in which they feature, and can reflect on the claim thus understood, and that the resulting reflective justification need not recur again to the particular experiences that played a role in concept acquisition. One might say that experience is 'screened off' from the justification by the conceptual understanding that it spawned. Thus, on the classical conception, experience yields concept acquisition, but it is the conceptual competence, and the resulting understanding of the claim employing those concepts, that suffices for reflective justification.[1]

On the classical conception, reflective justification is accessible to the individual epistemic agent who has acquired the relevant concepts. In keeping with tradition, to say that some informational item is accessible to an agent is (to a reasonable first

---

[1] Talk of justificatory reflection being 'accessible to anyone who has acquired the relevant concepts' can encourage one to think that a priori truths are conceptual truths—claims whose truth is fully guaranteed by the semantics of the concepts featuring in those claims. But the classical conception does not insist on this. Of course, in the empiricist tradition, one understands all a priori truths as conceptual truths of some stripe (reflecting only the relations between ideas, or expressing analytic truths, or something to this effect). But our formulation of the classical conception is intended to characterize a putative form of justification that, on its face, might be open to either empiricist or rationalist explanations of how there could be such justification. For reasons broached later, we have deep misgivings regarding the rationalist approach to the a priori, but rationalism is not ruled out of bounds by the classical conception itself.

approximation) to say that that item is available to be drawn upon in conscious cognitive processing. (In the intended sense of 'information,' an item of information need not be true. This non-success usage of the term 'information' will be the default in the present book, unless otherwise noted.) To say that some justification is accessible to certain agents is to say that such agents possess all the materials or information on which one would need to draw when undergoing processes that would give rise to, or sustain, a justified belief of the claim(s) at hand. For example, the character of an agent's own experience (or at least certain dimensions of it) is commonly thought to be accessible to that agent, since agents are thought to have an immediate 'grasp' of the character of their own experience. Undergoing the experience then provides the basis for generating judgments about that very experience, and provides or 'makes available' information that can inform myriad further justificatory inferences. Similarly, one's own beliefs are commonly thought to be accessible, as one is supposedly able to 'call to mind' one's beliefs. (Not all at once, of course, but agents are commonly thought to be able to draw upon those beliefs that are relevant and needed for the investigation at hand.) These beliefs are then thought to be available as the basis for all manner of inferential reasoning.[2] The obvious consequences of one's beliefs are also thought to be accessible—insofar as one's beliefs are accessible and the processes in virtue of which their obvious consequences can be determined are tractable—for us humans, or for the relevant cognitive system (since tractability is always tractability for cognizers of a type). Of course, to term a consequence 'obvious' is to say that the relevant processes are more than just tractable, it is to say that those processes are also particularly easy and common. The justification of the obvious consequences of one's (justified) beliefs is thus thought to be accessible. So, to say that the a priori justification for a claim is accessible to any and all who have acquired the concepts featured in the claim, and who can thus understand the claim, is to say that understanding it provides such agents with information that is sufficient to justify the claim and with the capacity to appreciate this justificatory connection, and that all this information is accessible to such agents.

Here, as in many other epistemological contexts, talk of tractable processes and accessible information involves some significant idealization, some abstracting away from limitations that may characterize an individual agent. Ultimately, the full extent of what counts as tractable inferential processes, and of what justification then counts as 'accessible' to a given agent, seems not to be determined by that individual agent's particular cognitive capacities. Instead what is tractable for an agent seems to be a matter of the general class of agents to which the agent belongs—standardly, humans constitute the type in question. Furthermore, what is tractable involves a moderate

---

[2] One's sprawling set of beliefs is supposedly a resource that can be piecemeal called upon as needed for the inquiry at hand, but it is also commonly acknowledged that this opportunistic recall is itself subject to the vicissitudes of the agent's ability to recognize which beliefs are relevant to, and need to be accommodated in, a stretch of cognition.

idealization for such agents: being determined by what processing such agents would be able to manage at their best. Again, to a first approximation, this may be thought of as a matter of what an ideally smart and conscientious finite human could manage. Thus, to say that a priori justification is accessible to agents who have acquired the relevant concepts is not to say that all who have acquired those concepts are also intelligent enough, and given to sufficiently dogged attention, that they can reflectively appreciate the justification that in some sense is 'accessible' to them. Consider: (at least a vast range of) mathematical truths are commonly supposed to be a priori justifiable. Yet the proponents of the classical conception would commonly recognize that many mathematical truths are beyond the capacities (and attention spans or motivations) of many of us. They would however insist that the justification is within the reach of at least some of the most intelligent, suitably trained, and best motivated and focused humans—and rests, for these individuals, on materials or information they possess solely by virtue of having learned the relevant concepts.

So on the classical conception, the a priori justification of certain claims is accessible to all who have acquired the featured concepts, because recognizing the truth (or necessary truth) of such a claim can be managed via a process that draws only on what is accessible by virtue of having acquired the featured concept, and that process is available to the relevant class of cognitive agents.

Furthermore, on the classical conception, experience plays no evidential role in the reflective justification of an a priori claim. As noted already, having acquired the needed concepts (perhaps by way of experience), the agent can understand a sentence in which they feature, and can reflect on the claim thus understood, and supposedly the resulting reflective justification need not recur again to the particular experiences that played a role in concept acquisition. The a priori justification is then thought to be uncontaminated by the empirical.

We will call an account of the a priori that preserves all elements of the classical conception, as set out just now, an account of the high-grade a priori.[3] Any such account is committed to three theses:

1. A priori claims are subject to a distinctive kind of justification, one that can be called justification by reflection. (A priori claims constitute an epistemically distinctive class.)

---

[3] What we are calling 'high-grade a priori' is different from what is often called 'strong' (as opposed to 'weak') a priori these days. To say that a claim is strongly a priori is to say that it is justified in a way that does not positively depend on experience, and that this justification is not subject to being undermined by subsequent experience. To say that a claim is weakly a priori is to say that it is justified in a way that does not depend positively on experience, but that this justification could be undermined by subsequent experience. Our formulation of high-grade a priori does not presuppose the sort of irrevisability thought to characterize the strong a priori. Our subsequent championing of an epistemically important place for the low-grade a priori certainly embraces a kind of weak a priori—however, it finds an even more robust place for experience in connection with a priori justification than most partisans of weak a priori justification have entertained.

2. Justification by reflection, for a given claim, is accessible to any epistemic agent who understands the claim, because it draws only upon what is accessible by having acquired the relevant concepts (and perhaps on similarly internalistically accessible—and nonperceptual—sources).[4] (The a priori is internalistically accessible.)
3. Because reflection draws only on understanding—on what is accessible by virtue of having acquired the relevant concepts and having understood the claim—it is not dependent on experience. (A priori justification is not contaminated by the empirical.)

2 Rationalist and empiricist variations

More developed accounts of the high-grade a priori differ in their understandings of the reflection posited in the generic characterization above. It is here that empiricists and rationalists have differed. Although precisely demarcating their differences can be tricky, it is standard to see one central difference between the two traditions emerging in a disagreement over whether there are synthetic a priori truths—whether there are claims whose justification can be provided by reflection alone, but whose truth is not determined by (the internalistically accessible elements of) conceptual semantics alone. Thus, empiricists and rationalists differ over what reflection can do—and, in particular, over what kinds of claims it can justify by itself and how it can manage to provide such justification.

Empiricists hold that reflection operates by tracking what is entailed by the internalistically accessible elements of the semantics of concepts. This is to say that reflection trades only on aspects of the satisfaction conditions of concepts that are individualistically accessible to anyone who has acquired the relevant concepts. On the classical (generic) conception of the high-grade a priori, experience gives rise to concepts, and in coming to possess a conceptual competence, one acquires certain minimal pieces of information (about what counts as satisfying the relevant concept, or about how the reference of the relevant concept is fixed in the actual world—details differ with differing understandings of conceptual semantics). The fundamental empiricist idea is that reflection works only by an essentially nonampliative use of this semantically given information. On such accounts, all a priori truths are conceptual truths.

On the standard way of differentiating the two traditions, rationalists believe that there are a priori justifiable synthetic truths. That is, rationalists hold that what is a priori

---

[4] This parenthetical point is intended to provide room for traditional rationalist treatments of a priori justification. The traditional rationalist believes that reflection can provide justification for synthetic a priori truths. To pull this off, the agent would need a source of information that could take one beyond what is learned in acquiring the concepts featured in the synthetic claim. Here, the rationalist commonly supposes that the agent has a capacity for a kind of 'rational insight' that allows the agent to 'see' further. (See the remarks on BonJour in the next section.) It seems that such rational insight needs to tap into information other than semantically given information, and to do so in a way that is not perceptual, and in a way that qualifies that information as accessible to the agent.

knowable is not limited to conceptual truths—rationalist reflection is advertised as (at least sometimes) providing essentially ampliative development on whatever information is acquired by virtue of having acquired the concepts featuring in the relevant claim(s). Rationalist reflection putatively somehow generates an understanding that runs beyond whatever an individual learns in acquiring the concepts, and beyond what is minimally involved in understanding the claim in question. Of course, it begins with what is given in the semantics of the concepts, but it purports to see further than that.[5] (Some readers may consider themselves rationalists, and yet not be committed to there being a priori truths that are not conceptually grounded. We believe that little really hangs on the terminology here. Self-proclaimed rationalists of this sort would be committed to some variant of what we ourselves term the empiricist position.)

In the present section we characterize the traditional positions as a preliminary to presenting our own understanding of an important kind of a priori justification. Doing so helps to situate our position. We do express certain misgivings regarding rationalist aspirations. But we do not here seek to decisively repudiate rationalism. The misgivings help to explain why we seek to develop our position without requiring the supposition that agents have recourse to rational insight of the sort that the rationalists have typically posited. The resulting account is naturally seen as falling roughly in the empiricist tradition—since it characterizes a kind of justificatory reflective inquiry that has to do with conceptually grounded necessary truths. Strictly speaking, however, our account is neutral in the dispute between rationalists and empiricists: since rationalists would also recognize conceptually grounded necessary truths as a priori knowable (they insist that such truths constitute a proper subset of what is a priori knowable), our account is not strictly incompatible with rationalism. Where we differ from most rationalists—and most empiricists, for that matter—is as follows. Most rationalists and empiricists have sought an account of a priori justification that conforms to the full package of doctrines set out in the previous section. They have sought to characterize high-grade a priori justification. In this chapter we characterize a low-grade kind of a priori justification. We do not insist that there are no claims subject to high-grade a priori justification—we remain largely agnostic on this matter. However, we do suggest that many philosophically interesting generalizations are best understood as low-grade a priori instead. This said, the way remains open for either rationalist or empiricist philosophers to make the case for high-grade a priori justification—as long as it is recognized as not having application where our account of low-grade a priori justification

---

[5] It is reasonable to suppose that 'seeing further' than conceptually grounded necessary truths—that seeing that certain synthetic a priori truths are indeed necessarily true—would require a source of information that runs beyond conceptual competence. One might then worry that our formulation in three clauses of the traditional conception of a priori justification is overly narrow, as it would rule out traditional rationalist conceptions. We have incorporated a parenthetical provision for such sources in our formulation of the second clause of our summary characterization. The central idea represented in the second clause is that the relevant justificatory processes and information are internalistically accessible to agents—and rationalist hand-waving in the direction of rational insight certainly intends to point to a nonperceptual process fitting the bill.

is better applied. Such philosophers should then want to think of our account as a supplement to their own. Of course, to the extent that there are processes that give rise to high-grade a priori justification, one should ultimately wish to incorporate a complementary account of these into a more developed account than can be produced here. While our account is compatible with there being high-grade a priori justification of either the empiricist or rationalist variety, it may be thought of as competing with the traditional accounts in this limited respect: some reflection that others have traditionally thought high-grade a priori, we ourselves claim to be low-grade a priori instead, and to the extent that our own account is widely applicable, it there supplants more traditional aspirations for high-grade a priori justification.

The standard way of characterizing rationalism and empiricism has ample basis in the history of philosophy. Hume, for example, famously distinguished relations of ideas, which he took to be all that could be justified merely by reflection, from matters of fact, which required more than reflection alone for their justification. The reflective justification of claims expressing the relations of ideas, could involve an active cognitive inquiry in which one might decompose various ideas and compare the contained ideas. One could express the results by saying that what would count as the one sort of thing would count as the other. Or, in a somewhat more material mode, one could simply note that anything that is a such-and-such also must be a this-and-that. But, whatever was done in coming to this reflective understanding of the relation of ideas, would not take one further. It would not take one beyond the 'what would count as' sort of claim—or beyond the mirroring material-mode articulations of such claims.

For example, by reflection, one supposedly could come to see that the idea of causation included the idea of spatio-temporal contiguity. This allowed one to see that those ideas were such that whatever pair of events satisfied the first would also satisfy the other. Whatever would count as the cause of a given event would need to be spatio-temporally contiguous with that event, or be connected to it by a chain of spatio-temporally contiguous events. This formal mode, 'what would count as what,' sort of claim—this claim about the character of our ideas—was mirrored by a material-mode claim that formulated the corresponding conceptually grounded necessary truth: all events that are related as cause and effect are either spatio-temporally contiguous or mediated by chains of spatio-temporally contiguous events. This material-mode claim supposedly employs just those accessible elements of the semantics of the concept CAUSATION that the formal-mode claim purportedly describes. It is then thought to be a priori and not to outstrip the formal-mode claim concerning what would count as what. It does not ensure, for example, that everything comes about by being caused—that all events are caused in the sense described. Such additional claims seem the aspired province of the rationalist.[6]

---

[6] It is worth noting that the prominent contemporary rationalist BonJour insists that Kant is not a rationalist, but is rather an empiricist. He charges that Kant really does not provide for synthetic a priori truths, because the claims Kant ultimately describes in such terms never address how things must be in the world (BonJour 1998, pp. 20–6).

To mention another example of the limited sort of claim that empiricists would allow as a priori, supposedly one might know by reflection that what would satisfy the concept GOD would also satisfy the concept all-powerful being. But, nothing here showed that there was a God. It was the rationalist—in the paradigmatic person of Descartes—who thought that one might arrive at a justification of such claims by reflection. In doing so, reflection would have to do more than simply discover what one's concepts are like and how they are related. Somehow it would need to allow one to see that the world must contain things that satisfy certain of one's concepts or ideas: that God exists, and that there are minds and bodies (and Descartes would even insist that he had reflective justification for the claim that they are distinct). Of course, it has long been common to talk in terms of concepts rather than ideas, but the general contrast remains: for the empiricist, reflection works by actively drawing only on accessible information about the semantics of the concepts themselves, and reflection does not take one beyond what is conceptually grounded truth, whereas rationalist reflection purports to do more.

Rationalism continues to find articulate and forceful voices in epistemology (witness BonJour,1998). Again, rationalist reflection is thought of as taking one beyond registering the implications of whatever elements of conceptual semantics are learned by anyone acquiring the relevant concepts; on BonJour's telling, it can track necessary relations between properties, relations that are not matters of such elements of 'meaning.' According to BonJour, an agent who has acquired the concepts and understood the claims can reflectively grasp (or make a good faith effort to grasp) the intrinsic relations between the properties that are themselves referred to in the claim under consideration. When all goes as it should, the sufficiently conscientious and nondogmatic person is supposed to be able to just directly 'see' that the claim in question is (necessarily) true by virtue of a metaphysical necessitation-relation between the relevant properties. It is this 'seeing' (or at least seeming to see) that the properties in question are thus related that makes for the justification.[7] Repudiating BonJour's rationalist story about high-grade a priori justification is not necessary for purposes of providing an empiricist account of a type of reflection yielding a low-grade a priori form of justification. Still, there is much to find puzzling in the rationalist model. Perhaps by way of background explanation for our developing our own account in terms of conceptually grounded necessary truths, and of our not supposing or positing rational insight into synthetic a priori truths, we should at least mention what we find most mysterious and troubling about the rationalist aspirations. The rationalist must posit a capacity for insight that at some crucial point goes beyond reflection on the internally accessible elements of

---

[7] Particularly interesting, as a challenge to empiricists, is the line of argument developed in 'In Search of Moderate Empiricism' (BonJour 1998, chapter 2). BonJour argues that even one's justification for putatively analytic truths turns on a rationalist insight—so that those in the empiricist tradition who have some place for a priori truths are committed to a species of rationalist insight.

the semantics of concepts—'insight that is not somehow reducible to the reflections on meaning,' as BonJour (1998, fn 16, p. 42) insists. He writes that, against a background of understanding the claim, one reflects on the properties and sees immediately how they must be related.[8] But, just what is the information on which such reflection is supposed to draw in tracking metaphysical-necessitation relations between properties? Reflection is supposedly accessible to all who have acquired the concepts referring to the relevant properties. So part of the story could be that reflection draws on whatever must be learned in acquiring the concepts. But this cannot be the whole basis, since the rationalist is claiming that insight takes one beyond what can be gotten from that alone. What must be learned by anyone acquiring a concept is presumably a conceptual truth, and rationalist reflection is purported to take one beyond such truths. But, on what other information can reflection draw? Of course, one acquires further information in the course of an experientially mediated engagement with things in the world possessing the relevant properties. But, reflection supposedly cannot recur to such information while still delivering (high-grade) a priori truths, since this would be tantamount to appealing to experience. In any case, the range of such information accessible to epistemic agents varies in ways that would then make for an inappropriate variation in what is a priori knowable. So the rationalist must posit a source of information that is neither conceptual nor experiential—something like a direct (non-experientially-mediated) grasp of the relevant properties. The picture seems to be as follows. By way of experience, an agent acquires concepts (the concepts of this and that property). But reflection (or 'insight') can take one beyond merely echoing such limited semantics—to synthetic a priori truths. In doing this, it makes no use of experience. Rather, it somehow grasps the properties themselves. (At least this is what reflection can supposedly do, when unclouded by 'dogmatism.') Frankly, we find this picture very mysterious.

---

[8] BonJour insists that, when all is working right, one who (a) considers the appropriate claims with reasonable care, (b) possesses the concept of metaphysical necessity, and (c) 'grasps' or 'possesses an adequate conception of' the relevant properties, can (d) see that the claims are necessary truths. The crucial question is just what is encompassed in (c)—'grasping' or 'possessing an adequate conception' of the properties at issue. Is rational insight to manage this, while standing on the shoulders of individualistically accessible conceptual semantics—drawing on such semantics while looking somewhat beyond it? This 'seeing' which amounts to getting information from something other than the accessible semantics (and other than from experience) is just what we ourselves find a deep and troubling mystery. There are those who would like to read BonJour as not needing any such source of new information. Albert Casullo once urged us to read BonJour as having less demanding aspirations for rationalist insight. It would be convenient to see BonJour as thinking of rationalist insight as just a matter of having acquired a deep appreciation for aspects of conceptual semantics. But this overlooks precisely the rationalist element in his position—the insistence on insight not being reducible to reflections on meaning. On the softer reading of BonJour, he qualifies as an empiricist (who is helping himself to an as yet ill-specified understanding of conceptual semantics). BonJour then adds that, in rationalist insight, one's use of conceptually ensured information has the phenomenology of an immediate judgment. We doubt that this soft reading of BonJour is one with which he would be comfortable.

For our purposes in this chapter (and book), we need not ultimately repudiate rationalism, since it purports to characterize one kind of high-grade a priori justification—where reflection must conform to the classical conception as set out above, and the rationalist form of such reflection must involve grasping metaphysical-necessitation relations that are not mere conceptually grounded necessary truths. Perhaps there are cases in which high-grade a priori justification can be had, and also cases in which the rationalist kind can be had. We do not pursue these matters here. We do argue that much philosophical reflection, much that is rightly thought to give rise to a kind of a priori justification, has not fully conformed to the classical conception—yet is low-grade a priori. Still, the doubts about rationalism, such as those just expressed, may help the reader to understand why we develop our account of the low-grade a priori so that it remains recognizably in the empiricist tradition: it purports to characterize a distinctive form of justification for claims that are conceptually grounded necessary truths, a form of justification accessible to agents by virtue of having acquired the concepts featured in the truths. In order to provide and defend our account, we need not insist that there are not other forms of reflective justification that are rationalist in character. We can remain agnostic for two reasons. First, our central contention is that there is a respectable notion of low-grade a priori justification complementing that of the high-grade a priori, and this indicates that we are open to the suggestion that a priori justification is somewhat heterogeneous—our central argument does not depend on showing that there is no rationalist insight delivering high-grade a priori justification. Second, while we develop our account of the low-grade a priori in terms that would fit comfortably within the empiricist tradition (since it is an account of the reflective justification of conceptually grounded necessary truths), we need not decisively eliminate the idea that there is some kind of rationalist insight at work behind the reflective processes we describe. That is, we need not decisively repudiate BonJour's suggestion that rationalist insight ultimately must inform even one's appreciation of conceptually grounded necessary truths. We have our misgivings regarding rationalist insight, expressed above. But little that we say turns on there not being some rationalist insight at work here. Should it turn out (somewhat implausibly, we think) that rationalist insight must come into play in one's appreciation of even the most rudimentary conceptually grounded truths—for example, the truth that capacitors store electrical charge—then such insight would doubtless come into play at points in the more elaborate reflective inquiry that we describe in this chapter. That would then be a dimension of such reflection that we omit from our account—but it would not be a dimension that we are committed to repudiating. (Importantly, it would not conflict with recognizing the empirical dimension that we argue characterizes much philosophical reflection.) Put simply, even a rationalist could allow that the account we now give of the reflective justification of conceptually grounded necessary truths correctly characterizes an epistemically distinct route to the justification of beliefs in such truths.

3 Some common ground and an orientation for the investigation

A point of agreement between rationalists and empiricists provides a landmark from which to orient. Rationalists and empiricists may differ regarding the scope or extent of a priori knowledge and justification. They may differ over whether there are a priori truths that are not merely conceptually grounded necessary truths—truths whose justification can be gotten merely by tracking internally accessible elements of the semantics of featured concepts—but they agree that such truths would be a priori justifiable. They agree that the following would make for a priori knowledge and justification:

A claim is a priori if (a) it is conceptually grounded and (b) individual epistemic agents can be justified in holding it by virtue of their reflectively drawing on their conceptual competence.

This may not be the only way in which a claim may qualify as a priori, but it at least expresses a prima facie sufficient condition for a claim being a priori.

An account that provides for conceptual-competence based reflective justification has good claim to providing an account of a priori justification, or at least of an important species of such justification. Accordingly we can claim to provide an account of such a priori justification, since we argue that there are claims that can be so justified—so there are a priori truths. However, we also argue for a particular understanding of reflective justification, or at least of the kind of reflective understanding that commonly features in philosophy. On our understanding, a priori justification itself must have an empirical dimension. We mark this somewhat paradoxical result by writing of 'low-grade' a priori justification—as opposed to the 'high-grade' a priori justification of epistemic lore.

One can think of the matter this way. Central to the concept A PRIORI JUSTIFICATION is the idea of epistemic justification by reflection—justification that can be obtained 'from the agent's armchair,' without 'going out' and collecting empirical evidence regarding what the actual world is like. Supposedly, such reflective justification is exhibited in familiar philosophical and mathematical cases and is distinct in kind from the empirical reasoning found, for instance, in the sciences. (It should be acknowledged that the relevant form of reflective justification does play some limited role in scientific contexts.) Empiricists hold that reflective justification turns on agents drawing on their competent understanding of their own 'ideas,' or 'meanings,' or 'concepts.'[9] Rationalists hold that that is part of the correct story—but insist that there are other kinds of justificatory reflection—kinds that give justification for truths that are not conceptually grounded. Finding the rationalist claims implausible, but not needing

---

[9] In this chapter we rely on various ideas about concepts, but we do not attempt a general theory of concepts and cannot recommend any account with which we feel consistently comfortable. For our purposes here, it is not necessary to have in hand any specific theory about the nature of concepts.

to decisively demonstrate their failings, we hope to develop a common ground on which empiricists as well as rationalists can agree: we give an account that vindicates reflection drawing on conceptual competence as a distinct justificatory route—though not as distinct as has commonly been supposed. One should be able to follow us in our focus and in our investigation without prejudice to the ultimate disposition of rationalist claims.[10]

So, we take as a starting point the idea that conceptually grounded reflection provides a priori justification:

(CGR) A claim is a priori if (a) it is conceptually grounded and (b) individual epistemic agents can be justified in holding it even if they do so simply by virtue of their reflectively drawing on their conceptual competence.

The picture is roughly this. All truths are true in part by virtue of the concepts there featured. This dependency holds no less for claims like, (1) 'There are brown dogs,' than it does for those like, (2) 'Water is H_2O,' or those like (3) 'Water is stuff with the same microstructure as the stuff in our prominent samples (filling lakes and rivers, etc.),' and (4) 'Capacitors store electric charge.' But there is this notable difference. Given the semantics of the featured concepts (thus, given whatever it is about the world that made or makes for the semantics of those concepts), and given their mode of composition, the latter three claims could not help but be true—they are necessary (true in all possible worlds). As we are putting it here, such truths are conceptually grounded—and this much is a matter of their semantics, and not of epistemology. CGR says that a claim is a priori if it is so conceptually grounded and (without 'leaving the armchair') agents can appreciate this fact by drawing solely upon their conceptual competence.

The three conceptually grounded truths above are of very different epistemic characters. The differences turn on the extent to which the elements of the conceptual semantics (which themselves fix the truth of the claims) may be accessible by virtue of one's possessing the relevant concepts. It is now a commonplace to note that, at least for some concepts, 'meanings are not in the head.' Sometimes, the semantics for a concept is not determined wholly by the internal states of one who counts as having acquired the concept. To use the familiar example, the concept WATER refers to stuff with the same microstructure as the stuff in a set of historical and contemporary samples. As a natural-kind substance concept, its reference is fixed by the historical interactions of a community (or set of related communities) with a stuff in the world. As a result, the (externalistic) semantics for water guarantees that water is H_2O. Because of this semantic guarantee, (2) counts as a conceptually grounded truth. But it is clearly not an a priori truth. The reason is that the

---

[10] The rationalist who is thus following our arguments will, of course, insist that, behind the reflective reasoning that we describe, there stands justifying rational insight into various supporting high-grade a priori truths.

conceptual guarantee here turns on elements of conceptual semantics that are not accessible. One is generally required to learn certain things in coming to possess a concept. The truths that may be counted among the internally accessible components of a concept's semantics are those that have both of these features: they are conceptually grounded necessary truths, and they also are (or readily follow from) truths that one has to learn in order to possess the concept. One need not have come to appreciate all that is conceptually grounded, but by virtue of having come to possess the concept, one must have come to appreciate or be sensitive to some of what is conceptually grounded. And, while (2) is a conceptually grounded truth, its semantic basis is beyond what is required for conceptual acquisition.

For contrast, consider (4). One does not count as having acquired the concept CAPACITOR if one does not appreciate that capacitors store electric charge. Thus, (4) is not just a conceptually grounded truth, it is also one that is grounded in internally accessible elements of semantics. As a result, one who has acquired the featured concepts should be able to reflectively appreciate that (4) is true, where this reflective appreciation draws on one's conceptual competence with those concepts. Unlike (2), (4) is grounded in internally accessible elements of the semantics of its featured concepts, and thus is a priori.

Claim (3), 'Water is stuff with the same microstructure as the stuff in the prominent samples (filling lakes and rivers, etc.),' is a delicate matter. It seems that a closely related claim is a priori: (3★) 'Water is stuff of the same natural kind as the stuff in our prominent samples.' But, one may certainly doubt that it is a priori that being of the same natural kind (of substance) turns on microstructure. After all, the discovery that natural kinds for substances turn on microstructural similarities and differences—as opposed to brute qualitative kinds—is a point that seems to have been empirically supported by the work of physicists such as Lavoisier, Dalton, and Maxwell. Also, it would seem that the prominent samples need not have been drawn from lakes and rivers; since folk on an arid world in which naturally occurring water is now subterraneous could yet share with us the concept WATER. Perhaps it would be best to say that, while (3★) like (4) may well be conceptually grounded and a priori, (3) is strictly speaking like (2): namely conceptually grounded in a way that involves an externalistic dimension, and hence is not a priori.

The preceding remarks suggest a distinctive route to a priori justification. When one has acquired the concepts featured in a claim, and when the claim itself expresses a truth that is grounded entirely in internally accessible elements of the semantics of the featured concepts, then, drawing on conceptual competence, the agent can come to appreciate that the claim must be true. Rather than consulting experiential evidence regarding features of the actual world, one comes to see that the combined semantics of the relevant concepts ensures that the world is as claimed—no matter what possible world is the actual world. Put simply (as will be seen, perhaps somewhat deceptively simply, but not falsely) the individual agent 'need only' access the internal elements of the semantics of the concepts that he or she has acquired (and perhaps trace out some accessible consequences) in order to appreciate that the claim is true. Insofar as one need only draw on one's conceptual competence, without looking beyond that to determine which possible world is the actual world, this justificatory route is indeed distinctive.

Since the epistemic justification just entertained would not depend on experiential evidence about what the actual world is like,[11] this form of justification is commonly held to be uncontaminated by the empirical. As will soon be seen, while reflecting a kernel of truth, this claim to empirical uncontamination is something of an overstatement. Here the focus will be on an important special case of reflective investigation, for which a modified understanding is in order: namely reflective inquiry as practiced in philosophical contexts—reflective inquiry into the kinds of concepts that figure importantly in philosophy. What we now hope to bring into focus is the character of philosophical reflection insofar as it conforms to the general understanding of a priori reflection advanced above—insofar as it involves reflection that draws on conceptual competence, and thus on the internally accessible elements of the semantics of concepts, and thereby leads one to appreciate that certain claims are necessarily true.[12] We hold that such reflective justification has rightly been understood as an epistemic breed apart—although just how apart is in need of discussion here—and that the long philosophical tradition that sees it as a priori justification is correct. However, we believe that this reflection also possesses an empirical dimension—and is not 'high-grade' a priori in the sense envisioned in much philosophical lore. Accordingly, we term it 'low-grade' a priori.

Philosophical reflection on philosophically important concepts, then, will serve as the principal example of low-grade a priori reflective inquiry. On the other hand, the considerations to be adduced are potentially generalizable to various other putative cases of the a priori. We will leave this generalizability issue largely open here.

4 Toward the low-grade a priori

4.1 The easy model, an easy mistake

The mode of philosophical inquiry often called 'conceptual analysis' has served as one prominent example of a priori reflection. Such reflection (which we will call conceptual-analytic reflection) can be understood as drawing on conceptual competence, and thus on internally accessible elements of the semantics of concepts featuring in the claims at issue. It is tempting to move freely from this understanding of reflection

---

[11] Or at least it does not depend on experiential evidence in the traditional fashion. As we will argue, in drawing on reflection one must sometimes treat the most direct deliverances of one's reflective thought-processes as empirical evidence for claims about the semantics of concepts. The investigation is not purely a priori in the sense of being free from empirical contamination—but neither is it devoted to determining whether the world is as advertised in the relevant claims. It has rather to do with drawing on the results of one's reflections to draw conclusions about the semantics of certain philosophically interesting concepts.

[12] This theme is also developed in Henderson and Horgan (2000a).

(which we ourselves believe to be essentially correct) to the idea that philosophically interesting results emerge 'fully formed,' as direct deliverances of conceptual competence. We will call this the 'easy model' of conceptual-analytic reflection. On the easy model, after 'turning ideas over in one's mind,' one 'just sees' on the basis of one's competence with the featured concepts that certain general claims are necessarily true. On this view, the philosophical claims somehow just 'float into consciousness' with a certain kind of obviousness—as conceptually guaranteed. (The model is suggested by BonJour's formulations in which general a priori results are 'grasped' in a 'direct' and 'immediate' fashion.)

We term this account the 'easy model' for two reasons. First, it makes conceptual-analytic a priori reflection a fairly straightforward affair. Turn over some ideas in your mind and, provided that you start with an adequate grasp of the concepts, the general results putatively stand out as immediately and obviously true. Insofar as one is then spared the toil of careful inferential moves of a sort that will soon be discussed, the model makes out conceptual-analytic reflection to be rather easier than it actually is. (The model can allow for some kinds of inference, however, viz., straightforward inferential extrapolations from judgments about concrete cases to abstract, conceptually grounded, necessary truths—where the appropriateness of the inferential extrapolation is itself reflectively obvious, thus the conclusion is rendered reflectively obvious too.)

Second, it is easy to simply fall into holding this model without careful examination: given that conceptual-analytic reflection draws on one's conceptual competence with the internally accessible elements of conceptual semantics, should not what comes in this way be simply or directly accessible? No. General claims can be grounded in elements of conceptual semantics, elements that are in an important respect internally accessible, without being direct deliverances of conceptual competence. This point is crucial; it and the supporting understanding of conceptual competence will be central to our account of low-grade a priori justification.

4.2 Three important observations, and the need for a two-stage model

If one is to have a sober understanding of what can be expected from reflection that draws upon conceptual competence, and if one is to have a considered view of how reflection itself can deliver justified beliefs, one must not succumb to unexamined presumptions regarding its workings. We submit that the following three conjectures are jointly more than reasonable.

First, a prominent way of drawing upon one's conceptual competence, conspicuously manifested in much well-received philosophical work, involves the generation of judgments about relatively specific and concrete scenarios. For example, one begins:

[Suppose that] somewhere in the galaxy there is a planet that we shall call Twin Earth. Twin Earth is very much like Earth; in fact, people on Twin Earth even speak English. In fact, apart from the differences we shall specify in our science-fiction examples, the reader may suppose that Twin Earth is exactly like Earth....

One of the peculiarities of Twin Earth is that the liquid called 'water' is not H_2O but a different liquid whose chemical formula is very long and complicated. I shall abbreviate this chemical formula simply as XYZ. I shall suppose that XYZ is indistinguishable from water at normal temperatures and pressures. (Putnam 1975a, p. 223).

In response to such a scenario, conceptual competence spawns fittingly specific and concrete judgments in a direct way:

On Twin Earth the word "water" means XYZ (Putnam 1975a, p. 223)

and,

The concept WATER refers to H_2O; it does not refer to the XYZ on Twin Earth.[13]

or simply,

Water is H_2O.

It should not be surprising that human conceptual competence is particularly suited to the generation of responses to such concrete specific scenarios. After all, in everyday contexts, where conceptual competence serves in a largely unnoticed way, it would seem to function largely in the direct and automatic generation of applications of concepts.

Second, conceptual competence is much less steady and reliable when called upon to directly generate conceptually grounded general truths. Perhaps conceptual competence can generate general truths with reasonable success when they turn on certain concepts of relatively straightforward sorts that do not commonly come to feature in philosophically interesting claims. For example, having acquired the concepts CAPACITOR and ELECTRICAL CHARGE, perhaps the general claim that capacitors store electrical charge comes fully formed when one pauses to wonder. But the sorry track record of philosophers, in their efforts to provide conceptually grounded necessary truths that would constitute untendentious conceptual analyses of philosophically interesting concepts that figure in key philosophical debates (debates about freedom and determinism, for example)[14] suggests that at least greater caution is needed. Particularly with respect to certain concepts that have commonly been significant for philosophers, one's conceptual competence may be much better at directly delivering presumably veridical judgments regarding specific applications of those concepts than it is at directly generating veridical judgments regarding generalities.

---

[13] The scenario drawn from Putnam itself builds in background information that is undeniably empirical: that the relevant samples of water on Earth are composed of H_2O. Reflection will ultimately need to accommodate these empirical presumptions of the scenario—making due allowance for them in formulating the results. These presumptions are not (or not all) a priori.

[14] Proposed conceptual analyses very often end up encountering counterexamples—including analyses that initially seem intuitively obvious, like the putative analysis of knowledge as justified true belief.

Third, by drawing upon what conceptual competence does provide, one can manage to justifiably believe certain conceptually grounded generalities that are not themselves the direct deliverances of that competence. Consider the justly famous result of Putnam's (and Kripke's 1972) reflections:

In all possible worlds, water is stuff with the same micro-structure as the stuff in the salient samples.

This conceptually grounded general truth is justified in terms of more particular judgments about the referent of 'water' in various concrete scenarios. We ourselves believe that such general results are rightly taken to be a priori. The central question becomes just how one can get to such truths.

The above three observations strongly indicate that, at least as it has application to philosophical cases, an adequate model of conceptual competence based a priori reflection will need to recognize at least two stages: one in which reflection on specific concrete scenarios generates correspondingly particular judgments (the direct deliverances of conceptual competence, mentioned in the first observation), and another in which one reflectively draws upon these particular judgments to inferentially support a judgment whose content is abstract and general (the need for this is evident in the second and third observations above).

4.3 An instructive parallel: investigations of syntax in theoretical linguistics

Traditional assumptions regarding the character of philosophical reflection have commonly been strongly constraining, owing in part to a lack of competing alternative ways of conceiving the a priori. To militate against their continuing to have an undue impact on one's thinking about the two stages of reflection, it will be helpful to consider a parallel two-stage epistemic process: the methodology typically employed by linguists in constructing and evaluating theories of natural language syntax. The empirical data for syntactic theory includes certain judgments of competent language-users—in particular, judgments concerning the grammaticality or ungrammaticality of various sentence-like strings, and concerning grammatical ambiguity or nonambiguity of various sentences. Notably, such judgments are relevant simultaneously to psychological theories of human language processing, and also to linguistic theories about the syntax of language itself. Native speakers, after all, can be expected to have judgment dispositions about these matters that reflect a solid mastery of their own language (or their own regional dialect, at any rate). So, when native speakers are intersubjectively consistent and also uniformly confident about such syntactic judgments, then normally these judgments reflect the natives' syntactic competence, their mastery of the syntactic norms or syntactic structures underlying their language. And this psychological hypothesis, in turn, has a direct implication for linguistic theory—namely that under an adequate theory of syntax for the natives' language (or dialect), those syntactic judgments will turn out mostly correct.

Although intersubjective consistency in grammaticality judgments is important, much of the crucial data for syntactic theorizing about one's own language is available from the armchair, in the form of introspectively accessible, confidently held, first-person judgments about grammaticality. The linguist's own grammaticality judgments already constitute a very rich, and evidentially very significant, body of empirical data vis-à-vis syntactic theory—because the default presumption in the first-person case too is that such grammaticality judgments are normally the products of one's own linguistic competence, and hence are mostly correct.

A two-stage structure is evident in linguistic inquiry concerning natural language syntax. When the linguist proposes certain abstract general syntactic principles, claiming that they are the rules of grammar for a given language, these proposals are not themselves the direct deliverances of the linguist's cognitive mechanisms of grammatical competence. Rather, the proposed rules of syntax are theoretical hypotheses about the language. Thus, first, grammatical competence generates grammaticality judgments about specific sentence-like word-strings. Although these judgments presumably are generated in a manner consistent with the general rules of syntax—so that the competent speaker possesses an implicit mastery of those rules, whatever they are—grammatical competence does not generate explicit beliefs whose contents are the syntactic rules themselves.[15] Then, second, the linguist's own grammaticality judgments, with their default status of presumptive correctness, are data vis-à-vis these proposed rules. The evidential connection between the data and the theoretical hypotheses—here, as elsewhere in science—is inference to the best explanation.

As is virtually always the case with inference to the best explanation, the evidential considerations involved, in proffering the proposed rules of syntax as the putatively best explanation of the data, operate via wide reflective equilibrium. Considerations of fit vis-à-vis wider theory, and with various kinds of facts less directly connected to the matter at hand, are potentially relevant. For example, some kinds of possible rules might fit less well than others with extant psychological understandings concerning human language-processing, or with extant theory in linguistics.

As this last point makes clear, the relevant wide-reflective-equilibrium methodology certainly need not be confined to armchair-obtainable data. Often a linguist can arrive at a reasonably well confirmed theoretical hypothesis from the armchair, but

(i) the linguist's background theoretical knowledge (e.g. knowledge of linguistic theory) may well play an important role in the overall evidential support the hypothesis possesses, and

---

[15] This leaves it open whether what we are here calling 'implicit mastery' is a matter of the subconscious deployment of *explicit* representations of general syntactic rules by human language-processing mechanisms, or instead occurs without the deployment of rule-representations even at the subconscious level. Either way, rule-mastery is implicit in the sense that language processing conforms to the rules without deploying *conscious* explicit representations of them.

(ii) this evidential status certainly can be further strengthened epistemically, or weakened, by potential evidence obtainable beyond the armchair.

Relevant considerations can include, for example, the grammaticality intuitions of other people. They can also include theories and results in cognitive science concerning natural language processing, since ultimately an adequate formulation of the rules of syntax would have to mesh with a detailed cognitive-scientific account of how those rules get accommodated, either implicitly or explicitly, by human language-processing mechanisms.

Another important dimension of the wide-reflective-equilibrium methodology employed in the nondeductive inference from the linguist's introspective data to the proffered rules of syntax is the availability of plausible supplementary hypotheses for 'explaining away' any recalcitrant data—in particular, recalcitrant grammaticality judgments, or judgment-tendencies, that do not conform with the proposed syntactic rules. Common examples are so-called center-embedded sentences, such as this one:

The man the cat the dog chased scratched sued for damages.

Such word-strings are difficult for humans to process, and are often judged ungrammatical. But, to the extent that cognitive science can provide independent reasons why such center-embedded strings are hard to process whether or not they are grammatical, ungrammaticality-judgments vis-à-vis such cases should not count heavily against certain proposed syntactic rules that count them as grammatical. Moreover, a recalcitrant grammaticality-judgment will be even less of a problem if it can be reversed or mitigated with the aid of a suitable paraphrase, such as this one:

The man sued for damages who was scratched by the cat that the dog chased.

We can bring together the above points, and make the two-stage model vivid, by imagining a linguist who is seeking to produce an account of his or her own idiolect. The linguist would begin with his or her own judgments, from the armchair—judgments about grammaticality that are defeasibly presumed to be the relatively direct results of his or her grammatical competence.[16] Generating such judgments in this first stage provides the data for subsequent inferential moves. While the set of such grammaticality judgments at least contains a healthy proportion that are direct products of the linguist's own grammatical competence, the full set of such judgments enters into subsequent (second-stage) linguistic theorizing in a somewhat different epistemic modality. The judgments become data for an overall theory that must provide an explanation of their status and their source. This theory will necessarily have dual

---

[16] It is not implausible to suggest that these judgments, when they are the products of properly exercised grammatical competence, are themselves (high-grade) a priori, being the product of the linguist's implicit mastery of the concept *grammatical in L* (where L is the linguist's own language). But this suggestion is not essential to the use of armchair syntactic theorizing in linguistics as a model for armchair philosophical inquiry in pursuit of conceptually grounded necessary truths.

dimensions—one regarding the rules of the grammar for the language, and the other regarding the extent of the informant's (linguist's) own grammatical competence. Accordingly, this second stage clearly involves an empirical abductive inference, rather than itself being the direct product of the linguist's grammatical competence.

The following points are worth emphasis. Consider what is needed to account for the data, the particular judgments produced in response to specific sentence-like word-strings. These judgments will conform to the grammar of the language to the (to be determined) extent that the rules of grammar are successfully tracked by the individual's (the linguist's) grammatical competence. A full psychological account of that competence would include an account of the grammar; to speak of such a competence is to speak of a capacity to conform to the rules. But any actual competence is subject to interferences, distortions, and systematic errors. Various performance errors are to be expected of one who is competent. Actual competence is imperfect.[17] Accordingly, any satisfactory accounting for sets of judgments will need to sort out both the grammar of the language and the character of the individual's competence. Given the judgments the individual makes, any account of the grammar will have implications for which judgments are competent judgments and which are performance errors. One's account of grammar thus makes demands on one's psychological theory of competence and of the ways that human competence falls short of ideal competence. Thus, if certain intuitive grammaticality judgments conflict with a proposed account of grammar, and if these judgments cannot be plausibly explained away as performance errors by appeal to credible psychological hypotheses about the limits of human grammatical competence, then the grammatical account is itself problematized. Any theory of grammar ultimately calls for an accommodating psychological account of competence.[18] Overall then, the linguist's proposed grammar will be informed by background and broadly empirical understandings of the finite and fallible character of people's actual (as opposed to ideal) grammatical competence; the account will then at least implicitly be committed to a rough understanding of this competence and its salient limitations; and this understanding will be rightly affected by, and answerable to, broadly empirical

---

[17] The present points are broadly empirical. The linguist approaches the study of any language with these points in mind; they inform how the linguist 'takes up' the judgments as data for further investigation. It is worth noting, however, that nonlinguists possess some inarticulate grasp of these points. After all, the ideas of performance error and competence would seem to be bound up with the notions of correctibility and correctness that are implicit in the everyday grammatical practice ultimately being accounted for. This observation is reflected in Brandom (1994). All grammatically competent speakers would seem to have in place some understanding of these matters.

[18] Linguists draw on various understandings of competence, and competence-related cognitive processes, when developing their accounts of grammar. The point is reflected in earlier remarks on expectations regarding center-embedded sentences, for example. But, again, linguists are not alone in having and making use of broadly empirical understandings of competence and tendencies for error. Everyone has and employs an appreciation of some of the dimensions affecting the rate of performance errors (or of those contexts where one may well need correction). For example, it would not be news to anyone that one is more likely to err when judging long and complex sentence-like strings. Furthermore, one's judgments may be expected to include rough judgments of complexity as well as judgments of grammaticality.

hypotheses about various human cognitive capacities and limitations. The results of such theorizing are clearly not the direct product of the linguist's grammatical competence. Nonetheless, syntactic theorizing can be effectively pursued by reflection in the armchair, drawing on the individual's own linguistic competence. But as just witnessed, there are also strong grounds for thinking that the justification of these results is not devoid of empirical elements. As we have argued, the investigation cannot plausibly be undertaken without one eye on a set of psychological issues having to do with the investigator/informant's competence. Psychological hypotheses about one's linguistic competence and its limitations on one hand, and linguistic theorizing about the rules of grammar on the other hand, are intimately interconnected, like mutually reinforcing strands.

So theorizing about the general rules of grammar, for a given natural language, deploys empirically informed abductive reasoning. Empirical considerations figure into the mix, inter alia, because of the need to develop the theory of grammar interactively with the empirical psychology of human language processing—where the relevant psychology covers both human linguistic competence and various kinds of performance errors to which humans are susceptible. Let us add some further remarks about the roles of matters empirical.

First, what about the concrete grammaticality/ungrammaticality judgments themselves—are they empirical claims? Here it is important to distinguish between a judgment's content and the fact of its occurrence. That a given grammaticality/ungrammaticality judgment occurs, in the linguist's own ongoing psychological history, is a contingent empirical fact, of course. But arguably, the content of such a judgment is, when true, a conceptually grounded necessary truth—a truth that is partially constitutive of the specific natural language under investigation. Hence, arguably the linguist's evidence for the grammaticality claim is non-empirical evidence: the linguist spontaneously finds the sentence (say) obviously grammatical, and in so doing is directly exercising his or her grammatical competence. Now, the armchair-based abductive reasoning deployed by the syntactic theorist actually incorporates grammaticality judgments both ways. Initially they are incorporated as (presumptive) non-contingent concrete grammaticality-facts about the given language, facts for which the linguist has (presumptive) non-empirical evidence. But eventually, when theory and data are being reciprocally adjusted to one another (with the possibility now under consideration that certain specific concrete grammaticality judgments were performance errors), the judgments are also incorporated as contingent psychological phenomena, and empirical evidence is brought to bear in sorting out the likely performance-errors.

Second, even though the concrete grammaticality/ungrammaticality claims constituting the linguist's initial data-points arguably are (when true) conceptually grounded necessary truths for which the linguist has competence-based non-empirical evidence, nevertheless the linguist makes an empirical assumption about the set of these data points, when reasoning abductively from that set. The assumption is that collectively, these data points are suitably representative of the full range of sentences in the language whose grammatical rules the linguist is seeking to discover. The truth or falsity of this representativeness assumption is an empirical matter, given the limitations of the linguist's grammatical competence: grammatical competence by itself simply does not yield up a verdict on the question of representativeness (just as grammatical competence by itself does not yield up the correct general rules of grammar for the language).

We conclude these remarks with some observations about the character of the wide-reflective-equilibrium dimension of the pertinent abductive reasoning—the reciprocal, equilibrational, adjustment of theory and data whereby some of the initial data points (namely grammaticality judgments) ultimately get rejected as performance errors and others get retained and counted as correct. One might wonder whether this dimension introduces a problematic relativism into the linguist's methodology, by privileging the linguist's own grammaticality judgments. But, although some uses of wide reflective equilibrium in some domains might spawn significant concerns about relativism (e.g. in seeking a moral theory that best systematizes one's own concrete moral judgments), such concerns really do not arise in the present context. For, the first-person grammaticality judgments that the linguist uses as data are presumed not to be highly idiosyncratic; and any judgments for which this presumption might turn out to be wrong thereby would become serious candidates for special theoretical treatment—e.g. being rejected as performance errors, or being treated as aspects of a regional idiolect rather than of the language writ large.

5 The reciprocal two-stage model of philosophical reflection

The observations of section 4.3 strongly suggest that the reflective investigation appropriate to many philosophically interesting and important issues is best understood as having a two-stage structure that parallels the linguist's reflective investigations of grammar. As in the case of linguistic investigation, philosophical reflection draws on the scattered concrete direct deliverances of a cognitive competence—conceptual competence, the analogue of grammatical competence. It seeks to arrive at conceptually grounded necessary truths, the analogues of the rules of grammar the linguist seeks to discover. Furthermore, the relevant conceptually grounded necessary truths are not reflectively generated in a direct way out of one's conceptual competence; so the ensuing reflection will need to employ the more particular concrete deliverances of conceptual competence as data for abductive inference. As will soon be seen, this reflective procedure has both psychological and conceptual faces, like investigations of grammar, and it is properly understood as having an empirical dimension.

In previous writings, we have used the term 'ideology' to refer to this kind of broadly empirical inquiry into the workings of concepts (cf. Horgan 1993, Graham and

Horgan 1994, Henderson and Horgan 2000a, 2003). Ideology, or conceptual-analytic reflection, is a philosophical enterprise continuous with relevant work in disciplines like cognitive science, linguistics, and sociolinguistics. Insofar as conceptual-analytic reflection relies primarily on armchair-accessible data, it can be effectively practiced by philosophers. Philosophical thought experiments, like Putnam's Twin Earth case, really are experiments: they generate data for conceptual-analytic theorizing, much as a linguist's intuitive grammaticality-judgments constitute data for syntactic theorizing. One makes a case for a certain conceptual-analytic hypothesis—for instance, the contention that the meaning of natural-kind terms depends on the language-users' environment—by arguing that it does a better job, all things considered, of accommodating the relevant data than do any competing hypotheses. Such reasoning is broadly empirical: inference to the best explanation. Although it can be conducted from the armchair and it is aimed at discovering conceptually grounded necessary truths, it is not high-grade a priori.

Again, a compelling reason for thinking of the results of such investigations as a priori is that one there draws on deliverances of one's conceptual competence—deliverances that are at least presumptively a priori—in a reflective process that can be pursued 'in the armchair,' to establish certain conceptually grounded necessary truths. Notably, the truth of such claims can be appreciated without looking to acquire data about whether the world is as there represented.

On the other hand, there are multiple reasons for recognizing that such investigation—and in particular, the second stage of conceptual-analytic reflection from the armchair—is not itself devoid of empirical aspects.

5.1 Preliminaries

Although the analogy to armchair linguistics will be a useful anchor to guide our discussion, the account we offer will include a number of features that arguably have no direct analogues in armchair linguistics. In particular, the data that feeds into conceptual-analytic reflection in philosophy are of various kinds. One kind is intuitive judgments about the applicability or non-applicability of philosophically interesting concepts to specific scenarios (actual or hypothetical); and these are the most direct analogues of grammaticality judgments in linguistics. But there are other kinds too. (In order to streamline exposition, we will defer discussion of other forms of data until sections 5.5 and 5.6, after the principal large-scale features of our account have been set forth.)

What we are offering is a proposed 'articulated reconstruction' of the structure of the evidential relations that we claim typically underwrite philosophical reflection. We do not mean to claim that in actual dialectical practice, philosophers explicitly present their reasoning in a way that conforms to this reconstruction. Nor do we mean to claim that it is typical for philosophers, when reasoning about conceptual-analytic matters, to consciously and explicitly entertain and embrace all the kinds of claims and assumptions that support such reasoning. On the contrary, we take it that often some of these claims and assumptions remain implicit, not only in the way philosophers articulate their arguments but also in the conscious reasoning process itself.[19] Articulated reconstruction seeks to thematize these features explicitly.

As the discussion unfolds, a number of subtle and complex issues will arise about whether or not certain specific aspects of the kind of reasoning we are describing are best viewed as empirical or non-empirical. In some cases we will just note such issues, without taking a stand on them. Our overall account will incorporate significant empirical elements in any case, while also remaining somewhat partial and incomplete because of the further issues about empiricality that we will here leave open. We have several reasons for remaining neutral about those issues. First, our overall argument will not require us to commit ourselves on these matters. Second, neutrality implements a 'big tent' strategy: some readers might find our overall argument compelling, while also maintaining that there are few (if any) elements of empiricality in philosophical reflection beyond those that we ourselves are committal about. There is no need to pick a fight with such readers by taking a stand on issues about potential further empirical factors. Third, we ourselves are unsure what to say about some of these additional issues, in any case.

5.2 Conceptual-analytic reflection as low-grade a priori abduction

Conceptual-analytic reflection in philosophy is importantly analogous to the reasoning that the armchair linguist employs. There are certain armchair-accessible facts, including in particular facts about how terms (e.g. 'water') and the concepts they express apply to various concrete scenarios, actual and hypothetical (e.g. Twin Earth). One's intuitive judgments about such matters are defeasibly presumed to emanate fairly straightforwardly from one's own conceptual/semantic competence. Given this presumption about the competence-based etiology of the concrete judgments—itself a broadly empirical assumption, notice—the occurrence of these various judgments constitutes empirical evidence in support of the philosophical hypothesis in question, e.g. the claim, 'Given that water is composed of H_2O, water is necessarily identical to H_2O' is a conceptually grounded necessary truth.[20]

The abductive reasoning in support of the hypothesis often will ultimately rest in part upon an available side-explanation concerning recalcitrant aspects of the data—for instance, why certain mistaken judgment-tendencies are present that go contrary to the philosophical hypothesis in question; and this explanation itself will often be an

---

[19] We would maintain that evidentially important assumptions and information can be—and often are—accommodated implicitly in human belief-formation not only without becoming conscious, but without being explicitly represented *at all* during cognitive processing—not even unconsciously. This theme will loom large in Chapter 7.

[20] Note that the *occurrence* of a specific concrete judgment is an empirical fact, even if the judgment itself happens to be high-grade a priori. The empirical fact of the judgment's occurrence, in combination with the empirical presumption that the judgment emanated fairly straightforwardly from the judge's conceptual/semantic competence, provides empirical support for the relevant philosophical hypothesis.

empirical (and partly psychological) hypothesis, whose credibility or lack thereof affects the overall wide-reflective-equilibrium credibility of the principal inference to the reflective claim that such-and-such is a conceptually grounded necessary truth. When discussing the case of theoretical grammar, we pointed out that accounting for the data demanded a coordinated account of grammar and competence—where the latter included an understanding of various performance errors. Similarly, the reflective abductive move from the data to an account of certain elements of the semantics for the relevant concepts, and to certain general conceptually grounded necessary truths, turns on mutually supporting understandings of both conceptual competence and certain corresponding performance errors.[21] Thus, not only do one's concrete-scenario judgments qualify as data for an account of conceptual semantics or conceptually grounded necessary truths by virtue of a background of broadly empirical understandings of one's own conceptual competence, but also the eventual evidential status of particular subsets of that data—concrete-scenario judgments—must be affected by understandings of one's own conceptual competence and tendencies to performance error.

Although the linguistics analogy is helpful and suggestive, the kinds of armchair-obtainable data that are pertinent to philosophical conceptual-analytic inquiry appear to be fairly diverse (more so than in the linguistics case), with some kinds being more directly analogous to grammaticality judgments than others. The types of data that can figure in philosophical conceptual-analytic reflection include the following:

1. Intuitive judgments about what it is correct to say concerning various concrete scenarios, actual or hypothetical.
2. Facts about conflicting judgments or judgment-tendencies, concerning the correct use of certain concepts in various actual or hypothetical scenarios.
3. Facts about standardly employed warrant-criteria for the use of various concepts.
4. Facts about the key purposes served by various terms and concepts.
5. General background knowledge, including untendentious scientific knowledge.

Data of all these kinds can go into the hopper of wide reflective equilibrium whereby conceptual-analytic claims are defended in philosophy. One makes a case for a certain conceptual-analytic hypothesis—for instance, the contention that the meaning of natural-kind terms depends on the language-users' environment—by arguing that it does a better job, all things considered, of accommodating the relevant data than

---

[21] As in the linguistics case, the operative understandings of conceptual competence and performance-error tendencies need not amount to a full-dress psychological theory about such matters. Rather, typically these understandings will take the form of plausible psychological hypotheses. Such hypotheses are themselves empirical, of course, being ultimately susceptible to vindication or to refutation by ongoing theoretical developments in cognitive science. And their status as empirical carries over to the status of the abductive reasoning in which they figure as background assumptions, since that reasoning typically relies upon such supplementary hypotheses (e.g. ones about performance-error tendencies) as a way of explaining away recalcitrant concrete judgments that do not accord with the abductive conclusion that such-and-such general claim is a conceptually grounded necessary truth.

do any competing hypotheses. Such reasoning, we maintain, is broadly empirical: inference to the best explanation, in which data of all the kinds 1–5 are potentially relevant and empirical elements of various kinds figure in various ways. Although it can be conducted from the armchair and it is aimed at discovering conceptually grounded necessary truths, it is not high-grade a priori.[22]

5.3 Core data: intuitive judgments about concrete cases

In this section we will focus on data of type 1, which is the kind most clearly comparable to grammaticality judgments in linguistics. Other kinds of data, such as those of types 2–5, will be discussed in later sections. A mainstay of conceptual-analytic investigation in philosophy is the posing of concrete scenarios (typically hypothetical ones, in which various pertinent features are built in by stipulation), and the formation of intuitive judgments about whether the concept(s) under scrutiny do (or do not) apply in the scenario. For instance, one specifies a concrete scenario in which an agent has specific kinds of evidence in favor of a proposition P, the agent believes P on the basis of that evidence, and P is true; and one forms the intuitive judgment that in such circumstances, the agent's belief that P would be a case of knowledge. Or, one specifies a concrete Twin-Earthly scenario in which the lakes and streams are filled with a clear, tasteless, potable liquid that has a chemical composition XYZ other than H_2O; and one forms the intuitive judgment that in such circumstances, that liquid would not be water. Or, one specifies a concrete scenario of the kind made famous by Edmond Gettier, and one forms the intuitive judgment that a specific justified true belief in the scenario is not a case of knowledge. And so on.

What logical form, or logical forms, do such concrete case-judgments exhibit? For present purposes this question can be left somewhat open. However, two kinds of statement-structure can be identified that look to be especially plausible, as a format for regimenting the pertinent concrete judgments. First are statements of this form:

Given that Φ, $\Psi(\kappa)$

where Φ is a stipulative specification of a scenario, and Ψ is a claim that deploys the target concept κ and that one judges to be true of that scenario. (Perhaps this logical form is best construed as a subjunctive conditional, or perhaps not—we leave that question open.) We will call them bare scenario-verdicts. Second are statements of this form:

It is necessarily true, by virtue of the content of the concept κ, that: given that Φ, $\Psi(\kappa)$

where $\Psi(\kappa)$ is a claim about how the concept κ (or its negation) applies in the scenario specified by Φ. We will call these conceptual-modal scenario-verdicts. An illustration

---

[22] See Henderson and Horgan (2003) for a similarly structured piece of conceptual-analytic reflection that illustrates the workings of each of these kinds of data vis-à-vis the hypothesis that folk-psychological concepts like belief and desire are 'austere' in such a way that the truth of folk-psychological ascriptions would not be undermined by the kinds of scenarios for mature science typically envisioned by eliminativists.

of an intuitive judgment of the second form, which in turn entails a corresponding claim of the first form, is this:

It is necessarily true, by virtue of the content of the concept KNOWLEDGE, that: given that
  (i) the teacher's only evidence that any student in the class owns a Ferrari is evidence that the student Nogot owns a Ferrari,
  (ii) the student Nogot does not own a Ferrari, and
  (iii) the student Hasit does own a Ferrari,
  (iv) the teacher believes that someone in the class owns a Ferrari because
    (a) the teacher believes (on the basis of the available evidence) that Nogot owns a Ferrari, and
    (b) the teacher has inferred this from the belief that someone in the class owns a Ferrari,

the teacher does not know that there's a student in the class who owns a Ferrari.

Initially in the process of conceptual-analytic inquiry in philosophy, such intuitively obvious-seeming claims are assumed to be true, and are treated as data to be accommodated as one seeks out conceptually grounded necessary truths that are general in content. In this respect they are analogous to the armchair linguist's own grammaticality judgments. The judgments are defeasibly presumed to emanate from one's competence—in the present case, one's semantic/conceptual competence.

Two questions can be raised about each kind of scenario-verdict. First, are such claims, when true and grounded in one's semantic/conceptual competence, necessary? Second, are they high-grade a priori? In the case of conceptual-modal scenario-verdicts, it seems clear that the answer to both questions is affirmative: the claim is necessary, since its very content is a conceptual-necessity claim; and it is high-grade a priori, because semantic/conceptual competence alone suffices to justify it.

In the case of bare scenario-verdicts, however, the matter is somewhat complicated and tendentious. Two pertinent kinds of bare scenario-verdict can be distinguished. The first kind is obtained from a conceptual-modal one, by dropping the conceptual-necessity aspect and retaining the rest. (For instance, one transforms the above statement about Nogot and Hasit by dropping the initial words 'It is necessarily true, by virtue of the content of the concept KNOWLEDGE, that'—so that the resulting statement begins with the word 'Given.') Such a bare scenario-verdict evidently counts as both necessary and high-grade a priori, since it clearly follows from a conceptual-necessity claim that itself has these two features.

But there is another pertinent kind of bare scenario-verdict too. Sometimes the explicit scenario-characterization one is given will not suffice, in combination with general, conceptually grounded, necessary truths concerning the target concept κ, to uniquely determine how κ applies in the scenario. For instance, perhaps one is given an explicit justified-true-belief scenario-description that leaves certain key details unarticulated, so that this description could be elaborated in either of two ways: either (i) in such a manner that the justified true belief counts as an instance of knowledge, or else (ii) in a manner that turns the scenario into a Gettier case, so that the justified true belief counts as not an instance of knowledge.

So suppose that one is given an explicit justified-true-belief scenario-description that could be elaborated either way, such as this:

You frequently see a student, Sally, from your class driving a Volvo. You ask her whether she owns a Volvo, and she replies 'Yes.' You have excellent evidence that she is truthful and reliable. You have no evidence that would call into question the statement that she owns a Volvo. You form the belief that she owns a Volvo, on the basis of your available evidence. And this belief is true.

Suppose that you intuitively form the bare scenario-verdict that in this scenario, one's belief that Sally owns a Volvo is an instance of knowledge. You simply never consider a possible elaboration of the scenario-description along the following lines:

Sally's Volvo has been in the shop for repairs, all the while she has been a student in your class. The Volvo you have seen her driving is not hers but mother's, on loan to her while hers is in the shop. She misheard your question about whether she owns a Volvo, because you asked it in a loud party and she misheard you as asking whether she owns a revolver, which she does.

In light of the fact that this elaboration is logically consistent with the original scenario-specification, one way to regard your original, bare, scenario-verdict would be to treat it as (i) true, (ii) contingent in content, and (iii) in effect amounting to this: if I were in a situation as thus described, then I would know that Sally owns a Volvo. On this construal, the justification for your scenario-verdict is empirical, even though your judgment-forming process does also deploy your semantic/conceptual competence concerning the concept KNOWLEDGE. The justification is empirical because certain contingent facts about your actual environment make it the case that in the 'closest possible worlds' in which the explicit scenario-specification obtains, Sally is driving her own Volvo and she clearly understands your question.

On the other hand, another way to construe the case would be as follows. Before you formed your bare scenario-verdict, you effectively 'filled in' the scenario yourself (at least implicitly), and in a manner guided by conversational implicature. The scenario you actually envisioned was one in which the Volvo you see Sally driving is her own, in which she clearly understands your question, and in which she answers it truthfully. Thus, the bare scenario-verdict at which you actually arrived is necessary rather than contingent, and indeed is conceptually necessary in virtue of the content of the concept KNOWLEDGE. The verdict concerns the scenario as envisioned, which is more detailed and specific than what was explicitly specified. This verdict emanates entirely from your semantic/conceptual competence, and thus it has non-empirical, high-grade a priori, justification. (Likewise for a corresponding conceptual-modal scenario-verdict, construed as keyed to the scenario as envisioned rather than as explicitly specified.)

For present purposes, we take no official stand on which of these two ways of construing the second kind of bare scenario-verdict is better (or whether one way is better in some cases and the other is better in others). This question about empiricality vs. non-empiricality is among those we can afford to leave to one side, since our overall account of conceptual-analytic reasoning in philosophy will go through in any case. (For what it is worth, though, we find ourselves more sympathetic with the second mode of construal, which would count both kinds of bare scenario-verdicts as non-contingent in content and high-grade a priori in epistemic status. And, as noted, conceptual-modal scenario-verdicts, when competence-based, clearly seem to have that status.) In short, we take no official stand on whether the core data for conceptual-analytic reflection have high-grade a priori justification, or they have justificatory status that is partially empirical, or they are an epistemologically mixed bag. However that may be, we will argue, crucial empirical elements enter elsewhere.

5.4 Abductive transitions and the representativeness assumption

Typically the aim of conceptual-analytic inquiry in philosophy is to seek out conceptually grounded necessary truths that are quite general in content. Sometimes these are metalinguistic or metaconceptual, e.g. 'The concept of knowledge is [is not] compatible with the concept of Gettier-style epistemic luck.' Sometimes they are first-order, e.g. 'Knowledge is [is not] compatible with Gettier-style epistemic luck.'[23] They do not always proffer necessary and sufficient conditions. But sometimes they do, either in a meta-level way or a first-order way, e.g. (to give a first-order example) 'Being a justified true belief is [is not] necessary and sufficient for being an instance of knowledge.'

Stage 1 of the pertinent reasoning process is the garnering of pertinent data—not only core data consisting of intuitive bare scenario-verdicts and conceptual-modal scenario-verdicts, but also other forms of data to be discussed below. Stage 2 is a transition from such data to a conceptual-analytic claim, or claims, of the sought-for kind. This transition, we maintain, is normally an abductive inference: the general conceptual-analytic hypothesis is embraced on the grounds that it yields the best explanation of the stage-1 data. For instance, individual conceptual-modal scenario-verdicts typically will be explainable as being direct consequences of the hypothesis. Individual bare scenario-verdicts will be explainable in the same way. And in optimal circumstances where there are no recalcitrant data-points to be dealt with, the distribution of bare scenario-verdicts in the data—in particular, the fact that the data does not contain any bare scenario-verdicts that conflict with the hypothesis—will be explainable by appeal to the modal force of the hypothesis: it purports to set forth not only a general truth, but a conceptually necessary general truth. (Recalcitrant data-points will be taken up in section 5.5 below.)

Sometimes the abductive transition will be very smooth and natural: the general hypothesis will immediately come to mind, without any conscious stepwise reasoning

---

[23] The example is inspired by Duncan Pritchard's (2010) distinction between Gettier-style epistemic luck and environmental luck.

of the kind experienced phenomenologically as a process of inference. In such cases, the general hypothesis will also seem intuitively obvious, in much the same way as are the concrete scenario-verdicts from stage 1. Even in such cases, however, the logical-evidential relation between the stage-1 data and the stage-2 hypothesis is an abductive one: the hypothesis is evidentially warranted by the data because of its explanatory force vis-à-vis that data. The nature of that logical-evidential relation is what we mean to be emphasizing here, whether or not the cognitive processing that mediates the transition from data to hypothesis is experienced psychologically as a conscious inference.

Other times, of course, the transition will be less obvious and immediate, and its abductive character will be reflected explicitly in the conscious experience of arriving at the hypothesis. One familiar kind of example in epistemology is the transition from (1) a body of stage-1 concrete scenario-verdicts about knowledge that include numerous subtle 'Gettier cases,' to (2) a general hypothesis about necessary and sufficient conditions for knowledge that includes some long, complex, multi-component, hard-to-survey, 'fourth condition' over and above the three familiar conditions of belief, justification, and truth. In cases such as this, the transition will not be phenomenologically immediate at all, and the general hypothesis is apt not to be intuitively obvious.

Full-fledged abductive reasoning about conceptual-analytic matters is not a simple, uni-directional transition from stage 1 to stage 2. On the contrary, normally there will be a considerable amount of reciprocal give-and-take, as theory and data get adjusted to one another and some of the erstwhile data gets rejected (e.g. as the product of performance errors). We will take up such reciprocal equilibration shortly. Before doing so, however, we wish to stress an important empirical element that enters into abductive transition from stage 1 to stage 2—and does so even apart from matters of reciprocal equilibration.

A key question to pose is this: Does this transition rest on any premise, over and above the data points themselves, that is contingent in its modal status and empirical in its own epistemic status? This question is important, because if the answer is affirmative, then that would inject an empirical element into the abductive transition. The transition thereby would be empirically infected, even if the data points themselves are all high-grade a priori, and also even if the applicable normative principles of abductive reasoning are also high-grade a priori. (We have already stated our official neutrality about whether the data points are all high-grade a priori. We hereby announce official neutrality, as well, about the epistemic status of normative principles governing rationally appropriate abduction.)

The answer to the question, we submit, is indeed affirmative. The abductive transition to a conceptual-analytic hypothesis H deploys a contingent assumption whose evidential status is empirical—namely that the core stage-1 data on which the transition is based is suitably representative vis-à-vis the class of potential scenarios to which hypothesis H applies. We will call this the representativeness assumption. Suitable representativeness is a somewhat vague notion, to be sure, but nonetheless is one of those vague notions that is fairly easy to understand (even if hard or impossible to analyze or precisify). The idea is that the various kinds of data points within one's actual data set match up reasonably well with the kinds of phenomena (both actual and potential) to which H would be applicable.

Abductive inference, in order to be reasonable and epistemically appropriate, needs to be grounded upon a body of data that one has good grounds for considering suitably representative of the phenomena to which the inferred hypothesis is applicable. Without such grounds, the inference will be too evidentially shaky to be reasonable. Moreover, in general the representativeness (or not) of one's data set will be a contingent matter, and thus one's evidence for the data set's representativeness will be empirical. Suitable principles of abductive reasoning, whatever exactly they might look like, therefore should acknowledge and incorporate this fact. Instances of such principles would then have a logical form something like this:

ABD[$\{d_1, \ldots d_n\}$,H]   If (i) one has the total set of relevant data points $\{d_1, \ldots d_n\}$, and (ii) one has good empirical evidence that collectively $d_1, \ldots d_n$ are suitably representative of the class of phenomena to which hypothesis H is applicable, then it is rationally appropriate to abductively infer H on the basis of $d_1, \ldots d_n$.

Even supposing that any principles of correct abduction are themselves high-grade a priori (a matter about which we ourselves remain neutral, remember), and even supposing that instances of such principles are also high-grade a priori (where these instances are statements with the lately mentioned logical form), nonetheless such an instance will inject an empirical element into the inferential transition—namely the element reflected in clause (ii) of the schema ABD[$\{d_1, \ldots d_n\}$,H]. This conclusion remains in force even supposing that all the data points $d_1, \ldots d_n$ are high-grade a priori themselves (another matter about which, remember, we ourselves remain neutral).

To illustrate the importance of the representativeness assumption and its empirical status, consider the epistemological history of attempts to analyze the concept KNOWL-EDGE. Suppose that one has entertained a diverse range of concrete scenarios of various kinds that are pertinent to the applicability or non-applicability of concepts like KNOWLEDGE, BELIEF, TRUTH, and JUSTIFICATION, and one has generated various bare scenario-verdicts and conceptual-modal scenario-verdicts about these cases. Suppose that all these verdicts are correct, and that they all reflect one's conceptual/semantic competence with the relevant concepts—no performance errors have slipped in. Suppose that one has never encountered any Gettier scenarios, and that none are included in one's data set. On the basis of one's actual data comprising a diverse range of relevant scenario-verdicts, one abductively concludes this:

JTB   It is a conceptually grounded necessary truth that for any cognitive agent A and any proposition P, A knows that P iff (1) A believes P, (2) P is true, and (3) A is justified in believing P.

This abductive inference might well be quite reasonable—indeed, normatively unassailable—given that one has good empirical grounds for assuming (perhaps tacitly) that one's data points are collectively representative of the full range of cases to which hypothesis JTB is applicable. And perhaps one does have good empirical grounds for that assumption—an assumption which, after all, evidently persisted in epistemology for many years before Gettier's landmark paper was published in 1963.

The conclusion of the envisioned abductive inference is false, of course—despite the fact that all the scenario-verdicts that served as data points are true. But this by itself is no normative indictment, because after all the inference is abductive rather than deductive—which means that it is not guaranteed to be truth-preserving. Moreover, insofar as the inference is evaluated in relation to the agent's own epistemic situation, arguably it is downright unassailable. The reason why seems clear: the agent had strong empirical evidence for a contingent assumption that figures in the inference at least implicitly, namely the representativeness assumption.

What Gettier brought to the attention of the philosophical world, of course, is that the pertinent, contingent, representativeness assumption is false. And, once one's overall data set comes to include scenario-verdicts about Gettier cases, that erstwhile representativeness assumption is no longer empirically well-warranted at all (given one's present, duly enriched, data set); quite the contrary.

Again, the key point we are emphasizing, as illustrated by the example just discussed, is that the inferential transitions from concrete scenario-verdicts to general conceptual-analytic hypotheses are mediated by an assumption that is contingent, and whose evidential status is empirical. Although the representativeness assumption typically is not explicitly stated when hypotheses are advanced, and typically is not consciously entertained either, nonetheless it figures crucially in an articulated reconstruction of the abductive logical/evidential relation between concrete core data and abstract, general, conceptual-analytic hypotheses.

Now, imagine an objector who wishes to maintain that conceptual-analytic reasoning in philosophy is a full-fledged high-grade a priori matter. This objector would have to claim not only (1) that stage-1 data (e.g. scenario-verdicts, both bare and conceptual-modal) are all high-grade a priori, and (2) that one's mastery and deployment of applicable principles of abduction is high-grade a priori, but also (3) that the representativeness assumption itself is high-grade a priori too. Claims (1) and (2) both look fairly plausible—and we have already declared ourselves neutral about them, for present dialectical purposes. But claim (3), which we deny, is enormously implausible—for two reasons. First, the proposition that one's data set is suitably representative is (if true) a contingent truth—not a necessary truth, let alone a conceptually grounded necessary truth. Second, it is very hard to see how the kind of evidence one could acquire in support of this proposition could be anything other than empirical evidence. For, even if the individual data points (the scenario-verdicts) are themselves all conceptually necessary and high-grade a priori in epistemic status, this fact does not in itself constitute evidence that the data points are collectively representative of the phenomena to which the abduced hypothesis applies. Rather, the sorts of considerations that would count in favor of representativeness are empirical ones—e.g. that one has deliberately sought out a wide range of concrete hypothetical scenarios, with an eye toward both quantity and variation; that the cases are significantly different from one another in various matters of detail; that one has not been able to think of any counterexamples to the abduced hypothesis; etc.

So the abductive reasoning deployed in conceptual-analytic reflection about the workings of philosophically interesting concepts is inevitably empirically infected, by virtue of the role in such reasoning of a representativeness assumption that is contingent rather than necessary, and whose evidential grounding is empirical rather than high-grade a priori. This means that the reasoning is not itself high-grade a priori, even though it can be effectively conducted from the armchair. And there are further empirical elements too, to which we now turn.

5.5 Reciprocal equilibration

Yet more is involved in the abductive reasoning about conceptual-analytic matters, beyond any simple unidirectional transition from data to hypothesis. In general, the abduction will involve a certain amount of mutual adjustment between theory and data, with some of the initial data being explained away rather than being straightforwardly accommodated by the hypotheses one settles upon. This two-way give-and-take process is a matter of reaching a specific form of reflective equilibrium, and so we hereby dub the process 'reciprocal equilibration.'

When thus equilibrating, one attends to stage-1 data in a somewhat different manner than just treating the data points as specific truths (many or all of which are conceptually necessary) to be accommodated by one's conceptual-analytic hypothesis. Rather, one now focuses on those stage-1 scenario-verdicts qua contingent psychological occurrences—i.e. as empirical phenomena. For each proposition p in the stage-1 data set, there is the corresponding empirical fact that one formed a judgment with the content p, a judgment in which p seemed intuitively obvious and may well have also seemed conceptually necessary. Likewise, there is the empirical possibility that one's judgment that p was a performance error, rather than emanating from one's competence.

Often the best overall theoretical position concerning the conceptual-analytic matters under consideration—the most appropriate abductively-generated position—will be one that treats some specific subset of the stage-1 judgments as performance errors; these judgments will get explained away, rather than being directly accommodated. Typically the debunking explanation will rest in part on certain plausible side-hypotheses about psychological tendencies toward the given kinds of performance error—in some cases, hypotheses that mesh fairly closely with the hypothesis that is the principal product of one's abductive reasoning. (Such debunking explanations will be the analogues, for conceptual-analytic inquiry, of the armchair linguist's debunking explanation of intuitive judgments about the putative ungrammaticality of center-embedded sentences.)

Here is an example of this kind of putative debunking explanation. Consider the kind of scenario that figures in the 'lottery paradox'—say, a hypothetical scenario in which

(1) an agent possesses a single ticket from a given lottery,
(2) the agent knows that exactly one million tickets have been sold and that exactly one of them has been selected as (but has not yet been announced as) the winner,
(3) the agent has no other pertinent information bearing on the chances of any specific ticket's being the winner, and hence
(4) the agent knows that the probability that his/her own ticket is the winner is one millionth.

Suppose that the agent forms the belief that this ticket is not the winner, and this belief is in fact true. Question: Does the agent know, in such a scenario, that his/her ticket is not the winner?

Many people who contemplate this kind of scenario (including we two authors, for what that is worth) form the intuitive verdict that that agent does not know that the given ticket is not the winner. On the other hand, some hypotheses about the concept KNOWLEDGE entail otherwise—namely accounts entailing that a justified true belief is an instance of knowledge if (a) the belief has an epistemic probability, for the agent, above some threshold lower than 999,999/1,000,000, and (b) there is nothing 'Gettierish' about the relation between the agent's justification for the belief and the fact that the belief is true. One equilibrational option, for those attracted to such a hypothesis, is to hold onto the hypothesis and to propose a debunking explanation of the recalcitrant scenario-verdicts. For example, such a debunking explanation might invoke the fairly plausible-looking psychological side-hypothesis that people are inclined to embrace the idea that a belief that p counts as knowledge, for an agent, only if the proposition p has epistemic probability 1 (for the agent). This side-hypothesis could be cited as a basis for treating the problematic scenario-verdicts not as veridical data to be accommodated by an adequate account of the concept KNOWLEDGE, but rather as easy-to-make performance errors.

For present purposes, it doesn't matter whether the reader agrees that the stage-1 scenario-verdict here being rejected is actually mistaken, or whether the reader finds the putative debunking explanation credible. (For what it is worth, we ourselves are strongly inclined to maintain that the scenario-verdict is correct, and we ourselves do not find the debunking explanation persuasive.)[24] Rather, the key points are these. First, reciprocally equilibrational dialectical moves of this sort are very common, as an aspect of conceptual-analytic reflection in philosophy. Second, such moves inject

---

[24] Here is what seems right to us to say about the issue. In typical situations in which an agent has a justified true belief that p, which counts as an instance of knowledge, the proposition p has no specific, quantitative, epistemic probability at all, relative to the agent's available evidence. (A fortiori, p does not have epistemic probability 1.) Rather, quantitative epistemic probabilities arise only under relatively unusual informational

additional empirical elements into the abductive process, over and above the empiricality that arises from the representativeness assumption (as discussed in the preceding section). It is an empirical hypothesis that a given scenario-judgment is a performance error (in the present example, the scenario-judgment that the agent does not know that his/her ticket is a loser). And the putative debunking explanation has recourse to psychological side-hypotheses about why and how such a performance error is apt to arise (in the present example, the hypothesis that people are prone to mistakenly think that genuine knowledge always requires epistemic probability 1). This kind of empirically tinged reciprocal equilibration is doable from the armchair, and thus does not prevent philosophical reflection from being low-grade a priori. But these further empirical elements do make such reasoning all the more different from a priori reasoning as traditionally conceived.

5.6 Real conceptual competence and noise elimination

Although one relies heavily upon one's conceptual competence in generating scenario-verdicts in stage 1 of conceptual-analytic reflection, and one relies heavily upon one's abductive competence in stage 2, nevertheless one needs to conduct reciprocal equilibration in a way that takes proper account of one's actual epistemic situation. Specifically, one needs to pursue equilibration in a way that is duly attentive to certain live empirical possibilities concerning the different potential sources of one's various individual scenario-verdicts. Although one's scenario-verdicts might often emanate quite directly from one's conceptual competence, sometimes they may (and do) reflect more than that. Other information, other processes, produce 'noise' within judgmental soundings taken of one's conceptual competence. As one does equilibration as a part of stage 2, often one will need to come to terms with significant noise in the data. Doing so introduces empirical hypotheses about which judgments are noise-infected, and about the sources of such noise. In this section we make some general observations about such matters.

Consider the typical situation in which one learns concepts. This is not a situation in which one's informants are interested solely, or even primarily, in one's acquiring the concept. Typically, the occasion for instruction arises when one is not capable of understanding some substantive point that the teacher wishes to convey. Perhaps one's instructor is trying to explain why a given monitor is better than another. The

---

circumstances. The actual conceptual relation between knowledge and epistemic probability is this: *if* a proposition *p* does have a specific epistemic probability for a given agent, *then* the agent knows that *p* only if the probability of *p* is 1. Hence the scenario-verdicts presently at issue are correct, rather than being performance errors. But this probability-1 constraint on knowledge, being conditional in form, has much less import than it is often thought to have, because it only kicks in under those relatively unusual circumstances in which the proposition in question has any quantitative epistemic probability at all. (We do acknowledge that there are further kinds of lottery scenarios to consider in which negative verdicts typically arise about whether one knows that one has a losing ticket—e.g. scenarios in which one knows that numerous tickets have been sold and only one will win, but one does not know exactly how many tickets have been sold. But this is not the place to pursue the matter further.)

instructor mentions the pixel-density of the two, and gets a blank look in return. One apparently needs to acquire the concept PIXEL in the course of this instruction. Instruction is then forthcoming both about certain concepts and about the particular monitors in question. And the two lessons may be given in a highly integrated and largely undifferentiated course of instruction. Similarly, early childhood lessons about morally right behavior probably are not well understood as lessons solely about what happens to be morally right or solely about the concept MORAL RIGHTNESS. The child (or colleague) is instructed in both within an integrated and largely undifferentiated lesson. Claims advanced in that lesson are not marked out as being conceptual instruction or 'substantive' doctrine—and many claims in the lesson may function both ways. Thus, the bottom line: what one learns while acquiring a concept is not (limited to) what one learns in or by virtue of acquiring that concept.[25] From the start, one acquires a mix of conceptually-based and nonconceptually-based information and transitions. The pieces in the mix do not come tagged, categorized, or otherwise reliably marked as either 'conceptually based' or 'other.' And this largely undifferentiated mix can then spawn largely undifferentiated judgments in response to concrete scenarios. The verdicts that the conceptually competent person finds intuitively obvious in response to scenarios may reflect this mix.

These observations force the following question upon the agent engaging in abductive conceptual-analytic reflection: Which of the intuitively compelling judgments really are the direct deliverances of one's conceptual competence, and which of them are not? While one's judgments reflect conceptual competence, they may and sometimes do reflect more—namely noise of one sort or another. Thus, one is not entitled to any flatly categorical presumption regarding the purely competence-based etiology of the intuitive judgments produced in response to the sort of concrete scenario that is common philosophical seed. Rather, as one engages in reciprocal equilibration, one must seek to distinguish which judgments are conceptually grounded and which arise from additional sources. We will mention three such sources of noise.

The first is the most important and the most daunting. It is also the source reflected in the foregoing discussion: typically concepts are acquired in a context that is marked by mixed learning agendas. As a result, what is learned is ultimately an undifferentiated mixed-bag of conceptually grounded and non-conceptually grounded information. The concrete judgments that a conceptually competent person finds compelling will likewise be a poorly differentiated mixed bag.

---

[25] There is seldom a test to pass. Seldom does one get certified as one who has acquired a set of concepts—in the sense of having 'mastered' or come to really 'possess' them. One commonly gets to employ concepts on which one has only a tenuous grasp, and one uses concepts in attributing beliefs to folk who have only such a tenuous grasp of some of the featured concepts. (Peacocke (1992) marks these contexts by distinguishing between possession conditions and attribution conditions.) So, even one who is employing a concept may yet be acquiring the concept in the same conversation.

There is a second kind of noise infecting the intuitive concrete judgments that serve as data-points for philosophical reflection: what is learned in acquiring a concept may itself be somewhat varied in its conceptual depth. Put differently, one's conceptual competence may itself encode and reflect more and less deep elements of the semantics of the relevant concepts—both deep and surface elements of conceptual semantics. To get a handle on what is intended here, consider the epistemological concept JUSTIFIED BELIEF. Plausibly, in order to possess this concept, one must be able to recognize instances of objectively justified belief of common (or paradigmatic) sorts. One must be sensitive to components of the scenario such as whether the belief in question arises by wishful thinking, or from a wide sample, or from a dream, or from a chemistry textbook, and so on. Some of the judgments identifying cases of justified belief may need to give way upon further investigation—for example, a judgment regarding a given case might respond to the role in that episode of belief-fixation of a widely employed heuristic, and one then may learn that that heuristic is unreliable, despite having been widely accepted in one's culture. Plausibly, these ready, everyday judgment capabilities are rooted in a sensitivity to certain indicators that may not themselves be conceptually deep, non-negotiable, or conceptually rooted, but which nevertheless serve to facilitate a capacity that is mandated for concept possession. The sample of everyday instances, and the capacity to identify such instances, has some sort of status in the semantics of the relevant concept—JUSTIFIED BELIEF—but not a status that is on the same level as the epistemically desirable and central features such as various forms of reliability, power, and the like. This difference in conceptual level is itself reflected in the judgment tendencies regarding scenarios in which it is stipulated that a commonly approved process is found to be unreliable (suppose that rather than being informed by well-tested theory, an experimental apparatus is revealed to be informed by a story hatched in a dream).

The present source of noise may be a special case of the first source—the mix of empirical and conceptual elements in the learning of a concept. At the very least, it is not easy to keep fully distinct. Consider the common suggestion that the semantics for the concept WATER might aptly be captured (perhaps partially) in the suggestion that water is stuff of the same sort as that potable, reasonably tasteless, material filling the lakes and rivers. This formulation seems to us to use 'ready indicators' to characterize the base homogeneous stuff to which water must belong. But such indicators are not conceptually non-negotiable—they are not necessary. A people from an arid planet with no surface water, all of whose water-sources were plant matter, might yet share the human concept of water. We humans and those non-humans would use different 'ready indicators,' and our own paradigmatic cases would be completely different from theirs, yet we could both possess the concept WATER. So, if our paradigmatic cases and ready indicators here serve as a component of the semantics of the water-concept, for us, they only serve as mere surface-indicators. Others may have different but fitting analogous paradigms and indicators that serve in like fashion, for them—and yet they can share our concept.[26] In any case, focusing too comfortably on these elements, resting content with surface elements of conceptual semantics, if that is what these are, would lead to errors in one's reflective understanding of the concept.[27]

A third general source of noise in the judgments that constitute data for conceptual-analytic reflection is a different kind of context effect: context effects that are not themselves rooted in the semantics of the relevant concepts. Alvin Goldman 'lump[s] together under the term "context"... various of [an individual's] other beliefs, background information, and so forth' (Goldman 1992c, pp. 145). Goldman argues that there are general psychological context-effects to which philosophers engaging in conceptual analysis will need to be attentive. Sometimes such psychological factors may distort one's judgments, by 'priming' a kind of over-sensitivity to certain elements of the presented concrete situation. Such priming may skew the individual's judgmental responses. One who wishes to produce an understanding of the semantics of concepts must ultimately 'control for' such distortions in evidential judgments by accounting for their nonconceptual roots.

It is undeniable that beliefs that the subject has, and which have been made salient by conversational or contemplative context, can affect the subject's judgment in ways that distort that individual's application of concepts. Recent harrowing experiences, or recently recalling or even reading about such experiences, could 'prime' an individual to categorize presented people, animals, or objects as objectively threatening, for example.[28] Attorneys in courts of law seek to induce context effects in jurors.[29] But, even without the able assistance of lawyers, humans are prone to some context effects

---

[26] Think again of Putnam's suggestion (1991, p. 11) that meaning and concepts may have an identity through time (and perhaps across worlds) while admitting differences—'with no essence,' he says.

[27] One can read Goldman's two-stage reliabilism as the suggestion that certain epistemological reflections on the concept of knowledge and the concept of epistemic justification have made such errors. Goldman argues that a flatfooted treatment of concrete judgments can yield an incomplete understanding of the relevant conceptual dynamics, and that this can foster intuitive judgments that obscure or distort deeper elements of the relevant conceptual workings (Goldman 1992b, 1999). He suggests that the best account of one's particular judgments regarding justification is that those judgments most directly reflect internalized lists of approved processes and methods. Ultimately, however, these list-structures are themselves influenced by a deeper evaluative basis: understandings of real-world reliability. The lists are a part of one's conceptual competence, and do have some (defeasible) conceptual and epistemic standing—and they strongly and most directly affect the judgments one makes about concrete cases. The underlying evaluative basis is, however, a deeper and more enduring element of the semantics—although it commonly affects concrete judgments only indirectly. At least this is one lesson that we would propose to take away from Goldman's two-stage reliabilism. We return to this matter in section 6 of Chapter 5.

[28] Plausibly, there is a contextual dimension to the semantics of the concept THREATENING. Thus different degrees of presented risk may qualify something or someone as threatening in different contexts. But, not all context effects can be chalked up to such conceptually appropriate variation. Sometimes context effects may make one more sensitive to presented risks than is (contextually) appropriate.

[29] It is commonly noted that defense attorneys seek to manipulate the context in which jurors approach a case so as to make *proof beyond a reasonable doubt* seem equivalent to *proof beyond any doubt*. They seek to frame convictions in terms of risks, and they focus on the bare possibility of mistaken conviction. Prosecutors may work to produce a mirroring set of conceptual mistakes—inducing the jurors to conflate *proof beyond a reasonable doubt* with a showing that something is merely *probable, given the balance of evidence*. While the standards for *proof beyond a reasonable doubt* are subject to conceptually appropriate and mandated variation,

that are not conceptually appropriate, and these conceptual performance errors are a noise in the set of concrete judgments that serve as one's basis for reflective generalization. The best explanation for one's judgments will occasionally explain away some of them as mistakes.[30]

The general point made here is that, realistically, there is an epistemic messiness to one's life around concepts. The epistemic situation of those who use concepts and who are reasonably competent with those concepts is a situation in which, for most any intuitive scenario-verdict, there is a live empirical possibility that the given verdict reflects noise in the data rather than emanating directly from conceptual competence alone. Doing one's best to filter out such noise, in the course of reciprocal equilibration, is a key component of abductive conceptual-analytic reflection—and it typically rests on empirical hypotheses about the nature of this noise and its sources.

5.7 Dual-pull phenomena and other data

Since section 5.2 we have been focusing on abductive conceptual-analytic reflection that employs the two kinds of scenario-verdicts as its stage-1 data: bare scenario-verdicts and conceptual-modal scenario-verdicts. But although such judgments are certainly one important kind of data in philosophical conceptual-analytic reasoning, they are not the only kind. As we remarked in section 5.2, the pertinent kinds of data can include each of the following:

1. Intuitive judgments about what it is correct to say concerning various concrete scenarios, actual or hypothetical.
2. Facts about conflicting judgments or judgment-tendencies, concerning the correct use of certain concepts in various actual or hypothetical scenarios.
3. Facts about standardly employed warrant-criteria for the use of various concepts.
4. Facts about the key purposes served by various terms and concepts.
5. General background knowledge, including untendentious scientific knowledge.

We will discuss each kind of data, in turn.

Scenario-verdicts, both bare and conceptual-modal, belong to the first category. Such judgments, qua occurrences, are contingent empirical phenomena—and are so treated in the reciprocal-equilibration component of conceptual-analytic abduction, where potential noise-infection is being taken into account. (On the other hand, recall that we did not commit ourselves as to whether the contents of these scenario-verdicts,

---

these do not encompass the standards for *proof beyond any doubt* or for *being probable, given the balance of evidence*. (At least they do not encompass the standards for these other concepts in the context of real law courts.) So, the competing strategies would seem to boil down to inducing errors by setting up various context effects.

[30] Both of the examples employed here are of non-conceptually-appropriate context effects involving concepts with contextual elements to their semantics. Perhaps it is to be expected that concepts with contextual dimensions should be subject to certain context effects as well. In both the cases considered here, the mistakes occur by a context-induced employment of standards that are beyond the range that is contextually appropriate.

when correct, are contingent or necessary, or whether the epistemic status of the correct verdicts is high-grade a priori.) Facts of types 2–5 typically are contingent and empirical too. Thus, their inclusion in one's data set for conceptual-analytic abduction introduces yet a third element of empiricality, beyond the two we have already discussed. (The first empirical element was the representativeness assumption concerning type-1 data, and the second was the need to invoke empirical hypotheses during reciprocal equilibration as a means of filtering out noise in type-1 data.)

The principal goal of conceptual-analytic inquiry in philosophy is to discover certain conceptually grounded necessary truths—ones that are general in content and are philosophically interesting. It is important to appreciate, however, that one can acquire empirical evidence for a hypothesis of the form 'It is a conceptually grounded necessary truth that p.' The situation here is analogous to the situation of someone who acquires empirical evidence in favor of some complicated mathematical proposition—for instance, the testimony of a reliable mathematician, who claims to have studied and understood a proof of the proposition. Often, the empirical evidence will bear upon a claim about a putative conceptually grounded necessary truth by virtue of the way the evidence fits into a wider web of justified beliefs and supplementary hypotheses—in the case of the mathematical proposition, for example, one's justified belief that one's interlocutor is a competent mathematician, and one's justified belief that this person is trustworthy about the matter at hand.

We turn now to data of types 2–5. In order to illustrate how such data can figure as empirical evidence in support of claims about putative conceptually grounded necessary truths, it will be useful to consider briefly a sample line of argumentation for a conceptual-analytic hypothesis concerning the concept KNOWLEDGE—a hypothesis that lately has been actively debated. This is the conjunctive claim that (i) the concept KNOWLEDGE is governed by implicit, contextually variable parameters of correct applicability, (ii) in typical contexts of application, the settings on these implicit parameters render numerous everyday knowledge-claims true, but (iii) in contexts where radical-deception scenarios are explicitly posed (e.g. scenarios involving Cartesian evil deceivers, or brains in vats), the settings on the implicit parameters tend to become so stringent that knowledge-claims about the external world become false in those contexts.[31] We will call this hypothesis, which posits contextually variable implicit semantic parameters, parameter contextualism about knowledge.

We will describe a multi-faceted philosophical argument for this hypothesis. What matters for present purposes is not whether the reader accepts this argument, but rather that it be recognized as a form of armchair-doable abductive reasoning in which data of types 2–5 serve as empirical evidence—and does so in part by figuring in a web of

---

[31] Lewis (1979, 1996), DeRose (1992, 1995, 2004, 2009), Cohen (1987, 1999, 2005). For critique, see Williamson (2005a, 2005b), Schaffer (2004).

empirically justified beliefs that includes various side-hypotheses. We begin by describing some pertinent data of the various types, and then we set forth the argument.

5.7.1 Type 2 It is notorious that one's judgment-tendencies are pulled in different ways, with respect to whether radical-deception scenarios establish the falsity of external-world knowledge claims. On the one hand are judgment-tendencies to classify certain paradigmatic beliefs as instances of knowledge: these judgments seem to respond to crucial features including strong justification, truth, and lack of 'Gettier features.' These judgment-tendencies take no notice at all of the possibility that the agent might be systematically and radically deceived. On the other hand is a judgment-tendency that almost invariably arises when radical-deception scenarios are explicitly raised in order to generate skeptical worries—namely a tendency to think (a) that external-world knowledge requires that the agent possess evidence precluding the possibility of radical deception, (b) that nobody ever has such evidence, and hence (c) that nobody has any external-world knowledge.

5.7.2 Type 3 The evidential standards that are normally employed, in one's practice of attributing external-world knowledge to others or to oneself (and also in the corresponding default assumptions one routinely and implicitly makes about oneself and others) are standards under which such knowledge attributions (and such default assumptions) are regarded as epistemically warranted independently of the fact that one's total experiential history is consistent with the possibility of being an envatted brain, or being the victim of a Cartesian evil deceiver, etc.

5.7.3 Type 4 Attributions and default assumptions of external-world knowledge figure ubiquitously in one's everyday activities, individually and collectively. The distinction between knowing that *p* on one hand, and on the other hand not knowing whether or not *p* is the case, is persistently and systematically reflected in virtually all of one's dealings with the world and with other people. If one knows that *p*, then one can safely act on the supposition that *p* is the case; otherwise not. If one believes that someone else knows that *p*, then one can safely act on both the supposition that *p* and the supposition that this other person will act on the supposition that p; otherwise not.[32] And so forth. There is a genuine distinction here of crucial practical importance, and people routinely deploy the concept KNOWLEDGE to track this distinction. Furthermore, it is plausible that, in competently employing the distinction, one has some reasonable sense for the practical significance of attributions of knowledge—a sense for the kinds of roles played by knowledge-attributions in regulating one's own practice

---

[32] Henderson (2009) develops a contextualist account that draws heavily on the idea that conceptually fitting applications of the concept of knowledge would be consonant with the everyday regulation of people's epistemic lives in a community of coordinated inquirers—which he understands as central to the point and purpose of the concept.

and that of one's epistemic community. To a first approximation, perhaps, one senses that one's belief or one's interlocutor's belief is so epistemically grounded that it amounts to actionable information—that one's self or one's interlocutor is here a good source of actionable information.

5.7.4 Type 5 There is overwhelmingly good scientific evidence that people's pre-theoretic, common-sensical conception of their embodied, sensory-perceptual communion with the external world is essentially correct. Much is known about the detailed workings of the various sensory modalities, and about how these modalities convey, via their effects on the central nervous system, accurate information about the external world to the experiencing agent. It doesn't happen via a non-veridical interface between an envatted brain and a fancy computer; rather, it happens via a by-and-large veridical, multi-modal, interface between body and world.

Consider now the hypothesis of parameter contextualism about knowledge. It nicely explains the type-2 data concerning the dual pull of skeptical scenarios, especially when parameter contextualism is deployed in combination with some supplementary psychological side-hypotheses which themselves are very plausible, given the hypothesis of parameter contextualism. One side-hypothesis is that people are so good at accommodating their judgment-making to implicit contextual parameters that typically they do not even notice them. Another is that in unusual contexts that generate a tendency for maximally strict settings of the implicit parameters governing the concept KNOWLEDGE, people are apt to experience both (a) an inclination to deploy the concept in accordance with those settings (which would mean denying all external-world knowledge), and also (b) a contrary inclination to deploy the concept in the usual ways. This package of hypotheses receives abductive empirical support from the dual pull, by providing an attractive-looking explanation of the phenomenon.

Data of type 3 reinforces these considerations. A plausible empirical side-hypothesis is that the epistemic standards one employs, when one makes confident attributions of knowledge—and when one confidently adopts and maintains default presumptions about knowledge possessed by oneself and by others—are appropriate epistemic standards, given the workings of the concept KNOWLEDGE itself. For, the use of grossly inappropriate epistemic standards, in the confident intuitive deployment of a concept, typically reflects a deficiency in one's conceptual/semantic competence with that concept. Parameter contextualism accommodates the epistemic standards governing normal application of the concept KNOWLEDGE, since it treats these standards as appropriate. 'Skeptical invariantism,' on the other hand, entails that such standards are much too lax; it entails that under suitable epistemic standards, external-world knowledge-attributions are warranted only if one's experiential evidence conclusively precludes the possibility of radical deception—which never happens. Ceteris paribus, a conceptual-analytic hypothesis that accommodates the epistemic standards normally accompanying a concept's deployment is better than a hypothesis entailing that those epistemic standards are seriously deficient. So in this respect, parameter contextualism does better than skeptical invariantism. (Non-skeptical invariantism fares well in this respect too, but badly in others. For instance, it cannot readily explain data of type 2.)

Data of type 4 also favors parameter contextualism. Human concepts emerge pragmatically, in ways that serve the purposes for which those concepts are employed. In general, therefore, concepts do not have satisfaction conditions built into them that are so demanding that they thwart the very purposes the concepts serve. Attributions and presuppositions of knowledge play a key action-guiding role both individually and interpersonally; the distinction between knowing that p and not knowing whether p tracks a genuine difference that is of ubiquitous importance in human affairs. So it would be purpose-thwarting for the concept KNOWLEDGE to possess satisfaction conditions that are both in-principle unsatisfiable and context-invariant. Parameter contextualism therefore accords better than does skeptical invariantism with the central purposes that the concept actually serves. (Here too, non-skeptical invariantism also does well—but again, at the cost of not explaining the intuitive pull of radical-deception scenarios.)

Data of type 5 reinforces these latest considerations. Given the plausible empirical side-hypothesis that humans normally deploy the concept KNOWLEDGE in a way that manifests conceptual competence, together with the conceptual-analytic hypothesis of parameter contextualism, the strong scientific-theoretical evidence supporting the by-and-large veridicality of sensory-perceptual experience really does underwrite common-sensical claims to know that such perceptual experience is mostly veridical. Indeed, this evidence also underwrites claims like 'I know that I am not an envatted brain,' even though these latter claims are somewhat elusive because affirming them (in language or in thought) tends to induce shifts to parameter-settings under which the claims become false.

When these kinds of considerations are fed together into the hopper of wide reflective equilibrium, they reinforce one another epistemically in such a way that their combined epistemic weight is very powerful. The hypothesis of parameter contextualism simply accords better with the relevant empirical data than does either skeptical invariantism or non-skeptical invariantism. Parameter contextualism, in combination with various psychological side-hypotheses that are plausible themselves (given parameter contextualism), explains the dual pull on one hand, while on the other hand according well with ordinary epistemic standards for attributing knowledge, with important facts about point and purpose concerning the concept KNOWLEDGE, and with the deeply held belief that scientific evidence about the workings of sensory-perceptual processes underwrites ordinary knowledge-claims. Collectively, empirical data of types 2–5 provide strong empirical evidence in support of the conceptual-analytic hypothesis of parameter contextualism.

As we remarked above, for present purposes in this chapter, the reader need not accept the argument just canvassed (although we ourselves find it quite compelling). Rather, the point we wish to make turns only on the following claims. First, the argument is indeed philosophical. Second, it has a large-scale structure that is not uncommon in philosophy. Third, it is abductive and empirical: it has the overall form of inference to the best explanation, the phenomena being explained are contingent and empirical, and the explanation deploys psychological side-hypotheses that are empirical themselves. Fourth, it can be conducted from the armchair. Reasoning with this combination of features counts as low-grade a priori.

5.8 The two-stage model elaborated

Let us now bring together the threads of the preceding discussion, and then add some further elaboration by way of brief discussion of recent relevant work by others. Initially (in section 1 of the present chapter) several central components of the classical conception of a priori justification were set forth. This provided a characterization of what we called the high-grade a priori:

1. A priori claims are subject to a distinctive kind of justification, one that can be called justification by reflection. (A priori claims constitute an epistemically distinctive class.)
2. Justification by reflection, for a given claim, is accessible to any epistemic agent (who understands the claim), because it draws only upon what is accessible by having acquired the relevant concepts. (The a priori is internalistically accessible.)
3. Because reflection draws only on understanding claims—on what is accessible by virtue of having acquired the relevant concepts—it is not dependent on experience. (A priori justification is not contaminated by the empirical.)

We then argued (particularly in sections 5.4–5.6) that there are compelling reasons for thinking that a greater appreciation for epistemic realities can be obtained by thinking of at least some a priori justification in ways that do not fully conform to this classical conception of the high-grade a priori. Of particular importance is the fact that philosophical reflection, which has historically served as a prominent sample of a kind of inquiry that gives rise to a priori justification, does not itself fully conform to these requirements. Our own account of low-grade a priori justification is then intended to gently 'warp' the classical conception in a way that allows one to accommodate this prominent putative example of a priori justificatory method. (Talk of 'warping' certain traditional planks in the classical or traditional conception of the a priori is intended to echo Quine's use of Neurath's figure of boat repair at sea.)[33] Low-grade a priori justification is provided by philosophical reflection on the workings of concepts.

To make vivid both the continuities with, as well as the departures from, the traditional conception, let us now summarize our conception of low-grade a priori

---

[33] Quine (1960, p. 4) writes, 'Our boat stays afloat because at each alternation we keep the bulk of it intact as a going concern. Our words continue to make passable sense because of continuity of theory: we warp usage gradually enough to avoid rupture.'

justification in three points, with some elaboration. In the case of low-grade a priori justification:

A. A priori claims are subject to a distinctive kind of justification, one that can be called justification by reflection—and one exhibited in historical and contemporary examples of philosophical reflection. (A priori claims constitute an epistemically distinctive class.)
B. Because it draws predominantly on what is accessible by having acquired the relevant concepts, justification by reflection on an a priori claim is largely accessible to epistemic agents who understand the claim.
   i. This is to say that the a priori justification is largely internalistically accessible.
   ii. Such justification can turn largely on what is accessible by virtue of having acquired the featured concepts because it has to do with claims that are conceptually grounded necessary truths.
C. Because reflection draws largely on what allows an agent to understand the claims at issue—on what is accessible by virtue of having acquired the featured concepts—its preponderant evidential base is constituted by the deliverances of the agent's own conceptual competence.
   i. Accordingly, reflection can be undertaken 'from the armchair' and without needing to 'go out' and gather experiential or perceptual evidence to support the claim that the world is as represented in the relevant claim. Instead one can appreciate that the claim is a conceptually grounded necessary truth.
   ii. However, it must be acknowledged that the relevant reflection is a two-stage affair. The first stage involves the accumulation of judgments regarding particular cases or scenarios—these are presumptively the direct deliverances of conceptual competence. The second stage involves an abductive inference in which these first-stage judgments serve as data-points (together with other data-points that are largely empirical but also are largely armchair-accessible) for an account of the workings of the relevant concepts and an associated understanding of the agent's conceptual competence.
   iii. As an important result, a priori justification is contaminated by the empirical.

The above presentation juxtaposes the classical conception—represented by (1)–(3) of our characterization of high-grade a priori justification—with the corresponding clauses (A)–(C) of our characterization of philosophical low-grade a priori justification. This juxtaposition makes vivid how we seek to gently 'warp' the classical conception in order to accommodate the salient sample of a priori knowledge presented by philosophical reflection. What is clearly exhibited is the respect in which we seek to replace the classical claim that a priori justification is not contaminated by the empirical (clause 3) with a claim (clause C) that recognizes the empirical dimension of conceptual analysis and yet which highlights those aspects of it that would have made it appear noncontaminated—its armchair accessibility and its concern with conceptually grounded necessary truths. These moves occasion an associated weakening of clause (2): clause (B) makes room for the empirical elements in armchair-accessible reflective justification.

Three kinds of empiricality were emphasized, all of which typically are present in low-grade a priori reasoning and justification. First is the empirical representativeness assumption, which figures in the initial transition from concrete scenario-judgments to a tentative conceptual-analytic hypothesis. Second are the empirical elements that figure in reciprocal equilibration between hypotheses and type-1 data, as one seeks to filter out the noise in the data—e.g. by explaining away some of the initial scenario-judgments as performance errors. Third are the empirical elements that arise when data of types 2–5 are incorporated: typically such data are contingent, empirical phenomena themselves, and typically the abductive reasoning to the best explanation of these data invokes in the explanation not just the conceptual-analytic hypothesis one seeks to establish, but also certain empirical side-hypotheses as well.

By way of further triangulation of our proposed model of the low-grade a priori, it will be useful to make some brief remarks comparing our approach to two related recent discussions: one by Christopher Peacocke (1993, 1998) and one by Alvin Goldman (1992b, 1999; Goldman and Pust 1998).

Peacocke has advanced a view of a priori knowledge that is in many respects like ours—but is also significantly at variance with our account. Like us, Peacocke is interested in accounting for a priori justification as a matter of drawing on conceptual competence—on what he terms the 'possession' or 'mastery' of the concepts featured in the relevant claims. His account of the character of concept possession leads him to a two-stage model of the a priori justification that one can have for general truths: various particular truths may be derived directly from one's conceptual competence, and the subsequent justification of general truths inferentially builds upon these particulars. In these respects, we and Peacocke are in agreement. However, Peacocke's over-idealized take on the epistemic situation of one who has acquired the relevant concepts leads him to understand the second stage (the generalizing stage) as devoid of empirical elements and thus as high-grade a priori.

Focusing on the conceptually competent agent, Peacocke explains that such an agent can generate a set of conceptually grounded judgments in response to concrete scenarios. The project is then understood as one of moving beyond those conceptually grounded particulars to conceptually grounded generalities. But, understanding the project in just such terms obscures questions of great epistemic moment that the agent must confront—since it supposes an idealized conceptual competence delivering a delimited set of conceptually grounded truths that can then be treated unproblematically as conceptually-given data points constraining a high-grade a priori inference to a subsuming generalization (when such is finally hit upon).

We do not deny that part of the epistemic action is finding a generalization that subsumes the direct deliverances of conceptual competence—since these latter are typically spawned in judgments responding to concrete scenarios. But we insist that there are additional families of questions that must be sorted out and answered at the same time. As indicated above, the result is an epistemic project with empirical as well as 'high-grade' a priori constraints. It is just these constraints that are most obscured in Peacocke's picture of an ideally competent agent with a clearly delimited set of conceptually grounded judgments awaiting an adequate subsuming generalization.[34]

To further locate our own proposed construal of conceptual analysis and the sort of a priori justification that it affords, it will be helpful to compare it with Goldman's treatments of these matters, as reflected in his recent writings. Three points are especially salient. First, although Goldman too proposes a somewhat revisionary account of the a priori, his revisions differ from ours. He holds on to the traditional idea that a key hallmark of the a priori is lack of empirical contamination. His revisionary approach then consists principally in these two features: (a) construing lack of empirical contamination in terms of a belief's being generated by a purely innate process; and (b) repudiating various trappings traditionally associated with the a priori, such as infallibility. Our own revisionary notion is different, of course. And we would maintain that our own notion of the low-grade a priori is more theoretically useful and more illuminating than is Goldman's alternative revision. Indeed, Goldman himself expresses a revealing point concerning his own revisionary a priori/a posteriori dichotomy. He writes of the 'need to transcend the traditional dichotomy between a priori and a posteriori knowledge'—of the need to overcome the idea that knowledge cannot, in some sense, exhibit elements of both at once (Goldman 1999, p. 23). With the dichotomy in place, he notes, an empirical dimension to a process or method leads one to categorize the beliefs it generates as a posteriori (supposing that it is a justificatory process at all). He worries:

Warrant is just a complex and multi-dimensional affair. Why try to force it into some neat little container or pair of containers that simply disguise its true contours? (Goldman 1999, p. 23)

The worry is essentially this: some beliefs might well come about via the interaction of innate processes (e.g. perceptual ones) and empirical input (e.g. sensory stimulation); and although their justification would officially count as a posteriori, the true contours of this justification would really incorporate elements from both of the traditional categories a priori and a posteriori. Thus, the proposed revisionary notion of the a priori is not very illuminating or theoretically useful.

Second, Goldman's construal of the enterprise of conceptual analysis in philosophy is strikingly similar in some respects to our own. Like ourselves, and like Peacocke, Goldman understands conceptual analysis as a two-stage affair, and as informed by empirical elements. However, unlike Peacocke and ourselves, Goldman denies that conceptual analysis gives rise to a priori justification or knowledge. Accordingly, one can see our own position as intermediate between Peacocke's—on which conceptual

---

[34] For a more detailed critical discussion of Peacocke's model of the a priori in comparison to our own account of the low-grade a priori, see Henderson and Horgan (2000a, 2003).

analysis gives rise to high-grade a priori knowledge—and Goldman's—on which it gives rise only to empirical, a posteriori, knowledge. We maintain that the relevant kind of abductive reasoning is epistemologically distinctive in important ways, including especially its heavy reliance on armchair-accessible data, and that this kind of distinctiveness merits the label 'a priori' (as qualified by the non-demeaning modifier 'low-grade').

Third, Goldman's general approach to the concept is highly psychologistic, and this is reflected too in how he thinks of conceptual analysis. He construes concepts as mental representations of a certain sort, and he construes conceptual analysis as the descriptive psychological account of how such representations are deployed in cognition. We ourselves cleave to a more traditional, more normatively laden, concept of concept (as does Peacocke). Accordingly, we also cleave to a more traditional, more normatively laden, construal of the goal of conceptual analysis—namely to uncover conceptually grounded necessary truths that are both general in scope and philosophically important in content.[35]

Finally, let us further triangulate our model of the low-grade a priori by addressing an objection raised by Nenad Miscevic (forthcoming) to earlier presentations of the model. Miscevic makes these striking observations:

> The phenomenology of philosophical thought experiments seems to speak against [the view that there are or should be constraining considerations at the level of psychology operative in the move from judgments to generalizations] .... Take the three examples [Berkeley's invitation to try to conceive of bodies with only primary qualities, the ship of Theseus, and Twin Earth cases pointing to composition as essential to natural kind stuffs]. In my own experience as well as in experience with students, there were no immediate problematic intuitions elicited. Everybody concerned just jumped from particular to general conclusion . . . without proposing counterexamples.

It seems to us that Miscevic is giving a correct description of many a philosopher's phenomenology associated with certain stretches of philosophical reflection: often, at the level of conscious reflective experience, one just jumps from particular to general, with no further ado. But although we claim that a suitable articulated reconstruction of conceptual-analytic reflection must incorporate the various complexities and empirical factors we have been emphasizing throughout section 5, it is no part of our view that all these elements must be fully manifested (or even partially manifested) in the phenomenology of reflection. On the contrary, we maintain that the phenomenology of reflection can make perfectly good belief-generating processes seem simpler than they in fact ultimately are. Indeed, we maintain that there is commonly a very substantial, phenomenologically hidden, depth and richness to epistemically justificatory cognitive processes—a theme that will loom large in

---

[35] For a more detailed critical discussion of Goldman's take on a priori and on conceptual analysis in comparison to our own take on these matters, see Henderson and Horgan (2000a, 2003).

Chapter 6. There we will argue—largely by appeal to recent developments in cognitive science, rather than in a low-grade a priori way—that processes and information 'submerged' below consciousness are typically essential for some of the more characteristic holistic elements of human cognition. Abductive inference is a paradigmatically holistic chore—and it would come as no surprise were important parts of the information relevant to an abductive inference to be accommodated by way of submerged processes.

6 Conclusion

We began with the idea that, while rationalist and empiricist philosophers may disagree concerning the extent of a priori knowledge, and concerning some purported ways of obtaining a priori justification, they agree on at least one point concerning what would be sufficient to make for a priori justification. When one has acquired a competence with the concepts featured in a claim, and when the claim itself expresses a truth that is grounded in internally accessible elements of the semantics of the featured concepts, then a rather distinct route to justification is available: drawing on conceptual competence, and reasoning from the armchair, the agent can come to appreciate that the claim must be true. We believe that there are cases of such justification to be had, and that such justification is epistemically distinctive enough and important enough to honor with the designation 'a priori.' Accordingly, we have set out to take a closer look at this a priori justification.

On the account we have developed here, with philosophical reasoning about philosophically important concepts as a paradigm case, a priori justification for interesting generalizations typically will come by way of a two-stage process. In the first stage, one employs one's conceptual competence to do what it does best: to generate particular judgments regarding concrete scenarios. However, such direct but particular results of conceptual competence do not have the generality that is sought in philosophy. This set of particular judgments provides the basis for a reflective generalization that is abductive in character. Our central objective here has been to urge on the reader an understanding of the epistemic character of this generalizing stage. We have argued that the abductive inference required to get one from the set of concrete judgments made in response to scenarios to general conceptually grounded necessary truths has an ineliminable empirical dimension.

What emerges is a route to epistemic justification that has been pointed to repeatedly by philosophers—although they have advanced various descriptions of what is there going on. We maintain that they have been dealing with samples of an epistemic kind: justification of (putative) conceptually grounded, necessary, general truths that draws upon conceptual competence. Philosophers' descriptions have commonly been mistaken, by ignoring the empirical abductive character of the relevant inquiry. Accordingly, while we are happy to retain the designation 'a priori' for the epistemic kind referred to, we add the qualifier 'low-grade' as a caution: the relevant inquiry does not have one feature that has commonly been thought to mark the a priori, namely it is not uncontaminated with the empirical. When philosophers undertake to reflectively discover interesting, general, conceptually grounded necessary truths, the kind of justification they should expect to obtain—and typically have obtained, despite widespread misconceptions about their own reflective methodology—is low-grade a priori justification.

3
Neoclassical Reliabilism

1 The agenda

Chapter 2 presented an account of low-grade a priori reflection that plausibly features in much philosophical investigation. Such reflection provides a justificatory basis for holding that certain claims are conceptually grounded necessary truths—truths that can serve to orient further empirical investigations. We believe that there are important such truths to be had in epistemology. These conceptually grounded truths orient further epistemological investigation. In particular, certain conceptually necessary general truths about what would be required for, and make for, objectively justificatory processes orient the empirical investigations necessary for understanding the more concrete character of realistic and fitting epistemological standards.

In this and the following two chapters we will put this understanding of low-grade a priori reflection to use, by investigating a central epistemological concept. In this way, we intend to clarify the role of low-grade a priori reflection in epistemological investigations. Take this as an extended practical demonstration of the method described in Chapter 2. Our investigation centers on the epistemic concept of *being (objectively) justified in believing*.[1] (Hereafter, when we speak of justification we will mean *objective* justification, unless otherwise noted explicitly.) We develop a low-grade a priori understanding of this central evaluative epistemic concept—and our investigation will self-consciously employ the type of reflection described in the previous chapter.

Reliabilists about justification typically advance the reliability of belief-forming processes, within the epistemic agent's actual environment, as a constitutive requirement for

---

[1] Here and throughout the book, we use the locution 'being justified' for what is often called *doxastic* justification: justification that accrues to an actual belief that a given epistemic agent actually possesses. Doxastic justification is our focus in this chapter and the next two. Being justified in believing a proposition *p* is to be contrasted with *having* justification for *p* (often called *propositional* justification)—where the latter is epistemic worthiness that accrues to *p*, relative to the information available to a given epistemic agent, whether or not that agent actually does believe *p*. (We will address the having/being distinction—i.e. the distinction between propositional justification and doxastic justification—in Chapter 7.) Throughout the book we also freely use the expression 'epistemic justification'; the default reading of this should be *objective doxastic justification*, unless it is clear in context that some other reading (e.g. *propositional justification*) is intended.

justification. They typically also emphasize that reliability is not the only feature that constitutes justificatory processes. They allow that epistemic justification does not require belief-fixation using the most reliable processes conceivable in connection with the formation of the relevant kind of belief. Instead, while justificatory processes must be reliable at some threshold level, facts about the cognitive systems involved, and what would be realistically tractable processes for such cognizers, can help determine what would be 'reliable enough' to be objectively justificatory on the part of such cognitive systems. Ceteris paribus, more guarded processes are more reliable. But objective epistemic justification should not require processes that are so loaded with checks, double-checks, and triple-checks, with cross-checks and cross-cross-checks, as to take unworkably long to yield a belief. Such alternative processes might be marginally more reliable (were they employed without error), but at the cost of yielding very few beliefs. Reliabilists commonly appreciate that such highly demanding and costly cognitive processes would not be fitting processes for humans—they would frustrate one's epistemic ends. With their attention to human cognitive capacities, reliabilists have typically allowed information regarding tractability (whether humans can consistently employ the process) and cognitive costs (whether humans can apply the process rapidly enough to yield the needed beliefs) to condition their thinking about what processes would make for the 'reasonable reliability' they require. Thus, on their accounts, objectively justificatory processes for humans would be reasonably reliable and would be serviceably fast and powerful.

In this chapter we will focus on the idea of reliability as it has featured in reliabilist epistemology, for we believe that there are aspects of reliability that need to be given greater articulation. Thus, we develop a distinction between two forms of reliability, hitherto not sufficiently appreciated in epistemology. Both forms figure importantly with respect to justification, and also with respect to knowledge. Our investigation provides a needed perspective on the current state of the art in reliabilist epistemology. Additionally, our discussion here provides a natural springboard for considerations we will put forward in the following chapter, in support of an account of justification involving yet a third kind of reliability that differs from either of the two kinds we discuss here.

We use the term 'standard reliabilism' for the generic form of reliabilism that emphasizes reliability within the worldly environment that the epistemic agent *actually occupies*—as opposed to various non-actual worldly environments such as that of an envatted brain. By 'classical reliabilism' we mean versions of standard reliabilism that do not explicitly distinguish between the two forms of reliability we will describe here. We use the expression 'neoclassical reliabilism' for the version of standard reliabilism that does make this distinction, and that deploys it in the way we describe in this chapter.

In this chapter we present neoclassical reliabilism as a plausible refinement of classical versions. Thus, we take it that neoclassical reliabilism is itself still a version of standard reliabilism, albeit an improved version. In Chapters 4 and 5 we will urge a departure from standard reliabilism, in favor of a significantly non-standard reliabilist account of justification. That new approach will still retain the broad spirit of reliabilism, however. Indeed, considerations much like those that motivate refining the classical version of standard reliabilism into a neoclassical version will also motivate transforming standard reliabilism into the non-standard version to be described in Chapter 4.

2 A fake-barn scenario: Athena and Fortuna

We begin with a variant of a familiar trope in recent epistemology, the fake-barn scenario. Suppose that two people, Athena and Fortuna, are driving in a car together from New York City to Memphis, and are on an interstate highway in rural West Virginia. They drive through a local area in which there happen to be numerous extremely realistic-looking, papier mâché, fake barns within view of the highway—although neither of them has any inkling of this fact or any reason to believe that they are traveling through such a region. As it happens, all the real barns in this local area are painted yellow, and none of the fake barns—or any other buildings in the area—are painted yellow. Again, they have no information to this effect. As they drive past a saliently presented yellow building, Athena, who has had reasonable experience with barns, gets a clear look at it, and on the basis of its barn-like visual appearance, she judges it to be a barn.

Fortuna gets only a very brief glimpse of the building out of the corner of her eye. As it happens, she saw her first barn just yesterday, and it happened to be yellow. (Barns are extremely rare in New York City.) She judges, on the basis of the briefly glimpsed building's yellow color, that it is a barn—even though she did not get a good enough look at it, and was thus unable to discern any other features that are distinctive of barns as opposed to houses or other kinds of buildings. It's not that she has a *general* belief that all and only yellow buildings are barns, or that all barns are yellow; she has never formed any such belief. Also, it's not that she has a *general* tendency to inductively extrapolate from old cases to new ones in a hastily-generalizing way, a tendency she might otherwise be exhibiting here. Rather, it just happens that *in the present circumstances*, a psychological process is present within her that takes as input both the brief glimpse of a yellow building and the yellow-barn memory, and generates as output the barn-belief about the briefly glimpsed object.

So Athena and Fortuna each form the belief that the building is a barn. And indeed it is. On the scenario as stipulated, it must be, because, although (unbeknownst to them) there are numerous fake barns in the local vicinity, it is also the case that the present building is yellow and (here again unbeknownst to them) that all the real barns in the vicinity are yellow and none of the fake barns—or any other buildings—in the vicinity are yellow.

What is one inclined to say intuitively about Athena and Fortuna, with respect to the question whether the given belief is justified, and also with respect to whether it counts as knowledge? First consider Athena. One's strong inclination is to say that her belief that the building is a barn is extremely well justified. After all, she has excellent perceptual evidence for the belief, and she formed the belief using a process of perceptual barn-categorization that generally works extremely well. On the other hand, as is commonly stressed in discussions of fake-barn scenarios, one is also strongly inclined to say that she does not *know* that the building is a barn, because her belief has been produced by a belief-forming process that happens to be *unreliable in this specific local environment*. Given all those fake barns around, any of which she would have mistakenly taken to be a real barn, the truth of her belief is too much a matter of epistemic luck to count as knowledge.

Now consider Fortuna. Here one has a very strong inclination to say that she *lacks* any significant degree of justification for her belief that the building she briefly glimpsed is a barn. This seems so despite the fact that this belief was produced by a belief-forming process that happens to be reliable—for reasons completely beyond her cognitive ken—in the local vicinity she is in at the moment. The trouble is that *this reliability is itself too fortuitous*, too much a matter of epistemic luck, for the belief to count as justified. And as a consequence, the truth of her belief is too much a matter of luck for the belief to count as *knowledge*—the reliability of the belief-forming process notwithstanding. (As should be expected, given the discussion of the previous chapter, these judgment tendencies constitute important data for the ensuing reflection. As should also be expected, this is just the beginning. There is much sorting out to do— including the matter of understanding what is at issue in the judgments that a belief, the process by which it is produced, and even the reliability of that process might be 'too fortuitous' or 'too risky.')

3 Local reliability versus global reliability

If one takes these intuitive verdicts to be correct, would this mean that we have here a case in which one person's belief (Athena's) is justified even though it is *not* produced by a reliable belief-forming process, and in which another person's belief (Fortuna's) fails to be justified even though it *is* produced by a reliable belief-forming process? That would be too flat-footed a moral to draw, in part because in both cases, the reliability of the relevant processes is not such a simple matter—one cannot flatly say that the relevant process is reliable, or that it is not reliable. There are respects in which Athena's belief-forming process is reliable, and respects in which it is not. Similarly, there are (different) respects in which Fortuna's belief-forming process is reliable, and respects in which it is not. There are at least two discernible dimensions commonly of some concern in discussions of the reliability of belief-forming processes, both of which figure importantly with respect to both justification and knowledge. On one hand is what we will call *local* reliability: relative to the specific, spatiotemporally local environment that the cognitive agent happens to occupy when the belief is formed, the given belief-forming process has a strong tendency to generate true beliefs.[2] On the other hand is what we will call *global* reliability: relative to the class of actual and potential local environments within the cognitive agent's global environment, the given belief-forming process has a strong tendency to generate true beliefs.

We pause now to elaborate upon the distinction between local and global reliability, before returning to Athena, Fortuna, and some additional thought-experimental colleagues of theirs who have yet to be introduced.

As is commonly recognized, reliability is always relative to an environment—either a wider or a narrower environment. Local reliability normally has currency only when there is something locally distinctive that influences the effectiveness of a given belief-forming process. Thus, the familiar fake-barn scenarios make contextually salient a rough region in which fake barns are abundant. Without such yarn-spinning that focuses on a region posing distinctive challenges, one commonly thinks in terms of the wider global, environment that human agents occupy. Several points of clarification are called for.

First, a possible global environment (whether actual or nonactual) typically includes a diversity of local environments that might be of significance. Thus, consider one's processes of determining one's location by reading street signs. It will be reliable in certain local environments, where official signage is 'good,' where tricksters are uncommon, and where one is familiar with the local language and conventions. It will be unreliable in local environments where these things are otherwise. A global environment also contains a diversity of local environments—certainly the actual global environment contains such a diversity.

Second, one may wonder whether an agent's global environment coincides with the whole of the actual cosmos the agent occupies. No. Rather, when one thinks of a global environment, the idea one wants to capture is basically this: while a cognitive process might have differing tendencies to produce true beliefs in differing local conditions, one can be concerned with what would be its tendency in the wider environment that comprises all the local environments into which the agent and like agents might enter and deploy it. This suggests that an agent's global environment is best understood as comprising not the whole actual or possible cosmos that the agent occupies, but just those portions of it into which the agent and like agents might venture (while yet remaining functioning cognitive systems).[3]

---

[2] Clearly our use of the terms 'local reliability' and 'global reliability' is different from Goldman (1986, pp. 44–5).

[3] The point of the parenthetical restriction can be appreciated by thinking of the various ways of taking the formulation without it. That formulation allows for various alternatives: an agent's global environment might include just those portions of the agent's cosmos that can readily sustain life, or just the agent's biosphere (if such agents are actually effectively planet bound), or are within the agent's light-cone (if such agents are high-tech travelers), or some combination. But, if one thinks of the agent's global environment as encompassing the whole of the agent's biosphere, or the agent's light-cone, it would seem that it then includes many local environments that would be irrelevant for purposes of gauging global reliability of a

Third, even were one to ignore the point just made—even were one to suppose that the agent's global environment encompasses the whole cosmos that the agent occupies (or a time-slice thereof)—a global environment would not be the same thing as a *possible world* (or a time-slice thereof).[4] A global environment, and likewise a total cosmic environment, will obtain (or have a counterpart) in multiple (similar) possible worlds. A possible world, by definition, has everything fixed—everything, including the space-time coordinates of all things or properties within it. In the actual global environment, the author's left index finger just landed on the 'I' of his keyboard. But, in this actual global environment, something else could have obtained just then (that finger might have been occupied grabbing his coffee cup, or the keyboard might have been at a slight angle so that the finger landed on the 'K'). One can take different trajectories through one's environment—which requires that the same environment obtains in different possible worlds. So can other things and people in one's environment—friends, enemies, predators, prey, winds, cars, and so on. They can take different trajectories in the same environment. (Think of a parallel observation from biology: in the environment of a greater-Yellowstone-ecosystem bison, the bison may cross paths with a wolf pack in a given day or may not. Both groups are present in the environment, and can take various trajectories through it. This fact makes a difference for the tendencies of both bison and wolves to have reproductive success in that environment.) When one says that a process is reliable in an environment, one is saying that it has the tendency to produce good results there, and this propensity must be understood in terms of nearby possible worlds involving that same environment (or its counterpart)—one's involving various alternative trajectories through that environment. In order to talk of tendencies in an environment, one must think of what would happen in a range of nearby possible worlds in which that same environment is still present.

4 Local reliability, global reliability, and the fake-barn scenarios

Return now to Athena and Fortuna, in their local fake-barn environment. In the scenario we described, Athena employs a barn-categorizing belief-forming process that is indeed highly reliable in one respect: it is globally reliable. (Recall that she has had reasonable experience with barns, and it is plausible to suppose that she has thereby come to have a globally reliable perceptual ability to discriminate barns from non-barns. After

---

process—those in which the agent could not possibly implement that process (for example, those in which the agent would be instantaneously crushed by gravity, or incinerated, or otherwise would cease to be a functioning cognitive system). It seems better to restrict the relevant global environment to those potential local environments that such an agent might enter *while remaining a cognitive agent*—letting the agent's global environment be constituted by the composite of these.

[4] The same is true of local environments.

all, in the world at large, there are few who are motivated to either camouflage their barns, or to construct fake barns, and so there are not many deceptive cases in Athena's global environment. Humans with reasonable experience typically do become reliable perceptual judges with respect to such generally straightforward common middle-sized physical objects.) But her barn-categorizing process is unreliable in another respect, for reasons unbeknownst to her and outside of her cognitive ken: because of all those fake barns in the vicinity, her barn-categorizing process is locally unreliable. Intuitively, the strong objective justification her belief possesses does indeed involve production by a reliable belief-forming process—namely a globally reliable one. On the other hand, intuitively, the fact that this strongly justified belief nonetheless fails to qualify as knowledge also involves a failure with respect to the reliability of the belief-forming process—namely a failure to be locally reliable. Both dimensions of reliability thus figure importantly, epistemically: the presence of global reliability figures in the fact that her belief is well justified, whereas the absence of local reliability figures in the fact that the belief nevertheless fails to be a case of knowledge.

Fortuna is a converse case. Her belief is produced by a barn-categorization process that is locally reliable (for reasons beyond her cognitive ken) but is globally unreliable. One judges that Fortuna's belief fails to be well justified. Intuitively, what appears to figure importantly in its lacking objective justification is the fact that the belief-forming process is not globally reliable. Given this lack of global reliability, the fact that the process happens to be locally reliable strikes one intuitively as a *lucky accident*, epistemically speaking; and for this reason, the belief does not count as a case of knowledge.

These intuitive judgments are plausibly viewed as the product of one's semantic/conceptual competence vis-à-vis the concepts of justification and knowledge, and thus are very likely correct. So taken, they point to important morals concerning justification and knowledge—morals that reliabilists should embrace. First, the reliability of belief-forming processes has the two dimensions we have described, and each may be important in its own right with respect to both justification and knowledge. Second, at least in the case at hand involving Athena and Fortuna, the way these two dimensions figure seems to be as follows. Global reliability of the process is required in order for the belief to be objectively justified (as this seems to be what Fortuna saliently lacks and what Athena possesses). Knowledge, on the other hand, requires this and more; knowledge seems to require local reliability as well. (In the scenario, it is local reliability that Athena lacks, while she seems to possess an objectively justified true belief.) Without local reliability, the truth of the belief is too much a matter of lucky accident for the belief to count as knowledge, despite its being well justified. Without global reliability, on the other hand, the belief is not objectively justified in the first place; so if the process that formed the belief happens to be locally reliable then this fact is just a lucky accident, epistemically speaking; and hence the belief is not a case of knowledge either. We might take these suggestions as provisional working hypotheses at this early stage in our reflective inquiry.

5 Global reliability as a robust disposition

We will call a disposition *robust* if it obtains relative to a fairly wide reference class of potential circumstances, situations, or environments. The idea is that a robust disposition is one whose possession does not depend heavily upon certain unusual or atypical features that are highly specific to the particular circumstance or environment which the possessor of the disposition might happen to occupy; i.e. the disposition does not obtain only relative to a narrow reference class of environments in which those particular features happen to be present.

A process may be robustly reliable or not robustly reliable (may or may not have a robust reliability). Reliability of a belief-forming process, of course, is the tendency to produce (mostly) true beliefs—and, like all dispositions, this disposition must be understood as relative to a reference class of actual or possible environments. If a process is globally reliable, it has this tendency with respect to the wide reference class that is the union of the local environments to which an agent *might* be exposed (or which the agent, or such agents, *might* come to inhabit for a period) within the agent's actual global environment. This formulation is intended to mark the contrast with mere local reliability. Alternatively, one could say simply that global reliability is reliability relative to such agents' actual global environment. This is to have reliability in a reasonably robust fashion. For a process to be globally reliable is for its reliability not to depend heavily upon atypical features that are highly specific to the particular circumstance or environment which the possessor of the disposition might happen to occupy; its reliability then does not obtain only relative to a narrow reference class of environments in which those particular features are present. This said, for a globally reliable process, there may yet be certain local environments involving atypical features in which the globally reliable process would be unreliable. A process can be globally reliable without being locally reliable with respect to some local environment afforded by the global environment (as illustrated by Athena's processes), and a process can be locally reliable without being globally reliable (as illustrated by Fortuna's processes). When a process is locally but not globally reliable, that process's reliability does depend heavily upon certain atypical features that are highly specific to the particular circumstance or environment which the possessor of the disposition occupies. Such merely local reliability is non-robust, because it involves a narrow reference class: a specific local environment that an agent happens to be in.

Compare automobiles. An old car with its somewhat compromised cooling system, worn tires, and the like, might well be reliable relative to a narrow range of potential environmental circumstances, but not relative to a wide range. It might be reliable in a local environment where the climate is temperate, it rains moderately and seldom snows, there are no long steep hills, and there is very little traffic. But it might be unreliable in local environments where there are, for example, temperature extremes, lots of traffic, demanding hills, or significant amounts of snow and ice. Although the car might be in service in an environment in which it happens to be locally reliable, it is not globally reliable. It thus is not *robustly* reliable. Its reliability depends heavily on the somewhat unusual combination of features particular to the environment where it happens to be employed.

On the other hand, there are fine new cars that qualify as globally reliable—that is, would stand up well to the demands of providing daily transportation with respect to the representative environments in which cars are ordinarily driven. Of course, such cars would fail in a few local environments—for example, those characterized by significant flooding, high electromagnetic surges (associated with nuclear explosions) or volcanic flows. But, with respect to the global environment taken as a whole, as a composite of the range of local environments presented within the global environment, the relevant cars would tend to provide daily transportation on demand.

Thus, if a belief-forming process possesses the robust property of global reliability, then it remains globally reliable even if it happens to be locally unreliable within a peculiar local environment in which an epistemic agent happens to be located. Such is the case with Athena. Her perceptual barn-categorization process remains robustly reliable even though, for reasons entirely outside of her cognitive ken concerning the peculiarities of the local region through which she happens to be driving, this process has become locally unreliable.

Compare automobiles again. Consider the Toyota Camry V6—a type of car that has recently received exemplary reliability ratings in the relevant edition of *Consumer Reports*. Since the survey on which this rating is based likely reflects a reasonable distribution of environmental situations, one can take these cars to be globally reliable.[5] Yet, even these robustly reliable automobiles can become locally unreliable in certain extreme local environmental circumstances. Suppose one were to relocate to a region where one's commute involved miles of sand or rough dirt and stone roads (perhaps one's spouse has accepted a position studying an isolated desert ecosystem). One might find that the globally reliable car proved unreliable (due to the tendency to break axles or get stranded in deep sand). Again, although a robustly reliable item—a car, a belief-forming process, or whatever—is reliable in a *wide range* of the potential circumstances within the reference class of the item's reliability, there can be *exceptional* local circumstances within which the item fails to be locally reliable. This is a ubiquitous feature of robust dispositions.

So a globally reliable automobile remains globally reliable even in circumstances where it is not locally reliable; likewise, a globally reliable belief-forming process remains globally reliable even in circumstances where it is not locally reliable.

---

[5] It may be that both tropical local environments and arctic local environments, while represented in the *Consumer Reports* survey, are somewhat under-represented. But we can set aside such qualifications here. If neither the cold of Minnesota and such states, nor the heat of the desert southwest or of Florida, elicit significant problems, we will let marginally more extreme environments be somewhat under-represented in our measure.

6 Safety: a constitutive requirement for justification

Return again to Fortuna, and consider what seems intuitively objectionable about her belief that the yellow structure she fleetingly glimpsed is a barn. The problem is that, although the process that generated this belief does happen to be locally reliable, its being so is too much a matter of epistemic *luck* for her belief to be justified.[6] Adopting the belief in the way she did—on the basis of a brief and fleeting glance in which the only salient feature she noticed was the structure's color, and in a way that arises somehow out of the fact that the one barn she has previously seen was yellow—is objectionably risky, epistemologically speaking. It is not epistemically *safe*. Fortuna has deployed a process that is not at all globally reliable, but coincidentally, she happens to do so in a rather special local environment in which that process is locally reliable. This seems an extraordinary lucky coincidence, for there is nothing about Fortuna that in any way 'tracks' the features of the local environment in virtue of which her yellow-building triggered barn-identification process is locally reliable. Without any relevant information about her local environment (in either the sense of 'information' that entails veridicality or the extended sense that does not), she employed a globally unreliable process that only by the sheerest of coincidences happened to be locally reliable and thus happened to produce a true belief here. It is precisely because the manner of belief-formation is so unsafe that its local reliability is too much a matter of luck to count for much, insofar as justification is concerned.

Compare the epistemically more delightful Athena. She, like most people, employs the sort of perceptual process that has been shaped by reasonable courses of experience with common objects. She got a good view of the object in question, and correctly judged it to be a barn. Experientially informed, or 'trained up,' perceptual processes having to do with common enough objects in clear view qualify as globally reliable processes. It strikes one as relatively safe to employ such a process in the absence of information suggesting that conditions are somehow exceptional.

Epistemic safety, of the sort apparently conditioning one's judgments in these cases, is then clearly associated with being a *suitably* truth-conducive belief-forming process. At least in the case of Athena and Fortuna, it is global reliability that makes for the difference that one senses in epistemic safety. One readily admits that Fortuna's process of forming beliefs about which structures around her are barns is locally reliable. But, one hastens to add, it is unacceptably risky nevertheless. Being highly dependent on unusual contingent features of the environment she happens to occupy, the local reliability of that process would likely disappear were she to come to inhabit a different local environment (and that is itself likely). So the fact that Fortuna here employs a locally reliable process is a matter of *epistemic luck*.

---

[6] In this book we use the phrase 'epistemic luck' and the related phrase 'epistemic safety' in an intuitive sense. This is not the sense associated with these phrases in recent knowledge-focused writings on epistemic safety and epistemic luck (see for example, Sosa 1991 and Pritchard 2005). Subsequently, we work to clarify the kind of epistemic luck and epistemic safety here objected to.

As we will soon discuss at greater length, one can imagine various cases in which one employs a process that is tailored to one's local environment. For example, perhaps one lives for a time in community V, where by convention or law, all and only the modes of mass public transport (trains and buses) are a distinctive violet color. From experience in community V, over time one will come to expect and judge that large violet vehicles glimpsed on the public roadways are buses—that is, one will tend to do so when one is in this increasingly familiar community. Here, the process of bus recognition by color clues would not be globally reliable in itself—but it is informed and called into play by general processes that are responsive to information specifically about community V. As so conditioned, as triggered and checked by these other processes, the tailored color-cued bus identification process comes to have a reasonable measure of global reliability.

This sort of conditioning of one process by others is a common aspect of human cognition, and we soon will need to consider it further. But, for now, the point is that little such conditioning or tailoring seems in play in Fortuna's case. She employs her barn-categorization processes in a largely uninformed manner, and would do so regardless of what region she happened to occupy—her epistemic luck in employing a locally reliable process is *blind* epistemic luck. This accounts for one's sense that Fortuna's belief-forming process is unacceptably risky—and that the resulting belief is not objectively justified.

So, there is reason to think that an idea of the *epistemic safety* (versus riskiness) of belief-fixing processes is at work in the judgments evinced in response to Fortuna and Athena.

A natural line of thought at this point represents what we believe is a significant insight into what is constitutively required for objective epistemic justification. The thought we now suggest is fully consonant with the above reflections on Athena and Fortuna, local and global reliability, and epistemic safety and risk—further, it is a line of thought that we think is well within the spirit of standard reliabilism:

First, embrace the idea that safety—a feature as yet to be more fully explained—is indeed a *constitutive requirement* for a belief's being objectively justified.
Second, look to give an account of safety as constituted by the belief's having been produced by some *suitably robustly reliable* belief-forming process.[7]

We now pursue this proposal. As we do, we will consider many scenarios and judgment tendencies (in keeping with the account of philosophical reflection advanced in the previous chapter). Over the course of this and the next two chapters, it will turn out that this proposal provides the seeds of a very workable understanding of objective

---

[7] There are various ways one might understand what is meant by saying that safety is thus 'constituted.' At a minimum, this constitution-claim entails that *it is a conceptually grounded necessary truth* that a belief is safe iff it has been produced by a belief-forming process that exhibits a suitably robust kind of reliability (where the nature of such robustness is yet to be elaborated).

epistemic justification. At this juncture we acknowledge that we have not yet provided an adequate account of the notion of epistemic safety that we believe to be pivotal for objective epistemic justification. We have not tried to do so. Rather, we expect a more adequate understanding to emerge by way of reflection on further scenarios. Still, we claim to have uncovered a significant clue from the cases of Athena and Fortuna—a line of thought to be further developed below—namely, that displayed in the two-part suggestion above.

How should one understand this idea of a suitably robustly reliable process? One might think, with an eye on the Athena/Fortuna cases, that global reliability per se is just the ticket. But a moment's reflection reveals that this proposal—while perhaps on the right track—is too crude as it stands. Suppose, for instance, that another traveler on Athena and Fortuna's highway, Diana, has full knowledge that the particular local region in question is full of very realistic fake barns, and of the location of this region. She has read all about it in the local morning paper, having spent the night at a hotel along the interstate located just a few miles from the region in question. She now finds herself knowingly driving through that peculiar local region. It remains true that her perceptual barn-categorization process is *globally* reliable; after all, her global environment is pretty much as it was before, so those processes remain globally reliable. Still, Diana most certainly would *not* be justified in coming to believe of a barn-looking structure off in a field, on the basis of its visual appearance, that it's a barn. After all, *she has excellent reason to believe—indeed, she knows full well—that, in her current local environment, the reliability of this belief-forming process is compromised (it is locally unreliable).* Considered in themselves, those perceptual processes remain globally reliable, but in this case would not give rise to objectively justified beliefs (unlike in the case of Athena). If Diana is to form beliefs in an objectively justified way, these perceptual processes must now be inhibited in keeping with the new information that she has acquired.

Likewise, consider the case of Elena. Suppose she knows both (a) that there are lots of barn facsimiles in that particular local area, and also (b) that in that local area, all genuine barns, and no other structures of any kind (including both other kinds of buildings and barn facsimiles) are bright yellow. Finding herself in that very location (and knowing it), she catches a fleeting glance at a bright yellow structure, and promptly forms the belief that it's a barn. Now, in itself, such a process of barn-categorization on the basis of yellow color, would be globally *un*-reliable. But, now, unlike in the case of Fortuna, although Elena formed her belief on the basis of a globally unreliable process (namely classifying briefly glimpsed structures as barns on the basis of their bright yellow color), one judges that this belief of hers *is* justified, even so. Her process is locally reliable, is globally unreliable, and yet here features in the production of objectively justified beliefs (unlike in the case of Fortuna). What is going on?

So there is a task to be undertaken in forging a neoclassical version of reliabilism that will incorporate the idea of the safety of belief-forming processes as a constitutive requirement of justification: one needs to give an account of such safety that makes clear its connection to some suitably robust form of reliability. The cases of Athena and Fortuna reflected the importance of safety, and provided some reason to think of it in terms of global reliability. But, as just demonstrated by the cases of Diana and Elena, global reliability per se won't fill the bill. But perhaps some refinement of it will. Notably, what seems different in the two sets of cases is how the processes in play—the perceptual barn-categorizing processes—themselves are related to further information and processes. So the suggestion to be developed is that epistemic safety might be understood in terms of suitably robust reliability. And furthermore, this will at least sometimes turn on how processes can be modulated by certain other processes.

7 Modulation

Compare Athena's and Diana's visual barn-categorization processes. Both are globally reliable. But Diana's categorization process is *more* globally reliable than Athena's. This is because Diana's process is selectively *inhibited* in this particular local environment in which it is locally unreliable, whereas Athena's is not. This inhibition is a form of what we will call *modulational control* of the belief-forming process by other cognitive processes within the agent's cognitive system. (In the present case, the inhibition works by way of relevant *beliefs* the agent has, ones pertaining to the question of local reliability of the perceptual process in question. But inhibitory modulation need not always work that way—it might work by way of information that is possessed subdoxastically.)

In Elena's case, another form of modulational control is taking place. It might be called *selection* or *spawning*. There is no such modulational control in Fortuna's case. In some respects, Elena's and Fortuna's barn-perception processes are similar—they generate a barn perception on the basis of the presentation of a yellow structure. That process, considered in isolation, is only locally reliable and not globally reliable. Of itself, it is not at all robust, and thus its use would be epistemically very risky and hence unjustified. That's the problem with Fortuna. Her process is employed without checks or balances from other processes, and without special occasioning by other processes. As a result, her process is employed unselectively, and is merely locally reliable, not at all globally reliable. In contrast, in the case of Elena, this process has been selected for use, spawned, by cognitive processes informing her perceptual processes— indeed, it has been selected *specifically for use in the present local environment*. Although the process is not globally reliable considered in isolation (or as used unselectively), *so delimited, so deployed*, it *is* globally reliable. It is globally reliable insofar as the cognitive system is only disposed to use it when it has been selected for local use by suitable wider modulating processes—as in the present case. (In Elena's case, the wider processes modulate her perceptual processes by spawning or selecting certain special-purpose processes for employment specifically in her current local environment. In her case, the modulation by selection works by way of relevant beliefs the agent has about the local environment, ones pertaining to the local reliability of this normally-unreliable belief-forming process. But, as noted already in the case of Diana, modulational control making for selective application need not work through such processes; a believer's cognitive architecture could employ other processes of modulational control that work subdoxastically.)

An important general point emerges from these considerations: Cognitive agents like humans deploy various belief-forming processes in ways that are *holistically integrated* within the agent's overall cognitive architecture. Very frequently, such processes are employed not in isolation, but rather under the control of various other cognitive processes that modulate them. When these modulating cognitive processes provide veridical information about the agent's local environments, the application of the modulated process is tailored to aspects of those local environments about which information is had. Its reliability is thereby enhanced. In principle, a whole host of different modulating relations might be epistemically important. For example, modulating processes might *trigger* a conditioned process in appropriate ways. (One's perceptual processes for spotting large, nonhuman, omnivores are primed when walking in known Grizzly territory.) They might *inhibit* it—making for a more selective use of the process. (One's perceptual processes for spotting large, nonhuman, omnivores are given less free reign when walking about the city.) In triggering or inhibiting the process, the wider processes inform it in ways that draw upon information that the wider processes generate or possess.[8] Many such kinds of modulation can and should be found among normal human cognitive agents.

Some terminology will be useful. A belief-forming process P may be under the conditioning control of a wider set of processes—with or without those wider processes having yet come by information that prompts changes in, or modulations of, P. When there is such a functional relationship between processes we will say that the process P is *under the modulational control of* the wider processes. This wider set of processes may be termed *modulating processes* with respect to P. Being under the modulational control of wider processes and being a modulating process is a matter of the dispositional relationship between wider processes and some narrower processes. This does not require that the modulating processes have actually effected changes in the modulated processes, or that they ever will, just that they are so 'positioned' in the agent's cognitive system as to stand ready to do this. When the modulating processes really *do* turn up information (veridical or not) bearing on the reliability of a process P, and when P or its use thus comes to be spawned, tailored, selectively triggered or inhibited, or in some like manner refined in ways that would (provided the information

---

[8] Here and throughout the book, unless otherwise noted, we use the term 'information' in a way that does not entail truth—so that an item of 'information' can be nonveridical. Commonly, the processes informing modulational control will not be perfectly reliable. It will turn out to be important that they be suitably reliable themselves (more on this soon). But their results will not always be veridical. Nevertheless, whether a result is veridical or not in a particular case, it will be epistemically good that such wider control processes are in place. The modulational control afforded is epistemically desirable and is important for objective epistemic justification.

is correct) make for greater reliability, we will say that P is *modulated by* those wider processes.

So a belief-forming process P is *under the modulational control of* a wider set of processes S within the agent's cognitive system, provided that S would tailor P (would trigger P, inhibit P, or the like), were S to come to generate or possess certain relevant information. P *is modulated by* S, provided that S has generated or come to possess information that prompts it to actually make some changes in how or when P is put in play.

Now, the modulating processes might have or provide specific information about the agent's local environment, or general information about the global environment (or some mix). When they employ veridical information about the local environment, the modulation afforded directly brings a gain in local reliability. The result is that P becomes *locally reliable as modulated* by S. Gains in local reliability (as modulated) are also marginal gains in global reliability. With enough modulation of this sort, enough gains in local reliability as modulated, a process that would not of itself (*sans* such modulation) be globally reliable, might become globally reliable as modulated. When the modulating processes employ general information about the global environment, they may afford gains in global reliability more directly. In either case, this makes for greater *global reliability as modulated* by those modulating processes.

What kinds of modulating mechanisms there are in humans, and what kinds humans are capable of developing and deploying, are empirical questions, principally within the purview of cognitive science. Although the example of Diana involved a kind of modulational control that did turn on certain articulable beliefs, there is no reason to think that all modulational control need be a matter of modulating processes that work at the level of belief. Indeed, it may be useful to think of many processes to which philosophers have commonly made reference as somewhat complex and as involving an important modulation of the core processes. For example, a competent perceptual agent must make subtle use of a great deal of information. Some of this information may be represented at the level of beliefs, of course, as in the case of Diana. But some of it may be had by the cognitive system, and modulate perceptual processes, without being so represented. A competent perceiver might be sensitive to much about the conditions of an observation without being able to represent those matters in a way even approaching belief. Light levels, degrees to which an object is obscured by other things, and the like, clearly are important for perceptual reliability, and these are matters to which a perceiver might be sensitive without consciously representing them. Such sensitivity could condition perceptual processing by giving rise to occasional states that might be described as hesitations, or warnings, indicating that the perceptual processes are compromised by conditions that might yet be somewhat nebulous. Still, this would make for a kind of inhibitory modulational control built into the perceptual processes themselves, triggered by information-processing below the level of conscious awareness. In later chapters, we will return to the issue of processes employing information that is not consciously or explicitly represented by the agent in any sense recognized by traditional epistemology. For now, it is enough to note that one would expect that some modulational control relies on information that does not rise to the level of belief-like states, or of other states commonly recognized by epistemologists.

As observed already, modulational control can convert an erstwhile only locally reliable process into one that, *as modulated*, is globally reliable. That's what happens with Elena. Further, modulation by controlling processes can enhance the global reliability of a belief-forming process that is already globally reliable, by inhibiting it in specific circumstances where it is locally unreliable (and where information pertinent to its local unreliability is available to the attunement processes); that's what happens with Diana (whose ordinary barn-categorizing belief-forming process gets *inhibited* by the modulatory influence of a controlling process).

Of course, modulating processes themselves can be reliable or unreliable, can exhibit either or both of the two kinds of reliability (local and global), and can be reliable (in either of these ways) to greater or lesser degrees. A fundamentally important feature that modulating processes presumably ought to possess is that they be globally reliable *themselves*. There are various ways of thinking about this matter. For present purposes, it is sufficient to connect this desirability to the idea of epistemic safety. The robustness of reliability of a belief-fixing process has been found to enhance the epistemic safety of that process and the beliefs that it spawns—reducing the riskiness of one's beliefs from an epistemic point of view. Belief-fixing processes that are merely locally reliable are unacceptably risky, those with global reliability are better off epistemologically. In a parallel fashion, if the modulating processes are merely locally reliable, this would seem to render the modulated processes themselves unacceptably risky. Typically, if the modulating processes are merely locally reliable, then whatever benefits in terms of reliability, or robustness of reliability, are there provided by their modulation, these gains are a matter of epistemic luck. Modulation by globally reliable processes is clearly less risky. Modulation by processes which are not themselves robustly reliable is something of a 'house of cards'—risky, even when, in the case of local context, it just happens to 'stand up.'

Susceptibility to modulational control is clearly an important and desirable feature for belief-forming processes—a feature that can significantly increase the overall reliability of the cognitive system in which the specific processes are situated. Also, insofar as modulational conditioning of certain kinds is normally feasible for, and operative within, creatures of a given kind (e.g. humans), the *unmodulated* use of certain belief-forming processes can be seriously objectionable epistemologically.

Fortuna is a case in point. Although the belief-forming process she used, in classifying the briefly glimpsed yellow structure as a barn, happened fortuitously to be locally reliable, this fact was entirely outside of her cognitive ken. But what sort of modulating processes would one look for—what sort of processes does one feel missing in Fortuna? One is inclined to say that Fortuna should have been sensitive to the extremely limited experiential basis informing her rather curious perceptual leap. She should have appreciated that longer courses of experience, experience with a range of cases, typically contribute significantly to one's perceptual competence—and she should have been sensitive to the fact that she had no such course of experience. Much of this could well be managed inarticulately, and in the background of consciousness. Still, as a result, there should have been a rather big 'warning flag' waving, one inhibiting or even extinguishing the rather half-baked perceptual process in question. Such perceptual cautions are common enough in human epistemic agents. They contribute to the global reliability of one's perceptual processes, and one expects and demands this much of human beings. Of course, perceptual processing can also be informed somewhat by general considerations at the level of beliefs. If, in Fortuna's general experience, office buildings have all been one distinctive color, stores a different color, gas stations another, and so on, then Fortuna might have justifiably formed general beliefs to the effect that one can judge the use of a building from its color, and it would have been reasonable to generalize from her one barn observation to all barns, and then to apply that generalization to this new experience. This would have been a very different case—a case of a set of modulating processes modulating her perceptual processes. But, in the scenario as stipulated, there was no such information and processing to be found in Fortuna. So, absent that, other modulating processes sensitive to the paucity of her experience regarding barns should have been operative in her, ones that would have *prevented* her from employing the perceptual process stipulated as at work in her. There were no such checks and her woefully risky perceptual processes were allowed to go their merely locally reliable way. Those processes were not under suitable modulational control.

From a reliabilist point of view, the presence and efficacy of suitable modulating processes, within the cognitive system viewed as an integrated whole, thus emerges as extremely important in relation to objective justification. What counts, though, as being a *suitable* modulating process? What counts as being under suitable modulational control? For reasons that will be the focus of our sixth chapter, this looks to be a question that cannot be answered in any great detail from the armchair—i.e. by low-grade a priori reflection alone. What ultimately makes for satisfactorily epistemically-competent belief formation cannot be settled in detail without taking into account what processes can be learned and tractably employed by cognitive systems of the relevant sort—adult human cognizers are a natural and common focus in much epistemology. So what counts as suitable modulating processes depends in part upon the cognitive architecture of the given kind of cognitive agent, and upon such an agent's susceptibility (by virtue of its cognitive architecture) to learning or internalizing various kinds of controlling processes that might not be innate to it. Also, whether *all* belief-forming processes are susceptible to modulation is itself an empirical question for cognitive science. One possibility is that all belief-forming processes are thus susceptible, at least to some extent; but another is that some belief-forming processes are not (though they might figure importantly in modulating *other* such processes). The notion of being under *suitable* modulational control is thus one that leads directly to a call for naturalization in epistemology—a theme to which we will return in later chapters.

8 Safety as constituted by global reliability under suitable modulational control

With the notion of modulating processes in hand, and also the notion of suitable modulational control, we can return to the question posed at the end of section 4, of this chapter: Is there a form of robust reliability that is a plausible candidate for what constitutes the *safety* of a belief-forming process? The discussion up to this juncture points in a natural-looking direction (but some care will be needed). The proposal is this: a belief-forming process is safe just in case it is *globally reliable under suitable modulational control*. (The preposition, 'under,' here indicates that it is the disposition to modulate, and not actually having modulated, that is at issue.)

It is worth emphasizing at this point that our talk of 'suitable modulational control,' and the associated notion of what counts as 'epistemically competent,' for cognitive systems of the relevant sort, say for normal adult humans, should be understood as reflecting the familiar idea that along with robust reliability (under suitable modulational control), fitting processes will also be workably fast and powerful. This part of the picture is given attention in Goldman's writings.

At this stage, we are suggesting that *epistemic safety* may stand in place of global reliability in an adequate understanding of what it is to be objectively justified in holding a belief. We have begun to explore that notion of epistemic safety. It provides a very natural way of getting at what has made various forms of reliabilism so attractive. That is, it captures the judgments and core reasoning that have motivated reliabilism. Thinking about epistemic safety is intuitively sensitive to how processes can be embedded within a cognitive system and can thus be modulated by yet wider processes and information. Such modulational control can contribute significantly to epistemic safety.

It is notable too that some ways in which processes can be affected by others have been given a crucial role in Goldman's reliabilism; he holds that it is necessary for objective justification that the process by which the relevant belief is fixed also be one that is itself acquired by a process that tends to the acquisition or production of tendencies to reliable belief-fixing processes. This provides further reason to think that we are developing the idea of epistemic safety in a way that is continuous with much reliabilist thought.

So the centerpiece of neoclassical reliabilism is the conjunction of the following two claims. First, a constitutive requirement for a belief's being (objectively) justified is that it is produced by a belief-forming process that is *epistemically safe*. (Again, in addition to being epistemically safe, justificatory processes must also be workably fast and powerful.) Second, a belief-forming process is epistemically safe just in case it is *globally reliable under suitable modulational control*. This much comes from low-grade a priori conceptual analysis, says the neoclassical reliabilist. And the analysis points the way toward naturalizing epistemology, for two reasons: first, because cognitive science has a lot to say about which cognitive processes are reliable and which are not, and second, because a cognitive-scientific account of human cognitive architecture will heavily inform (via the theory of cognitive competence it subserves) what counts as *suitable* modulation of belief-forming processes by wider processes.

While it is not possible to say in detail what counts as suitable modulational control, as this must be informed by work in cognitive science, one could suggest a partial understanding of the matter that is suggested by the neoclassical reliabilist focus on global reliability. A central idea for neoclassical reliabilism is that mere local reliability is not enough for epistemic safety. Rather, the needed safety is understood as a matter of global reliability and associated modulational control processes. Thus, it would seem reasonable to understand neoclassical reliabilism as looking to modulational control processes that enhance global reliability by modulating belief-forming processes—such processes enhance the local reliability of belief-forming processes, and cumulatively enhance global reliability. This is to say, the core idea in neoclassical reliabilism, as distinct from classical reliabilism, is to pay heed to the pivotal idea of epistemic safety, and to understand it as intimately associated with global reliability of belief-generating processes and modulational control processes that augment this global reliability (commonly by enhancing local reliability). It seems reasonable to take this as the key to a neoclassical take on suitable modulational control.

If this neoclassical reliabilist account were to hold up on further reflection (it is challenged in the two chapters to follow), it would be a low-grade a priori result. It would represent a necessary truth grounded in the concept of epistemic justification: that being justified requires one's belief to be the product of processes that are globally reliable under suitable modulational control. Although it would be impossible to determine from the armchair just what constitutes suitable modulational control in humans, nevertheless one would have some (low-grade a priori) guidance as to what the required modulational control processes would need to be like: they would be ones that enhance the global reliability of controlled processes in light of information obtained by processes that themselves have significant global reliability—and they would be *suitable for humans* in that they are sort of processes that humans *can* develop and deploy.

9 Applying the account to the cases

To illustrate, let us consider how this account of justification applies to the cases of Athena, Fortuna, Diana, and Elena.

Athena's belief-forming process counts as safe, and thus objectively justified, on this account. To see this, one should keep in mind several distinctions from the previous section. Athena is a normal, competent, adult perceiver, who is supposed to have had some reasonable run of sporadic barn encounters. In the course of this, she has come to be reasonably sensitive in perceptually recognizing barns. Furthermore, it has been supposed that she is rather like Diana in one important respect: her perceptual processes are under the ongoing modulational control of processes that make use of her information about the conditions of observation. It may be supposed that these wider processes are themselves open to new information of the relevant sort—open in the ways reflected in the case of Diana. (If one has not been supposing that, let it be stipulated now for purposes of further discussion.) That is, had Athena been exposed to information regarding the prevalence of fake barns in the curious region through which she now travels, she would have refrained from the otherwise confident generation of perceptual beliefs regarding barns. That her perceptual processes are under the modulational control of suitable processes is a standing fact about her and how her cognitive processes influence each other. Thus, not only is the perceptual process by which she forms her beliefs globally reliable, it is indeed under the control of suitable globally reliable control processes. However, because Athena has not encountered any basis for believing that she has entered a region with many fake barns, these modulating attunement processes have not attuned her perceptual processes *to the local circumstances*. Because her perceptual processes are under suitable modulational control, they are predictably (generally) sensitive to common circumstances involving perceptual difficulties (such as those presented by low light levels or great distances, for example). But they are not sensitive *to the particular circumstances* of the fake-barn region—to the facts about these local circumstances that make her process locally unreliable. This lack of sensitivity reflects no deficit regarding the processes of modulational control she has in place. Rather, these processes do not here locally modulate her perceptual processes because no input-information is *available* to her about the existence of lots of fake barns in the local vicinity.

Diana's belief-forming process also counts as safe. Indeed, Diana's process is not merely under modulational control (as is Athena's), and it is not merely thereby sensitive to a range of common perceptual circumstances (as also is Athena's), but additionally it is *sensitive to her specific local circumstances*. Here the processes of modulational control (which she largely shares with Athena) have been provided information about the peculiar difficulties confronted in that local environment. Because that information has become available to her, her modulational control processes have come to check her normal barn-categorizing perceptual processes, to inhibit them in a way that is epistemically desirable in this relevantly difficult environment. That information led her to appreciate that her local environment was a rather special one in which her generally globally reliable process is not locally reliable, and to inhibit its normal operation. So modulated, her processes became more globally reliable than they would have been without modulation. Thus, Diana is right to *withhold judgment* about whether the object she sees is a barn. She would be unjustified in believing it to be a barn, since that would be contrary to the inhibitory influence of the modulational control processes which in fact are currently (and appropriately) inhibiting her from categorizing it as a barn on the basis of its visual appearance. The difference between Athena and Diana is not a matter of the normal (experientially informed) perceptual barn-categorization processes that each brings to her road trips, nor is it a matter of the modulational control processes that each generally has in place, allowing for information about local environments to produce modulations in those perceptual processes.

Rather, the difference is with the information that is afforded Diana but not Athena. Both have in place processes that do well with the information accorded them. Thus, Athena is objectively justified in believing that there is a barn yonder, whereas Diana would not be justified in forming such a belief and is therefore right not to.

Fortuna's belief-forming process does not count as safe, and thus she is not justified in her belief. Even though the process happens to be locally reliable, one intuitively feels that it lacks a kind of epistemic safety, and one senses that this is importantly relevant to her lack of objective justification. This is just how the case is treated by neoclassical reliabilism. The fact that her process is locally reliable contributes virtually nothing to epistemic safety (as understood here and as intuitively gauged), and thus counts for virtually nothing justification-wise. For one thing, the process is not globally reliable, and thus is epistemically risky on its face. Furthermore, with respect to Fortuna's unusual barn-categorizing perceptual process, there seems not to be in play any significant modulational control processes of a sort that would be needed for the global reliability of the processes under their control. That is, it is not as though her barn-categorizing process is globally reliable despite being unchecked by modulational control processes, and furthermore this process (in her) is not under the modulational control of wider processes.

In contrast, Elena's belief-forming process counts as safe, and she is justified in her belief. Considered in isolation, this process that moves from presentations (even glimpses) of yellow buildings to the belief that the structure in question is a barn certainly would *not* be safe. But, in Elena, it does not work in isolation. In fact, it works only at the invitation of a process that is informed about the peculiarities of the local environment. It is modulated, thus it is globally reliable under suitable modulational control, and thus it is epistemically safe.

10 Local reliability as a constitutive desideratum for justification

Under the neoclassical reliabilist account of justification, being produced by a *locally* reliable belief-forming process is not a constitutive requirement for a belief's being justified. Athena's barn-belief, for instance, is very well justified, even though the perceptual process that produced it is not locally reliable. Being produced by a *globally* reliable belief-forming process, on the other hand, one that is at least globally reliable under suitable modulational control, is taken to be constitutively required. But, what should neoclassical reliabilism say about the role of local reliability, in connection with justification?

Values can be internally related to an evaluative concept in various ways. The evaluative epistemic notion of epistemic justification has internal relations to a range of other concepts, such as epistemic situation, true belief, a system of true beliefs, a locally reliable process, a globally reliable process, epistemic safety, and the like. The evaluative notion of epistemic justification conceptually entails that several of these pick out something, or some feature, that is valuable (that is good from the epistemic point of view). But, not all are valuable in quite the same way. As argued above, one cannot be justified in a given belief unless one has produced or maintained that belief by processes that are epistemically safe. We have drawn upon and refined classical reliabilism to suggest that epistemic safety might be understood as being produced by a process that is globally reliable under suitable modulational control. Something along these lines is *constitutively required* for being a justified belief.

On the other hand, one can be objectively justified in holding a given belief even when that belief is not part of an integrated system of true beliefs, or even when that belief is not true—despite the fact that systematic true belief is valuable in a way that is constitutively connected to the concept of epistemic justification. The truth of one's beliefs is not required for being objectively justified in holding the belief, although it is conceptually given as valuable. Indeed, attaining systems of true beliefs is conceptually given as the end around which the concept of epistemic justification is itself oriented— it is, as we shall say, *a constitutive-desideratum-as-an-end*. If one has developed cognitive processes that are epistemically safe in the relevant sense (are globally reliable as suitably modulated), and if such processes operated in an uncompromised fashion in forming a given belief, then one is objectively justified in the resulting belief, even if one fails in this case to believe a truth. Famously, even the most wonderful of cognitive processes can fail in certain perversely difficult local environments.

Other characteristics of cognitive processes are valuable in a manner that is constitutively linked to the evaluative notion of epistemic justification in yet other ways than as constitutively required or as constitutive-desideratum-as-an-end. Sometimes a certain feature will have the status, relative to a given process, that we shall call *constitutive-desideratum-as-manner-and-means*, vis-à-vis the constitutive-desideratum-as-end (producing systems of true beliefs). Let us explain. We have already noted that within the agent's global environment are local environments that may pose special difficulties. We have noted that the local reliability of one's belief-forming processes within the local environment that one happens to occupy is not necessary for objective justification. Still, it is plausible to think of such local reliability as a constitutive-desideratum-as-manner-and-means for objective justification. Crudely, one might say that concern for the local reliability of such processes is itself required for objective justification, although the local reliability of one's processes is not itself required.

This formulation can be sharpened and refined by thinking of the modulational control processes discussed in the last section. We noted that it is epistemically desirable that there be cognitive processes that condition, tailor, trigger, inhibit, or generally modulate one's belief-forming processes in ways that tend to attune those processes to one's local environment. This contributes to the robustness and thus epistemic safety of one's belief-forming processes. Thus we formulated neoclassical reliabilism as requiring that one's processes be globally reliable under suitable modulational control. In effect, such modulating processes contribute to global reliability and thus to the truth of beliefs produced, and do so *by tending to yield or enhance local reliability*. Tending to produce or enhance local reliability is a manner and means for enhancing global reliability—and this idea is itself built into the idea of epistemic-safety-enhancing modulation processes. The concept of epistemic justification thus requires such modulational control (directed to local reliability) to be necessary for its satisfaction. The cognitive system as a whole is required to operate in a manner sensitive to information bearing upon local reliability. In this sense, local reliability is a constitutive desideratum-as-manner-and-means for justification. So the value and importance of local reliability vis-à-vis justification are honored and upheld within neoclassical reliabilism, notwithstanding the fact that local reliability is not constitutively required.

11 Brain lesions and clairvoyants

Various well known thought-experimental scenarios are sometimes put forward as putative counterexamples to reliabilism. In this section we argue that regardless of what force such cases have against *classical* reliabilism, the neoclassical version of standard reliabilism handles the cases very naturally.

The cases in question are ones where the agent has a belief that intuitively is not justified, and that nevertheless has been produced by a reliable belief-forming process. The generic point that the neoclassical reliabilist can make, concerning such scenarios, is this: although the belief might well have been produced by a process that possesses *some* form of reliability, it has not been produced by a process that possesses the especially robust kind of reliability that constitutes epistemic *safety*—namely a process that is globally reliable under suitable modulational control.

BonJour (1985, pp. 38–42) discusses four cases in which an agent comes to believe by virtue of a reliable clairvoyant faculty that the President is in New York. In each scenario, the clairvoyant faculty is reliable in a range of circumstances that include those of the case in question. Presumably, the faculty generates cognitively spontaneous beliefs—beliefs that are in a fashion analogous to perceptual beliefs, but perhaps without an attendant distinctive phenomenology. Each scenario then has to do with a case in which the relevant agent retains or maintains the belief that is generated by the clairvoyant faculty.

In the first, Samantha believes that she has a reliable clairvoyant faculty, and maintains her belief that the President is in New York by attributing this belief to such a faculty. However, she has strong evidence (from reputable news reports) that the President is in Washington instead.

In the second, Casper believes that he has the clairvoyant faculty on which he also relies in fixing the belief that the President is in New York. However, Casper has reason to believe that he (at least) does not have any such faculty. Indeed, he has labored to verify that he does have that faculty, and the results have been consistently negative—but only because the cases he happens to have examined were ones outside the range of the faculty's reliability.[9] The present belief is generated within the range of circumstances in which Casper's faculty is reliable.

In the third variation, Maude also believes that she has a reliable clairvoyant faculty on which she relies to fix her belief that the President is in New York. Unlike Casper, Maude has no evidence regarding her own clairvoyant faculty or its track record. However, Maude has massive general evidence that there is no clairvoyant faculty to be had.

In the last variation, Norman possess a clairvoyant faculty that is reliable under conditions that normally obtain. The belief that the President is in New York arises in Norman by virtue of his reliable clairvoyant faculty, operating in its favorable circumstances. However, he possesses no evidence, general or specific, for or against his having such a faculty. Further, he has no evidence supporting or undermining the belief regarding the President's whereabouts. The belief just arises, by the reliable process, in Norman, who then just retains the belief.

Most who consider these cases (ourselves included) are strongly inclined to judge that all the agents in each of the scenarios are not justified in believing that the President is in New York.

In the first three cases, the agents supposedly have strong evidence either directly against the belief, or against the supposition that the generating process is reliable. Ignoring such evidence seems to clinch the case. In the absence of stronger contrary evidence (evidence supporting either the belief itself or the belief in the reliability of its generation), the agent is not justified in persisting in believing that the President is in New York.

Of course, what to make of such judgments (indeed, what to make of all the judgments mentioned in this chapter) is an issue that will occupy us for several chapters. While commonly presented as refutations of reliabilist epistemologies, these scenarios do not have such an unambiguous force. Reliabilists might reasonably insist that the first three cases are not well-described flatly as ones in which the belief in question was fixed for the agent by a reliable process. This response to the cases is given principled form by neoclassical reliabilism—and its application to the first three cases is particularly straightforward. Let us then focus on this application. To consider the cases in neoclassical reliabilist terms, it is helpful to add a stipulative clarification of the cases themselves: one can presume that the clairvoyant beliefs arise spontaneously in the agents (presumably in ways that are analogous to perception—the agents suddenly find themselves believing as they do). This is apparently how BonJour would have us understand the cases. However, even if the clairvoyant process in each case is, of itself, globally reliable, the neoclassical reliabilist would want to know whether it was so reliable under suitable modulational control. In each of the first three cases, the

---

[9] One sometimes finds it said that Casper has excellent reasons to think that he lacks a clairvoyant faculty. One may wonder, however. For, it seems Casper has examined a nonrepresentative sample of supposed cases. But the point can presumably be finessed.

cognitively spontaneous belief arises and survives only by ignoring evidence that should, at the very least, occasion a kind of balancing accommodation. It is highly plausible that further cognitive processes ought in each case to have inhibited the retention of the clairvoyant belief. Neoclassical reliabilists would be within their rights (would be insisting only on a careful application of their approach) when they insist that the belief at issue in these scenarios did not result from a process that is globally reliable under suitable modulational control.

Compare the perceptual cases that we have considered already. Perceptual processes are plastic in significant respects; they are permeable to information possessed by virtue of earlier perceptual successes and failures, for example. This is why one can become progressively better at many perceptual tasks. When a perceptual process is of a sort that could be refined in terms of such track records, one tends to demand such refinement. This envisions a plasticity in the perceptual process—its being subject to ongoing, diachronic, modulation, so that it gives increasingly better outputs (as when one learns to perceive distinct spices in cooking by ongoing trial and feedback regarding errors). Sometimes, however, one may find that one just does not have the capacity to be a good perceptual judge (perhaps one finds that, try as one will, no course of training makes one a good judge of particular notes on some standard tonal scale—that one is 'tone-deaf' with respect to such perceptual discriminations). This sort of information can be used to block or inhibit the relevant perceptual belief-forming processes. Again, such modulational control is clearly a good thing, and the neoclassical reliabilist insists that, where feasible, such modulational control must be in place. To neglect such information is to be unjustified in the resulting beliefs.

On the other hand, some elements of human perceptual processes may not be so plastic. The Müller-Lyer illusion seems recalcitrant to information about the illusion. That is, one's rudimentary perceptual processes here do not seem responsive to information about deceptive cases, do not seem to be plastic. Whereas one might cease to have even the tendency to judge that some tone is middle C, one will never lose the tendency to judge the one line longer than the other in the familiar diagram. Still, even here, one demands a certain form of modulational control. The rudimentary perceptual processes in question may not themselves be plastic, and may not be such that one can simply 'turn them off.' Still were one to encounter an agent who knew of the Müller-Lyer illusion and who yet would insist that the one line really was longer, one would judge that agent to be cognitively defective and unjustified in the perceptual belief. One knows that, however things appear, and however recalcitrant those perceptual tendencies, one can come to be disposed to set aside the verdicts that result from those tendencies—the appearances may be had, but should not result in the associated beliefs. When rudimentary perceptual processes are not plastic, one may yet choose to reject their verdicts as mere appearances in select classes of cases, drawing on information about those very processes and their reliability. Again, this is a form of suitable modulational control.

Returning now to BonJour's clairvoyants, we are still supposing that the clairvoyant processes in question yield cognitively spontaneous beliefs or judgment tendencies analogous to the outputs of rudimentary perceptual processes. Samantha has strong evidence that the President is not in New York. This evidence should at the very least temper her tendency to believe as she does. She should weigh the character and quality of evidence on the two sides. Without this, something important is missing, one judges. The neoclassical reliabilist would agree, and would have a very plausible account of what is missing. Human cognitive agents possess reasoning capabilities that can be used to filter cognitively spontaneous beliefs or judgment tendencies by checking these against other information that the agent possesses. To fail to make use of such filters, when readily applicable, would be to employ a set of processes (an overall process) that is jointly less globally (and locally) reliable than one might. The problem appears to be one of a lack of suitable holistic control processes.

Similar problems are to be diagnosed in the cases of Casper and Maude. Casper has reason to believe that he has no clairvoyant capacity. Maude has reason to believe that human beings as a class (and herself as a member of that class) do not have a clairvoyant capacity. If the clairvoyant process is plastic, one would want to see it modulated and thus blocked by such information. Furthermore, even if the relevant rudimentary process is, like the processes behind the Müller-Lyer illusion, subject to neither refinement nor extinction, the curious cognitively spontaneous beliefs or belief tendencies that are produced might be resisted at the level of considered belief. Of course, in these cases as stipulated, there will be a cost: foregoing the output of a somewhat isolated but reliable cognitive process (at least until new information is obtained indicating its reliability). However, the almost pervasive benefits of suitable modulational control processes (the apparent role of such processes, from the rudimentary processes of modulated, informed, perception to the subtle holistic judgments of scientists) pays its way epistemically. If one sets aside the sporadic deliverances of an isolated globally reliable process (for which investigators seem unable to find evidence), then this seems a small price to pay. The neoclassical reliabilist insistence on suitable modulational control processes seems difficult to fault.

The case of Norman is not as straightforward. Although neoclassical reliabilists can consistently hold that Norman's belief is unjustified, this turns, in some measure, on certain natural ways of understanding the case that require care, involving suitable modulational control. Norman has a somewhat isolated but reliable cognitive process giving rise to a belief that seems just to spring to mind. This seems at least a little out of the ordinary. It certainly seems so to those who consider the scenario. But, should it also seem so to Norman? Compare perception. One has rather extensive experience with perception—one has generated a significant track record in connection with various kinds of cases. (It is through training that individuals have each gotten as good as they have at perception.) Furthermore, one has some sense for these track records. This sense for classes of cases, topics, conditions and the like certainly informs one's ongoing perceptual processes and one's confidence in their output. But, while Norman may be presumed to be perceptually normal in these respects, he seems otherwise situated with respect to the clairvoyant beliefs that just pop into his mind. Their very isolation seems to some extent troubling. One wonders why questions were not asked. For the neoclassical reliabilist seeking to come to terms with Norman's case, these are the pivotal matters: Should Norman have asked further questions? Should he have been sensitive to the unusual cognitive isolation of these cognitively spontaneous beliefs? In what ways should processes generating cognitively spontaneous beliefs be integrated into wider cognitive processes? (Compare Goldman 1986, p. 112.)

It has been common since Harman (1988) to appreciate that there are very real limitations to the extent to which one must keep track of what exact information and sources underlie one's beliefs. It is not uncommon to recall a fact without being about to recall where or how one came to know it. One of the authors of this book believes that Admiral Halsey commanded the U.S. aircraft carrier group during important battles against the Japanese during the Second World War. That same author does not remember where or how he came to believe this. What kind of questions should or must this author ask—given that one need not possess 'sourced' reasons for everything? As we admitted earlier, the exact character of the neoclassical reliabilist requirement concerning 'suitable modulational control' is open to investigation. Without more exactness than is possible at this point, it is difficult to determine what that position would need to say regarding the case of Norman. We find our own judgment tendencies regarding this case to be somewhat less clear and determinate than those in the other cases. It does seem strange that the agent would have a highly reliable process, one with significant applicability, without having noticed something about its reliability—or, at least, without having learned or 'internalized' significant information regarding that faculty. This suggests that there may well be something amiss with Norman's standing processes of modulational control. Perhaps one would need to stipulate more about the case (as well as determine more about the character of suitable modulational control in humans) to determine whether the case poses any real problem for neoclassical reliabilism.

BonJour takes the four clairvoyant scenarios as pointing to one central lesson:

> [E]xternal or objective reliability is not enough to offset subjective irrationality. If the acceptance of a belief is seriously unreasonable or unwarranted from the believer's own standpoint, then the mere fact that unbeknownst to him its existence in those circumstances lawfully guarantees its truth will not suffice to render the belief justified and thereby an instance of knowledge (BonJour 1985, p. 41).

This certainly is one way of running with the judgments one tends to make in response to these scenarios. But the problematic irrationality involved here is more than merely 'subjective.' The neoclassical reliabilist can capture this fact, by offering the following alternative diagnosis:

External or objective reliability of some narrowly characterized generating process is not enough to offset the lack of suitable (reliability-enhancing) processes of modulational control within that agent's cognitive system. If, from the objective point of view, the acceptance of a belief turns on processes that are not subject to modulation by suitable control processes—and some such failings are characteristic of believers who fail to make use of their own individual standpoint—then the mere fact that unbeknownst to that agent a given belief is generated by a narrow, isolated process that happens to be globally reliable need not suffice to render the belief justified and thereby an instance of knowledge.

This neoclassical reliabilist response not only honors the intuitive judgment of irrationality-based unjustifiedness that BonJour seeks to elicit, but also explains why the pertinent kind of irrationality is not just 'subjective.' Thus, this position evidently has no problem with BonJour's classic objections.

We turn now to Plantinga, who provides a recipe for generating scenarios that he believes decisively refute reliabilist epistemologies:

It is easy to see a recipe for constructing examples here. All we need are cases where some phenomenon is in fact a reliable indicator of the truth of a proposition, but my believing the proposition in question on the basis of that phenomenon arises from cognitive malfunction (Plantinga 1993a, p. 192).

Plantinga is notoriously partial to brain lesions, at least in his examples. In one variant on the case of the epistemically serendipitous brain lesion, there is a rare but specific form of lesion associated with a range of cognitive processes—commonly yielding absurd beliefs. But, one associated process led the agent with the lesion to believe that he has a brain lesion—where reasons really do not play a supporting role. As Plantinga 1993a, p. 199) notes, one tends to judge that the agent is not warranted in this belief. More generally, one judges that, 'a ground, or indicator, or a belief-forming mechanism, can be reliable just by accident—due, for example, to a freakish malfunction; and in those cases there will be no warrant' (Plantinga 1993a, p. 192).

Plantinga insists then that being (objectively) justified in believing—in his terminology, having *warranted* belief—cannot result from 'pathological' processes; rather, it can only 'occur in someone whose faculties are functioning aright.' One senses that there is an important truth lurking in this insistence which, as it stands, is not particularly informative. It does little more than raise the important question of what makes for the right functioning of processes. But for now, we want to point out that the neoclassical reliabilist should have no problem with Plantinga's cases, which can be naturally accommodated in much the same way as BonJour's.

In Plantinga's case of the epistemically serendipitous brain lesion one is asked to consider a rather far-fetched logical possibility in which a brain lesion results in a very narrow, and apparently isolated, process which yields as output the single belief that the agent has a brain lesion. This is an extraordinarily fine-grained way of characterizing a process, and one wonders whether there might be a more natural way of characterizing the agent's processes. (Perhaps remarks in the next section have some relevance just here, but we simply note the question and move on.) In any case, this extraordinary process, so understood, is highly isolated—and thus seems completely uninfluenced by modulational-control processes. The belief produced obviously has many important implications for the agent, and it seems striking that the belief would go unchallenged (given that it is said to be completely without support from other information had by the agent and other processes on which the agent might draw). Even were the tendency to believe in this fashion not susceptible to complete eradication (even were this tendency as difficult to extinguish as is the Müller-Lyer illusion), still, at the level of considered belief, the belief in question ought to have been challenged and rejected by tractable modulational control processes. One demands such modulational control on the part of human cognitive agents. The neoclassical reliabilist has available a (completely non-ad-hoc) basis for demanding this as well: such checking is in keeping with the demand for suitable modulational-control processes in human cognitive agents.

12 The generality problem

A challenge sometimes raised against reliabilism is the so-called generality problem: the problem of finding some principled way to determine which of various process-types, all instantiated by a given belief-forming *token* process on a particular occasion of belief formation, is the process-type whose reliability or nonreliability is supposed to determine whether or not the agent's belief is justified. Here we will briefly address this matter, in light of the neoclassical account of justification we have set forth on behalf of standard reliabilism. (What we say largely will carry over, mutatis mutandis, to the non-standard version of reliabilism to be set forth in the next chapter.)

According to neoclassical reliabilism, global reliability under suitable modulational control is required for objective epistemic justification. That is the feature that must be possessed by the belief-forming process that produces a given belief, in order for that belief to be justified.

But now enters the generality problem. Reliability of any kind (and hence reliability of the especially robust kind that the neoclassical reliabilist focuses upon) is a property of a process *type*. But any given *token* belief-forming process will invariably instantiate numerous different process-types, some of which may well have different reliability-statuses than do others. How, then, is one supposed to decide which process-type instantiated by the particular process-token is the one that counts, for purposes of its epistemic safety or unsafety?

What we will say about this does not depend on the details of the neoclassical version of reliabilism, and it should not. The generality problem poses the question: Which, among the different process-types instantiated in the generation of the given belief, is the one that *matters* with respect to the possession (or non-possession) of the epistemically crucial kind of reliability? This question is important, regardless of whether the relevant form of reliability is local, global, global under suitable modulational control, or alternatives to be discussed in the next chapters.

We have four points to make, in addressing this question. (In what follows, the singular and plural forms of the word 'process' will normally refer to process *types*. When we mean to be speaking of a token process, we will say so explicitly.)

12.1 Point one

Too little has been made of the scientific context in which this question can best be addressed. Processes that are posited or described in science are generally the sort of thing for which certain kinds of differences at one time yield a systematic difference at later times. They are the sort of thing that can in principle be described and understood in terms of generalizations with at least a moderate degree of invariance (Woodward 2000). The fitting source for understanding what cognitive processes there are, for understanding to what they are sensitive and what they tend to produce (and thus for the extent of reliability they would have in varying environments) is thus the special sciences that study cognitive processes. As these sciences develop, they come to settle upon a set of theoretical resources characterizing sorts of processes and associated dimensions of sensitivity, courses of development, and the like—the sort of theoretical resources that one finds set out, for example, in a reasonably advanced textbook on the psychology of perception. Admittedly, such resources may provide a basis for understanding one token bit of processing at various levels. Thus a perceptual response to an environment might be characterizable at various, neurological or psychological, levels—and thus understood as instancing processes at various levels. What we are observing here is simply that the results of settled science, where it obtains, provide the resources for thinking about the processes in play—and thereby a starting place for thinking about what process kinds are epistemically relevant.

The present point is not troubled by the suggestion that there might be multiple scientific explanations of any one phenomenon—in this respect, we ourselves find the erotetic model of explanation congenial. Thus, given the exact question being answered, one might explain a perceptual verdict in terms of certain salient objects in the agent's environment, or in terms of background training and resulting sensitivities, or in light of contextual priming, and so on. (These explanations do not compete.) This variation with respect to what is taken as explanatory in a context should not distract one from the point that the same set of processes (at interrelated levels), understood in terms of some range of more or less settled science, is at issue in each explanation. Thus, the processes of concern across the differing explanations are essentially those to which scientific results direct one's attention—scientific resources provide strictly the best characterizations of their boundaries and tendencies.

Properly understood, this allows for some convenient redescription of tokens of these processes in everyday nonscientific language, as long as one can reasonably expect that the items and tendencies so characterized are those to which settled science would direct one's attention. To take a familiar sort of example, the process consisting in the projectile with a certain mass, velocity, and surface structure, undergoing a certain acceleration by virtue of gravitational force, and deceleration by virtue of resistance, can be conveniently characterized as the baseball flying out of the park—here, what is instanced is one process despite the different ways of referring to it.[10] One implicitly appreciates that its being a baseball is not relevant for purposes of its trajectory. Similarly, one may refer to the confident perceptual verdicts of a conscientious agent concerning familiar and everyday objects in his or her environment (perhaps the agent's car, or pet, or house). Plausibly the process at issue is ultimately a matter of a certain richness of input to a neural net that has undergone a long series of verdicts with feedback, and has thus become differentially sensitive to the multifurious aspects of the rich information embodied in its impats.[11] The process type of ultimate concern remains that which cognitive science (or the relevant science) would ultimately find operative here.

It is worth noting several ways in which this constraint is commonly violated in the philosophical literature. One sometimes finds processes characterized in terms of particular times and locales that no scientific account would find significant—e.g. some particular time of day (say, 3:00 p.m.) or some locale (say, the northwest corner of the house at 2557 Van Dorn in Lincoln, Nebraska). Of course, by virtue of training, background information possessed, or primed salience, some specific time or location might have significance (thus by virtue of a course of sensitizing experience and motivated salience, one is likely to readily identify one's own house from a familiar vantage point). But, then, mention of times and locations really is a convenient proxy for what ultimately presumably matters—namely the effects of training, familiarity, or interests, in a psychological process-kind that—independently of the specifics of individual training or information—does not depend upon some particular environment. One can be trained to recognize locations, and one's training rather than some particular location is what matters in the science and in the individuation of processes. Similarly, one sometimes finds processes characterized in terms of highly specific doxastic outputs—such as the belief that 'Yonder is a barn.' This commonly seems wildly gerrymandered from the point of view of cognitive science or any science with a plausible bearing on perceptual processes. (Recognizing particular, familiar, dear objects should instead be understood along the lines lately suggested.) Of course, it is plausible that the relevant perceptual process types are sensitive to ranges of past experience—often including quite particular matters such as barnhood/non-barnhood (as in the contrasting cases of Athena and Fortuna).[12] Thus, it is

---

[10] We do not always use the more canonical scientific terms in formulating our examples in this book—although we suppose that one might reformulate these, at least with difficulty, in such terms. Framing scenarios in familiar terms has certain advantages when eliciting ready judgments from one's conceptual competence.

[11] When thinking about such processes in connection with evil demon cases, one would want to abstract away from sensory sensitivity to distal objects in the actual environment, and focus instead on process types (such as would be tokened both in normal humans and in an envatted brain) that operate on more proximate inputs.

[12] The cases of Athena and Fortuna are admittedly somewhat cartoonish, and might seem to violate these strictures. But they can be otherwise understood. The processes in play in the two cases obviously turn on

plausible that behind conveniently sketched scenarios, and behind common responses to them, is some sensitivity to processes understood in terms of such diachronically modulational effects of experience and training. This concludes our elaboration and discussion of our first point concerning the generality problem—the need to bear in mind the relevance of scientific modes of process individuation.

12.2 Point two

A process that matters cannot be *degenerate*. There are two ways in which a process might be degenerate. First, it might be so specific—so packed with detailed circumstantial features of the particular occasion of belief-formation—that the question of the process's reliability-status essentially just reduces to the question whether, *on the given occasion*, the generated belief was true. Rather, the process-type must be sufficiently general in scope that it could be instantiated in a variety of different specific circumstances. It is plausible that this form of degenerate process-typing can be seen to be inappropriate in view of the considerations above. Typically, such degenerate cases are also marked by the invocation of properties that (a) ultimately have no standing in scientific understandings of the relevant process, but (b) in which the scientifically extraneous elements make a real difference to the reliability of the process individuated in those terms. Thus, one reads of a process of consulting one's watch at exactly 3:00 p.m. (as luck would have it)—where it is built into the process (by stipulation) that the watch is broken and perpetually reads 3:00, leading to the belief that it is 3:00. (The irrelevance of such degenerate processes can be understood as a special case of our first point, about the pertinence of scientific modes of process-individuation. No scientific theory plausibly makes anything of 3:00 p.m. per se, although the 'process type' envisioned turns on this.)

A second form of degeneracy, slightly milder but nevertheless unacceptable, obtains when a process is specified so that an essential feature of it is that it is operative only in one narrow environment (or one narrow class of environments). For example, uncritically accepting others' testimony in a local environment where all interlocutors are trustworthy would be a degenerate process. It should always be possible to ask the question of how a process would fare, whether it would be reliable or not, in a diversity of environments. The point requires care. Of course, with modulational control, a narrow process may come to be triggered by information about a local or global environment. It might then, *as so modulated*, come to be operative only in the relevant

---

very different histories—very different acquired information, training, and the like. In this respect, there is little to worry about. But, we write of processes in terms that suggest that these are individuated by their production of a single kind of verdict—verdicts regarding the presence of barns. Ultimately, however, the processes in question should be understood as perceptual/categorization processes of types that are not restricted to barn verdicts. In Athena's case, the process type involves perceptual categorization rooted in what is a significant (if informal) course of training; in the case of Fortuna, there is perceptual categorization that seems to be rooted in exceedingly limited background (so that the association relied on something like rare physiological conditions obtaining at her first barn exposure). These process types make no mention of barn verdicts.

environment. (With long experience in shopping at Summit Hut, and in contrasting retail outlets, one might have information that leads one to trust the sales staff uncritically, but only when shopping *there*.) Here, *the process as triggered* might be applicable only in the relevant environment-kind. But this does not make for degeneracy because the narrow, modulated process is here understood as under the modulational control of wider processes. These would modulate the narrower process differently in different environments. The reliability of *the process under such modulational control* can be determined for various environments in which the modulational control and controlled processes are then envisioned as at work. One can ask the question of whether the process under such modulational control would be reliable with respect to a diversity of environments. (The irrelevance of this second kind of degeneracy also can be understood as a special case of the requirement that pertinent processes be those that science would posit or describe.)

12.3 Point three

The question, 'Which, among the different processes instantiated in the generation of the given belief, is the one that *matters*?' has a false presupposition. There need not be any *single* process-type that matters. Rather, in general there might very well be a genus-species hierarchy of several process-types, all of which are instantiated in the etiology of the given belief, and all of which are equally pertinent with respect to their epistemic safety or lack thereof. As long as all the members of the hierarchy have the *same* epistemic-safety status, there need be no reason to choose among them.

12.4 Point four

If a given belief-generating process-token instantiates two nondegenerate process-types P and P★ such that P★ is more specific than P, and if the safety-status of P★ differs from the safety-status of P, then normally P★ will 'screen off' P with respect to the justification-status of the given belief. That is, the safety-status of P will not count. (Whether the safety-status of P★ itself counts will depend upon whether or not P★ gets screened off, in turn, by a yet more specific nondegenerate process-type P★★, where P★★ has a safety-status different from that of P★.)

This last point explains why it is sometimes appropriate to drop to some fairly specific process in doing safety assessment, whereas at other times it is appropriate to focus on some much more generic process. Elena's barn-belief is justified because the token process that produced it instantiates a quite *specific* nondegenerate process-type that is safe: categorizing something (in this case, as a barn) based on reliably produced information about an environmental correlation (in this case a local environmental correlation of yellow-colored structures and barns) as suitably modulated by processes that select this process only under very specific informational circumstances. Although Elena's token process presumably also instantiates non-safe process-types of a more generic kind—e.g. *classifying structures into functional kinds based on their color*—these are screened off by the more specific process-type that is safe—namely classifying structures into functional kinds based jointly on their color and on reliable information regarding relevant color-involving environmental correlations.

13 Summary: the neoclassical version of standard reliabilism

Reflections on the cases of Athena and Fortuna, on local and global reliability, and on epistemic safety and risk, suggested a central line of thought:

First, embrace the idea that safety—a feature as yet to be more fully explained—is indeed a *constitutive requirement* for a belief's being objectively justified.
Second, look to give an account of safety as constituted by the belief's having been produced by some *suitably robustly reliable* belief-forming process.

This line of thought both organized this chapter and will organize the two chapters to follow. Here we have begun to work through ideas regarding what makes for the kind of epistemic safety constitutively required for objectively justified belief, and, in particular, regarding what is the safety-constituting form of robust reliability.

Because global reliability is more robust than mere local reliability, it seems plausible that suitably robustly reliable processes might be globally reliable processes. Pursuing this idea in the present chapter, we developed a form of classical reliabilism that we term neoclassical. Neoclassical reliabilism represents a refinement on classical reliabilist positions in its close attention to how human cognitive competence often involves using information from wider processes to modulate (selectively inhibit, selectively trigger, even design or spawn) narrower processes. A narrow process, considered just in itself, is not the primary subject of epistemic evaluation when it is under the modulational control of wider processes. If it is under such modulational control, then the robustness of reliability it enjoys, and its safety, are best gauged in terms of its tendencies under that control. We discussed how the reliability of a narrow process can be enhanced under such modulational control.

The central proposal of neoclassical reliabilism is this: a belief-forming process P is safe just in case it is *globally reliable under suitable modulational control*. This does not require that the modulational-control processes have actually acquired information and have then actually modulated the processes under such control.

We showed that neoclassical reliabilism accommodates a range of cases, including several that have been advanced as objections to classical reliabilist positions (such as BonJour's clairvoyant cases). While we ultimately criticize and abandon neoclassical reliabilism in the next two chapters, the discussion of the present chapter should prove highly instructive. Our ultimate position will retain the central line of thought that a form of epistemic safety is constitutively required for objective epistemic justification, and that the relevant epistemic safety is a matter of belief-fixing processes being robustly reliable under suitable modulational control. What will be challenged (in the next chapter) is the neoclassical understanding of sufficiently robust reliability.

4
Transglobal Reliabilism

In this chapter we raise problems for standard reliabilism, including the neoclassical version set forth in Chapter 3; and we propose replacing it with a version of reliabilism we call 'transglobal reliabilism.' Although transglobal reliabilism is certainly nonstandard, it remains within the broad spirit of reliabilism even so. As shall be seen, considerations strikingly parallel to those that motivate moving from classical to neoclassical reliabilism motivate moving further—from neoclassical to transglobal reliabilism. Some of the central ideas in this and the following chapter were initially presented in Henderson and Horgan 2001.

The motivation for adopting transglobal reliabilism will emerge in this chapter concurrently with the articulation of the position. As in Chapter 3, we begin with some concrete thought-experimental scenarios—in this case, scenarios prompting intuitive judgments about justification that make trouble even for the neoclassical version of standard reliabilism. Then we fashion a version of reliabilism that is both independently plausible and also accommodates one's intuitive judgments about the key scenarios.

In Chapter 5 we will elaborate more fully the case for transglobal reliabilism, by feeding into the low-grade a priori reasoning process certain additional forms of armchair-accessible data and certain additional abductive factors that affect the non-demonstrative reasoning from such data to theoretical conclusions about what is (and is not) constitutively required for a belief to be justified.

In this chapter and hereafter, our talk of epistemic justification is again to be understood as referring to *objective* epistemic justification, unless otherwise indicated.[1] Also, we will hereafter use the expression 'neoclassical reliability' to refer to the feature that neoclassical reliabilism claims is constitutive of epistemic safety (and hence claims is required for epistemic justification)—namely global reliability under suitable modulational control.

1 Epistemic safety without neoclassical reliability: the new evil demon problem

The scenario to be presented here was first set out by Cohen (1988) and was labeled the 'new evil demon problem' for reliabilism by Sosa (1991a). In keeping with

---

[1] And in this chapter and the next one, we continue to focus on being justified as opposed to having justification—i.e. on doxastic justification as opposed to propositional justification.

philosophical mythology, suppose that there is an evil demon—malicious and very powerful—out to deceive the agent. Seeking to epistemically defeat the agent at every turn, the demon provides the agent with compellingly consistent appearances or experiences that seem to indicate the nature of the agent's ambient environment—at least as compellingly consistent as are the ongoing perceptual experiences of normal humans. As the agent undertakes to do things in that world, the demon responds by giving the agent the fitting appearances. But, the world that the agent and the demon inhabit is radically other than the world that the agent is led to imagine and theorize about—thus the deception. Of course, if the demon is really good at deception, then the agent is presented with sufficient epistemic problems to 'solve'; these keep the agent engaged making sense of the imaginary world.

These days, radical-deception scenarios often involve powerful computers in place of evil demons. Typically, one supposes that the supercomputer has charge of a brain in a vat. The supercomputer has been programmed to provide the brain with ongoing input that is systematically false.[2] More fully, the computer has been programmed with a model of a world for the agent to inhabit, and it gives the brain input appropriate to, and indicative of, that modeled world. But, since the world that the computer and brain really inhabit is quite different from that world modeled in the computer and presented to the brain, this brain is deceived thereby. (As it is commonly put, the computer takes into account the brain's output, and gives it just the input it would receive were it walking down the street, playing tennis, or so on for various standard life activities.) Whether the deceiver is a malicious demon or an ingeniously programmed computer, the agent subject to deception has no real chance.

Now, to focus one's judgments on pertinent concrete scenarios, consider several agents inhabiting such a demon-infested environment. To begin with, suppose that some agent, call her Constance, is remarkably like the intelligent, educated, and conscientious epistemic agents one would want to include in one's own epistemic community. She avoids fallacious ways of reasoning, both formal and inductive. Constance avoids inconsistency as well as the best of us. She maintains a high degree

---

[2] We realize that the appeal to such scenarios is rendered problematic by recent trends in philosophy of mind, according to which the content of most or all of one's intentional mental states allegedly depends on certain kinds of actual connections between occurrences of such states in oneself (and/or in one's evolutionary ancestors) and the actual environment. Those who favor certain versions of content-externalism will doubt whether a brain in a vat has systematically false beliefs. (Some will doubt whether such a brain has beliefs at all, or any other intentional mental states; and some will doubt whether it has any mental states, even sensations.) We lack the space to address this issue in detail here, so we will make just two remarks. First, we think that versions of content-externalism denying that brains in vats have systematically false beliefs are deeply wrongheaded, despite their current popularity; this denial should properly be viewed as a *reductio ad absurdum* of such views. (See the critique of a hypothetical content-externalist called 'Strawman' in Lewis 1994, especially pp. 423–5; also Horgan, Tienson, and Graham 2004). Second, we suspect that the points about objective epistemic justification that we will be making in this paper, resting partly on considerations about demon-infested environments and brain-in-vat scenarios, probably could also be made by appeal to more complicated hypothetical scenarios that finesse content-externalist considerations. We will not pursue such complications here.

of wide reflective equilibrium in her belief system. In keeping with the facts as just stipulated, she only generalizes when (apparent) samples are large enough for statistical confidence at some high level, and then only when the samples are either random or characterized by a diversity that seems to match the distribution of likely causal features in the population. Furthermore, Constance has taken note of where her observational judgments have seemed untrustworthy in the past, and discounts certain observational judgments accordingly. In crucial respects, she is like the best perceptual agents among us. She is like those who, on the basis of long experiential refinement, prompted by successes and failures, have come to be sensitive, careful, and discriminating perceivers of everyday things. In a parallel fashion, Constance has trained herself in a long process of refinement in her perceptual judgments, drawing on apparent successes and failures, to be a sensitive and careful perceptual agent. (Of course, because she is subject to demonic deception, her training has of necessity been reflective of false-successes and false-failures. But otherwise it reflects the sort of training and shaping of perceptual-experience based judgment that makes for systematic success in our global environment.) Put simply, if one were picking epistemic teams to play in our actual global environment one would not hesitate to pick Constance for one's own team, as long as she could join us in our own environment. In that global environment, Constance would be a model epistemic citizen.

Suppose then that Constance, in her demon-infested environment, hears familiar noises clearly emanating from the phone on her desk (or so things appear), and that she then forms the belief that someone is calling. Of course, no one is calling. The belief is false and arises by way of a highly unreliable process. All processes are both locally and globally unreliable in a world where a powerful and resourceful evil demon (or analogous supercomputer) is at work on the inhabitants.[3] Still, there is a very strong tendency to judge that Constance is justified in holding this belief. Of course, one does not find this scenario to be an epistemically felicitous scenario. But, one is strongly disinclined to find fault with the agent. The problem lies with the agent's extremely inhospitable environment—its demon infestation. There, no agent and no process will help. So, one judges that the problem lies with the environment, and not the agent. Fine agent, lousy environment. In keeping with this, one judges that Constance is objectively justified and has done nothing epistemically wrong or inappropriate in believing that someone is calling. Of course, Constance's epistemic biography, in such an inhospitable environment, will be an unhappy one—its heroine will have few

---

[3] One could imagine various wrinkles. These would affect formulations, and might call for refined stipulations of the scenarios, but they would not affect the substantive points made here. For example, in a global environment where the deceiving demon or computer operates locally, on only some inhabitants, this would make for localities where all processes were locally unreliable, but there might yet be processes that are globally reliable. For our purposes here, we will suppose that the deceiver is an equal opportunity deceiver—deceiving all inhabitants (other than itself). Operating throughout the global environment, all local environments (in whatever sense can be made of these) are ones where all processes are doomed to unreliability, and they are then globally unreliable as well.

successes, and this is clearly objectively epistemically undesirable. But one's judgments employing the concept of epistemic justification focus on a different matter. One senses that Constance is not to be faulted; one would not have her do other than she does—she employs fitting processes in the sense of fitting processes to which the concept of epistemic justification seems sensitive. Again, if one were picking epistemic teams to play in any of a wide range of environments where some processes would be reliable, one would not hesitate to pick Constance for one's own team, as long as she could join us in such a more hospitable environment.

This judgment poses a clear challenge to reliabilist accounts of justification that view the global (or local) reliability of processes to be at least a central necessary condition for justified belief. If this judgment is honored, such accounts must be abandoned. Neoclassical reliabilism is not immune to the challenge. This refined position takes neoclassical reliability, i.e. global reliability under suitable modulational control, to be constitutively required for objective justification—to be a necessary condition. Constance has in place very significant modulational-control processes of a sort that in less inhospitable environments would suitably contribute to global reliability, but these cannot contribute to global reliability in her global environment, because of all that systematically misleading sensory input that is guaranteed to be provided by a deceiving demon or computer. Despite all her modulational-control processes, Constance's processes lack the core feature demanded by neoclassical reliabilism—namely global reliability. So, on the neoclassical reliabilist view, Constance's beliefs are not justified. But one's strong pre-theoretic judgment is that, on the contrary, Constance's perceptual-experience based beliefs are extremely *well* justified.

To make the problem yet more vivid, it may help to consider, by way of contrast, a different agent who is also beset by a powerful deceptive demon (or computer). However, this agent, call her Faith, is provided with the appearance of a community that holds certain epistemic standards that are quite at odds with those that most of us have come to approve. For example, folk, or rather apparent folk, in Faith's epistemic community engage in the gambler's fallacy, and consistently approve of such inferences. They have no notion of the representativeness of samples, to take another example, and do not have evaluative practices that would lead to the associated caution in forming generalizations from instances. It is as if Faith has been raised in such a community—and has come to have the predictable inferential tendencies. Faith is not unreflective, however, and attempts to get at the truth as best she can. She conscientiously applies her epistemic standards—such as they are. (When bets or strategies informed by instances of the gambler's fallacy lead to disappointments, this is written off as cursed luck.) One day, Faith notes that it has been quite a while since the fair die used in a game has turned up a six. So, she forms the belief that a six is due—and that the probability of a six on the next toss is rather higher than 1/6—let us say she believes it is greater than 0.5. What is one to make of Faith's belief here?

One may well find oneself pulled in two ways, and it will be helpful to keep in mind the distinction between objective and subjective justification. People who conscientiously employ their own epistemic standards (which they believe, on the basis of reasonable reflection, to contribute to the satisfaction of the epistemic end of systematic true belief) and who thereby draw on the relevant sources of information, count as subjectively justified in the resulting beliefs. On the other hand, this is not enough for being objectively justified. Arguably, Faith may be subjectively justified in believing that a six is due, and one tends to evaluate her conscientiously formed beliefs accordingly. Given her recent experience as-of observing a long enough run of non-six tosses, and her beliefs or standards, she is subjectively justified in her belief that a six is due. Still, one is far less inclined to judge that Faith is objectively justified. Of Faith, one is not inclined to say (as one was of Constance), 'Fine agent, lousy environment.' One is inclined to judge that there is something about Faith's processes themselves (and not just the lousy environment) that makes them objectively inappropriate, and that makes her belief objectively unjustified.

Of course, Faith's disposition to commit the gambler's fallacy is no more unreliable, as a guide to what is really going on in the demon world, than were the processes that Constance employed. Even so, one is inclined to judge that there is something wrong—objectively wrong—with Faith's processes, *and not with Constance's*. One is inclined to judge that Faith is not objectively justified in believing as she does, *although Constance is*. The case of Faith here serves as a useful contrast, helping to clarify the character of one's judgments regarding Constance. Constance is objectively *and* subjectively justified, while Faith seems only subjectively justified.

Apparently then, the global reliability of belief-fixing processes is not a necessary condition for being justified in believing. At least this is what is indicated by one's intuitive judgments about Constance in her demon-infested environment. (Of course, in a conceptual analysis, judgments can be accommodated in various ways, including being explained as an understandable error. So what ultimately to make of such judgments, and such suggestions, will need to be determined.)

Intuitively speaking, there does seem to be a reason for thinking that Constance's beliefs are justified, whereas Faith's are not: just as one sensed that Athena's processes were *safe* despite their lack of local reliability, here one senses that Constance's belief-forming processes are epistemically safe despite their lack of *neoclassical* reliability, while Faith's are not. Even though Constance's processes lack the feature that neoclassical reliabilism took to constitute epistemic safety, they strike one as epistemically safe nonetheless. And intuitively speaking, Faith's belief-forming processes are deficient with respect to this kind of safety possessed by Constance's. But the problem is that as far as the feature stressed by neoclassical reliabilism is concerned—namely neoclassical reliability—Constance and Faith are both equally badly off with respect to justification.

One can think of the pertinent scenarios this way. In the case of Athena and Fortuna (supported by the cases of Diana and Elena), one found that local reliability (while a concern) was not what made for the differences in justification that one judges to be manifested there. Rather, one felt that the difference had to do with the relative epistemic safety of the various agents. In these cases, at least, sensed safety corresponded rather well with global reliability, and even better with neoclassical reliability (i.e. global reliability under suitable modulational control). This led to neoclassical reliabilism as a refinement on classical reliabilist positions: taking neoclassical reliability to be constitutively required for objective justification. But there is good reason to reconsider neoclassical reliabilism itself. The cases of Constance and Faith again point to epistemic safety as crucial. The most ready of intuitive reasons, when one asks what motivates one's judgments in these cases, seems to be that Constance's processes are epistemically safe, while Faith's are not. A reasonable conjecture is that epistemic safety is indeed what is constitutively required for objective justification—all the cases (Athena, Fortuna, Diana, Elena, Constance, Faith) point to this—but that it is not itself simply a matter of neoclassical reliability. That is, it is not a matter of *global* reliability under suitable modulational control. The neoclassical reliabilist suggestion may have been on the right track without being quite right, without managing to correctly identify what constitutes epistemic safety.

The new evil demon problem involves a thought-experimental scenario in which one has strong intuitions that a certain cognitive agent in the scenario has beliefs that *are* well justified, even though these beliefs do *not* meet the conditions that the neoclassical version of reliabilism claims are constitutively required for justification. We turn next to a case involving the converse mismatch between intuitive judgments and theory: scenarios in which the agent has certain beliefs that *do* count as justified according to neoclassical reliabilism, but about which one has strong intuitions that the beliefs in fact are *not* justified.

2 Neoclassical reliability without epistemic safety: Ashley the 'Valley girl'

A leading idea in Chapter 3 was that belief-forming processes that are locally reliable for fortuitous reasons beyond the epistemic agent's cognitive ken, but that are not globally reliable, are too risky to be a source of justified beliefs. (The case of Fortuna illustrates the point.) An analogous idea will serve as the basis for thought-experimental cases suggesting, in parallel fashion, that belief-forming processes that are *neoclassically* reliable for fortuitous reasons beyond the epistemic agent's cognitive ken, are too risky to be a source of justified beliefs.

Before proceeding, some remarks about the notion of suitable modulational control are in order. Actual and potential modulational-control mechanisms must score well on each of two distinct dimensions, in order to count as suitable. One dimension was already emphasized earlier: for creatures of a given kind, a modulational-control mechanism must be tractably implementable in the cognitive architecture of creatures of that kind. (As we stressed, filling in the details of this dimension of suitability is largely a matter for empirical cognitive science.) The second dimension of suitability is enhancement of the pertinent kind of reliability—in the case of neoclassical reliabilism, *global* reliability. Because of this second dimension, potential modulational-control mechanisms will only count as suitable, from the perspective of neoclassical reliabilism, to the extent they really do enhance the global reliability of the belief-forming processes they modulate. This point needs to be borne well in mind concerning the thought-experimental cases now to be discussed. In particular, the *lack* of a given kind of modulational control, in an epistemic agent inhabiting a given global environment, will only count—according to neoclassical reliabilism—as the absence of *suitable* modulational control if that such modulation would enhance global reliability *in that specific global environment*.

Our scenario involves a young lady, Ashley, who is a somewhat upper-middle-class, highly wasp-y, 'Valley girl'—the type one finds portrayed in popular American culture. (The prototypes are Caucasian teenage females in the San Fernando Valley, north of Los Angeles.) Her experience with people and the world is highly limited, and she is prone to generalizations that are not at all suitably sensitive to her sample size or the narrow range from which her sample is drawn. However, Ashley lives in a world rather unlike the world that constitutes the actual global environment here on earth. The real earthly global environment is diverse and heterogeneous (culturally, economically, technically, climatically, biologically—in terms of flora and fauna, and so on). As most people are aware, this makes generalizing regarding humans a tricky matter. In order to reliably form true beliefs about populations in general, it is necessary to give some care to one's samples. But Ashley is otherwise situated. In her global environment, the human population is homogeneous—just one big population of Valley folk, throughout the total global environment. So, although Ashley herself knows very little of the wider world, and although she has garnered virtually no relevant evidence on the matter, the kinds of inductive generalizations she is prone to make are by and large true—because, fortuitously for Ashley (but not for human flourishing, one suspects), the overall global environment she inhabits is so extremely homogeneous in numerous respects that her inductive processes are globally reliable. Even without concern for, or sensitivity to, sample size and representativeness, generalizing freely about people from small samples is globally reliable, in this homogeneous global environment in which Ashley finds herself.

Let us be specific about Ashley's modulational-control processes. She does have some, and they do serve to modulate her inductive belief-forming habits. Concerning most matters, she pays suitable attention to relevant evidence (including sample size, potentially undermining evidence, and the like) when forming beliefs inductively—i.e. she is by no means clueless. It is only when forming inductively-based general beliefs about humankind that she ignores sample size and fails to seek out undermining evidence—a feature of her cognitive makeup that has been strongly reinforced by the intensely parochial Valley culture prevalent in her local environment. (Such parochialism is also prevalent throughout the various locales that collectively constitute her *global* environment—although this fact is unbeknownst to her.) So Ashley has globally reliable inductive processes here, and they are under the modulational control of certain wider processes. Are they under *suitable* modulational control, by the lights of neoclassical reliabilism? Indeed so. For, on one hand, these control-mechanisms appropriately take into account available information she has about matters like sample size, potential undermining evidence, and the like when she is forming beliefs that are not generalizations about humankind; the modulational-control processes thereby enhance the global reliability of her overall belief-forming cognitive architecture. And on the other hand, from the perspective of neoclassical reliabilism, the fact that such control-mechanisms do not modulate her inductive belief-forming processes concerning humankind does not constitute a *lack* of suitable modulational control at all; this is because such mechanisms would not enhance the global reliability of those humankind-involving inductive processes.

The key thing to stress here is that as far as global reliability is concerned, her belief-forming practices and also her modulational control processes are just fine *in her actual global environment*. Modulational control processes are in place, and from the point of view of neoclassical reliabilism, they do what they should do.

Now, suppose that Ashley overhears her mother and her mother's best friend talking about some antidepression medication that they both take. She immediately generalizes that all women between 35 and 50 years of age take antidepressants to cope with the horrible and crushing boredom of their lives—and she is right because, well, it is a highly homogeneous global environment that she inhabits. This belief is the product of a globally reliable inductive process, and one that is modulated by processes that satisfy the neoclassical reliabilist standard for being under suitable modulational control—they are disposed to make the modulations that would enhance global reliability (in Ashley's actual global environment).

Still, to jump freely from such small and narrow samples of humankind locally, to such sweeping generalizations about humankind in general, seems *intuitively* highly problematic epistemically. Intuitively speaking, Ashley's generalizations about humans are not well justified. One judges that they are not epistemically safe—even though they do have the feature that neoclassical reliabilism claims constitutes epistemic safety. These judgments provide prima facie reason to think that, while the neoclassical reliabilist position may represent an improvement on classical reliabilism, its understanding of epistemic safety in terms of processes that are neoclassically reliable—i.e. are globally reliable under suitable modulational control—is yet flawed. So, here is another basis for thinking that global reliability may not hold the key to understanding epistemic safety. The new evil demon problem suggests that global reliability is not needed for justification. The case of Ashley suggests that global reliability, even with modulating processes that serve to enhance local and global reliability, is not enough for epistemic safety and for epistemic justification.[4]

3 Analogues of the Athena/Fortuna contrast

The case of Ashley resembles in key respects the earlier case of Fortuna: whereas Fortuna employs a belief-forming process that is locally reliable but intuitively is not epistemically safe, Ashley employs certain belief-forming processes that are neoclassically reliable but intuitively are not epistemically safe. Thus, just as the case of Fortuna supports the claim that global reliability is more robust than mere local reliability and hence is more important for epistemic justification than mere local reliability, the case of Ashley supports the suggestion that there is some form of reliability that is yet more robust than neoclassical reliability—and hence is yet more important for epistemic justification than mere neoclassical reliability. However, the Ashley case does not involve a contrasting pair of believers, and in that respect is not like the case of Athena and Fortuna as a contrasting pair. We turn now to some cases that do involve suitably analogous contrast pairs. The two cases exhibit a common abstract structure: one member of the pair (the analogue of Athena) deploys belief-forming processes that are intuitively safe but are not neoclassically reliable; the other member (the analogue of Fortuna) deploys processes that are neoclassically reliable but are not intuitively safe.

3.1 A 'Truman Show' scenario: Harry and Ike

The case of Athena and Fortuna indicated that the local reliability of a belief-forming process is not a constitutive requirement for its justification, and that some form of epistemic safety apparently is. Athena's barn-belief is justified because the process that produced it is safe, even though that process is not locally reliable. Fortuna's belief is unjustified because the process that produced it is *not* safe, even though that process *is* locally reliable. Although local reliability remains an important epistemic desideratum, it is not constitutively required for justification; nor is it sufficient for justification. Neoclassical reliabilism embraces these morals, and proposes to construe epistemic safety as a specific form of robust reliability: namely neoclassical reliability (i.e. global reliability under suitable modulational control).

The scenario we will now describe is designed to be structurally parallel to the Athena/Fortuna scenario, and to elicit intuitive judgments suggesting that neoclassical

---

[4] Ultimately, the case of Ashley points to a problem in the neoclassical reliabilist approach to suitable modulational control: when one thinks of safety in terms of global reliability, and one then thinks of suitable modulational control in terms of contribution to global reliability, one has the wrong take on both. Once one recognizes that there is a form of reliability yet more robust than global reliability—once one recognizes the epistemic importance of what we term 'transglobal reliability' (later in this chapter)—one can think of suitable modulational control as contributing (not just to global reliability but) to transglobal reliability. Ashley's processes do not do this. So, while neoclassical reliabilists (and reliabilists who do not focus on transglobal reliability) do not have the resources to understand her as failing to have the makings of epistemic safety, the transglobal reliabilist has those resources.

reliability is *itself* not constitutively required for justification—and instead is, like local reliability, a constitutive epistemic desideratum-as-manner-and-means. This in turn will suggest that neoclassical reliabilism is mistaken in its construal of epistemic safety. Although epistemic safety does indeed appear to be constitutively required for justification, an alternative account of safety is needed.

In the 1998 movie *The Truman Show*, the main character has been raised from childhood on a movie set where he has lived his entire life being the subject of a massive deception by skillful actors. The result has been a 24-hour a day television program in which viewers are treated to Truman's life from birth (which, one supposed, wasn't staged) to his being a young adult. We want to consider a competing show in which two friends, Harry and Ike, have been similarly deceived and observed. Harry and Ike spend their entire lives in carefully contrived circumstances in which everyone else they ever interact with is an actor playing a part in an elaborate conspiratorial deception within an elaborate local stage-set. The conspiracy is so well orchestrated that it has rich 'counterfactual depth': for various potential actions that Harry or Ike might engage in, including actions such as undertaking to change jobs or to travel to distant lands, the conspirators (the actors, directors, and stage-hands) stand ready and able to maintain the verisimilitude of the ongoing deceptive play-acting. The deceivers are good and the production is well-financed. Thus, they are capable of doing their deceptive work within whatever alternative local environments Harry or Ike might venture into. That is, they are capable of going on location anywhere that Harry or Ike would plausibly find accessible. Put simply, the deception potentially extends to such an extensive set of local environments that it is, for all intents and purposes, global.

Harry is highly paranoid, in one specific way. He believes that everyone around him, except Ike, is an actor playing a part, and that every local environment he ever finds himself in is an elaborate stage-set being manipulated behind the scenes. Harry possesses not a single shred of significant evidence for these paranoid beliefs, and he never obtains any evidence for them throughout the entire course of his life. Ike, on the other hand, exhibits no such paranoia. He takes his ongoing experience at face value, and has no tendency at all to believe or even suspect that he is being duped by a bunch of actors or that all his local environments are elaborate stage-sets. Ike believes that his friend Harry is just hopelessly paranoid, and he considers Harry's paranoid beliefs far too silly to take seriously for even a moment. (Ike too never receives even the slightest positive evidence in support of Harry's beliefs.)

Let us say more about the etiology of Harry's curious belief-forming processes. (The goal is to elaborate the scenario in such a way that these processes count as being under *suitable* modulational control, from the perspective of neoclassical reliabilism.) Harry sometimes engages in generalizing practices that other people around him would regard as highly paranoid, and as totally unwarranted. These are practices that result from certain very strong emotions, ones that affect his modulational-control processes vis-à-vis his inductive-generalization processes. As it happens, he is so constituted psychologically that these emotions would kick in only with respect to relatively few matters. Also, it happens that the unusual, emotion-based, modulational-control mechanisms coincide with facts about his global environment in just such a way that these mechanisms have a systematic tendency to spawn specific belief-forming tendencies that (coincidentally) are globally reliable within his specific global environment. In his particular biography, the pivotal instance came when he became very upset upon having learned that his parents and all other adults were lying to him about Santa Claus. His being so upset provoked a very striking generalization: he came to his belief that everyone but his friend Ike (who has been his best pal since childhood) is constantly play-acting an elaborate deception.

Now, Harry's paranoid belief-forming processes produce an excellent track record of true beliefs over the course of Harry's life. Moreover, objectively these processes have an extremely high propensity to produce true beliefs within Harry's actual global environment—since all those actors and stage hands do indeed stand ever-ready to accommodate themselves to whatever choices Harry might make about moving from one local environment to another. They maintain the deceptive conditions flawlessly, and yet Harry believes that he is being deceived in all those things that he would otherwise tend to believe.

Furthermore, by the standards of neoclassical reliabilism, Harry's modulational-control mechanisms are entirely suitable. Although the unusual belief-forming processes they spawn are ones that produce beliefs that intuitively are wildly paranoid, nonetheless such beliefs are generally *true* in Harry's global environment. Thus, these peculiar modulational-control processes enhance global reliability—which means that they count as *suitable*, from the perspective of neoclassical reliabilism.

Intuitively, however, Harry's paranoid beliefs are epistemically unjustified even so: they are highly *risky*, rather than being safe. In this respect, they seem rather like the beliefs of Fortuna. Unlike in the case of Fortuna, however, this lack of safety cannot be understood in terms of a lack of global reliability. For, the reliability of Harry's processes does not depend on special or peculiar features of that particular locality or environment. All local environments are ones into which Harry and Ike's deceivers would freely follow (or even precede them). So, all local environments are ones in which these agents would be subjects of deceptive presentations. For any potential local environment, E, within Harry's global environment, if Harry *were* to go into E then his processes *would* end up being reliable in E. The cumulative effect is that, inhabiting a global environment with able deceivers as his constant traveling companions, Harry's paranoid belief-forming processes are globally reliable. Still, these processes seem unacceptably risky.

Recall from Chapter 3 that Fortuna's locally reliable process seemed risky, despite being locally reliable, because its local reliability seemed dependent on peculiar aspects of her environment that her cognitive processes did not track and for which she had no informational basis. Similarly, Harry's processes seem risky, despite being globally reliable, because their *global* reliability is highly dependent on peculiar aspects of his *global* environment that his cognitive processes seem ill-suited to track, and for which he has no real indication.

Ike's belief-forming processes fare differently. In the numerous cases in which his non-paranoid beliefs are at odds with Harry's paranoid ones, Ike's beliefs are systematically mistaken. But despite this very poor track record with respect to the goal of systematic true belief, intuitively these beliefs of Ike's are well justified nonetheless. This is because the processes that generate the non-paranoid beliefs are intuitively epistemically *safe*—even though they happen to be systematically non-veridical because of all that conspiratorial play-acting and behind-the-scenes set designing. As in the case of Athena, this epistemically laudable safety seems closely tied to the fact that Ike's belief-forming processes here have a kind of robust reliability—but one that we have not yet managed to articulate. It is not simply that those processes are neoclassically reliable—which does make for a greater robustness of reliability than afforded by mere local reliability (as discussed in the previous chapter). For, Harry's processes are neoclassically reliable and yet lack the relevant epistemic safety, while it seems that Ike's lack neoclassical reliability and yet possess the relevant epistemic safety.

3.2 Two envatted brains: Constance and Sextus Pessimisicus

In our earlier case of Constance the envatted brain, deployed in section 1 of this chapter to illustrate the new evil demon problem, we introduced a contrasting character too—Faith. However, Constance and Faith do not jointly constitute a contrasting pair analogous to Athena and Fortuna, because Faith is not an epistemic agent whose pertinent belief-forming methods are neoclassically reliable. So it will be useful to contrast Constance with yet another envatted brain—this one being relevantly analogous to Fortuna (with Constance being analogous to Athena).

Suppose that there is an epistemic agent, call him Sextus Pessimisicus, who is a lifelong envatted brain and who forms beliefs in the following way: whenever he has experiences that would generate in an ordinary epistemic agent a belief with content *p*, he forms a belief expressible this way: 'The Great Deceiver is deceiving me into being tempted to believe that *p*.' (He uses the label 'the Great Deceiver' to name the putative external device or agent, whatever it is, that he believes is systematically deceiving him about the external world.) Now, this process, as deployed by Sextus, is neoclassically reliable, because it meets the requisite criteria. First, it is globally reliable, within the global environment that Sextus actually occupies. (Wherever he might get transported to, in that global environment, he will remain envatted and will remain hooked up to the computer that monitors his motor outputs and generates his sensory inputs.) And second, by the standards of neoclassical reliabilism, his habit of converting each initial temptation to believe a proposition *p* into a Great-Deceiver belief vis-a-vis *p* counts as a stunningly suitable form of suitable modulational control; for, it reliably replaces false but tempting potential beliefs with actual beliefs that are true.

As we remarked in section 1, one is strongly inclined to judge that when Constance forms the belief, on the basis of her sensory-perceptual experience, that someone is calling, she is using a belief-forming process that is epistemically safe (despite not being neoclassically reliable)—and hence that her belief is justified. Suppose now that Sextus forms the belief, on the basis of the same kind of sensory-perceptual experience, that the Great Deceiver is deceiving him into being tempted to believe that someone is calling. One is not inclined to give epistemic approval to Sextus or this belief of his; one is not inclined to judge that he is justified in so believing. Quite the opposite: one senses that Sextus would be too far out on an epistemic limb, and without epistemic motivation. The process in question seems unacceptably risky, since it is only truth-conducive in extraordinarily jerry-rigged global environments like the one he happens actually to inhabit. Furthermore, nothing seems to tip Sextus off to the fact that he is in such an inhospitable environment. Apparently, Sextus would have needed to have jumped blindly to this process—without the benefit of modulational-control processes that deployed pertinent information about that environment. The fact that Sextus happens to be using a globally reliable process in this scenario strikes one as the most extraordinary result of the blindest of epistemic luck—as a limiting case of being epistemically unsafe. Also, the fact that his paranoid way of modulating his initial belief-tendencies counts as suitable modulation, by neoclassical standards—i.e. as modulation that systematically enhances global reliability—also strikes one as the blindest of epistemic luck. Intuitively, suitable modulational control is the kind that enhances epistemic safety, whereas Sextus's wildly paranoid kind of modulational control does exactly the opposite.

So the moral of the case of Constance and Sextus as a contrast-pair is the same as in the case of Ike and Harry: one epistemic agent in the pair (Ike in the one scenario, Constance in the other) forms beliefs in a manner that seems intuitively safe but fails to be neoclassically reliable, whereas the other agent in the pair (Harry in the one scenario, Sextus in the other) forms beliefs in a manner that is neoclassically reliable but fails to be intuitively safe. And the overall moral of the various scenarios posed so far in the present chapter is this: although one's intuitive judgments about the cases conform well with the idea that a constitutive requirement for a belief's being justified is the process that produced the belief is epistemically safe, these intuitive judgments also provide strong evidence that—contrary to neoclassical reliabilism—epistemic safety is not constituted by neoclassical reliability.

4 Experiential safety versus de facto safety

The cases just considered do not in any way impugn the apparent importance of epistemic safety for objectively justified belief. On the contrary, they reinforce it. With respect to Constance and Ike, one is strongly inclined to say that their processes *are* epistemically safe, and that this is *why* they are justified. Furthermore, with respect to Ashley Harry, and Sextus, one is strongly inclined to say that their processes *are not* epistemically safe, and that this is why they are unjustified.

What the intuitive judgments impugn, rather, is the neoclassical reliabilist account of what epistemic safety consists in. There is a notion of epistemic safety at work in these judgments that is not to be understood in terms of the specific form of reliability that neoclassical reliabilists point to—namely global reliability under suitable modulational control (where 'suitable modulational control' is itself understood, neoclassical-reliabilist-fashion, in terms of conduciveness to global reliability).

Neoclassical reliability does constitute a certain kind of safety. A belief-forming process with this form of robust reliability constitutively affords a matter-of-fact safety within the actual global environment. Within a given global environment, an epistemic agent with neoclassically reliable processes is not likely to go wrong. Let us call this *de facto* safety. We do not, of course, deny that neoclassical reliability, and the de facto safety that it constitutes, are epistemically desirable. But, de facto safety does not seem to be the form of safety that is constitutively required for objective epistemic justification. Rather, it is epistemically valuable in a way that is rather like local reliability—i.e. that it is a constitutive desideratum-as-manner-and-means.

We will advance, explore, and defend the following suggestion: what is wanted, as constitutively required for justification, is a form of safety that is more intimately tied to the agent's own epistemic situation, and specifically to the agent's own experiential vantage point on the world—what we will call *experiential* safety. What is constitutively required for epistemic justification is experiential safety, not de facto safety—with the notion of experiential safety, obviously, needing explication.

So we return to the question of what constitutes epistemic safety, now with this suggestion in mind. Notice too that although the neoclassical reliabilist answer is evidently inadequate, this fact does not undermine the thought that epistemic safety is some kind of *suitably robust reliability* of the belief-forming process. On the contrary, that thought still looks very promising, and well worth pursuing. And pursue it we shall.

5 Transglobal reliabilism characterized

In this section we set forth, briefly and succinctly, the version of reliabilism that we recommend. (Elaboration and further elucidation will then follow in subsequent sections.) The core idea is to invoke a form of reliability that is more robust than global reliability, and that is connected to epistemic agents' experiences in a manner that conforms well to the intuitive, pre-theoretic, notion of experiential safety. We call this *transglobal* reliability. It stands to global reliability in much the same way that global reliability stands to local reliability. Transglobal reliability is reliability relative to a reference class comprising not just the actual global environment, but rather a certain wider range of *possible* global environments. We call these the *experientially* possible global environments; they are possible global environments in which there are epistemic agents who have experiences of roughly the character of the common, everyday experiences of human beings. Thus, transglobal reliability is characterizable this way: reliability relative to the reference class comprising the experientially possible global environments.

The notion of modulational control also will figure importantly in our proposed version of reliabilism, in much the same way it already figures in neoclassical reliabilism (and with much the same rationale). The main difference will be that suitability of modulational-control mechanisms is to be understood in terms of the enhancement of the transglobal reliability of belief-forming processes, rather than the enhancement of global reliability. Neoclassical reliabilism's core notion of neoclassical reliability, i.e. global reliability under suitable modulational control, is to be replaced by what we will call *postclassical* reliability—i.e. transglobal reliability under suitable modulational control.

So our proposed version of reliabilism, which we will call *transglobal* reliabilism, makes the following core claims. First, epistemic safety is constituted by postclassical reliability. Second, epistemic safety is constitutively required for epistemic justification. Hence, third, postclassical reliability is constitutively required for epistemic justification.

In addition, transglobal reliabilism claims that local reliability and neoclassical reliability are both constitutively involved in epistemic justification too. Although neither of these forms of reliability is constitutively *required* for justification, each of them is a constitutive desideratum-as-manner-and-means. Whereas neoclassical reliabilism already treated local reliability this way, postclassical reliabilism extends the same treatment to the feature that neoclassical reliabilism treated as a constitutive requirement—namely neoclassical reliability. (Thus, de facto safety too is construed by postclassical reliabilism as a constitutive desideratum-as-manner-and-means, since de facto safety is constituted by neoclassical reliability).

6 Transglobal reliabilism elaborated

We turn now to a more extended, more detailed, elaboration of the various claims and ideas embraced by transglobal reliabilism. More needs saying about several matters: the notion of an experientially possible global environment, the nature of transglobal reliability, the role of modulational control, and the status of neoclassical reliability as constitutive desideratum-as-manner-and-means. We will address these matters in the order just mentioned, in the successive subsections of the present section.

6.1 Experientially possible global environments

Experientially possible global environments can be understood in terms of this leading idea: having the experiences that one has (or roughly similar experiences) is compatible with one's inhabiting any one of a range of global environments. This is not to say that the various global environments are all compatible with the *content* of the experience, but rather that *having those experiences* is compatible with being in any of some range of global environments. (A global environment in which one is an envatted brain is an experientially possible global environment, but one not compatible with the contents of one's experiences.) An epistemic agent could have experiences very much like the experiences that we-common-epistemic-agents have and yet be in a very different environment. Some such environments would be ones in which the agent with those experiences would be correct in taking much of the experience 'at face value'—ones in which much of that agent's experience is correct. Others would be ones in which the agent would have experiences much like one's own, but would be largely misled by them. This might conceivably happen in two ways. In one, the experiences would be misleading because of the coloring of appearance by socialization into a belief system. (Perhaps one 'sees' the night-time fog in the swamp, illuminated by the full moon, as a ghost.)[5] The second is the more radical sense in which experience can be misleading: it would be a matter of even the appearances (with whatever coloring) being misleading—as would obtain were that agent to be a brain in a vat, for example, or were the agent to be afflicted by an evil demon. The set of experientially relevant possible global environments runs this gamut of global environments in which an agent would have experiences of roughly the character of one's everyday experience.

To talk of possible environments being compatible with agents 'having experience with roughly the character of one's common, everyday, experience,' is vague primarily in the characterization of the experiences at issue—where it appeals to a notion of rough similarity in experiences. In the remainder of this subsection we will elaborate upon this idea, in order to help provide a fix on the character of the rough similarity at issue.

To begin with, the idea of a range of environments in which the agent could have certain experiences is not particularly difficult to understand. Thus, consider the familiar idea that you might be a brain in a vat hooked to a very powerful and well-programmed computer, and that you could then be made to have the exact same experiences that you actually do (and will) have. This scenario, which readily induces one to think of an environment in which one would have *exactly the same* experiences as one actually has, provides a clear special case of an environment in which experiences are similar to those had in one's actual environment. The environments in which an agent could have *exactly the same experiences* as those experiences actual agents have obviously constitute a proper subset of the set of environments in which agents could have experiences of at least roughly the character as actual agents. This set of such environments in which one could have exactly the same experiences (as one actually has) is thus a proper subset of the set of experientially relevant possible global environments.

---

[5] This source of misleading experience turns on a 'theory-ladenness' or 'training-ladenness' of (at least some) experience. The actual extent of such theory-ladenness need not be specified, for our purposes here. Furthermore, nothing that we need or use here turns on the pessimistic view that theory-ladenness produces distortions that cannot be overcome.

Before turning to the less restricted set of *experience-similar* environments, it is worth saying a little more about the diversity of environments in which one's experience would be exactly the same as one's actual experiences. Again, demon-infested environments can provide clear cases. As long as one's counterpart-agent makes the same choices, and as long as the demon (or computer) responds by giving the appropriate identical input, the experiences had would be identical. But these would seem to be only the most extreme of the alternative environments in which experiences could be identical. They are extreme in the matter of deception. In other environments, one's perceptual processes could conspire with conditions in less deceptive ways to give rise to the same experiences. One can imagine cases in which conditions and perceptual processes make for one's having exactly the same experiences, and where these would be more illusory or deceptive than one's experiences in the actual global environment, but less illusory than those same experiences would be in the demon-infested global environment. Examples are easy to imagine. For example, the world (planet and cosmos) might have been recently created (say, 75 years ago) by a deity set on testing the faith of agents. Suppose that, as part of the original equipment of the world, the deity provides the agents with a book explaining that the world is of relatively recent origin. Suppose that the deity also provides agents with perceptual processes like our own. Thus, such an agent's experience of most everyday objects is just as veridical as our own—one's car, house, computer, and dog are really as they seem (provided that the content of this experience does not involve them seeming to be more than 75 years old). However, the deity also populated the world upon creation with items that seem to indicate that the world had an existence long ago—antiqued documents and other 'faux-artifacts' seeming to come from an earlier technological era (arrow heads, steam engines, frigates, and so on), even geological strata and 'fossils.' An agent in that world who lacks faith will experience the fakes as real, just as we experience the old artifacts we encounter as real. The 'dinosaur fossil' will be seen as the fossilized remnants of a very old and long extinct creature.

In yet other possible environments, one could have the exact same experiences one actually has, and yet these would be less misleading than they actually are. Humans actually experience the images on a cinema screen as changing in a continuous fashion, even though they are not. These experiences, which are non-veridical in the actual global environment, would be veridical in an experientially possible global environment in which the images projected on television and movie screens really change continuously (rather than changing in a series of small and unnoticed steps or stages).

Against the background of an understanding of global environments in which one could have *exactly the same* experience, one can begin to get some purchase on the relevant notion of global environments in which epistemic agents could have *similar* experience—'experience with roughly the character of one's common, everyday, experience.'[6] There are several ways in which experience might come to differ, and

---

[6] The shift from talking of environments compatible with an agent having similar experiences, or in which an agent *could* have such experiences, to talk of environments in which an agent *would* have such an

yet be relevantly similar. One involves alternative possible trajectories through the actual global environment. Consider a global environment like our own with respect to the inhabiting agents, their cognitive (including perceptual) processes, and the objects to be found in the environment. But, now focus on one agent—you the reader. Perhaps you had breakfast this morning. There is an alternative trajectory you might have taken through this global environment—say, a trajectory in which you awoke later than you actually did this morning. If you use an alarm clock, perhaps it did not go off, or at least you did not hear it. As a result, your spatio-temporal trajectory through the environment begins to diverge and already there is a difference in experience (not hearing the alarm, noticing a different time upon awaking). Next, perhaps you forego breakfast for reasons of time. Again, a difference in experience due to a divergence of trajectory through the environment.

Such differences can become truly significant epistemologically. Röntgen might have moved in somewhat different ways about his lab in 1895, and then might not have noticed out of the corner of his eye that a piece of paper, coated with barium platinocyanide and shielded from his cathode ray tube by an opaque barrier, glowed when his cathode ray tube was turned on. He may not have then investigated further to note that the effect persisted when the coated paper was moved to an adjoining room. Alexander Fleming might not have had occasion to notice that a mold which had accidentally developed in a culture had produced a bacteria-free circle about itself. An investigator, such as Fleming, who chanced upon a situation that prompted a line of investigation, might not encounter it when taking a different path through much the same environment.[7] Still, despite the difference in experience that accrues as the result of taking somewhat differing paths through the environment, the agent's experiences have 'roughly the character of one's common, everyday, experience.'

Differences in environments, rather than differences in an agent's path through an environment, can also lead to experiences that are roughly of the same character as one's common, everyday, experience. Again, as noted already, the envatted brain inhabits an environment very different from our own—but, if the brain makes parallel choices and is given appropriate input, the brain may have experiences that are

---

experience is made here for a certain vivacity of image. Typically the second turns on the agent taking a particular trajectory through that environment. Because we are interested generally in how processes would fare in various possible global environments, without supposing that the agent takes some particular trajectory through that possible environment (and thus occupies just some particular set of local environments within that environment), we are primarily concerned with environments being compatible with having experiences similar to those that actual agents actually have (with the 'could' formulation rather than the 'would' formulation).

[7] Rough-skinned salamanders produce very powerful toxins in their skin—each produces enough to kill many humans. Why so much? It turns out that they are eaten by garter snakes that have developed a resistance to the toxin. Thus a kind of evolutionary arms race has resulted. This interesting fact came to light after three fishermen were found dead—and a salamander was found in the coffee pot (most of us are more careful when making coffee). Had the fisherman been more careful, their paths would have been different, and so would that of the biologist who discovered this nice evolutionary example.

identical to our own. Now, suppose that, while you awoke as usual this morning and had breakfast, the envatted brain is allowed to 'oversleep' and is not given experiences of an alarm clock going off, and the envatted brain then decides to forgo breakfast. As a result, the brain has experiences that are different from your own. Still, parallel to the case of differing paths described above, the envatted brain has experiences that are roughly of the same character as those you had.

Less radical (but still deep) differences in the global environment could give rise to agents with experience of roughly the character of one's own. For example, consider inductive practices in global environments whose populations are markedly more homogeneous than those found in the actual global environment we inhabit. (Ashley the Valley girl inhabits such a global environment.) In such global environments the same causal factors operate uniformly on the members of those populations that are the focus of most scientific investigations. As a result, looking at a few members of a population would give an investigator a fair idea of how things are in the population as a whole. While an investigator's experience in such an environment would be different from that of investigators in our own world, there will be very significant similarities. We may, for concreteness, suppose that many of the same general sorts of animals, processes, and things are to be found in the alternative environment. It is rather as though the contrast has been turned down and the variation that is to be found in the sustained investigation of the actual global environment is not to be found in the alternative world. Clearly, by virtue of trajectory, selective investigation and attention, and the like, some agents in the actual environment can be exposed to unrepresentatively homogeneous samples taken from populations that are more heterogeneous than they appear on casual inspection. In the actual environment, such experience is typically the result of cognitive laziness, selective attention, and the like. But, in the alternative environment imagined, such experience of homogeneity would result from the homogeneous causal character of that environment. The idea is that sustained inspection in the alternative global environment would not turn up the more fine-grained variation. In this alternative environment, if one has encountered one stupid cat, then one can freely generalize to all members of the cat population (they are homogeneously stupid). If one has encountered one unfriendly Frenchman, then one can safely generalize to the whole (there homogeneous) lot. In any case, for our purposes, such alternative global environments will count as environments in which agents have experience with roughly the character of one's common, everyday experience.

Differences in agents also can obviously make a difference in experience. As reflected above, lazy investigations and more sustained investigations can make a difference in the experience of the heterogeneity of populations. Furthermore, differences in training and expectations can color experience. One of the authors of this book experiences most pit bulls as lovely, cute, cuddly dogs of an even disposition (although that same author is troubled by the heterogeneity in the population—and finds even more troubling the variation in the population of pit bull owners). However, this author also notes that others have very different experiences when seeing a pit bull heading in their direction. Similar variation in experiences obtains among people confronted by spiders. In other contexts, some have the experience of 'seeing' supernatural phenomena, where others see only natural phenomena of particular sorts. Still, at an appropriate level, the experiences folk have are of much the same character. All see a dog trotting down the street, in roughly such-and-such a spatial location relative to one's self, in such-and-such surroundings. All see a spider, or small eight-legged creature. All may see a light hovering over a swamp. Variations in 'coloration' aside, the experiences have much the same character.

We have just been seeking to give articulate form to the somewhat intuitive notion of an *experientially possible global environment*. The notion picks out those environments that are compatible with agents having experiences of roughly the character of actual people's common, everyday, experiences. We have elaborated upon this notion by considering kinds of cases and allowable variations—seeking thereby to give the reader a better grasp of the idea. This was to allow one to better understand transglobal reliability, which we have characterized as reliability relative to a reference class comprising experientially possible global environments. We turn next to some elaborative remarks about transglobal reliability.

6.2 *Transglobal reliability*

How can one understand the idea of 'being reliable in a wide range of experientially relevant possible global environments,' construed in such a way that the complement-property is being non-reliable in only a *narrow* range of those environments, so that one makes good sense of the ideas of a wide range and a narrow range? One might try to explain this idea as follows: the number of members in the class of pertinent global environments in which the given process is reliable is much higher than the number of members in the pertinent environments in which the process is not reliable. But this assumes that both classes are finite; yet presumably they are really both infinite (even though possible global environments are individuated in a less fine-grained way than possible worlds). One might instead try to explain the operative wide/narrow distinction this way: as regards the space of experientially possible global environments, the volume of the region of this space in which the given process is reliable is much larger than the volume of the complementary region in which the process is unreliable. But this would require specifying some kind of quantitative metric over that space, and it is far from obvious whether that could be done—and if so, how. We will have more to say about such challenges in the next chapter. At this juncture we want to focus attention on what is for us the crucial point. Our formulation of what it is for a process to be transglobally reliable is intended to circumvent the difficulties just mentioned. Rather than thinking in terms of relative numbers of possible global environments, or in terms of the relative volumes of regions of possible global environments, we propose thinking in terms of more primitive, intuitive ideas: that of (comparative, non-quantitative) degrees of variation across possible global environments, and that of a process being reliable (robustly reliable) across greater or lesser ranges of such variation.

To begin to see how one might make sense of transglobal reliability along these lines, it is appropriate to focus on three kinds of scenarios, with an eye toward guardedly abstracting from them some powerful, intuitive ideas.

Type-1 scenarios: an agent's belief-forming process is globally reliable but nevertheless counts intuitively as not transglobally reliable,
Type-2 scenarios: an agent's belief-forming process is not globally reliable but nevertheless counts intuitively as transglobally reliable, and
Type-3 scenarios: an agent's belief-forming process is both globally and transglobally reliable. [8]

Cases of type 1 include Ashley the Valley girl (in her highly homogeneous global environment), and paranoid Harry (in his Truman-Show global environment). Cases of type 2 include both an envatted brain and non-paranoid Ike (in his Truman-Show global environment). Cases of type 3 include those of Athena, and a twin of Constance, Connie, who occupies a more epistemically hospitable global environment (such as ours) and who there employs processes for generalizing from samples that is attentive to the sorts of sampling and statistical safeguards covered in standard statistics classes.

Let us reflect on these cases, observing how different processes fare with respect to global reliability as one considers variations in the possible global environments. One can compare Ashley (a type-1 case, employing 'sloppy' induction) with Constance when inducing from samples (a type-2 case involving statistically safeguarded induction), and Connie (a type-3 case also involving safeguarded induction).

Type-1 cases (such as Ashley's) exhibit a striking general feature: the global-reliability status of the given belief-forming process is *highly dependent on specifics of the agent's actual global environment that are systematically outside the agent's cognitive ken* (in that the agent lacks wider cognitive processes which might be suited to registering these specifics and modulating her processes accordingly). That is, relatively minor potential variations in global-environment features that the agent systematically lacks information about would produce fairly dramatic changes in the global-reliability status of the given processes. Indeed, one can formulate a recipe for developing type-1 cases: first take some process that seems 'out on a limb' in that it is very easy to imagine possible global environments in which it would be an utter flop. Second, suppose that the process is in operation in a way that is not modulated by information about the global environment. Third, imagine a global environment that is as it needs to be in order to make the process globally reliable—provide environmental 'scaffolding' for the process in the form of an environment that is as needed to make the 'limb' hold. Here one is *tailoring the imagined environment to the process* (rather than the reverse, tailoring the process to an environment, which is commonly what happens when a process is under suitable

---

[8] One could consider a fourth kind of case: that of processes that are both globally and transglobally unreliable. But, its treatment would be obvious, given what is said of the cases considered here.

modulational control). One tailors the imagined environment to 'cover for' the epistemically possible ways in which the given process could go wrong. For sloppy induction, we can imagine several forms of special-purpose environmental scaffolding. One, already imagined in Ashley's case, is a global environment with highly homogeneous populations. Another would be an environment with a powerful friendly demonic character who notes the input that sloppy inducers happen to receive, anticipates the sloppy induction that will follow, and changes the population in the agent's global environment to conform. Another would contain a different friendly demon, one who provides the sloppy inducer with just the input (the apparent samples) necessary to allow even sloppy induction to derive results that accord with the characteristics of the population antecedently obtaining in the agent's environment. In each of these cases, there is an intuitive sense in which the global environment here has been engineered or 'scaffolded' to 'cover for' the many ways that sloppy induction can go wrong (many of these are, notably, ways that safeguarded induction would not tend to go wrong). Remove that scaffolding and sloppy inductive processes will flop.

It is a straightforward matter, for carefully crafted thought-experimental global environments like these, to discern the pertinent 'scaffolding'—and thus, how to imaginatively alter such features in order to alter the reliability-status of sloppy induction. Ashley's environment is highly homogeneous, so begin to vary the heterogeneity of populations, across alternative experientially possible global environments in which Ashley might find herself, and her processes quickly become unreliable.[9] Similarly, remove just your friendly demon from either of the other environments, and the other imagined sloppy inducers are also in trouble.

Type-2 cases are the hostile mirror image of type-1 cases. Here one starts with a process that seems *not* 'out on a limb'—that is, one starts with a process that holds up well under much qualitative variation of possible global environments. (Safeguarded induction is a paradigmatic example of such a process.) But then one thought-experimentally 'engineers' an experientially possible global environment with behind-the-scenes features that would be enough to bring down the reliability of such a process—one imaginatively places 'landmines' in the envisioned environment, in a special purpose way. Here we find an inversion of what was found in the type-1 cases: a little variation of the envisioned environment—simply varying it by eliminating the narrowly engineered landmines—and global reliability is restored.

Contrast the type-1 and type-2 cases just discussed with the type-3 case of Connie, who is using safeguarded induction. For purposes of comparing Ashley with Connie, start with Ashley's highly homogeneous global environment of a sort that would make even sloppy induction globally reliable. Safeguarded induction is also globally reliable here. Then begin varying the degree of heterogeneity within populations—thereby

---

[9] To paraphrase a well known character from television, 'It's the heterogeneity, Captain. She can't take much more.'

considering a series of possible global environments. As one thus 'turns up' the population heterogeneity across these experientially possible global environments, safeguarded induction will continue to be globally reliable far after sloppy induction will have become unreliable. It is certainly globally reliable in the actual environment. Of course, at some point, with heterogeneity in populations far more extreme than in the actual global environment, safeguarded induction might cease to work—perhaps due to limitations in memory to hold information about samples of adequate size to reveal statistically significant patterns reflective of the wildly heterogeneous populations. But it will not readily become globally unreliable.

For purposes of comparing Constance with Connie, start with Constance's global environment, one in which she is an envatted brain subject to a perfectly well orchestrated, ongoing, non-veridical sensory-perceptual experience. Constance's use of safeguarded processes is not globally reliable there. Then begin varying the degree to which Constance's sensory-perceptual experience operates in a way that generates non-veridical visual-mode representations of her ambient environment—thereby considering a series of possible global environments. As one 'turns down' the degree of behind-the-scenes, special-purpose, 'engineering for deception' of her sensory mechanisms, across these experientially possible global environments, safeguarded induction will very quickly become globally reliable. It will remain unreliable only insofar as the degree of such deception-maintaining engineering remains extremely high—e.g. as it does in an experientially possible global environment in which Constance is in a Matrix-style 'body pod,' receiving computer-generated sensory inputs, for 364 days per year, but then on Christmas is allowed out into a wider local environment that happens to be very much like the kind of environment that she experiences herself to be occupying every day. Here one finds an inversion of what was found in the type-1 cases: a little variation of the environment—simply varying it by eliminating the narrowly engineered landmines—and global reliability is restored. Once restored, one is again in a type-3 case, and much further variation tends to preserve global reliability. Similarly, Connie also has little need for either sort of benign demon—she does well without them, and by the time Connie is ready to generalize from her samples (say when it makes for statistical confidence at level .001), the benign demon will seldom have occasion to change population characteristics in anticipation of her results. (Even were the demon set on making Connie's process perfectly reliable, it would have occasion to intervene only one time in 1,000 inductions by Connie.) The other demon is no more helpful. So, take the demons away—they do little good. Then continue intuitively to vary the global environment. Across much of the variation, safeguarded induction will succeed.

There are, of course, epistemically possible global environments that would make for the global unreliability of safeguarded induction. For example, one might introduce a deceiving demon—and one gets to the case of Constance. Or one might vary the environment by introducing a Humean demon who simply changes the global environment every decade or so, or as soon as one comes to an inductive conclusion on some matter. Either way, the inductive conclusions which had been derived would be rendered false.

Such, intuitively, are the relevantly different cases. The key dimension making for the differences is this: the extent to which the global-reliability status of the given belief-forming process is highly dependent on specifics of the agent's actual global environment that are systematically outside the agent's cognitive ken. The type-1 cases (processes that are not transglobally reliable, but are globally reliable) depend on the environment having some specific features that cover for ways that the process in question could go wrong—so that varying the environment on just that feature is enough to render the process unreliable. Across widely varied possible environments lacking that feature, the process would remain globally unreliable. With respect to the type-2 cases, one has to imagine specific ways of engineering the environment so as to make them unreliable. Their global unreliability depends on such special purpose possibilities—epistemic landmines. Vary one of these, and the process readily becomes globally reliable. Across widely varied possible global environments which lack a special purpose landmine, the process is globally reliable.

6.3 Modulational control

According to transglobal reliabilism, the kind of safety that is constitutively required for epistemic justification, namely experiential safety, is to be understood in terms of a form of reliability more robust than global reliability—namely transglobal reliability. We take transglobal reliability to be constitutively required for objective justification. But once one refocuses on transglobal reliability, one can recognize that neoclassical reliabilism's general insights about the importance of modulational control processes carry over: suitable modulational control can yield a desirable extra measure of transglobal reliability, and thus of epistemic safety.

In this subsection we elaborate upon both the similarities and the differences between how the notion of modulational control figures in neoclassical reliabilism and transglobal reliabilism respectively. We also elaborate upon various aspects of modulational control, beyond what was said in Chapter 4, that figure importantly in its constitutive role in epistemic justification.

6.3.1 Suitability In one respect the notion of suitable modulational control works the same way within both neoclassical reliabilism and transglobal reliabilism: suitability depends upon whether the given kind of modulational control is tractably implementable in epistemic agents of a particular kind (e.g. humans), given the cognitive architecture of such agents. In another respect, however, what counts as suitability is different within the two kinds of reliabilism: neoclassical reliabilism says that a tractably implementable form of modulational control is suitable if it enhances global reliability, whereas transglobal reliabilism instead gears suitability to enhancement of transglobal reliability.

Several of the thought-experimental scenarios we set forth earlier in the present chapter can be harnessed in support of the claim that the notion of suitable modulational control should be tethered, first and foremost, to transglobal reliability. For example, in the case of Ashley, the form of modulational control that one feels is missing is not one that would contribute to *global* reliability. (Her tendency to form sweepingly general beliefs about people at large, on the basis of small samples from her immediate local environment, is quite globally reliable in her actual global environment, because of the fact (unbeknownst to her) that the global environment is so dramatically homogeneous socially and culturally.) Rather, the modulational control that one judges she lacks, and should possess, is control contributing to *transglobal* reliability. Global reliability is undoubtedly epistemically desirable—a point to which we will return—and so is the measure of de facto safety afforded by modulational control processes contributing to global reliability. But, that is not the right kind of safety that is required for epistemic justification, as reflected in the case of Ashley. Nor is de facto safety, as constituted by global reliability, necessary for the epistemic safety that is required for justified beliefs, as reflected in the cases of Constance and Ike. Turn now to the case of Harry. He employs processes that are globally reliable but not transglobally reliable. Their global reliability depends on how things work in Harry's global environment—on the way in which there is a crew of talented and devoted deceivers ready to anticipate his moves and present a consistent deception. Harry's distinctive mode of modulational control—namely persistently believing that they are actors playing a part and are not sincere in what they do or say—does extremely well at enhancing the global reliability of his belief-forming processes. Nonetheless, these modulational control processes revolve around a wildly hasty generalization from a single emotional disappointment (upon finding that there is no Santa). His generalization regarding the pervasiveness of deceivers is true, and the belief-forming processes that are modulated by this belief are globally reliable. Furthermore, the emotively driven generalizing process that generated this belief is itself so finely circumscribed as to be globally reliable in this global environment. Thus, it itself is a globally reliable form of modulational control, as are the ongoing influences in Harry's belief-forming system of his paranoid belief that everybody other than Ike and himself is an actor playing a part. Harry's paranoid belief-generating processes are thus globally reliable and under globally reliable modulational control. But that is not sufficient for the kind of safety that is constitutively required for epistemic justification. Intuitively, his modulational control processes are far too risky a way of coming to beliefs about the global environment, and thus put him out on too tenuous a limb. Intuitively, these processes are highly unsuitable, despite the fact that they greatly enhance global reliability. The problem, evidently, is that they do not at all enhance—on the contrary, they detract from—*transglobal* reliability.

The case of Sextus Pessimisicus is much the same. He, like Harry, has an idiosyncratic modulational control process that on one hand inhibits the formation of beliefs that a normal person would form in normal ways (e.g. via perceptual experience), and on the other hand triggers the formation of beliefs whose content is obtained from the content of the inhibited erstwhile-beliefs by prefixing the 'Great Deceiver' operator. This modulational control process routinely and systematically suppresses any initial tendency to believe that *p*, while triggering a belief of the form 'The Great Deceiver is trying to deceive me into believing that *p*.' Such modulational control greatly enhances the global reliability of Sextus's belief-forming processes; thus, under neo-classical reliabilism it qualifies as *suitable* modulational control. Intuitively, however, it is far from suitable, despite greatly enhancing global reliability, because its use is highly risky, epistemically speaking. Once again, the apparent problem is that the process detracts from, rather than enhancing, the kind of reliability that is constitutively required for justification—namely transglobal reliability.

6.3.2 Two kinds of modulational enhancement It is important to distinguish and appreciate that there are two broad ways in which modulational control processes can enhance transglobal reliability. We will now elaborate on this theme, in a way that focuses on an instructively illustrative kind of case: scientific experimentation and its contributions to the formation of scientific beliefs.

The first kind of modulational control is manifested by building into the experimental processes, and into the associated belief-generating processes, features that themselves make for transglobal reliability. For example, the belief-generating cognitive processes may themselves include features such as sensitivity to sample size, to representativeness, and the like. General-purpose belief-forming processes such as induction, with safeguards such as sensitivity to sample bias, sample size, and the like, do not themselves suppose that the environment is one particular way rather than another. That is, such safeguarded inductive processes commonly are designed to avoid pitfalls that the agent might confront in various possible global environments. (If the environment is a highly hospitable one for induction from samples, one characterized by homogeneous populations, they will be globally reliable; if it is a moderately challenging one, one characterized by significantly heterogeneous populations, they would yet tend to be globally reliable.) Admittedly, they would fail in global environments of certain highly hostile kinds. (For example, those in which a powerful demon shuffled regularities after significant but unpredictable periods of regularity). Thus, such processes are reliable in a wide range of (but not all) experientially possible global environments. Of course, such processes will take input in the form of putative information about how things are in the world. For example, general inductive reasoning from samples to populations clearly relies on information about samples, which is information about how things are in a certain piece of the environment. But these inductive processes do not themselves make special substantive presumptions in moving from that information to the resulting conclusion about the population. Such extremely general-purpose processes can be said to be *transglobally reliable, considered in themselves*. (Since such features typically take input from other processes that may or may not be transglobally reliable, one could perhaps better write of them as *conditionally* transglobally reliable, considered in themselves. One can say that they, of themselves, contribute to the transglobal reliability of one's yoked cognitive processes.)

But this cannot be the full story, because scientific/cognitive processes commonly 'go out on a limb'—i.e. they are designed to be globally reliable, drawing on extant understandings of that environment. One is then tailoring processes to certain beliefs about one's global environment—one is relying on those beliefs to modulate one's belief-fixing processes. One thereby relies on the global environment being certain ways and not other ways. There is always some measure of epistemic risk here—but then uncertainty is a fact of epistemological life. The question is whether one's limb will ultimately support safe inquiry. Insofar as a specific cognitive process relies on the global environment being certain ways and not other ways, that process, *considered in itself*, will not qualify as significantly transglobally reliable. This noted, one can recognize the second way in which the spawned, tailored, or modulated processes can be transglobally reliable—it is that way that depends on suitable modulational control. While certain processes may not be transglobally reliable considered in themselves, they may yet be indirectly transglobally reliable, that is *transglobally reliable considered as being under the modulational control of transglobally reliable modulational control processes*. Here it is crucial that the modulating information on the basis of which one designs the spawned processes not be overly risky. It is crucial that it be 'good information' in the sense of being the result of transglobally reliable processes. (Recall that we are using the term 'information' in a way that does not presuppose an item of information is true. In order to be 'good,' however, information must itself be epistemically justified.) If the modulational control processes would work (would tend to produce true beliefs) in a wide range of experientially possible global environments, then the tailoring of controlled processes to the environment that they afford would tend to enhance global reliability across a correspondingly wide range of experientially possible global environments. The processes under such modulational control would be reliable in a wide range of experientially possible global environments. Under this suitable modulational control of transglobally reliable processes, the processes are transglobally reliable. Processes spawned in this fashion are thus *transglobally reliable under suitable modulational control* (of transglobally reliable processes).

Thus, the strength of the limb on which one is situated in experimental work is a joint product of two factors: (a) the components of experimental/inferential design that incorporate features making for the transglobal reliability of processes generally (these can be thought of as general features of good inference), and (b) being under the modulational control of transglobally reliable processes. To work from such strong limbs is demanded by our postclassical reliabilism.

In light of the preceding remarks, let us now make a distinction between two ways that a belief-forming process can be postclassically reliable (i.e. reliable under suitable modulational control), and two associated ways that modulational control can enhance transglobal reliability. First, a process can be transglobally reliable when considered in itself, and apart from modulational control; we will call such a process *inherently* transglobally reliable. When an inherently transglobally reliable process is under suitable modulational control, it becomes yet *more* transglobally reliable; we will call this *incremental* enhancement. Second, a process can fail to be transglobally reliable when considered in itself (i.e. can fail to be inherently transglobally reliable), and yet can be transglobally reliable when considered as under suitable modulational control. In such a case, the modulational control enhances the *overall* transglobal reliability of a cognitive agent's various belief-forming processes, by harnessing a process that is not itself inherently transglobally reliable for use in particular informational contexts where, by virtue of the specific information available to the cognitive agent in the given context, the process becomes transglobally reliable. (It is globally reliable in a wide range of experientially possible global environments *in which such information is available to the cognitive agent*.) We will call a process of this kind *non-inherently* transglobally reliable; and we will call the relevant kind of enhancement of transglobal reliability *threshold-crossing* enhancement. (The reason for the latter label is that the process considered in itself is below the threshold for qualifying as transglobally reliable, whereas the process considered as under modulational control is above the threshold.)

For a vivid illustration of threshold-crossing modulational enhancement, consider concrete cases of cognitive processes (and associated experimental processes) that are 'out on a limb' and yet transglobally reliable under suitable modulational control: those striking processes by which scientists develop, measure, or observe certain quantities or features that have been theorized about, but which previously could not be observed. In these cases, the investigator may move freely from certain simple indicators to beliefs about theoretical processes—so freely that they claim to have observed those processes. In the background stands impressive modulational control. Results gotten in antecedent cognitive processes spawn a cognitive process—cobbling together variations on already developed or possessed processes. The new cognitive process will be cobbled together out of more rudimentary processes that are reshaped and coordinated—so that the fashioning of a new process might also be thought of as the refinement and coordination of belief-forming processes that were already a part of the cognitive system. Shapere (1982) describes how experimental physicists designed a process for observing the interior of the sun, by measuring the flux of high-energy neutrinos, by looking for certain trace impurities showing up within 300,000 liters of dry-cleaning fluid deep in an old mine. Associated with the relevant manipulations within the physical world, and particularly with the interpretation of the results, are cognitive processes by which investigators formed beliefs about the interior of the sun, the flux of neutrinos, and the like, based on relatively simple perceptual data. The experimentalists designed the experimental apparatus and spawned the cognitive processes as joined twins under the direction of theories they had previously generated (theories having to do with certain processes) and on the basis of previous experimental results. The preexisting scientific/cognitive practices (in theoretical physics, applied chemistry, and the like), together with the processes within experimental physics whereby one designs or fashions such processes, constitute a broad and impressive set of modulational control processes—and they spawned a belief-forming process that takes chemical observations of the dry-cleaning fluid as input and yields beliefs about the prevalence of high-energy neutrinos and the processes at the center of the sun as output. Very plausibly, this process is not inherently transglobally reliable; for, there is no good reason to think that it is globally reliable in a wide range of experientially possible global environments and is globally unreliable in a narrow range of such environments. However, as modulated in light of all the background information available to the scientists who used it, it becomes highly transglobally reliable: it works in a wide range of experientially possible global environments in which such informational modulation spawns its use, and fails to work in only a narrow range of such environments. This is a dramatic case of threshold-crossing modulational control.

6.3.3 Modulational refinement Not all modulational control works by spawning a new process—by designing an inferential process associated with a new experimental practice, or by fashioning a cognitive process for which the agent or agents would not have antecedently had some inclination to some forerunner. Instead, modulational control often works by refining existing processes in various ways. (It is even plausible that when a new process is spawned, this is a matter of cobbling together sets of existing processes, which are shaped and coordinated into what we are calling a new process.) Refinement will typically be diachronic, happening over time rather than all at once. And it will typically be a matter of modulational enhancement, rather than modulational threshold-crossing; i.e. the unrefined process will be transglobally reliable already, but will become more so as it gets diachronically refined.

Processes can be refined in various ways. A pre-existing process may be extended, coming into play where it previously would not have been in play. Here it comes to be triggered by wider processes, and its being so triggered typically is informed by those wider processes. Or a process may be curtailed, not coming into play where it previously would have been in play. Here it is inhibited, or its results are rejected, by wider processes, and in respects that are informed by those wider processes.

Refinement of either sort (extending or curtailing) can be appropriate for either perceptual processes or for inferential processes. Suppose, for example, that one has a rather special-purpose process for judging that one was in high northern latitudes: where one perceives a prominent display of the aurora borealis, one infers that one is in high latitudes. Furthermore, one appreciates that the aurora is itself a result of radiation being channeled by the earth's magnetic field, and that this has focused such effects at the poles. But, recent work has suggested that the earth's magnetic field has repeatedly entered periods of shift, followed by full reversals, followed by periods of reasonable stability. This information leads one to constrain one's inference by requiring at least the absence of information to the effect that one is then in a period of instability. Were one informed that the earth had entered a period of magnetic field instability, this would then inhibit one's standing inferential tendency.

Perceptual processes are commonly both extended and refined by various modulational processes that operate diachronically. Constance is said to be like those who, on the basis of long experiential refinement (learning from successes and failures), have come to be sensitive, careful, and discriminating perceivers of everyday things. Perceptual processes typically come to be shaped and attuned by the apparent successes and failures to which the agent has been exposed. Apparent successes or failures may be revealed in ways that turn on subsequent perception—in which case the perceptual process will itself be shaped by further perceptual processes. As a child, perceiving as a child, one was trained to distinguish poison ivy from other plants—training that came in the form of messages perceptually gotten. Perhaps one learns to distinguish ripe, but not overly ripe, melons—commonly by way of subsequent experiential investigation of purchased melons. Apparent successes or failures may be revealed by processes that are partially inferential. Suppose one perceptually judges that an individual bird in one's desert environment is of some species. But upon receiving testimony regarding the ranges and lives of birds of the relevant species (relying on inductions by others) and then inferring that one's individual bird is very unlikely to have been of that type, given where it was observed, one may then abandon one's belief. Whether perceptually or inferentially revealed, apparent successes may lead to the reinforcement or extension of the perceptual process under modulational control. Apparent failures may lead to an extinguishing, or at least a curtailing, of the perceptual process under modulational control.

In a wide range of experientially possible global environments, such diachronic refinement would make for an increasingly sensitive and globally reliable perceptual agent. As a result, except in those extremely inhospitable environments where they are subject to input that is pervasively deceptive, trained perceptual processes tend to be globally reliable, and to become increasingly so in the course of ongoing training. This is to say that trained perceptual processes are reliable relative to a reference class comprising *experientially* possible global environments—they are reliable in a wide range of such environments—they are postclassically reliable. Thus, while Constance's perceptual processes are not globally reliable in her unfortunate environment, they are transglobally reliable under modulational control. It is this virtue that is missing in Sextus, who systematically rejects the results of his perceptual processes, and who does so on the basis of modulational control processes that are not transglobally reliable.

We can sharpen these observations regarding the postclassical reliability of perceptual processes by employing the distinction between being inherently transglobally reliable and being non-inherently transglobally reliable, and the correlative distinction between incremental modulational enhancement and threshold-crossing modulational enhancement. Typically, perceptual processes start off being transglobally reliable, for numerous kinds of perceptual beliefs that these processes generate. But perceptual processes can and do become increasingly better, with diachronic modulation through experience and training. (One can learn to recognize, upon very brief exposure, a particular kind of bird, or tree, or foreign accent, etc., etc.) And some perceptual processes start off not being inherently transglobally reliable at all—e.g. visual word-recognition processes in children just starting to learn how to read. Diachronic modulation through experience and training initially is threshold-crossing (the child becomes able to read about Jack and Jill), and then becomes incremental as reading skills progressively improve.

Here in section 6.3 we have discussed how various cognitive processes of general and familiar sorts are postclassically reliable. We considered processes that are variously spawned, selectively triggered, or selectively inhibited (with an eye to their local and global reliability), and in each case noticed gains in transglobal reliability provided that the modulational control processes themselves have a measure of transglobal reliability. We also considered an important special case of processes under modulational control—perceptual processes—noting the ways in which these can be informed by antecedently possessed information and acquired sensitivities. Our conclusions draw upon information that is largely accessible from the armchair (if one includes reflections of a reasonably common-sensical sort about one's perceptual and reasoning processes). The picture of modulational control presented here is subject to significant further elaboration and refinement in light of ongoing cognitive scientific results regarding processes of the sorts here discussed. Still, two general points seem firmly established: (1) processes of modulational control of the sorts here outlined are surely exhibited by humans, and (2) they contribute to the transglobal reliability of human belief formation. Each point is important. Were such modulational control processes not to contribute to transglobal reliability, they would not make for the form of epistemic safety that is pivotal to being objectively justified in believing. They do, and thus are epistemically good. On the other hand, one might imagine many possible powerful cognitive systems exhibiting elaborate and wondrous forms of modulational control. While these forms of modulational control might be epistemically nice to the extent that they would enhance transglobal reliability, some of them would doubtless not be tractable or fitting for human cognitive agents. Our talk of *suitable* modulational control is intended to honor this last point. Among various possible forms of modulational control that would enhance transglobal reliability, only those that are tractable to humans are fitting or suitable to humans. (Only *suitable* modulational control is constitutively required for being objectively justified in believing.) Thus, detail regarding just what processes make for suitable modulational control (and thus objective epistemic justification in humans) depends on information regarding humans as cognitive systems—information of sorts not available from the armchair. A more detailed understanding of suitable forms of modulational control will turn on a spectrum of epistemological inquiry, characterized in Chapter 6. Ideas about how humans can manage some of the informational chores associated with those forms of modulational control suitable to them then feature importantly in Chapters 7–8.

6.4 De facto safety as a constitutive desideratum for justification

Under transglobal reliabilism, de facto safety does not count (as it did under neoclassical reliabilism) as a constitutive requirement for justification. De facto safety, recall, is *global* reliability under suitable modulational control. This is as it should be, insofar as one's intuitions about cases like those described above are manifestations of one's conceptual competence with the notion of *being objectively justified*. Folks like Constance and Harry have beliefs that are very well justified, even though these beliefs lack de facto safety. Their beliefs do possess *experiential* safety, and this latter kind of safety is what constitutes the distinctively *epistemic* form of safety that *is* constitutively required for justification.

What, then, should be said about the status of de facto safety? As reflected in scattered remarks in sections above, one should say of de facto safety the same thing that neoclassical reliabilism says about *local reliability*: namely de facto safety is a constitutive desideratum for justification. More specifically, it is a feature that is constitutively desirable *as manner and means* toward achieving the fundamental constitutive desideratum-*as-goal* of justification—namely systematic true belief.

So de facto safety still gets its due, within transglobal reliabilism. But it is critical to appreciate the difference between a constitutive desideratum and a constitutive requirement. De facto safety is constitutively *desirable* for objective justification, whereas experiential safety is constitutively *required*. (And, in a wide range of experientially possible global environments, processes that are transglobally reliable are also globally reliable.)

Suitable modulational control remains a constitutive requirement. This does not mean that agents whose processes are postclassically reliable will necessarily engage in a conscious, intentional pursuit of de facto safety or global reliability. Instead what is required is that the agent, as cognitive system, be so constituted as to 'pursue' de facto safety by suitable processes of modulational control. There must be in place modulational control processes that (at least in global environments that are not extraordinarily hostile) enhance global reliability and de facto safety by producing information about local and global environments and modulating belief-producing processes. It is in this sense that the pursuit of de facto safety must be built into an agent whose beliefs are epistemically justified. But it is the 'pursuit' of de facto safety, not the attaining of it, that is mandated for objective epistemic justification.

Unless a cognitive agent is unlucky enough to be in a pervasively deceptive global environment, the constitutively required kind of safety (namely experiential safety) will further the form of safety that is a constitutive desideratum (namely de facto safety): insofar as the epistemic agent's global environment cooperates—insofar as experiences of cognitive agents within their global environment are not systematically and radically deceiving—experiential safety will *bring in its wake* de facto safety. And de facto safety, in turn, conduces toward systematic true belief. These points could be extended to local reliability, too: The constitutively required experiential safety conditionally furthers the de facto safety, which turns on processes being globally reliable under suitable modulational control. And, this, in turn, furthers local reliability. So, for objective epistemic justification, local reliability also remains a constitutive desideratum-as-manner-and-means, as does global reliability.

The upshot is this. Attaining the constitutive desideratum of de facto safety, a desideratum that is constituted by neoclassical reliability, is certainly desirable, and certainly does *contribute* as manner and means toward achieving the constitutive desideratum-as-goal of epistemic justification—it contributes to achieving systematic true belief. Still, it's doing so *suitably*, rather than *fortuitously*, depends upon the belief-generating process's having a more fundamental feature, the key feature that is actually constitutively *required* for justification: experiential safety. Thus, while the global reliability and de facto safety of Ike's, Ashley's, and Sextus's processes contributed to their achieving systematic true beliefs, it did so in ways that were yet unsuitably risky—too much a matter of epistemic luck. According to transglobal reliabilism, the relevant form of safety, missing in these cases, is experiential safety (that is, being transglobally reliable under suitable modulational control).

7 Applying the central idea to the cases

Transglobal reliabilism can smoothly accommodate one's intuitive judgments about epistemic justification with regard to the various thought-experimental cases with which this chapter began. Likewise for the various cases we set forth in Chapter 3. These facts constitute part of the case in favor of transglobal reliabilism. (Further evidential considerations will be adduced in the next chapter.) In the present section we revisit these cases, and we explain why and how transglobal reliabilism accommodates one's intuitive judgments about them.

Recall Constance and Faith. Both are victims of radical deception, but Constance's belief-forming processes are, nonetheless, intuitively beyond reproach, whereas Faith's are intuitively sloppy.

There is a very strong tendency to judge that Constance is justified in holding her perceptual belief that someone is calling her on the phone. One is not inclined to think that the scenario represents a particularly happy or epistemically desirable case, of course. But, one is strongly disinclined to find fault with Constance or her processes. The problem lies with her extremely inhospitable, demon-infested environment. There, no agent and no process would be able to attain significant true beliefs. Fine agent, lousy environment. Thus, one is inclined to judge that Constance is justified and has done nothing epistemically wrong or inappropriate in believing that someone is calling.

Faith's disposition to commit the gambler's fallacy is no less reliable in her demon-infested environment than are the processes that Constance employs. Even so, one is inclined to judge that there is something wrong—objectively wrong—with Faith's processes, *and not with Constance's*. One is inclined to judge that Faith is not objectively justified in believing as she does, *although Constance is*.

One might think that neoclassical reliabilists should simply soften the tone of their judgments regarding agents in demon-infested environments. For example, they might insist that, in global environments where there are no reliable processes possible, and thus no possibility of objectively appropriate processes (or of objectively justified beliefs, they might insist), it seems best to say that processes are neither appropriate nor inappropriate. The neoclassical reliabilist might write of all processes in a demon-infested environment as 'nonappropriate,' and of all beliefs as 'nonjustified.' While this wrinkle would give neoclassical reliabilism a kinder, more sympathetic face, it really does not respond to the core objection. It does not provide a basis for distinguishing between persons, or between processes, in demon-infested environments. The core of the new evil demon problem is the intuition that there can be differences in the objective appropriateness of processes of agents in such environments. It is that the reliabilist has missed something of epistemological importance, not that the reliabilist has been too harsh in characterizing a homogeneous class of possible epistemic cases. The solution is not an epistemological form of 'political correctness.' While all agents in a demon-infested environment would be 'epistemically disadvantaged,' we cannot leave the matter there. Some agents may employ processes that are epistemically appropriate, while others may fail to do so—and that is just what our judgments about the cases suggest (Constance is justified in believing as she does, while Faith is not). The neoclassical reliabilist cannot say that Constance is justified in believing that someone is calling her on the phone.

Transglobal reliabilism, on the other hand, has no difficulty accounting for these judgment tendencies. As stipulated, Constance is, in certain crucial respects, like the best perceptual agents in the actual global environment.[10] She is like those who, on the basis of long experiential refinement (learning from successes and failures), have come to be sensitive, careful, and discriminating perceivers of everyday things. Constance's perceptual processes have been shaped by the apparent successes and failures to which she has conscientiously attended. In many global environments, she would have thereby come to be a sensitive and globally reliable perceptual agent. In a wide range of experientially possible global environments, such trained and shaped perceptual processes are subtly sensitive to the things confronted in that environment. (Although, in her particularly inhospitable demon-infested environment, such trained perceptual processes are not globally reliable.) Thus, while the use of trained perceptual

---

[10] The case focuses on a perceptual belief, and its objective justification becomes the issue. Still, given what has been said about Constance's reasoning processes, one could have focused on inferential beliefs with equal force.

processes, such as Constance's, might fail to be globally reliable in some environments, and even in her actual environment, such processes would seem to be reliable relative to a reference class comprising the set of experientially possible environments. The transglobal reliabilist thus finds it natural to see Constance as forming perceptual beliefs as she should—as objectively justified by virtue of forming her beliefs via a transglobally reliable process.

Perhaps there are experientially possible global environments in which Faith's sloppy reasoning processes (including the gambler's fallacy) would be globally reliable. It seems plausible that there would be some environments compatible with having experiences with roughly the character of one's everyday experiences in which Faith's cognitive processes would be globally reliable. (For example, in one such environment, there might perhaps be a gambling deity who (marginally) influences the course of events in what would otherwise be random processes, and who does so in a way that nudges sequences of events so as to have them conform to patterns that naively 'seem more random.') But, even if there are such experientially possible global environments, they would be rather exceptional. With respect to the reference class of experientially possible global environments, Faith's processes are not reliable. Were she to happen to be in a peculiar experientially possible environment in which her sloppy inductive processes were globally reliable, this would be a curious stroke of epistemic luck. As her luck would have it, such is not Faith's world—the demon is in the business of deceiving her, and her processes are not globally reliable. But, considered without supposing that one knows what experientially possible global environment Faith inhabits, her processes are risky. They would not be globally reliable in a wide range of demon-infested environments, and they would not be globally reliable in a wide range of experientially possible variations on our actual global environment: They simply would not be reliable in a wide range of experientially possible global environments. As a result, with or without a stroke of epistemic luck, they seem unacceptably risky. So, the transglobal reliabilist has no difficulty seeing Faith's processes as objectively unjustified.

The cases of Harry and Ike come in for similar treatment. Much like Constance, Ike is subject to systematic (if somewhat more limited) deception. Still, his processes would seem to be transglobally reliable, even if they fail in his global environment. Clearly, one wants to say of Ike and of Constance, something parallel to what was said about Athena. For Athena, while the peculiarities of her local environment may have rendered her processes locally unreliable (unbeknownst to her, of course), her processes were nevertheless such as to possess a more robust form of reliability, global reliability. The robustness of reliability of her processes afforded them an epistemically desirable measure of safety. For Ike and Constance, while the peculiarities of their global environments may have rendered their respective processes globally unreliable (unbeknownst to them, of course), their processes were nevertheless such as to possess a yet more robust form of reliability, transglobal reliability. This greater robustness of reliability of their processes affords them a yet more epistemically desirable measure of safety. Such safety cannot ensure that one is not unlucky, that one does not inhabit a demon-infested environment. But nothing can guard against that. On the other hand, it minimizes the epistemic risks, and that is all that can be asked.

In contrast, Harry (and Sextus Pessimisicus) can be compared with Fortuna. The (unappreciated) peculiarities of the local environment rendered Fortuna's processes locally reliable, but those processes were globally unreliable and thus epistemically risky. The local reliability of Fortuna's processes was too much a matter of epistemic luck, depended too much on (unappreciated) peculiarities of Fortuna's local environment. The case of Harry is parallel: the peculiarities of his global environment render his processes globally reliable, but those processes are themselves transglobally unreliable. The global reliability of Harry's and of Sextus's processes is highly dependent on peculiarities of the experientially possible global environments that they happen to occupy, and this renders those processes unacceptably risky.

Ashley too is not justified in her general beliefs about humankind, according to transglobal reliabilism—despite the fact that her processes are neoclassically reliable. They are not postclassically reliable, and thus are globally unreliable in a wide range of experientially possible global environments, and thus are unacceptably risky.

Furthermore, transglobal reliabilism has no difficulty with the judgments that served as data in Chapter 3. Just as Constance's trained, sensitive, perceptual processes count as transglobally reliable under suitable modulational control, so do both Athena's and Diana's. Of course, in Athena's and Diana's more hospitable global environment, this has resulted in their also employing processes that are globally reliable under suitable modulational control (for, in these cases, the modulational control would contribute both to global reliability—apparently satisfying the neoclassical reliabilist demands for modulational control—and to transglobal reliability—satisfying transglobal reliabilist demands for modulational control). Of course, Diana's process has *actually* been modulated, in a way that Athena's process has not—enhancing its global reliability. But, once one has come to appreciate the epistemic safety afforded by transglobal reliability, one can see that the global reliability afforded here is a good thing—even a constitutive desideratum-as-manner-and-means—without thinking that it is what makes for objective justification here. Athena is justified in her belief that there is a barn before her, and Diana (who produces no such belief) would be justified in those beliefs in which she would perceptually judge that there was a barn at some location. Fortuna's processes lack global reliability, transglobal reliability, and any significant modulational control. The transglobal reliabilist has no difficulty accommodating the judgment that she is unjustified in her belief. One also judges that Elena is justified in the belief that she produces—and one notes that her process is here spawned by information and processes in a way that makes it, under such modulational control, globally and transglobally reliable (considered as under such ongoing control). Finally, all those clairvoyant friends of BonJour and those with serendipitous brain lesions are deficient with respect to the modulational control processes which seem to be in play, and their processes certainly are not, of themselves (without modulational control) transglobally reliable.

So transglobal reliabilism vindicates one's intuitive judgments about epistemic justification, for all the cases considered in the present chapter and in Chapter 3. And it also offers a satisfying, plausible, rationale for those judgments—namely (a) that experiential safety of belief-forming processes is a constitutive requirement for epistemic justification, and (b) that experiential safety is constituted by postclassical reliability. These facts constitute strong evidence in favor of transglobal reliabilism.

8 Knowledge

Our main concerns in this book have come to revolve around the concept of (objective) epistemic justification. However, one can look up from the reflective analysis of that concept to briefly consider, from the perspective of transglobal reliabilism, the other central epistemic evaluative concept: the concept of knowledge. There is clearly significant variation in how the word 'knowledge' is employed, and it is plausible that there might be some contextual elements to this notion. This said, it is reasonable to advance the following working hypothesis: at least in *many* ordinary contexts, the notion of knowledge works in such a way that not only is objective epistemic justification constitutively required (and thus experiential safety, which is constitutively required for such justification), but in addition the various features that are constitutive *desiderata* for justification become constitutive *requirements* for knowledge. If this is correct, then for a given belief to count as knowledge, that belief must be (a) true (since truth is a constitutive desideratum-as-end), (b) the product of processes that are postclassically reliable (since that is constitutively required for justification), and (c) the product of processes that are also neoclassically and locally reliable (since these are constitutive desiderata-as-manner-and-means for justification).

One can consider a few of the cases that have served in the above reflections. Obviously, those in which the agent's beliefs are false do not count as knowledge, so we need not tarry over the cases of Constance, Faith, and Ike. Also, those cases in which the agent fails to be justified on transglobal reliabilist grounds probably do not require extended comment. Just as BonJour's clairvoyants and Plantinga's victims of brain lesions do not strike one as justified, they also do not strike one as having knowledge—even though their beliefs are true. The same goes for Sextus Pessimisicus, Harry, Ashley, and their ilk. There is simply too much amiss with respect to their cognitive processes, they are too unsafe to give rise to knowledge, one judges, and our working hypothesis would predict this much. The more interesting cases are those in which the agent arrives at true and justified beliefs, but one would yet judge intuitively that the agent does not have knowledge. Athena seems a good example. Here, there is not so much something wrong with her belief-forming processes, per se, but with something about those processes in the peculiar global or local environment. They are transglobally reliable under suitable modulational control, and they are even globally reliable—so at least this one constitutive desideratum-as-manner-and-means is attained. But, due to the peculiar features of the local environment, they are not locally reliable.

132   THE EPISTEMOLOGICAL SPECTRUM

Our working hypothesis would thus have Athena's belief count as a justified true belief but not as knowledge.[11] If the working hypothesis is correct, then there should be similar cases in which an agent generates a true belief by way of processes that are transglobally reliable under suitable modulational control, and yet fails to have knowledge there because the process lacks global reliability. Ashley provides such cases, via the true beliefs she forms by using processes whose global reliability depends upon the fortuitous homogeneity of her global environment. An example is Ashley's belief that all middle-aged women take antidepressants.

So there is good reason to advance the working hypothesis. We will return to the matter in the next chapter.

9   Summary: replacing neoclassical reliabilism by transglobal reliabilism

We began this chapter with a set of scenarios that provoke judgments at odds with neoclassical reliabilism. Of course, such judgments could be mistaken. There is a reasonable presumption that they arise out of one's competence with the concept of epistemic justification—and that they thus serve to reflect important conceptually grounded necessary truths. However, it is possible that these judgments are some form of performance error. Ultimately, we will need to reflect further on the range of cases and judgments featured in this and the preceding chapter. We will need to expand the range of cases somewhat, and we will need to bring into our reflection certain observations regarding the point and purpose of various evaluative epistemological concepts, including that of *being objectively justified*. We will need to determine which account of that concept and of one's competence provides the best explanation for the judgments. The full investigation awaits in the next chapter.

For now, we can consider the tentative results gotten in the present chapter. While the cases with which we began constitute a set of significant objections to neoclassical reliabilism, they do not pose a challenge to the idea that a form of epistemic safety is constitutively required for objective justification. Indeed, they seem to reinforce this point while, at the same time, indicating that the neoclassical reliabilist understanding of the requisite safety is flawed. Still, drawing on an insight from neoclassical reliabilism, we have begun to investigate the idea that epistemic safety might be understood in terms of a highly robust form of reliability—a reliability that is not unduly dependent on features of the local or global environment. While global reliability is a relatively

---

[11] It is worth noting that, insofar as Athena's belief is the product of perceptual processes that are subject to the sort of suitable modulational control that we have envisioned throughout our discussions, her belief also is the result of processes that are locally reliable under suitable modulational control. This is because those processes are subject to eventually turning up the sort of information that induced Diana to modulate her processes—and under that control, the perceptual processes are locally reliable. What this suggests is that global reliability and local reliability of one's processes (as well as such reliability under suitable control) are constitutive desiderata-as–manner-and-means for justifications. Local reliability is lacking in Athena's case.

robust form of reliability, it appears not to be robust enough, and we propose that the needed epistemic safety is found in transglobal reliability—or, more fully, transglobal reliability under suitable modulational control. This both makes good sense of the pivotal idea of epistemic safety and allows us to accommodate the intuitive judgments made in response to the scenarios that trouble neoclassical reliabilism. Further, we can make good sense of the judgments featured in the previous chapter. This makes a rather strong case for transglobal reliabilism—one that will be further developed in the next chapter.

5

Defending Transglobal Reliabilism

1 Overview

The defense of transglobal reliabilism began in Chapter 4, and proceeded in a way that conforms to the account of low-grade a priori reflection in Chapter 2. Judgments made in response to concrete scenarios were treated (in Chapter 3, as well as Chapter 4) as data to be accommodated in abductive inference about the nature of objective justification. Upon some reflection, transglobal reliabilism emerged as a particularly promising approach; it accommodates the judgments featured in those chapters rather naturally.

In this chapter, we will develop the defense further, and in a way that continues to conform to the characterization of low-grade a priori reasoning in Chapter 2. Additional data will be considered. It will include scenarios about which one tends to experience certain sorts of competing judgment-tendencies. Also, observations regarding the point and purpose of the evaluative epistemological concepts of justification and knowleledge will need to be factored into the reflection. We will argue that transglobal reliabilism is correct because ultimately it provides the best overall explanation of a broad range of data.

Various aspects of abductive reasoning will be at work. For example, it will be important to provide a plausible and natural explanation of why and how competing judgment-tendencies arise in some cases of competing attributions of justification or of knowledge. (One potential form of explanation accommodates both by introducing context-sensitive factors that vindicate each judgment under certain specific contextual uses but not others. Another potential form of explanation repudiates some of these statements as just mistaken, but offers a plausible explanation of why and how such mistakes or mistake-tendencies somehow arise naturally.) Consideration needs to be given to whether this approach conforms well with key aspects of the point and purpose of the concepts under investigation, namely justification and knowledge. Alternative potential explanations of the data need to be considered, and need to be compared to ours in terms of comparative theoretical benefits and costs. Ultimately, the strength of the abductive argument for transglobal reliabilism turns on whether the proposed account does better, in terms of overall theoretical plausibility and explanatory power, than extant alternative approaches.

Before proceeding to the main business of the chapter, we address a potential objection to transglobal reliabilism: the allegation that the notion of transglobal reliability of belief-forming processes is an inherently problematic concept. We argue, in reply, that comparable issues arise for dispositional concepts in general, and thus that they do not appear to raise any *special* problem for the concept of transglobal reliability. This line of argument is an aspect of the abductive-inferential component of low-grade a priori reasoning in favor of transglobal reliabilism: maintaining that the key concept deployed in this position is sufficiently clear to bear the theoretical weight assigned to it. We do not purport to 'clear everything up'; but we would insist that one will not get far in either science or epistemology if one dispenses with dispositional notions.

2 The problem of infinities

There are infinitely many members of the class of experientially possible global environments. As discussed already (in sections 5.3 and 5.5 of the preceding chapter), this calls for caution when developing one's account of transglobal reliability. It is tempting to gloss our talk of a process being reliable across a wide range of experientially possible global environments in terms that we have avoided. One cannot understand transglobal reliability (reliability across a wide range of experientially possible global environments) as a matter of a ratio—the number of such environments in which the process is globally reliable divided by the total number of such environments. For, there is no such ratio. Thus, one cannot say that transglobally reliable processes are 'reliable in most experientially possible global environments.' (Not only is the class of experientially possible global environments infinite, so also are both the subclasses in question.) Nor can one make sense of the idea by saying, concerning the space of experientially possible global environments, that the volume of the region of this space in which the process is reliable is very large, compared to the volume of the complementary region in which the process is not reliable. For, this would require some pertinent, well-defined, quantitative *metric* over the space of experientially possible global environments, and it is very far from clear (to say the least) what such a metric could be.

We have suggested a way of thinking about transglobal reliability—about wider and narrower ranges of global environments across which different processes would be reliable—without running afoul of the problem of infinities just noted. Rather than thinking in terms of relative numbers of possible global environments, or in terms of the relative volumes of regions of possible global environments, we proposed thinking in terms of comparative degrees of variation across possible global environments and in terms of a process being reliable (robustly reliable) across greater or lesser ranges of such variation. Furthermore, we identified a highly general feature of transglobally reliable processes: a process's *global reliability status is not highly dependent on specifics of the agent's actual global environment*. This suffices for making sense of a serviceable comparative notion of transglobal reliability—and we have deployed these resources in a discussion of the scenarios motivating transglobal reliabilism (in section 5.3 of the previous chapter).

In the present section, we seek to bolster these ideas by making several additional points about the problem of infinities. Briefly, the points are these. First, the problem of infinities arises quite ubiquitously for dispositional notions: typically for such notions there are infinitely many 'positive' cases (actual or possible) and also infinitely many 'negative' cases, and typically there is no well-motivated quantitative metric over the space of cases that would allow one to make good sense of the idea of a quantitative ratio between the 'volumes' of the two subspaces that respectively contain the positive cases and negative cases. Second, there is a natural and plausible way of handling this general issue—a way that does not invoke such problematic-looking quantitative notions. Third, the account we have already offered fits well within this treatment of the generic problem of infinities. The upshot will be to bolster our proposed account in two ways: first, by showing that it is not ad hoc, and second, by showing that its lack of quantitative precision is not objectionable. Let us take up these points in turn.

First

It is important to observe that something like the problem of infinities arises extremely generally for dispositional notions. Take *global* reliability of belief-forming processes, for example. Even if one holds fixed the actual global environment, the fact remains that there are infinitely many potential trajectories that humans or other cognitive creatures could take through that environment, and the track record that would result from the operation of a given process will vary across different trajectories through the environment. One might say that global reliability is a matter of the process's generating a true belief in a 'wide range' of the episodic trajectories in this infinite class (where there are infinitely many episodic trajectories in which a true belief results, and there are also infinitely many episodic trajectories in which a false belief results). No natural-looking quantitative metric is even remotely in sight, over the space of possible trajectories in which a given belief-forming process is employed, for purposes of assessing whether that process is globally reliable. Yet global reliability looks to be a perfectly respectable dispositional notion, nonetheless. Parallel points could be made using a common garden-variety dispositional feature, such as *flammability*. There are infinitely many specific ways for a given kind of substance to be subjected to circumstances that sometimes cause something to burn, even if one restricts the reference class fairly severely (e.g. to actual earthly environments in temperate climates). So the *problem of infinities* arises quite ubiquitously for dispositional concepts.

Second

One can abstract from our earlier treatment of the specific version of the problem of infinities that arises for the notion of transglobal reliability (sections 5.3 and 5.5 of the previous chapter), to formulate a plausible sketch of a response to the problem of infinities that is intended to treat dispositions generally. The core ideas are as follows. First, associated with a well-behaved dispositional concept will be some canonical *qualitative-ordering* relation over the members of the reference class, based on some *canonical ordering-property*. (In the case of flammability, the feature might be something like *pertinent overall similarity to paradigmatic circumstances in which some familiar substances catch fire*.) Second, this ordering-property can be exhibited by members of the reference class in differing qualitative degrees, but not in any well-defined *quantitative* degrees. That is, although one member can exhibit the property to a greater degree than another (or a lesser degree, or the same degree), there is no meaningful interval-scale or ratio-scale measure for the property such that it makes sense to say that an item in the reference class exhibits the property to some particular numerical degree. Third, some items in the reference class exhibit the canonical ordering-property to a *very great* extent, others exhibit it to a *very small* extent (or perhaps not at all), and still others exhibit it to a *moderate* extent—where again, these are *qualitative* categories that are not grounded in an interval-scale or ratio-scale quantitative measure. Fourth, for any position in the ordering, there are infinitely many items in the reference class occupying that specific position; as we will put it, the members of the reference class constitute a *fully distributed infinity* with respect to the canonical ordering-property. Finally, fifth, the idea that the relevant dispositional property obtains relative to a 'wide range' of items in the reference class now gets explained this way: the disposition is manifested for all items except those that exhibit the canonical ordering property to an extreme extent—i.e. either to a *very great* extent or else to a *very small* extent (or not at all). (In the case of flammability, for example, a substance is flammable—and thus catches fire in a wide range of situations in the reference class of 'flame-encouraging' circumstances—provided that it catches fire in all such situations apart from those that differ from paradigmatic fire-inducing circumstances *to a very great extent*.)

No doubt there is more to be said at the generic level, by way of elaborating the general approach we have sketched to the problem of infinities. We suspect, for example, that one's interests and purposes, in employing a given dispositional notion, sometimes can play a role in determining what counts as correct usage—and that dispositional notions will often be fairly context-sensitive, since correct employment in a context is answerable to matters of interest and purpose. Contextual factors could enter in either or both of the following ways. First, they might partially determine what counts, in context, as a suitable kind of canonical ordering-property. Second, even with the canonical ordering-property already fixed, contextual factors might partially determine how items in the reference class get ordered with respect to that very property—for example, by partially determining what counts as a minor difference concerning the ordering property and what counts as a *substantial* difference. (Comparative similarity is often a vague and somewhat amorphous affair—even comparative similarity with respect to a specific ordering property—and so it plausibly is context-sensitive.)

Third

How should this generic approach to the problem of infinities be implemented in the case of the notion of transglobal reliability? When reflecting on processes that are postclassically reliable—that is, processes that are transglobally reliable under suitable modulational control—the most pertinent general feature exhibited in such cases was said to be this: the global-reliability status of the given belief-forming process is *not* highly dependent on specifics of the agent's actual global environment. This suggests that the canonical ordering-property for epistemically possible global environments is the following: being a global environment with specific features on which that process's qualitative degree of global reliability is highly, and sensitively, dependent. Of course, there will typically be global environments in which a process that intuitively strikes one as transglobally reliable will fail to be globally reliable—but it will be easy to identify the rather special characteristics of that global environment making it inhospitable (deceiving demons, mad cognitive scientists, or wild variations in natural laws, for example) and making the process there globally unreliable. Remove this special pitfall, and global reliability results. The environment becomes one of various environments in which the intuitively transglobally reliable process is globally reliable, and this reliability is not highly dependent on some specific characteristics of those global environments. Thus, a qualitative ordering of the overall reference class (of experientially possible global environments) would be as follows. At one end is the 'narrow' class of environments with specific features on which a process's qualitative degree of global reliability is highly, and sensitively, dependent. The rest of the overall reference class constitutes the 'wide' class: environments lacking specific features on which the process's global reliability are highly dependent.[1]

---

[1] Processes that are highly transglobally *un*reliable can be treated as the mirror image. Such a process might be globally reliable in some experientially possible global environments—but typically it will be easy to identify the rather special characteristics of that global environment which make it strikingly hospitable to just such a process, as though the environment has been tailored to cover for the ineptness of the process (special benign demons or benignly mad cognitive scientists, or highly homogeneous populations, or the like) and making the process there globally reliable. Remove this special helper, or add some simple pitfalls like some heterogeneity in populations, and global unreliability results. When the global environment is tailored for the process that intuitively is not transglobally reliable, the global reliability of the process is highly dependent on some feature special to that environment (the demon, neural scientist, nomic roulette, or the like). Once removed, the environment becomes one of various environments in which the process is globally unreliable, and this unreliability is not dependent on some highly specific characteristics of those global environments. Then it is easy to imagine significant ranges of variation that do not reinstate the global reliability of the process.

Thus, for an intuitively transglobally *un*reliable process: in a global environment in which it is globally reliable, (a) this status *is* highly dependent on specifics of the global environment, while (b) in a global environment in which the same process is not globally reliable, its unreliability is *not* highly dependent on specifics of that environment and it maintains that status across wide variation. Conversely, for an intuitively transglobally reliable process: in an inhospitable global environment in which it is globally *un*reliable, (c) this global unreliability is highly dependent on specifics of that global environment, while (d) in a global environment in which it *is* globally reliable, this status is *not* highly dependent on specifics of that environ-

So the notion of transglobal reliability looks to be a respectable dispositional notion. It does face the problem of infinities, but so also do most dispositional notions. We have sketched a plausible-looking way to address that problem generically, without recourse to inherently problematic attempts to do so in quantitative terms. And we have explained how our earlier non-quantitative explication of transglobal reliability is an instance of this generic approach. Card-carrying members of the Society for Exact Philosophy might yet hanker for a quantitatively precise explication of transglobal reliability, but such a hankering would be misplaced. As Aristotle famously said in Book 1, Chapter 3 of the *Nicomachean Ethics*, 'Our discussion will be adequate if it has as much clearness as the subject matter admits of, for precision is not to be sought for alike in all discussions, any more than in all the products of the crafts.'

3 Epistemic safety, postclassical reliability, and the truth connection

The normative notion of epistemic justification is intimately bound up, constitutively, with the goal of believing truths while avoiding belief in falsehoods. Neoclassical reliabilism clearly honors this constitutive aspect, since global reliability of belief-forming processes is a matter of their producing beliefs that are by-and-large true. On the other hand, one might wonder whether transglobal reliabilism fails to honor sufficiently the concern for truth that figures constitutively in the concept of epistemic justification. After all, as we ourselves have emphasized—for instance, in discussing the new evil demon problem—a cognitive agent's belief-forming processes could be transglobally reliable under suitable modulational control, and yet could systematically fail to generate true beliefs. (Such is the unfortunate situation of the envatted brain.) Does transglobal reliabilism manage to deliver a suitable truth-connection despite this fact? If so, what is the nature of that connection, and is it strong enough to honor the central and constitutive role that the concern for truth plays in the concept of epistemic justification?

As we pointed out in Chapter 4, transglobal reliabilism does incorporate at least one kind of constitutive link to the truth-goal: it treats global reliability as a constitutive *desideratum* governing epistemic justification. One might well wonder, however, whether this is enough. Shouldn't an adequate account of epistemic justification build in some kind of constitutive *requirement* that yields an appropriate connection to the truth-goal?

---

ment and it maintains that status across wide variation. Thus, for either transglobal reliability or transglobal unreliability, the canonical ordering-property is the extent to which a process's global reliability or unreliability is dependent on specifics of the agent's actual global environment. The global unreliability of a transglobally reliable process will be highly dependent on specifics, while the global unreliability of a given transglobally reliable process will be highly dependent on specifics.

Indeed it should, and in fact it does. In order to say what this constitutively required feature is, and why it suffices, we will now bring together several of the closely intertwined conceptual threads in the preceding discussion, in a way that views from a somewhat new angle the fabric that results. The guiding questions, at present, are these. First, what kind of truth-related attribute, if any, does transglobal reliabilism treat as a constitutive requirement for epistemic justification? Second, if there is such an attribute, does its role as a constitutive requirement adequately honor the pre-theoretic idea that epistemic justification is intimately and constitutively bound up with the truth-goal?

In Chapters 3 and 4 we emphasized the role of *safety* in the concept of epistemic justification: belief-forming processes that are excessively risky yield unjustified beliefs. We emphasized too that the pertinent kind of safety—what we termed epistemic safety—is not plausibly construed as simply a matter of global reliability of the operative belief-forming processes (or of global reliability under suitable modulational control). For, processes that happen to be globally reliable for reasons that are outside of the agent's cognitive ken might yet be unacceptably risky in relation to the agent's own experiential vantage point on the world—so that the actual global reliability of these processes is a *lucky accident* relative to the information actually possessed by the agent. Various of our thought-experimental characters illustrated this point, such as Ashley the Valley girl and paranoid Harry. Although global reliability under suitable modulational control does constitute safety of a kind—namely what we termed *de facto* safety—it is not the sort of safety that is constitutively required for epistemic justification, i.e., epistemic safety. Rather, epistemic safety of belief-forming processes is constituted instead by a form of reliability that is modally robust, relative to the class of experientially relevant possible global environments: namely postclassical reliability, i.e. transglobal reliability under suitable modulational control.

How does this modal kind of reliability link up with the goal of truth? One thing it does not do, of course, is guarantee that belief-forming processes that possess it are actually globally reliable and therefore are actually apt to produce true beliefs and not false beliefs. Nonetheless—and this is the crucial point—processes that possess this feature are *likely* to be globally reliable, relative to the agent's own experiential vantage point on the global environment. We will call this property *transglobal likelihood of global reliability*. This likelihood-feature is *qualitative*, and may not be refinable into any kind of quantitative probability. It is *modal*: it obtains relative to the reference class consisting of experientially possible global environments, rather then being a matter of what is likely relative to the epistemic agent's actual global environment itself. Nonetheless, it is a property that is *actually possessed*, in the actual global environment, by belief-forming processes of the kind that make for epistemic justification. And according to transglobal reliabilism, it is a property that is constitutively required for epistemic justification.

Can adequate sense be made of transglobal likelihood of global reliability? Yes, and in fact we have already done so. In effect, the explication we have given (in section 5.3

of Chapter 4 and section 2 of the present Chapter) of the idea that a belief-forming process being globally reliable 'in a wide range' of experientially possible global environments, while failing to exhibit global reliability only in 'a narrow range' of such environments, also constitutes an explication of the pertinent, modal and qualitative, kind of likelihood of global reliability. This explication is already on hand; one only needs to recognize and appreciate that it does indeed amount to a plausible and satisfying explanans for the intuitively natural explanandum-notion of transglobal likelihood of global reliability.

Let us return now to the questions at hand. To the question, 'What kind of truth-related attribute, if any, does transglobal reliabilism treat as a constitutive requirement for epistemic justification?,' the answer is this: transglobal likelihood of global reliability. To the question concerning this attribute, 'Does its role as a constitutive requirement adequately honor the pre-theoretic idea that epistemic justification is intimately and constitutively bound up with the truth-goal?,' the answer is affirmative. Likelihood of global reliability brings in its wake likelihood of producing a preponderance of true beliefs; so, here one has a strong, constitutively required, connection to the truth-goal. And the kind of likelihood that matters epistemically is one that is appropriately tethered to the experiential vantage point of the agent, and thus to the information possessed by the agent. Neoclassical reliability—i.e. global reliability under suitable modulational control—is neither necessary nor sufficient to play this role: not necessary, because the agent's experiential vantage point might systematically fail to deliver veridical representations of the actual global environment (as with an envatted brain), and not sufficient, because belief-forming processes that happen to be neoclassically reliable might nonetheless be enormously risky relative to the agent's own experiential vantage on the world (as with Ashley and Harry). The right truth-related attribute to treat as a constitutive requirement for epistemic justification is not the global reliability of belief forming processes, but rather the transglobal likelihood of such global reliability. Transglobal reliabilism delivers the goods.

4 Key purposes served by the concept of epistemic justification

The present chapter is aimed at further developing the case for transglobal reliabilism, by incorporating considerations in support of it over and above those we put forth in Chapter 4. In sections 2 and 3 we considered two potential objections—the problem of infinities, and the charge that the transglobal reliabilist account of epistemic justification does not adequately accommodate the constitutive goal of systematic truth—and we argued that both objections can be satisfactorily defused.

We turn next to some further positive evidence in favor of transglobal reliabilism. We will discuss a range of familiar uses of the concept of epistemic justification and the purposes served by those uses, and we will argue that those uses are smoothly and naturally accommodated by transglobal reliabilism. Such accommodation counts in its favor, as a component of the overall abductive case for the view.

The data we will draw upon in the course of the discussion will include not only common-sensical observations about the uses and purposes of the notion of objective epistemic justification, but also certain conflicting judgment-tendencies that arise when one asks how to apply this notion to some specific concrete scenarios. These conflicting tendencies will bring into sharper relief the different evaluative purposes that the concept can serve, and will generate theoretical pressure to incorporate a contextualist element into one's account of epistemic justification. The notion of suitable modulational control can be smoothly and naturally construed as exhibiting the sought-for contextual variability—a fact that constitutes yet another positive component within the overall package of considerations in favor of postclassical reliabilism.

4.1 The generic purpose: safe truth-seeking under uncertainty

What is the most generic, most fundamental, evaluative purpose that is served by the concept of epistemic justification? We will argue that a very plausible-looking answer to this question fits nicely with the account of this concept delivered by transglobal reliabilism. We discuss this generic evaluative purpose in this section—attending to how it makes for a compelling concern for postclassical reliability. In the following sections we consider various more specific evaluative purposes, all of which are species of the genus we are about to discuss.

Our proposed understanding of the generic evaluative purpose served by the concept of epistemic justification turns on three leading ideas. First, the over-arching goal of attaining systematic true belief—including the avoidance of *false* belief— clearly figures centrally when beliefs are being evaluated in terms of epistemic justification. Second, this pursuit of systematic true belief must be undertaken in the face of a form of uncertainty characteristic of epistemic life: one's epistemic chores must be managed while possessing only a fallible understanding regarding the global environment in which one is situated—which also entails uncertainty regarding which belief-forming processes will work in one's global environment. Third, the question whether a given epistemic agent A is justified in holding a belief with content p is closely tied to the experience-based evidential situation of A himself/ herself—i.e., this question is closely tied to A's own experiential vantage-point on the world.

When one brings these three leading ideas together, what emerges is the following conception of the generic purpose of the evaluative concept of epistemic justification, and of the teleological structure possessed by this concept in light of this generic purpose. The form of epistemic evaluation for which the concept is employed involves a certain goal or end—a certain *telos*—that is a constitutive desideratum-as-end— namely systematic true belief. But although this *telos* does have a constitutive role to play, its role is subtle. Truth of a belief is not constitutively *required*, in order for that belief to be justified; on the contrary, a belief's being true is neither necessary nor sufficient for the agent to be justified in holding it. What is constitutively required, however, is the *experiential safety* of the process that formed the belief. (As we stressed in section 3, a belief that is produced by an experientially safe process is *likely* to be true, given the agent's experiential vantage-point on the world. Such experience-relative likelihood of truth answers directly to the second and third key ideas mentioned in the preceding paragraph—uncertainty as a fact of epistemic life, and the centrality of the vantage point on the world that is occupied by the agent whose belief is being appraised for epistemic justification.) Experiential safety thus becomes an end or goal itself—another *telos*—that is constitutively involved in the evaluative notion of epistemic justification. It is a constitutive requirement for the justification of a given belief, whereas truth of the belief is a constitutive desideratum-as-end. As one might put it, experiential safety is the *primary telos* of objective justification (a *telos* that is constitutively required), whereas truth is the *secondary telos* (a *telos* that is constitutively a desideratum-as-end around which such evaluation is oriented). The secondary *telos* figures essentially in the nature of the primary one, because the experiential safety of a belief-forming process is a matter of that process's proclivity to yield beliefs that exhibit the feature that is the secondary *telos*, namely systematic truth.

So the notion of epistemic justification, on the account here offered, expresses a form of epistemic appraisal that is both fundamentally teleological and teleologically complex. It is fundamentally teleological because of the centrality and fundamentality of the primary *telos*: experiential safety of the belief-forming process. And it is teleologically complex because of the role of the secondary *telos* as constitutive desideratum-as-end, and also because experiential safety is a matter of a belief-forming process's proclivity for yielding beliefs with this secondary-*telos* feature (namely truth).

To say that the evaluative concept of epistemic justification is fundamentally teleological is not to deny, of course, that it can figure in deontological epistemological appraisal—in epistemic 'ought'-judgments. On the contrary. But the point is that this kind of epistemological 'ought' is conceptually dependent upon the underlying epistemological *telos*, namely experiential safety.

The conception just described of the generic purpose of the concept of justification, and of the teleological structure the concept possesses in order to serve that purpose, is very plausible from the perspective of reflective common sense. In effect, low-grade a priori reasoning is here being brought to bear—in the present instance, as a way of thematizing one's everyday, commonsensical, understanding of *what one is up to* when one characterizes a given belief of a given agent as being justified or unjustified. This way of construing the concept's generic purpose 'feels right,' intuitively: not only does it look very likely to fit well with one's intuitive applications of the concept in actual and hypothetical concrete cases (including the various cases set forth earlier in the present book), but it looks very plausible as a way of explaining the rationale for those justification-judgments.

The strong plausibility of this construal of the generic purpose of the concept of epistemic justification constitutes significant positive evidence, beyond what was said in Chapter 4, in favor of transglobal reliabilism. Experiential safety of belief-forming processes is at the heart of the construal, since it figures as primary *telos* and as constitutive requirement. And, as argued already in Chapter 4, experiential safety itself is constituted by postclassical reliability. Thus, the generic purpose of the concept of epistemic justification—namely experientially safe truth-seeking under uncertainty—points straight to transglobal reliabilism.

In addition to the generic purpose of the concept of epistemic justification, there might well be more specific purposes too, each of which would fall under the generic purpose we have just described. Transglobal reliabilism, with its emphasis on postclassical reliability as constitutively required for epistemic justification, has an aspect that is potentially promising for accommodating various specific purposes. Postclassical reliability is transglobal reliability under suitable modulational control. Different specific purposes for which the notion of epistemic justification might be employed could involve distinct, contextually determined, standards governing what kinds of modulational control count as *suitable*. This theme will be pursued presently.

Although the focus in this chapter and the preceding two chapters is the concept of *objective* epistemic justification, a few remarks are now in order concerning subjective justification. This notion too seems to have a complex structure in which the goal of systematic truth figures as a secondary *telos* and experiential safety figures as a primary *telos*. But actually exhibiting experiential safety is not a constitutive *requirement*, in the case of subjective justification, but instead is itself a constitutive desideratum. What is constitutively required, rather, is accordance with a set of normative standards for belief-formation which a given epistemic agent—or a community of epistemic agents to which the given agent belongs—adheres to in pursuit of true beliefs. If an agent's belief has been formed in accordance with the pertinent normative standards—the agent's own standards as the case may be, or the standards of the agent's community—then the belief thus formed counts as *subjectively* justified. The notion of subjective justification, like that of objective justification, can be used for either teleological appraisal or deontological appraisal: teleological when one's principal interest is in whether the agent formed a belief in a manner that *exhibits experiential safety by the agent's own lights* (or those of the community), and deontological when one's principal interest is whether the agent formed a belief in a way that the agent *ought to, by the agent's own lights* (or by those of the community).

4.2 Cases evincing a dual pull toward crediting and gatekeeping: Sophie and Hypatia

A number of different (and less generic) purposes can underlie applications of the concept of epistemic justification, and vary in their salience from one specific circumstance or application to another. In order to highlight this fact, and to bring into focus two important types of more-specific purpose that can lie behind one's judgments about the justification-status of an agent's belief, it will be useful to set forth some illustrative cases that evince a pull toward each specific purpose—where the justification-status one is inclined to assign to the agent's belief depends upon which purpose governs one's judgment.

In the mid-1950s, experimental works were emerging that would make salient several pitfalls facing those who sought to determine whether or not a given drug regimen was effective. Apparently, of particular moment was a compelling study by Beecher (1955) reporting that about a quarter of patients reporting back pain who were administered a placebo subsequently reported relief or diminution of their pain. This, and perhaps other studies at that time, provided significant evidence for a placebo effect that could vitiate studies of the effectiveness of new drug treatments. Other phenomena also threatened to lead researchers to spurious findings of effectiveness. For example, observer-expectancy effects obtain when an experimenter, anticipating certain results, inadvertently either manipulates subjects or misinterprets data to 'find' the results hoped for. With the salience of such pitfalls becoming apparent, proper processes of modulational control would require experimenters to look for ways of structuring experiments to mitigate or eliminate such risks. The indicated refinements in such experimental processes are double-blinding and placebo control groups (or control groups employing already well-understood treatments). With postclassically reliable background processes making evident the threat posed by placebo effects and observer-expectation effects, suitable modulational control would refine experimental processes to incorporate such innovations.

Now imagine that a medical researcher named Sophie, at that time at which these pitfalls have just become salient to the medical-research community, recently grew a social consciousness and joined a fledging group called Doctors without Boundaries. She then departed the cosmopolitan city of Chicago to bring medicine to the somewhat backward natives of Kansas—where, for example, Darwinian biology would remain controversial in public schools for yet another half century or more! Communication into such a backwater is, we will stipulate, slow and uncertain. Now Sophie is a respectful person, and is intrigued by the idea that there may lurk some significant truth in folk remedies. Being trained in hitherto cutting-edge science, she endeavors to treat folk practices as sources of hypotheses—giving them careful and rigorous tests in her field laboratory. However, having been isolated for a few years now, Sophie's experiments, and her associated inference tendencies, will not have been informed by those results in the wider community now indicating the need for double-blind, placebo-controlled testing. Her specific experimental process then does not incorporate features that the cutting-edge methodologists and medical researchers have come to understand as needed for neoclassical reliability—they do not exhibit the actual modulation from which her contemporary research community benefited. Nonetheless, Sophie has been careful and responsible in designing and implementing her empirical studies. Through no fault of her own, she just isn't aware of all those pitfalls associated with failure to employ double-blind methodology.

Sophie has good modulational-control mechanisms in play, and certainly would have taken appropriate steps to avoid pitfalls were she to have acquired the relevant information. But modulational-control mechanisms operate on pertinent information that is actually possessed by the epistemic agent—and she lacks that information, for reasons that do not reflect any irresponsibility on her own part.

So, imagine that Sophie hears of a folk remedy for problems of balance and coordination—it seems that the Kansans urge that one ingests the ground up brains of an animal recognized to have superior coordination: the common cat. Sophie then undertakes a systematic study of the benefits of eating cat brains for one's sense of balance. On the basis of her meticulous study, involving sizable human (and cat) populations, and apparent positive correlations at levels of statistical significance there obtained, she forms the belief that eating cat brains does tend to enhance one's sense of balance. Her experiment did not involve giving a placebo to a control group, nor was it double-blinded.

Let us now describe a second, partially similar, thought-experimental scenario. Imagine a medical researcher named Hypatia who is living and working in Chicago at the turn of the nineteenth century—some fifty years before the medical-research community will become aware of the pitfalls underlying the need for placebos and double-blind methodology. Hypatia is intrigued by the idea that there might be significant truth to the idea, prevalent in Kansas, that eating cat brains will improve one's balance. She undertakes careful and extensive research to investigate this idea, using the very best medical-research methodology of her day. On the basis of her meticulous study, involving sizable human (and cat) populations, and apparent positive correlations at levels of statistical significance there obtained, she forms the belief that eating cat brains does tend to enhance one's sense of balance. Her experiment did not involving giving a placebo to a control group, nor was it double-blinded.

Ask oneself, now, these questions. Is Sophie objectively justified in believing that eating ground-up cat brains improves one's balance? Is Hypatia objectively justified in so believing? (Both of them are *subjectively* justified in so believing, surely; but that is not the issue here.)

In both cases, one is apt to feel a strong dual pull—on one hand, toward judging that agent's belief is indeed justified, and on the other hand toward judging that it is not. We now set forth an account of these competing judgment-tendencies that adverts to the differing specific evaluative purposes that apparently lies behind them. The account will have a contextualist aspect: the specific purpose that governs (in context) a particular justifiedness-judgment will be construed as a contextual parameter that figures in the concept of epistemic justification. And the account will accord well with transglobal reliabilism: the implicit contextual purpose-parameter is most naturally construed as attaching to the notion of suitable modulational control—as governing what kinds of modulational control count, in context, as suitable. Thus, the fact that one feels a dual pull in cases like those of Sophie and Hypatia, along with the most natural and plausible way of explaining that dual pull, will together constitute further evidential considerations in favor of transglobal reliabilism.

One kind of purpose, often at work, is squarely concerned with whether an agent holds a given belief on the basis of processes that exhibit, relative to the information available to the agent (and only that information), the primary *telos*. In such contexts of epistemic appraisal, the appraiser is not especially interested in whether the agent's belief is indeed true, or whether it is even likely to be true given the nature of the agent's actual global environments. Thus, certain constitutive desiderata, such as systematic truth and global reliability of the belief-forming process, are regarded in context as unimportant. Rather, the appraiser is mainly concerned with whether the processes that produced the belief in the agent, operating as they did on the information available *to the agent*, were suitably safe. This may be termed the *crediting* use of the concept of epistemic justification. A key question guiding evaluative appraisal is whether the agent is *worthy of approval* for holding the belief in question.

A second kind of purpose has to do with the regulation of one's epistemic community and how beliefs are fixed there. Commonly, human inquiry is organized community inquiry. Others serve as sources and repositories of beliefs on which one draws. Judgments about objective justification in others serve to regulate who is to be treated as an unproblematic source. People need and want to make such judgments, since this is an integral component of a kind of 'gatekeeping' by which agents are accorded full or partial partnership in one's community of inquiry. Accordingly, we will call this the *gatekeeping* purpose. In contexts where gatekeeping is one's principal evaluative concern, factors that are constitutive desiderata within the concept of epistemic justification—e.g. global reliability and local reliability of the agent's belief-forming processes—take on considerably more importance (despite still being only constitutive desiderata rather than constitutive requirements). Specifically, it now becomes contextually appropriate to deploy more demanding standards concerning the kind of modulational control that counts as *suitable*. Although one's epistemic appraisal of the agent's belief still remains tethered to the information that the agent herself/himself possessed and deployed in forming the belief—the information that the agent's own belief-forming processes operated on, to generate the belief—nonetheless one's criteria of suitable modulational control no longer remain *fully* tethered to information possessed by the agent. Rather, one evaluates the modulational-control aspects of the agent's belief-forming processes in light of what counts, given the full range of modulation-relevant information *available to the evaluator's own community*, as suitable modulational control.

Return now to our thought-experimental cases, beginning with Sophie. Insofar as one's principal evaluative purpose is crediting rather than gatekeeping, one will judge her justified in her beliefs about cat-brain therapy. Her belief-forming processes are transglobally reliable under modulational control that has accommodated all the information that her own background cognitive processes have afforded. Thus, insofar as the credit-worthiness of her beliefs is concerned, these processes count as being transglobally reliable under *suitable* modulational control. Thus, given the contextually appropriate standards for suitable modulational control, Sophie's beliefs are rightly judged to be epistemically justified.

In an important respect, however, Sophie is an epistemically flawed generator of beliefs about the matter at hand. Her specific experimental process, while subject to suitable modulational control relative to the information that she herself possesses, has not benefited from the information extant in her community of contemporary medical researchers—and is subject to pitfalls that this community now appreciates and insists on avoiding. Her belief about the medical benefits of cat-brain therapy is thus tainted by its basis solely in this flawed process, and thus tainted *as a source* on which to draw in the community of inquirers. Drawing on Sophie as a source of beliefs on the relevant matters is as epistemically problematic as are the processes that Sophie there employs. Thus, one would not want to 'take it from Sophie' that cat brains are effective. Put starkly, one would not want to include such an agent in one's epistemic community in the same way that one would want to include a more fully informed experimentalist. One would not want to include such an agent as a full participating member whose beliefs may be treated as resources on which to presumptively draw.[2] An agent whose belief-forming processes one knows to be defective should not serve as a repository of beliefs on which one can or should presumptively draw, and one commonly marks this kind of gatekeeping by judging that the belief so produced does not count as epistemically justified. Our proposed contextualist element in transglobal reliabilism accommodates such judgments: in context, Sophie's belief-forming processes count as failing to be under suitable modulational control, and hence the beliefs produced by those processes are rightly judged to be epistemically unjustified.

These observations about the two different ways of appraising the objective justification-status of Sophie's cat-brain beliefs also apply mutatis mutandis, to the corresponding beliefs held by Hypatia. Comparing the two cases side-by-side is useful, however, because doing so further underscores the plausibility of the contextualist element we are here proposing to incorporate into transglobal reliabilism. When one is considering a case historically, as situated at a time when the wider epistemic community did not itself possess information pertinent to modulational control that is possessed by one's own contemporary epistemic community, in general it will be less likely that one will find oneself evaluating the historical agent's belief with an eye toward whether or not that agent, using those very belief-forming processes, would be a candidate for unqualified admission into *one's own* epistemic community. One *can* evaluate the historical agent's beliefs in the gatekeeping way, certainly: one can ask whether or not it would be appropriate to 'take it from Hypatia' that cat-brain therapy is effective, even though Hypatia herself may be long dead. (In effect, one thereby thinks of one's epistemic community as diachronically extended, and as

---

[2] A given agent can be included in one's epistemic community in various ways. In any actual case, agents would have learned or shaped processes of varying objective epistemic worth—and one would want to treat the agent as a good source of information on some matters, and a suspect source on other matters. A fishing guide may be a fine source regarding streams and flies, for example, without being a good source of information regarding the virtues of various political figures. The Nobel Award-winning physicist need not be a good source of anthropological information.

including persons perhaps now deceased.) Nonetheless, one will be more likely to evaluate the agent in a way that is tethered to information available to the agent herself, and/or tethered to information available to the agent's own synchronic epistemic community. Thus, although there is a dual pull in the case of Hypatia too, in this case one is apt to feel more strongly the tug toward judging her cat-brain beliefs epistemically justified than in the case of Sophie—and one is apt to feel less strongly the competing tug toward judging these beliefs unjustified.

Notice, too, yet another plausible-looking contextualist element that emerges when comparing Hypatia with Sophia. One contextually appropriate way to judge the epistemic status of Hypatia's cat-brain beliefs would be to adopt an evaluative stance of 'synchronic gatekeeping,' so to speak. That is, one asks whether Hypatia, in forming her cat-brain beliefs in the way she did, deserved full membership in her own *synchronic* epistemic community—a community in which nobody had yet uncovered the need for placebos and double-blind experimental methodology. And the answer is yes, just as it is when one considers Hypatia's beliefs under the crediting mode of evaluation. (One might well be evaluating her beliefs both ways at once, since here the two perspectives yield the same evaluative verdict.) This further contextualist wrinkle is one that itself deserves inclusion as an aspect of the contextualism that we are here proposing to incorporate into transglobal reliabilism.

Once one goes contextualist within the framework of transglobal reliabilism, as we are here proposing to do, it becomes a live open question whether there are yet further kinds of specific purpose—yet further species of the generic purpose of experientially safe truth-seeking under uncertainty—that can guide epistemic-evaluative uses of the concept of epistemic justification, in specific contexts. One plausible-looking purpose, for instance, is *self-monitoring*—i.e. the purpose of attending, perhaps with special diligence, to one's own current processes of belief formation, with an eye toward revealing potential flaws and/or discovering potential improvements. We will not pursue such matters further, in this book. But, if indeed there are such further context-specific purposes that can and do play a role in real-life uses of the concept of epistemic justification, it looks very likely that these too can be readily accommodated within the framework of contextualized transglobal reliabilism. Different contextual purposes will make for differences regarding what kind of modulational control counts, in context, as suitable.

So one can rightly judge both that Sophie's cat-brain beliefs are justified and that they are unjustified—although not both ways at once. Likewise for Hypatia's cat-brain beliefs. Transglobal reliabilism accommodates these facts smoothly and naturally, by treating various specific purposes that might be dominant in specific contexts of epistemic evalauation—e.g. crediting, gatekeeping, historical-synchronic gatekeeping—as contextually variable parameter-settings governing the notion of suitable modulational control. Judgments regarding epistemic justification are all applications of the generic notion, with its generic constitutive requirement that the belief is produced by a postclassically reliable belief-forming process—a requirement that is grounded in the generic primary *telos*, namely experientially safe truth-seeking under uncertainty. One's principal evaluative purpose determines which usage is contextually operative, and hence which judgment is correct in the present context. Under the crediting usage, the operative processes must be postclassically reliable, with the criterion of suitable modulational control being fully tied to the *agent's* transglobally reliably produced information. Sophie's and Hypatia's cat-brain beliefs count as objectively justified, under this usage. Under the typical gatekeeping usage, on the other hand (and setting aside the wrinkle about evaluating historical cases relative to the agent's own synchronic epistemic community), the operative processes must be postclassically reliable, with the criterion of suitable modulational control incorporating reliably produced information available to *the evaluator's community*. Sophie's and Hypatia's cat-brain beliefs count as epistemically unjustified, under this alternative usage.

Given that the specific evaluative purposes are all species of the generic epistemical-evaluative purpose of experientially safe belief-formation under uncertainty, and given that this generic purpose counts strongly in favor of transglobal reliabilism about epistemic justification, the fact that transglobal reliabilism can be so readily contextualized, as a way of accommodating the various specific purposes that fall under the common evaluative genus, constitutes yet further evidential support for transglobal reliabilism.

5 Knowledge and the dual pull

In view of the contextual dimension of the concept of epistemic justification, it seems that one should now look more closely at the concept of knowledge and consider whether there are contextual dimensions here. Of course, the suggestion that there are is much discussed in the literature. We will not attempt to survey this literature, or to survey all respects in which the matter of knowledge might or might not have a contextual element. (Among the matters we will not pursue is whether and how the lately-discussed contextual aspects of the concept of objective justification might get transferred to the concept of knowledge, by virtue of epistemic justification itself being a constitutive requirement for knowledge.) Instead, we here want to focus more narrowly on the working hypothesis advanced in the previous chapter: at least in *many* ordinary contexts, the notion of knowledge works in such a way that not only is justification constitutively required (and thus experiential safety, which is constitutively required for justification), but in addition the various features that are constitutive *desiderata* for justification become constitutive *requirements* for knowledge. If this is correct, then for a given belief to count as knowledge, that belief must be (a) true (since truth is a constitutive desideratum-as-end), (b) the product of processes that are postclassically reliable (since that is constitutively required for justification), and (c) the product of processes that are also globally and locally reliable under suitable modulational control (since these are constitutive desiderata-as-manner-and-means for justification).

A scenario will now be considered that tends to elicit a dual pull in judgment-tendencies regarding knowledge. It suggests that, in some contexts, what counts as knowledge may be marginally less demanding than the working hypothesis would suggest. There look to be certain potential, contextually appropriate, uses of the concept of knowledge under which not all features that are constitutive desiderata for justification become constitutive requirements for knowledge.

This scenario involves an agent, Trevor, who, body and brain, spends most of his life in a Matrix-like pod in which he receives ongoing non-veridical experiential input that represents himself, to himself, as moving about in the environment around him—even though in fact he is lying motionless in the pod, with the sensory areas in his brain being directly stimulated by computer-generated inputs. The pod and the lab where it is located are Trevor's normal local environment. The local environment that is used as a frame of reference for his non-veridical sensory input is real enough—but Trevor is typically nowhere near it, and is certainly not making his way through that local environment as he is led to believe. However, occasionally, Trevor is removed from the pod during his sleep and is allowed to wake up in the local environment that is used as the model for the illusions he is normally provided. He then makes his way about, without any clue that there is anything unusual about his day.

Typically, when Trevor seems to be sitting at a kitchen table, he is really supine and motionless in some technically sophisticated slimy pod. The cognitive processes that generate his everyday beliefs, such as that he is sitting at his table eating breakfast, thus are not globally reliable—not for Trevor, who is em-podded on most days. Furthermore, on most days, those processes are not locally reliable either, since typically he is not in a local environment of the kind he thinks he is in, and is not interacting with the objects in such a local environment in the ways he thinks he is.

Now, concerning epistemic justification, one's judgments about such beliefs are pretty unequivocal: like the everyday beliefs produced by Constance, Trevor is fully, objectively, justified in his belief that he is sitting at his kitchen table eating a bowl of cereal. Transglobal reliabilism accommodates this judgment: the processes involved in generating his belief are postclassically reliable, even though they are not globally reliable and are only rarely locally reliable. (Further support for transglobal reliabilism!)

Consider a day in which the belief in question is true—one on which Trevor is out and about in the local environment as represented, and thus really is at his table eating a bowl of cereal. Now, one feels a dual pull when one asks whether that everyday belief is knowledge. On one hand, one is inclined to say no. Look, he spends most of his life radically deceived; he cannot tell the difference between the mere-appearance cases and the reality cases, and in fact he has no idea that it is mostly mere appearance. The truth of his present belief is far too much a matter of epistemic luck for this belief to count as a case of knowledge. He does not *know*. In many contexts of epistemic appraisal, this is surely what one would say, and it fits well with the working hypothesis about knowledge.

On the other hand, it is not hard to imagine contexts where one would be strongly inclined to judge that Trevor knows that he is eating a bowl of cereal. Suppose, for instance, that one is conversing with Trevor while he is eating his breakfast, and in this specific context one is concerned with things he knows and things he doesn't know. He knows that there is a bowl of cereal on the table in front of him, and that the milk in the bowl is still cool, but (perhaps) he does not know whether there is any cereal left in the cupboard, or (more clearly) that he will be in a pod by tomorrow. One's interaction with Trevor gives rise to certain immediate short-term purposes, framing one's thinking about Trevor in terms of distinctions having to do with what Trevor can and has here successfully come to track. Here, epistemic appraisal seems sensitive to the interest in such matters, and is not controlled by facts about the agent's longer-term situation. For now, and for present purposes, he has not only formed these beliefs in epistemically good (justificatory) ways, but has thereby come to possess bona fide knowledge about his present situation.

We do not advance any firm proposal regarding how to formulate the contextual element that is suggested by these judgment tendencies. The Matrix-style case does suggest that some qualification of the original working hypothesis is in order—and that such a qualification would need to reflect a certain weakening of standards for knowledge in some contexts. At the same time, it still seems very plausible that in *numerous* contexts of usage, the standards for knowing operate in such a way that a belief does not count as an instance of knowledge unless it is produced by a process that is reliable in all three ways—locally, globally, and transglobally.

6 Comparative theoretical advantages

It should be evident that transglobal reliabilism accommodates the various judgment tendencies adduced over the course of this and the previous two chapters, and that it does so without epicycles. In the notion of epistemic safety, unpacked in terms of postclassical reliability, one finds a unified way of treating these cases which seems to embrace both the underlying motivation for reliabilism and the concerns that have moved more internalist epistemologists. This is particularly clear in the discussion of the new evil demon problem for traditional and neoclassical reliabilism. Of course, reliabilists such as Goldman have advanced ways of accommodating apparent counterexamples, as has Sosa, who holds an interesting hybrid position. We maintain that transglobal reliabilism ultimately enjoys certain theoretical advantages over these alternatives. These derive in significant measure from the way in which the devices to which these authors advert reflect concerns for epistemic safety that are better accommodated in terms of the notion of postclassical reliability. Here we focus on two different proposals that Goldman has offered for dealing with cases that pose a challenge to standard reliabilism: his attempt to explain away judgment tendencies in the new evil demon problem as performance errors, and his attempt to accommodate clairvoyant cases by demanding meta-reliable processes that form cognitive processes. We also consider two proposals by Sosa: in one he deploys a notion that he himself calls 'safety' in order to handle certain cases that challenge standard reliabilism; and in the other he recommends an approach to the new evil demon problem. The upshot will be that transglobal reliabilism treats the pertinent issues in ways more plausible than are the proposals advanced by Goldman and by Sosa—which constitutes yet further evidence in support of transglobal reliabilism.

6.1 Goldman on approved belief-fixing processes

There are various ways in which one might attempt to accommodate the judgment tendencies discussed in recent chapters. Goldman, for example, construes the judgments made in response to scientifically benighted cultures, and judgments of the sort discussed in Chapter 3, as revealing of the deep evaluative basis for the concept of epistemic justification. He then treats the demon-world scenarios as eliciting what might be termed mere elements of the common *conception* of objective justification rather than deep elements of the *concept*. That is, he holds that the first judgments are correct and revealing of the semantics of the concept, while the judgments conflicting with his version of reliabilism are mistaken. Although judgments of the latter kind reflect elements of psychologically common ways of conceiving justification, they are said to obscure the real workings of the concept of justification, as tied to its deep evaluative basis.[3]

According to Goldman, the concept of epistemic justification is psychologically embodied as a list of approved belief-fixing processes. Typically, one applies the concept by checking to see whether the agent is employing only such approved processes in fixing the relevant belief. An agent who relies only on such processes is judged to be justified in the resulting belief. However, says Goldman, it is important to note that the internalized list of approved processes, insofar as it serves as a conceptualization of what it takes to be justified, is itself influenced by extant beliefs about what is truth-conducive (in the real world in which humans live, of course). Internalization of this list-conception is supposedly a largely implicit matter; often it is already managed as standards are learned in one's culture; Goldman believes that people's judgments about

---

[3] The discussion in this section is based on one natural reading of Goldman's work, one emphasizing (Goldman 1992b). Goldman (1999) pursues a different approach, roughly this: the concept of epistemic justification is correctly applicable to an epistemic agent's beliefs if those beliefs are produced by processes that are reliable, for humans, in the global environment that humans actually occupy; hence, the external-world beliefs of a radically deceived epistemic agent are indeed epistemically justified, even though the processes that produce them are not reliable *as deployed by that agent in that global environment*. But this alternative proposal of Goldman's is extremely implausible, since what matters intuitively and pretheoretically is the reliability-status of the processes *as deployed by the epistemic agent*. (See also Sosa 2001.) To appreciate the point, consider an agent whose processes of modulational control have led to the development of processes that are globally reliable in the global environment the agent inhabits, but which would not be reliable in the actual global environment that we and our readers inhabit. Perhaps the agent relies on indicators that would not work in the global environment that humans actually occupy, but work fine in the environment that that agent occupies. It seems strange to evaluate the agent as having unjustified beliefs.

counterfactual scenarios do not readily take the respondent beyond the list-structural conception to the deeper evaluative basis that is essential to the concept itself.

As remarked above, there are different ways in which one might attempt to accommodate apparently conflicting intuitive judgments. Goldman's (1992a, 1992b) way is to write off as mistaken the judgments concerning demonic scenarios—mistakes that reflect something about the psychological structure of one's conceptualization rather than about the evaluative concept and its deep evaluative basis. The intuitive judgments are performance errors.

Our own response has been different. We have offered an account of epistemic justification that fully accommodates one's intuitive judgments about the justification-status of the beliefs possessed by an agent in a demonic scenario. Transglobal reliabilism treats such judgments as the products of one's conceptual competence, rather than as performance errors. Furthermore, our approach also provides an independently plausible, theoretically well motivated, account of the deep evaluative workings of the concept of epistemic justification—an account that stresses the idea of experientially safe belief-formation under uncertainty. All else equal, an approach to epistemic justification that treats one's strong intuitive demon-scenario judgments as the products of conceptual competence is theoretically preferable to an approach that is forced to write off such judgments as performance errors. All the more so when the former kind of approach is theoretically well motivated independently. (And indeed, recall that part of the theoretical motivation for transglobal reliabilism emanates from the underlying spirit of classical reliabilism itself: the classical reliabilist should welcome the refinements that lead to neoclassical reliabilism, but the considerations much like those that motivate this refinement also motivate the further move to transglobal reliabilism.) So transglobal reliabilism offers a better treatment of the new evil demon problem than does Goldman's performance-error approach.

6.2 Goldman on meta-reliability

Goldman has recognized that (global) reliability is, at best, a necessary, but not sufficient, condition for appropriateness of processing. On his account, an additional necessary condition is that the reliable process must itself have arisen from a meta-process (a process-generating process) that is conducive to the production of truth-conducive first-order processes (Goldman 1992a). In imposing this additional requirement—the requirement of 'meta-reliability'—Goldman's reliabilism points to an epistemological concern that is akin to the concern for postclassical reliability. If the epistemic processes employed by agents get generated in an inherently risky fashion, and if the generated processes fortuitously turn out reliable because the local and global environments just happen to be among a limited number of ways for which such processes are reliable, then the agents are the undeserving beneficiaries of dumb luck. The central idea behind attention to meta-reliability seems to be an *aversion to an epistemic role for dumb luck*. The local or even global reliability of belief-spawning processes is not sufficient for the objective propriety of a belief, and this is shown when one reflects on cases where that reliability is significantly a matter of dumb luck on the part of the agent (Fortuna, Sextus, Harry, and Ashley).

Cases like those of Ashley and Harry provide compelling examples of situations in which a belief-forming process is neoclassically reliable but not epistemically safe—and in which one therefore judges that the agent is not justified in the beliefs formed via this process. In Chapter 4 we used such cases to argue for the inadequacy of neoclassical reliabilism, and as partial motivation for turning to transglobal reliabilism. However, it appears that incorporating a meta-reliability requirement into a more traditional version of reliabilism, as Goldman proposes to do, also handles such cases. Although Ashley and Harry both employ belief-forming processes that are neoclassically reliable, these processes were not themselves produced by meta-reliable processes. Modifying neoclassical reliabilism by incorporating Goldman's meta-reliability requirement thus allows one to sustain as correct one's intuitive judgments to the effect that Harry's paranoid beliefs, and Ashley's small-sample-based beliefs about humankind at large, are not justified.

How does transglobal reliabilism stack up against an amended version of neoclasssical reliabilism that incorporates a meta-reliability requirement, as regards scenarios with features like those of Harry and Ashley? Transglobal reliabilism fares better. This is because it is not difficult to construct analogous cases that have these same features *even though the belief-forming process in question is itself the product of a globally reliable meta-process*. Such cases would vividly illustrate the superiority of transglobal reliabilism over an appeal to global meta-reliability.[4]

One such case is an experientially possible global environment with the following features. Over the past 10,000 years, this global environment has been qualitatively exactly similar to the actual global environment; however, 10,000 years ago a divine being instantaneously created it, with all the many features constituting evidence of much greater age—strata in its Grand Canyon whose best available scientific explanation invokes geological theories according to which some of the rocks date back two billion years, red-shifted light from celestial objects whose best available scientific explanation invokes theories in physics and cosmology according to which the light from these objects has been traveling through intergalactic space for 12 billion years, and so on. The divine creator of this cosmos also created humans 10,000 years ago, instantaneously—all the evidence of evolution notwithstanding. She instilled in them, as a feature of their cognitive architecture, a strong predisposition toward accepting verbatim the doctrines they encounter as children in their society's 'sacred texts'—even in the face of overwhelmingly strong evidence against these doctrines.

---

[4] Actually, if the reader carefully reviews our discussion in Chapter 4 of Harry, it will be found that this case already has the sought-for features. In order to build into the case the presence of globally reliable modulational-control processes, we told the story of Harry in a way that included, in effect, a globally reliable *meta-process* as the source of Harry's proclivity toward certain specific kinds of (globally reliable) paranoid belief-forming processes.

(As a result, many humans tend to insist that the cosmos is only 10,000 years old, because it says so in a 'sacred text' they call the Holy Bible.)

This act of hers was a *globally reliable external meta-process*, since the belief-forming processes that result from it—widespread in the human population in this cosmos she created 10,000 years ago—are themselves globally reliable. And the divine act instilled in most humans a *globally reliable internal meta-process*—namely a process that engenders in them certain specific belief-forming processes that implement and maintain internal consistency within an overall belief system according to which the doctrines in the 'sacred text' are true. (Notice that the modulational-control mechanisms in such humans are themselves globally reliable, in this global environment; thus, from the perspective of neoclassical reliabilism, they constitute *suitable* modulational control.)

One's strong intuitive judgment is that the anti-scientific beliefs of these religiously zealous softheads about the age of the cosmos, about the age of the rocks in their Grand Canyon, about their own origins as a species, etc. are grossly lacking in epistemic justification, even though (i) they are systematically true, (ii) they are produced by belief-forming processes that are neoclassically reliable, and (iii) these belief-forming processes are themselves produced by globally reliable meta-processes. Transglobal reliabilism accords with this judgment. But neoclassical reliabilism, as supplemented by a requirement of global meta-reliability, does not. So much the better for transglobal reliabilism, by comparison with the alternative view.

The cases so far discussed are ones in which an agent's beliefs are not justified even though the processes that produce them are neoclassically reliable. Cases like those of Constance and Ike are compelling examples of the converse: situations in which the agent's beliefs are justified even though the processes that produce them are not neoclassically reliable. Now, one might think that such cases can be handled by treating global meta-reliability as a constitutive requirement for justification, and demoting neoclassical reliability to a constitutive desideratum: think of Constance and Ike as having normal human evolutionary-ancestral histories, so that the globally reliable meta-processes produced Constance's and Ike's first-order belief-forming processes. This proposed alternative to neoclassical reliabilism—call it *global meta-reliabilism*—is a potential competitor to transglobal reliabilism. Global meta-reliabilism too would vindicate one's intuitive judgment that Constance and Ike both have numerous justified beliefs, even though the processes that produce these beliefs are not neoclassically reliable.

How does transglobal reliabilism stack up against global meta-reliabilism, as regards scenarios with features like those of Constance and Ike? It is not difficult to construct cases that have these same features and in which the belief-forming process in question *also fails to be the product of a globally reliable meta-process*. Such cases would again illustrate, in a converse way from the case described in the preceding paragraph, the superiority of transglobal reliabilism over an appeal to global meta-reliability.

An example of such a case is the well known philosophical thought-experimental creature, Swampman. This creature is just like an ordinary human except that he came into being as a result of random spontaneous chemical interactions when a lightening bolt struck a swamp rich in organic molecules. Swampman could well have epistemically impeccable belief-forming processes, even though these processes were generated by utterly unreliable meta-processes. Swampman's belief-forming processes will be impeccable provided that they are postclassically reliable, regardless of their etiology.[5] So much the better once again for transglobal reliabilism, by comparison to an alternative view that requires global meta-reliability but not neoclassical reliability.

6.3 Sosa on Safety

Ernest Sosa (2000) deploys a concept that he expresses with the word 'safety,' and argues that the feature dubbed with this expression is a necessary condition for knowledge. The feature he calls safety is not the same as the one we have been discussing in this book—although the pre-theoretic connotations of the word 'safety' make it appropriate to use it either our way or his. Here we will briefly explain his notion, and how it differs from ours. (It seems fitting to do so, if only because he uses the same word for a different notion.) We will also argue that the specific work for which Sosa deploys his notion gets smoothly handled by the approach to knowledge that we have briefly advocated in this book—an approach that builds upon transglobal reliabilism about epistemic justification. This fact constitutes yet another consideration in favor of transglobal reliabilism itself.

As Sosa uses the term, what are 'safe' are particular beliefs of particular agents, while what we have termed 'epistemically safe' are, in the first instance, belief-fixing processes—and secondarily the beliefs to which they give rise. Sosa characterizes safety as follows:

Call a belief by S that p "safe" iff: S would not believe that p without it being so that p. (Alternatively, a belief by S that p is "safe" iff as a matter of fact, though perhaps not as a matter of strict necessity, S would not believe that p without it being so that p.) (Sosa 2000, p. 378.)

Sosa maintains that a belief can be generated by a reliable process and yet not be safe, although he also allows that the two matters are closely related: 'the reliability requirement jibes especially well with the belief/fact conditional ["S would not believe that p without it being so that p", or $B(p) \rightarrow p$, which is used to characterize safety]' (Sosa 1999, p. 375). Although it seems that reliable processes commonly produce safe beliefs, Sosa claims that this connection is not invariant—that a reliable process can produce a belief that is not safe. He offers as a putative example the following case. An agent believes that it is 3 p.m. as the result of looking at a watch; however, a demon has gained control of the agent's watch and determined its display according to the roll of a

---

[5] We realize that the appeals to Swampman scenarios are rendered problematic by certain prominent recent trends in philosophy of mind, according to which a creature who lacks a suitable evolutionary pedigree would thereby lack intentional mental states (or would lack mental states altogether, even qualia). But our remarks in note 53 of Chapter 4 about brain-in-vat scenarios apply here also, mutatis mutandis.

die; by coincidence, the die reads three (thus the watch reads 3:00) and the agent happens to look at the watch at 3 p.m. Sosa (2000, pp. 374–5) claims that the epistemically salient process is reliable, but that the belief does not track the truth about time in a way that ultimately makes it safe.

Suppose that an agent holds a belief that p, and that this belief is safe in Sosa's sense. Again, this means that the agent would not believe that p without it being so that p—symbolically, $B(p) \rightarrow p$. One evaluates this subjunctive conditional by looking to nearby possible worlds in which the agent believes that p, and determining whether p is true in those worlds. Of course, the agent's own world is the nearest possible world to the agent's world. So, where the belief in question is true, p is true in *the* nearest possible world. Thus, on pain of triviality, the conditional must be understood as requiring that p be true, not only in the nearest possible world, but also in other nearby possible worlds. That is clearly how Sosa understands the conditional. Furthermore, sameness of process is crucial to nearness of possible worlds; in all the relevantly near possible worlds, the agent employs the same process by which p is produced in the agent's own world. Since the sameness of process determines nearness, for purposes of gauging safety, one may characterize Sosa's notion of *safety* this way: in the nearby possible worlds where the same process generated a belief that p, that belief was true—where nearness now is presumably a matter of local environmental similarity (since that would be largely left over after the process is held constant). This would seem to be a very special form of local reliability—special because it is *reliability for the special purpose of producing just a belief with the content here produced*. That is, it seems to be a matter of the process in question being *reliable with respect to whether or not it is the case that p*.[6]

Sosa's 'safety' is not at all what we ourselves have called epistemic safety. As noted already, Sosa's safety is a matter of how a particular belief-content produced by a particular process would fare in highly similar environments. It is thus a special case of what we have called local reliability. In contrast, what we ourselves call epistemic safety is a matter of how a process would fare in a *wide range* of experientially possible global environments. The contrast can be made vivid by recalling Sextus Pessimisicus, whose beliefs would seem to qualify as safe in Sosa's sense—but his processes are not safe in our sense. Sextus' belief that the Great Deceiver is leading him to think that it is time to wake up is arguably Sosa-safe, since it is likely that Sextus would not believe that without it being true that the Great Deceiver is leading him to believe that it was time to wake up. But the general process at work here would be reliable only in certain demon-infested environments (namely nearby environments)—and these are not a wide range of experientially possible global environments.

Sosa uses his notion of safety for epistemological purposes that are quite different from those that have motivated our own discussion of epistemological safety. In particular, Sosa's notion is intended to capture a condition on which true beliefs

---

[6] By the standards suggested in our discussion of the generality problem (Chapter 3, section 12), the process on which Sosa focuses seems a pretty degenerate process type.

count as knowledge, while ours is intended in the first instance to capture something about what it is for one to be epistemically justified in holding some belief.

But despite the differences just alluded to in the notions of safety on which we and Sosa focus, Sosa's demand on knowledge seems to be closely related to our working hypothesis regarding the demands on knowledge, suggested in the previous chapter. The hypothesis was that, at least in *many* ordinary contexts, the notion of knowledge works in such a way that not only is justification constitutively required (and thus experiential safety as well, which is constitutively required for justification), but in addition the various features that we have identified as constitutive desiderata for justification become constitutive requirements for knowledge. This is to say that, for a given belief to count as knowledge, that belief must be (a) true (since truth is a constitutive desideratum-as-end), (b) the product of processes that are postclassically reliable (since that is constitutively required for justification), and (c) the product of processes that are also globally and locally reliable (since these are constitutive desiderata-as-manner-and-means for justification).

If something like this is correct, then it is plausible that the sort of local special-purpose reliability that Sosa terms 'safety' is indeed required for knowledge. But this is a derivative requirement, since it is entailed by our own proposal. (Local reliability entails the special-purpose kind of local reliability that Sosa calls safety; hence, our own proposed local-reliability requirement on knowledge entails Sosa's safety requirement.) Our own proposal already handles, in a smooth and natural way, cases like Sosa's stuck-watch case: since the agent in that scenario forms the belief that it is now 3 p.m. by means of a process that is not locally reliable, on our account this fact already disqualifies the belief from being an instance of knowledge.[7] Thus, although Sosa's own requirement gets vindicated under our proposal, it is also derivative and hence redundant. The upshot is this: since transglobal reliabilism leads naturally to an account of knowledge that already automatically generates the intuitively correct 'not knowledge' verdict for scenarios like the case of the manipulated watch, this happy fact constitutes yet further evidence in support of transglobal reliabilism itself.[8]

6.4 Sosa on the new evil demon problem

Sosa's notion of safety does not help him deal with the new evil demon problem. But he does not intend to deal with this problem in such terms. Instead, he attempts to deal with it by thinking in terms of the 'aptness' of processes, where aptness is relativized to 'worlds' (i.e. global environments). Thus, an agent such as Constance employs processes that would be apt relative to the world that humans actually occupy, but

---

[7] This presupposes that the process is understood in a natural non-degenerate fashion—one that leaves out what is surely gerrymandering language about just happening to look at the watch at exactly 3:00.
[8] Recently, Duncan Pritchard (2005) has discussed forms of epistemological safety that are closely related to the safety that concerns Sosa—and has done this with an eye to understanding what is required for knowledge. We have not discussed Pritchard's fine work here, for reasons of space, but we can say that many of the points developed in this section largely carry over in application to it.

not relative to demon worlds; by contrast, Faith's processes would not be apt relative to either. Constance's beliefs thus have a form of positive epistemic status that Faith's beliefs lack—namely being the product of processes that are apt relative to the actual global environment. However, BonJour responds that this really is not an adequate response to the issues posed by judgments regarding agents in demon-worlds: 'surely the main intuition is that the demon victim's beliefs are justified without qualification in the environment that he inhabits, not merely that they are justified in relation to a quite different environment' (BonJour 1995, p. 211). We agree that the new evil demon problem cannot be managed by a relativized notion of aptness, and that it demands a different treatment. Accordingly, we maintain an important advantage of our account is that it smoothly and fully accommodates one's intuitive judgments made in response to evil-demon scenarios.

7 Summary: the case for transglobal reliabilism

In this and the preceding two chapters, a significant array of scenarios and judgment tendencies have been considered. Transglobal reliabilism has the resources to easily accommodate the judgments to which most people find themselves drawn. Furthermore, this is not managed by piling on epicycles within the account of the concept of epistemic justification. Instead, the main lines of transglobal reliabilism, those relied on here, are found to be rooted in strong trends within the judgment tendencies themselves. Prominent here is the tendency to find the cognitive processes of certain agents (such as Fortuna, Harry, and Sextus) to be unacceptably risky from an epistemic point of view, and the complementary tendency to find the cognitive processes of other agents (such as Athena, Diana, Elena, Constance, and Ike) to be epistemically safe. Such judgments arose in connection with the parallel judgments that those beliefs arising in the risky fashion were not epistemically justified, while those arising in the safe manner were. This attention to epistemic safety and risk is not itself special to transglobal reliabilism; rather, it is already reflected in the move from classical reliabilism to the more refined and more nearly adequate neoclassical reliabilism. At the same time, the neoclassical reliabilist focus on global reliability seems incapable of adequately accommodating the range of judgments concerning safety; transglobal reliabilism provides a better analysis of the form of epistemic safety that seems constitutively required for objective epistemic justification. Transglobal reliabilism is thus found to provide a strongly unified explanation of these judgments.

The unified character of the resulting account is reflected in the requirement that belief-forming processes be themselves under suitable modulational control. This necessary condition for objective epistemic justification is not some epicycle needed to cover some otherwise recalcitrant cases. Instead, it is motivated by the ways in which such modulational control can enhance various forms of reliability and make for greater robustness. This general idea already emerged in the neoclassical reliabilist position developed in the third chapter—modulational control tends to enhance reliability in a range of local environments, making for greater global reliability. When one comes to appreciate the epistemic importance of transglobal reliability and the experiential safety it affords, one then also comes to appreciate how modulational control of belief-generating processes by wider processes (themselves transglobally reliable) constitutes the kind of epistemic safety—namely experiential safety—that is necessary for epistemic justification.

Showing how transglobal reliabilism readily accommodates a very impressive set of judgments—elicited by a very wide set of scenarios—was largely accomplished in the preceding two chapters. On exhibit there (particularly in the fourth chapter) was the unifying concern for transglobal reliability and experiential safety. This much made for a very strong initial case for transglobal reliabilism—since it was found to be able to accommodate much of the evidential base appropriate to philosophical reflection on the concept of epistemic justification. The agenda for the present chapter has then been threefold—with each agenda item serving in certain respects to expand the evidential base for the abductive argument, via inference to the best explanation, for transglobal reliabilism.

First, if transglobal reliabilism deployed notions with certain special difficulties or obscurities, this would make it relatively problematic. The problem of infinities might be thought to be just such a problem. However, we have argued that the problem, which is certainly of theoretical interest, is not a special problem for transglobal reliabilism, or for reliabilism generally. Rather, the issues raised are ones that need to be faced by any account that has a place for dispositional notions. We sketched a plausible-looking general way of addressing these issues, and we explained how it can be applied to the notion of transglobal reliability specifically.

Second, as explained in the second chapter, low-grade a priori philosophical reflection seeks to find the best explanation for a range of armchair-accessible data. Included in that data are the judgments that tend to be elicited by scenarios—and transglobal reliabilism does particularly well on this score. But also included are common-sensical observations regarding the purposes served by the concept under investigation. Here we discussed a generic purpose served by the concept under investigation, and two different specific purposes that all fall within the genus. The generic purpose is evaluation with respect to *safe truth-seeking under uncertainty*—a teleological form of evaluation that incorporates both the secondary *telos* of systematic true belief, and the primary *telos* of experiential safety in pursuit of the secondary *telos*. The two specific purposes are crediting and community gatekeeping. Transglobal reliabilism not only honors the generic purpose very well, but also lends itself easily and naturally to the incorporation of a contextualist dimension which nicely accommodates each of the more specific purposes sometimes served by the evaluative notion of epistemic justification.

Third, when engaged in inference to the best explanation, one ought to consider alternative ways of accommodating the data. To some extent this project was already pursued in the previous two chapters—e.g. in setting forth the comparative advantages of neoclassical reliabilism over classical reliabilism on one hand, and of transglobal reliabilism over neoclassical reliabilism on the other hand. But in this chapter we considered some alternative accounts of some of the phenomena that transglobal reliabilism purports to explain. Goldman has developed a very influential reliabilist account that explicitly treats scenario-judgments of many, but not all, the sorts we address. On Goldman's proposal, while some of these judgments reflect conceptual competence, a significant number are treated as reflecting performance errors. We argued, however, that transglobal reliabilism provides a better account of the data. Not only does transglobal reliabilism accommodate more intuitive judgments than Goldman's (without the need to explain away some of these judgments as putative performance errors), but transglobal reliabilism also accommodates the intuitive unity of the judgments made in response to the various scenarios. The unity in question has been highlighted in terms of experiential safety, explicated as postclassical reliability. It then seems unnecessary, unnatural, and pointless to attribute performance errors in cases (like the new evil demon problem) where a concern for experiential safety seems in evidence. We also argued that the approach to knowledge suggested by transglobal reliabilism handles the kinds of cases that motivated Sosa to claim that knowledge requires the kind of special-purpose local reliability that he calls 'safety,' and also that transglobal reliabilism handles the new evil demon problem decidedly better than does Sosa's appeal to what he calls aptness.

Assuming that one's belief-forming processes possess at least an acceptable level of postclassical reliability, additional postclassical reliability must be balanced against costs in terms of the productivity of processes—their power, speed, and conduciveness to systematic true belief. And again too, epistemic agents are limited in the processes they can implement, and in how quickly and consistently they can implement what processes they can. So, what makes a fitting balance depends in crucial ways on the psychological-cognitive facts about human beings—about the processes they can develop and deploy. Such matters are crucial in thinking about what counts as *suitable* modulational control and *adequate* transglobal reliability. They highlight the fact that conceptual analysis in the low-grade a priori mode, which has been under way in this and the preceding two chapters, itself points toward a role for a more thoroughly empirical dimension to epistemology—a scientifically informed, naturalizing dimension. That dimension will come prominently into focus in the next several chapters.

6

Epistemic Competence and the Call to Naturalize Epistemology

The phrase 'epistemology naturalized' has been prominent in epistemology ever since Quine's classic paper by this title. The label has been applied to various (and somewhat sundry) doctrines and positions (see Goldman 1999), and these doctrines and positions have been vigorously debated. In this chapter we describe, and argue for, a general approach to epistemology that we contend deserves the appellation 'naturalized epistemology.' One leading idea is that epistemology comprises a spectrum of different, and complementary, types of inquiry all organized around certain common themes and concerns (see also Henderson and Horgan 2008). At one end of the spectrum is low-grade a priori inquiry, of the sort exhibited in preceding chapters of the present book, aimed at uncovering conceptually grounded necessary truths concerning notions like knowledge and justified belief. At the other end are certain parts of richly empirical cognitive science, including in particular the cognitive-scientific account of what we will call *human epistemic competence*. And there are various intermediate points in this spectrum too—e.g. forms of inquiry that draw upon scientific theorizing about human competence without themselves falling clearly within that theorizing. (Examples of such mid-spectrum inquiry will occur in subsequent chapters of this book.)

A second key feature of naturalized epistemology, as we propose to construe it, is that this approach does not by any means eliminate the element of *normativity* from epistemology. On the contrary, it presupposes that notions like knowledge and justified belief are essentially normative, and it puts heavy emphasis on the idea that the pertinent normative standards are constrained by the nature of human cognitive architecture and by facts about human cognitive capacities and their limits. Indeed, normativity is present even within those aspects of a posteriori cognitive science that belong to the spectrum of epistemological inquiry, because the notion of epistemic *competence* incorporates normative standards itself.

Thirdly, naturalized epistemology as we conceive it does not by any means eliminate from epistemology a role for conceptual analysis or a priori theorizing. On the contrary, although pertinent normative standards in epistemology are always constrained by facts about human cognitive architecture and cognitive capacities, *some* important aspects of epistemological inquiry can be conducted without detailed information from cognitive science about such matters. Typically, scientific information will become increasingly relevant to epistemology as the inquiry reaches a fairly high level of specificity. (A case in point is our own preceding low-grade a priori conceptual analysis of the notion of justified belief: cognitive-science-level information is needed as one seeks a detailed filling-in of the analysis—a filling-in that includes, for instance, a specific account of what counts as suitable modulational control, in humans.)

It will turn out that the various claims made in this book all fit comfortably within naturalized epistemology, as here construed. Yet the present chapter provides something of a transition in terms of the comparative importance of considerations from cognitive science. Whereas the inquiry in Chapters 1–5 has not needed to make much use of such considerations, they will play a considerably more prominent role in the chapters hereafter.

1 Engineering for truth-seeking

In the present section we sketch in more detail the overall conception of naturalized epistemology we advocate. Yet further elaboration—focusing on the idea of epistemic competence—will then occupy the rest of the current chapter.

The orientation that Quine (1969) originally called 'naturalized epistemology' is sometimes accused (e.g. by Kim 1988) of eschewing epistemic normativity altogether. Although Quine's seminal text perhaps can be read that way, eschewing normativity is certainly no part of naturalized epistemology as we ourselves propose to construe it. Nor, evidently, was this Quine's own intention either, as evidenced by the following passage from Quine (1986):

> Naturalization in epistemology does not jettison the normative and settle for the indiscriminate description of ongoing processes. For me normative epistemology is a branch of engineering. It is the technology of truth-seeking (Quine 1986, p. 664–5).

We are very much in sympathy with these remarks: epistemology is usefully and plausibly construed as being unified by a fundamental concern for appropriate 'cognitive engineering' vis-à-vis the goal of truth-acquisition—i.e. the goal of forming a rich, systematic body of beliefs about matters of concern to a cognitive agent, a body of beliefs with a high proportion of true beliefs over false ones. (See also Henderson and Horgan 2008). One important objective of epistemological inquiry, then, is to articulate *design specifications* for an effective truth-seeking cognitive agent: principles of design to which such an agent should largely conform, in its belief-forming cognitive processes. The design specifications being sought are to be both normative and descriptive: normative insofar as they characterize how a given kind of cognitive agent (typically, a human) *ought* to proceed in its belief-forming operations vis-à-vis the goal of truth-acquisition, and descriptive insofar as cognitive agents of the given kind actually *do* proceed that way when they are exercising their belief-forming competence rather than exhibiting performance errors. Descriptive, also, insofar as the prescriptions are constrained by descriptions of human cognitive resources and the possibilities for alternative processes these afford (see section 3 of this chapter). Thus, a full articulation of these design specifications would constitute an account of *epistemic competence*, for agents of the given kind.

Thinking of normative standards for belief-formation as constituting an account of epistemic competence is not enough, however, to merit the label 'naturalized epistemology.' For, one might think that the standards being sought—standards that would collectively characterize epistemic competence—can be uncovered without recourse to richly empirical science.[1] One might then conceive of the enterprise in the following way (a conception that informs much traditional epistemology). First, the sought-for epistemic design-specifications are supposed to be applicable not just to some specific class of cognitive agents (e.g. humans), but rather to all *possible* rational-belief-forming agents. Second, these design-specifications are ascertainable from the armchair, in a manner that is a priori (perhaps low-grade a priori) rather than being informed by richly empirical, a posteriori, scientific theory. We will call this approach to the discovery of epistemic standards *armchair epistemology*.

Naturalized epistemology, as we conceive it, does more than embrace the idea that normative standards for belief-formation constitute design-specifications for a truth-seeking cognitive agent (and thereby constitute an account of epistemic competence). For, as just explained, armchair epistemology does that too, in effect—even in the hands of practitioners who do not articulate their project in these terms. Naturalized epistemology incorporates this further claim: a complete and fully detailed articulation of the design-specifications that characterize epistemic competence cannot be discovered by a priori methods, but instead must rely at least in part upon a posteriori scientific theory—in particular, upon richly empirical cognitive science.[2] And a corollary of this claim is that such a scientifically informed account of epistemic competence would apply to a specific class of cognitive agents (typically, humans); this leaves open whether other possible kinds of cognitive agents might conform to epistemic design-specifications different than those applicable to humans.

We have already committed ourselves to naturalized epistemology as thus described. We have argued that objective epistemic justification is a matter of a belief's being produced by a process that is transglobally reliable under suitable modulational control, and that the question of what counts as *suitable* modulational control is one whose answer cannot be completely ascertained from the armchair, but instead depends in

---

[1] In calling a subject matter *richly* empirical, we mean that its claims are not knowable a priori—not even low-grade a priori. Although low-grade a priori inquiry does incorporate empirical elements, it is not *richly* empirical in the a posteriori manner that is typical in science.

[2] While richly empirical results are needed when filling in details—when fully articulating the design specification—these results can constrain the general outlines of normative models as well. This is reflected in the general points advanced in the chapters to follow.

part upon results from richly empirical cognitive science about the nature of human cognitive architecture. The need to embrace naturalized epistemology thus emerges directly out of low-grade a priori conceptual analysis, since such analysis reveals an aspect of the concept of epistemic justification whose full elucidation cannot be provided by a priori methods. Yet further reasons to embrace naturalized epistemology will emerge as this chapter unfolds.

Naturalized epistemology, as here characterized, includes a spectrum of different types of epistemological inquiry. We will hereafter call it the *E-spectrum*, letting 'E' go proxy both for 'epistemology' and for 'engineering.' The different, mutually complementary, forms of inquiry falling within the E-spectrum are unified by a common concern with engineering for truth-seeking.

At one end of the E-spectrum are portions of what we are here calling 'richly empirical cognitive science'—in particular, those portions that elaborate the overall account of epistemic competence beyond what can be ascertained from the armchair. The phrase 'richly empirical cognitive science,' as we here intend it, covers experimental and theoretical inquiry of the kind typically pursued by scientists seeking to understand human cognition and its neurobiological basis. Such inquiry normally is not pursued from the armchair, but rather in laboratory and clinical settings. Typically it employs careful and systematic data-gathering, self-conscious experimental design, statistical analysis of data, and the like. The theories and models put forward in a posteriori cognitive science normally are subjected to fairly elaborate experimental and clinical testing. (To call such inquiry *richly* empirical is to remind ourselves and our readers that empirical elements can and do enter into other forms of inquiry as well, albeit sometimes in ways that do not require leaving the armchair and thus do not require scientific experimentation and data-gathering; indeed, we have stressed that this is so even for low-grade a priori reasoning aimed at uncovering conceptually grounded necessary truths.)

Although this portion of the E-spectrum is straightforwardly a part of science (while also being a part of epistemology too), this does not mean that it is 'merely descriptive' and lacking in normativity. In reading much of the pertinent scientific work, one finds on display a concern for epistemically right and wrong ways of fixing belief, that is, for what we are here calling human epistemic competence. This concern is often explicit (see the range of work mentioned in this chapter) and is seldom far from the surface. The pertinent kinds of scientific inquiry will give pride of place to providing a scientific account of epistemic competence for a class of agents (typically, normal human agents). The distinction between exercises in cognitive competence on one hand, and on the other hand 'performance lapses' that fall short of one's cognitive competence, will be drawn largely on *normative* grounds. Epistemic competence is a matter of capacities for forming and sustaining beliefs in *good ways*—good with respect to truth-seeking. It is a matter of being appropriately engineered for truth-seeking.

At the opposite end of the E-spectrum is low-grade a priori inquiry, often aimed at uncovering conceptually grounded necessary truths concerning concepts especially important in epistemology—e.g. the concept of knowledge and the concept of justified belief. This kind of inquiry typically can be effectively pursued from the armchair, often with much of one's attention directed to suitably instructive thought-experimental scenarios. Our own preceding discussion of justification, in Chapters 3–5, falls under this form of inquiry (as we have stressed already).

Each end of the E-spectrum exerts constraining influence over the rest of the spectrum. The low-grade a priori end, for instance, heavily informs the fundamental *evaluative* aspects that go into engineering for truth-seeking. An effective truth-seeking cognitive system will be one that tends to generate *justified* beliefs and tends not to generate unjustified ones, that does so in ways that exhibit a suitable mix of speed, power, and the like, and produces systematic and useful beliefs relative to its own goals and needs. The constraining influence of these aspects of evaluation will be operative all across the E-spectrum—including within richly empirical cognitive science, for instance with respect to how the distinction is drawn between epistemic competence and cognitive phenomena that constitute lapses in such competence.

Conversely, the end of the E-spectrum that falls within richly empirical cognitive science also constrains the entire spectrum. An important example of this, as stressed already, is the need for theoretical cognitive science to supply the details about what counts as suitable modulational control, even though this notion itself emerges as a conceptually grounded prerequisite for being a cognitive agent that is well engineered for truth-seeking. Also, applicable normative standards for truth-seeking must be standards that are *tractable* for creatures of the kind one is considering (typically humans). And questions of tractability are, to a large extent, ones whose answers are to be found within richly empirical cognitive science. (The demand for tractability is the subject of the next section.)

The E-spectrum also includes forms of inquiry that lie between the two ends. For instance, it can include claims or assumptions about human cognition that on the one hand are not the products of low-grade a priori reasoning and do not purport to be conceptually grounded necessary truths, but on the other hand emanate fairly directly from untutored common-sense reasoning rather than arising within richly empirical cognitive science. It can also include more *tutored* common-sense reasoning that draws upon lessons from richly empirical cognitive science and perhaps calls into question certain of the untutored claims. (In the next chapter we will focus on an instance of the relatively untutored kind of intermediate-spectrum theorizing that can be found, at least implicitly, in much recent epistemology. We will also engage in the more tutored kind, in a way that draws upon lessons gleaned partly from recent developments in richly empirical cognitive science.)

Quine famously held that epistemology, once naturalized, becomes a branch of psychology. Is the analogous claim true on our own recommended conception of epistemology—that is, as an E-spectrum of mutually constraining forms of inquiry? In other words, is the E-spectrum, in its entirety, a branch of cognitive science? Well, that depends on how broadly or narrowly one employs the expression 'cognitive science.'

On the one hand, one might use it relatively narrowly, so that it comprises only *richly empirical* scientific inquiry about belief-forming processes and other related aspects of human cognition. Under that usage, only a portion of the E-spectrum, and not all of it, belongs to cognitive science. On the other hand, one might instead employ 'cognitive science' more broadly, in a manner that incorporates any pertinent considerations that exert important constraining influences on richly empirical theorizing about the mind—in particular, considerations that affect how the competence/performance distinctions should be drawn. Under this wider usage, it appears that the whole E-spectrum is indeed a branch of cognitive science.

Our own view is that this is a non-substantive terminological issue. Furthermore, it appears to us that categories like 'cognitive science' and 'psychology' can legitimately be used in a variety of different ways—some fairly wide and others more narrow—depending on one's specific purposes in a given context. But the following two claims are the important substantive ones. First, a fully articulated theory of competence cannot be discovered from the armchair, but must draw, in part, on richly empirical cognitive science. Second, the different forms of inquiry within the E-spectrum exert mutually constraining influences upon one another. These two facts are enough already to make the entire spectrum deserve the label 'naturalized epistemology'—whether or not one chooses to classify all forms of inquiry within the spectrum as parts of cognitive science per se.

2 Systematizing epistemic normativity: a priori aspects and richly empirical aspects

A perennial goal in epistemology has been to set forth normative principles governing rationally appropriate belief-formation. On one hand, such principles would be general in scope; but on the other hand, they would yield specific recommendations about what to believe in various concrete epistemic situations in which cognitive agents might find themselves—situations involving the possession of various kinds of perceptual and non-perceptual evidence and information, for instance. Ideally, a complete set of such principles would fully *systematize* epistemic normativity, and in a manner that provides specific *guidance* for belief formation: they would specify how an epistemic agent ought to proceed in belief-formation, and proceeding in that manner would be a route to objectively justified belief. In effect, then, such a systematization of epistemic normativity would constitute a theory of epistemic competence—even though attempts in epistemology to articulate such normative principles in epistemology have not typically been described that way.

Traditionally, philosophical attempts to articulate normative principles for belief formation often have been conducted from the proverbial armchair, and thereby have been conducted in an a priori manner (at any rate, a low-grade a priori manner). Naturalized epistemology need not repudiate such attempts, or principles that emerge from that approach. On the contrary, important *parts* of the sought-for systematization of epistemic normativity might very well be ascertainable by inquiry conducted at or near the a priori end of the E-spectrum. However, if indeed a *complete* account of human epistemic competence must draw in part upon richly empirical cognitive science—as naturalized epistemology contends is the case—then armchair methods alone will not be enough to do the whole job.

With these observations as the stage setting, let us briefly consider a representative example of the traditional armchair-style epistemological treatment of normative principles of belief formation. The following passage from Van Cleve (1979) nicely illustrates how the sought-for principles are often discussed, specifically in the context of foundationalism:

> Foundationalists often set forth principles specifying the conditions under which propositions of various types are justified. Usually called *epistemic principles*, they fall into two groups: principles that tell us that propositions of certain types are justified independently of their logical relations to other propositions, and principles that tell us that if some propositions are *already* justified, then any propositions that stand in such-and-such relations to them are *also* justified. Principles of the first sort I call *generation principles*... and those of the second sort I call *transmission* principles.... The general form of an epistemic principle is 'If... then P is justified for S'.... Descartes's C & D Rule [clearness and distinctness rule] is a generation principle. It tells us that if someone is clearly and distinctly perceiving a proposition... then that proposition is certain for him. Another example of a generation principle is Chisholm's Principle (A), which says that if a subject is in any of a designated group of 'self-presenting states,' then it is evident to him that he is in the state in question. An obvious example of a transmission principle is the principle that deduction transmits justification.... This is the *only* transmission principle Descartes allows. But most foundationalists countenance several others, including, perhaps, principles whereby justification is transmitted to propositions about the physical world and propositions about the past. (pp. 75–76)

These further remarks by Van Cleve nicely illustrate the way principles are typically discussed by armchair epistemology in connection with coherentism:

> Some coherentists espouse principles that are neither generation principles nor transmission principles, but a sort of hybrid between the two. An example would be 'If P coheres with the system of propositions accepted by S (or scientists of our culture circle, etc.), then P is justified for S.' This is like a generation principle in that its antecedent contains no epistemic terms, but like a transmission principle in that its antecedent specifies relations to other propositions. (p. 75)

Several points deserve emphasis concerning epistemological discussions conducted in this vein. First, often they proceed largely at a meta-level, at which more attention is given to the logical structures that such principles might have than to the specific contents of the principles. (Sometimes this is because the author's immediate purpose is not so much to articulate specific normative principles, but rather to inquire about the overall structure of a system of justified beliefs—e.g. whether such a system would have a foundationalist structure, or a coherentist structure, or some other kind of global structure. We turn to such matters ourselves in Chapter 8.) Second, various substantive, and fairly plausible, first-order normative principles have indeed been proposed on the basis of armchair methods—for instance, Chisholm's Principle (*A*), and the principle that deduction transmits justification. But third—and most importantly in the present context—the principles that have actually been proposed appear to fall far short of constituting a *complete* systematization of epistemic normativity. Foundationalists, for instance, have had relatively little to say by way of articulating *non-deductive* transmission principles, such as principles that would codify epistemically appropriate abductive inference. And coherentists have had relatively little to say by way of articulating principles that would explicate the vague notion of 'coherence' and would provide specific guidance about how to form beliefs that collectively exhibit this feature.

The upshot of this third observation is the apparent need for supplementation from richly empirical cognitive science, in the search for a more complete systematization of epistemic normativity. A less sketchy and partial, more thorough and complete, inventory of normative principles of belief-formation evidently will have to draw in part—probably in *large* part—upon aspects of the theory of epistemic competence that are not ascertainable from the armchair but instead are to be sought within richly empirical cognitive science. Nature has engineered a class of cognitive agents with rather impressive epistemic competence, namely, humans—a fact that needs to be appreciated and respected, notwithstanding the many kinds of performance error to which humans are susceptible. The most promising-looking route to a more complete understanding of epistemic competence, beyond what can be gleaned by armchair reflection alone, looks to be richly empirical scientific investigation of the design that nature has instilled in humans. So says naturalized epistemology. Our present point is that the rather limited success that armchair methods have met, in seeking principles that would systematize epistemic normativity, constitutes good evidence for this key claim of naturalized epistemology.

One final observation, before moving on. In this section we have been discussing the perennial ambition in epistemology to find some set of general normative principles that collectively provide a full systematization of epistemic normativity. If there is such a set of principles to which humans conform when they are exhibiting epistemic competence and avoiding performance errors, then those principles would together constitute a theory of human epistemic competence. And if there is such a set of principles, we have been arguing, then they are largely to be discovered within richly empirical cognitive science, rather than just from the armchair. But the following possibility should be acknowledged: perhaps normatively appropriate belief-formation, of the sort exhibited in epistemically competent human cognition, is actually too subtle and complex to be completely systematizable by any set of general normative principles. If so, then there is no *fully comprehensive* set of general epistemic principles to be discovered—not even by deploying all the resources of richly empirical science. But even if things should turn out that way, it would still be the case that normatively appropriate belief formation, in humans, is the kind of belief formation that manifests human epistemic competence; and it would still be the case that richly empirical cognitive science can reveal a great deal about the nature of that competence that cannot be ascertained by armchair methods alone. Indeed, cognitive science might well provide the theoretical resources to explain why, and how, humans are capable of generating beliefs in ways that accord with a form of epistemic normativity that simply outstrips full systematization by exceptionless general principles. We will recur to this theme below, later in this chapter and again in Chapter 7.

3 Tractability: ought implies can

So far in this chapter we have been stressing two principal motivations for embracing naturalized epistemology: first, the need to rely on richly empirical cognitive science for a full specification of what counts as suitable modulational control in belief-formation, and second, the need to rely on richly empirical cognitive science in order to ascertain more about epistemic normativity, and more about principles that systematize epistemic normativity (to whatever extent it is systematizable), than can be learned within armchair epistemology. We turn now to a third important motivation.

Epistemology is largely concerned with normative matters—specifically, with how one ought to proceed in the matter of belief-formation, with an eye toward truth-seeking. What is normatively appropriate for a class of epistemic agents (typically, humans provide the intended class) cannot be determined in grand isolation from questions of what processes those agents can or could employ. Put simply: 'ought' implies 'can.' That an epistemic agent ought to produce and sustain beliefs in certain ways, that the agent ought to think in certain ways, entails that the agent can. In developing an account of how humans should fix belief, one must not lose sight of how such agents *can* fix belief. Which, *among the processes that humans could employ*— including those that humans could come to employ with training—have an acceptable mix of postclassical reliability, power, and speed? Which *among those humanly possible processes* have the best balance of those factors? If an account of objectively appropriate processes is to be appropriate *for a class of agents*, it must be sensitive to such issues.

That ought does imply can is clear—at least when 'can' is understood relative to a class of cognitive systems rather than to the individual agent. The matter is easily understood when reflecting on evaluative judgment-tendencies and the motivations for such epistemological evaluations. One wants to regulate one's own cognition, through training and through such self-monitoring as humans are capable of, and one wants to do so in conformity with standards that are fitting for humans. One would be foolish to try to train oneself to undertake the impossible, and one is wise to evaluate one's own performance in terms of standards that do not call for what are humanly impossible processes. One looks for members in one's epistemic community who likewise employ such processes. One wants partners in a cooperative epistemic endeavor, and one wants one's partners to employ processes at least as good as those one wants oneself to employ. But, again, it would make little sense to ask them to use processes that no human could manage. It would make little sense to condemn one's belief-forming processes when they conform to what is appropriate, even optimal, for humans. It would make little sense to 'hold out' for 'ideal' processes that no human, or even no finite system, could implement. So, to say that an individual ought to reason in a certain way implies at least that agents of the relevant kind (through training and with motivation) can manage to reason in that way. (At any rate, the ought claim implies that such agents can at least *approximate* the recommended mode of reasoning, even if they cannot conform to it perfectly invariantly—that is, without the occasional slip.)

On the other hand, at the level of individuals, there is a respect in which the implication fails. A particular individual, through poor training or motivation, or cognitive deficits, may be so strongly disposed toward certain suboptimal cognitive processes that there is a sense in which that individual cannot do other than reason in a given epistemically undesirable manner. Even so, one has an epistemic motivation (gatekeeping) to restrict that individual's epistemic standing in the community of inquirers. Thus, one judges that such an individual ought to have employed certain processes, even though that individual could not employ those processes—given *that individual's* training or motivation, or cognitive deficits. One evaluates the agent's processes as epistemically inappropriate, and the individual's resulting beliefs as unjustified, even though the individual might be doing his/her best.

Concern for the tractability of a set of epistemological standards is at least as old as Aristotle. More recently, it finds expression in a range of writers—for example, Cherniak (1986)[3] and Goldman (1999).[4] However, it is not uncommon in reading modern and contemporary epistemology to encounter accounts of putatively appropriate processing that are overly idealized in the sense that they are almost oblivious to issues of tractability. Epistemologists have commonly worked in an epistemology-for-a-world-of-propositions tradition. Work within that tradition can help call attention to general informational tasks facing epistemic agents. But, too often, the informational demands are flatfootedly translated into simple-minded prescriptions of certain kinds of cognitive processes—e.g. processes in which all the information would need to be occurrently represented, and in a way that would make the information reflectively accessible to the agent. (We address this specific demand in Chapter 7, at some length.) The move from informational demands to prescriptions regarding processing is commonly made without attention to the tractability of the

---

[3] Cherniak gives a strikingly illustrative application, concerning standards for how humans ought to gauge the internal truth-functional logical consistency of global belief-sets. To think, for example, that one's cognitive processes for the determination of the truth-functional consistency of one's belief-set should involve a manipulation of representational states and judgments that parallel those found in truth-tables, is to be insensitive to how finite cognitive systems could manage their cognitive lives in real time. For sets of beliefs approaching those of the size of those we humans possess, truth-tables-in-the-head would take an astronomical amount of time to work out. The needed sensitivity to truth-functional inconsistency must be managed in other ways.

[4] Goldman (1999) provides a nice overview of motivations for various forms of naturalized epistemology, along with references. Our own approach is similar to Goldman's moderate naturalism in several respects.

processes there prescribed. Somewhat predictably, the standards that result from such empirically unconstrained reflections are commonly not fitting for the cognitive system to which they are then applied.

BonJour's (1985) coherentism provides an instructive illustration. BonJour quite rightly identifies holistic information to which a cognitive agent would need to be sensitive in arriving at judgments.[5] He is led to the view that justified empirical beliefs should form a globally coherent reinforcing system. He then supposes that justification requires the cognitive system to somehow 'survey' a structure of representational states that constitutes the agent's entire set of beliefs—it must survey for the kind of coherence he identifies. Only after announcing this rather demanding standard does BonJour consider whether human agents could ever implement it. He doubts that this is ultimately humanly possible—and thus is led to doubt that humans can ever be justified in empirical believing. From our perspective, the crucial misstep comes in formulating standards first and not asking about tractability until later. Somewhat predictably, the standards that result from such a procedure are not fitting for the kind of cognitive system to which they are then applied.

In the next chapter we will sketch an account of belief-formation that incorporates tractable processes by which humans can manage the informational demands that BonJour helps to identify. That theoretical approach will be informed by general developments in cognitive science that suggest kinds of processes that are not considered by BonJour or much other traditional epistemology. We will argue that such processes would allow humans and similar creatures to aptly manage their epistemic tasks, handling informational demands identified by BonJour and other traditional epistemologists. A cognitive-science account of such processes can then be incorporated within fitting epistemological standards—thereby avoiding the problematic intractability that threatens epistemological accounts that are not informed by helpful developments in cognitive science.

4 Idealization and epistemic competence

Although some traditional epistemology may be inappropriately idealized because it fails to attend to the tractability of the standards that it would impose, there is yet room for a suitable kind of idealization in understanding epistemic justification. Suitable idealization will be the kind appropriate for distinguishing between epistemic competence on one hand, and on the other hand, performance errors stemming from factors like fatigue or limitations in the information-storage capacity of working memory. Such idealization will be keyed to the actual 'engineering design' for truth-seeking belief-formation that natural selection has instilled in humans, and thereby will be keyed to matters of tractability as well.

---

[5] Holistic information plays a crucial role in the justification of many beliefs, whether or not coherentism is the right account of the overall structure of a system of justified beliefs. This theme will loom large in Chapters 7 and 8.

The epistemic competence of a class of agents is constituted by a *select, idealized, subset* of the various dispositions that such agents possess or might possess. All actual human cognizers have dispositions to various performance errors, and all possible human cognizers *would* have dispositions to performance errors. For actual human cognizers, the dispositions or capacities by which they manage their epistemic tasks well (to whatever extent they do) are then the pertinent subset of their dispositions. Moreover, the dispositions in this select set are apt to require a *somewhat* idealized characterization within a theory of epistemic competence, because the competence is apt to be most perspicuously characterized in a way that abstracts away from resource limitations such as memory capacity. (Compare human grammatical competence, as conceived within Chomsky-style linguistic theory: it is to be characterized in a way that applies to grammatical natural-language sentences of any finite length whatever.) This constrained kind of idealization is apt to be necessary in order to filter out all dispositions to performance errors, since some such error-dispositions (though not necessarily all) will result from resource limitations themselves. But it will be a significantly constrained form of idealization nonetheless, because it will be firmly tethered to the actual cognitive architecture of humans—the engineering-design for truth-seeking that nature has actually installed in humankind. This select, idealized, subset of human belief-forming dispositions constitutes the *actual* epistemic competence of humans.

An account of actual human epistemic competence is in some ways a relatively unambitious normative standard, however. More demanding forms of epistemic competence—higher standards for epistemic competence—involve dispositions that human cognitive systems *could* acquire. Here one thinks in terms of possible human beings with better training and refined processes. Yet, even with the best possible training and motivation, human cognizers would exhibit a mix of epistemically desirable and undesirable dispositions. Hence, the dispositions or capacities by which such possible humans would manage their epistemic tasks well still would be a select, and somewhat idealized, subset of the dispositions that they would possess. These constitute *humanly possible* epistemic competence. There is room for a range of more or less ambitious or demanding standards of humanly possible epistemic competence, standards setting out increasingly demanding models for the capacities humans might acquire to further their epistemic project—a theme to which we recur below. However, all fitting standards—all pertinent competence-theories—will be constrained by information about the kinds of cognitive processes that are tractable for humans, and so about the nature of human cognitive architecture.

The distinction between actual human epistemic competence and humanly possible epistemic competence is best thought of as a graded one, and also as somewhat contextual. It is graded in the sense that one can envision a whole range of different types of, and different degrees of, better-than-minimal competence. These could involve a variety of different forms of humanly achievable expertise, problem-solving skill, creativity in hypothesis-generation, and so forth.

The distinction is also contextual, insofar as such variations can be thought of in either of two ways, depending on one's specific theoretical purposes in addressing them—either as different *forms of competence* on one hand, or as different ways of applying the *same* fundamental epistemic competence on the other hand. (Learned skills, after all, arise by dint of one's applying one's innate capacities for learning to a specific regimen of training, practice, and the like.)

Some might imagine that despite the normative elements embodied in a theory of human epistemic competence that draws upon richly empirical cognitive science, there is nonetheless a problematic tension between naturalized epistemology and normative epistemology. To appreciate how such a concern might arise, consider a hypothetical conversation between a rather traditional epistemologist and someone with naturalizing tendencies. Suppose that the two are discussing a traditional epistemological account, for example, a coherentist account that requires that a massive amount of argumentation be accessible to the agent in sustaining a perceptual belief. The naturalist might object that the account is psychologically implausible, because it grossly distorts the belief-forming processes that are employed in the context in question. There is then a recognizable tendency for the traditional epistemologist to attempt to brush off the objection with the following considerations:

Epistemology is not in the business of describing how we *do*, in fact, undertake certain tasks—not even when we are doing as well as we humanly can, exercising our epistemic competence and avoiding performance errors. Rather, epistemology is in the business of saying how such tasks *might ideally* be undertaken. This is to set out ideals that may not be paralleled, even in part, by actual human cognition. Such ideal accounts result from reflection on what combinations of evidence and information would provide reasons for holding a belief. Thus, deductive logic and systems such as Carnap's account of logical probability have central place. If, for example, certain forms of holistic coherence involving a given belief would support that belief, then such coherence is to be called for generally in the normative account that epistemology provides. Thus, the normatively engaged epistemologist should ruthlessly abstract away from all implementing systems (computing devices or particular psychological entities) and demand belief-forming processes that are maximally good at generating beliefs in a way that fully reflects the actual evidential relations among the items of information available to the epistemic agent.

This view of idealized accounts has deep roots in the philosophical tradition and is bound to give pause to some would-be friends of naturalization. (Note that the view could be grafted onto transglobal reliabilism, too: the traditional epistemologist insists that what constitutes transglobal reliability under suitable modulational control is nothing less than belief-forming processing that tracks and reflects, fully and completely, all the evidential-support actually present in the epistemic agent's available information.)

Now, we grant that such 'pure reflective' idealization has something to contribute to epistemology. Its place in more inclusive epistemological investigations is ultimately that of a kind of 'brainstorming' of *abstract* possibilities for belief-formation. But some of these abstract possibilities may turn out not to be real possibilities for the actual cognitive systems of concern.[6]

If reflection on 'pure ideals' is to inform a normative epistemology fitting to humans, it will need to be by calling attention to practices within the set of *learnable* methods—to processes that are tractable for humans. Accordingly, pure ideals will only characterize ways of reasoning that human cognitive agents *ought* to employ to the extent that these ideals characterize ways that humans (with complementary training and high motivation) *can* reason. So, although pure reflection might call attention to various cognitive processes that *would* be desirable, *were* they tractable for systems of the relevant kind (typically for humans), these would need to *be* tractable in order to be fitting standards for such systems. (Or at least, there would have to be tractable processes available to those systems whose deployment would *approximate* those standards.)

Furthermore, even if 'pure reflection' picks out a method that also happens to be tractable, it does not follow that that method must be adopted as a part of a fitting normative standard. There are yet further considerations to be factored in. Learnable methods may be more or less consistently implementable (Cherniak (1986) writes of feasibility orderings), may be variously demanding in terms of one's cognitive resources, and may promise small or large gains in global or transglobal reliability over alternative methods.[7] In order to be normatively appropriate, a cognitive procedure will need to be learnable and feasibly implementable without interfering with the implementation of other processes or methods that promise (as implemented) greater gain in valuable beliefs. Thus, although epistemology may be concerned marginally with 'pure ideals,' this hardly has central place. And although it may be concerned centrally with normative ideals, ultimately these are not going to be pure ideals.[8]

---

[6] One set of very general limitations on the force of such 'pure ideals' can be seen as arising from the limitations of any finite system, or of any physically realizable system, or of any such system within the life of the physical universe. Cherniak (1986, ch. 4) argues, from results in the field of computational complexity, that most algorithms for deductive logic are, when generally applied, intractable for such systems.

[7] One place that such considerations become prominent is in the discussion by Gigerenzer and Hoffrage (1995) about 'how to improve Bayesian reasoning without instruction' (viz., by couching problems in terms of sampling frequency formats rather than in probability or relative frequency formats). The 'improvement' envisioned is itself understood as a matter of conforming to Bayes' theorem. The human tendency to ignore base rates when presented with a problem in standard probability formats can be seen as revealing that, when given information in probability formats, such problems call for processes that are somewhat lower on Cherniak's feasibility orderings for humans than are the processes that would address such problems when provided information in sampling frequencies. Such problems and processes are marginally tractable for humans, but difficult and soon give rise to significant errors and lapses. Gigerenzer and Hoffrage's suggestion is, in effect, that different information formats make for equivalent problems that are much more feasible—less costly and more consistently managed.

[8] The inverse tendency is sometimes in evidence in the work of champions of forms of naturalized epistemology. For example, Bishop and Trout (2005b, p. 696) say that, 'a naturalistic theory of epistemology takes as its core, as its starting point, an empirical theory.' (See also, Bishop and Trout 2005a). But, as they themselves would recognize, the empirical work or theory to which they themselves appeal (what they term Ameliorative Psychology) is unabashedly normative itself. When one asks just what really is the 'starting point' here, one is therefore likely to find more than one. It is better to think in terms of the E-spectrum, with

What these last few paragraphs indicate is that, while epistemological standards may well best be articulated in idealizing accounts, the nature of those ideals is easily misconceived. They are not properly pure ideals. Once epistemologists are freed of misconceptions regarding the sort of ideal standards one should seek, the place for ideals in epistemology is worth preserving. The appropriate sort of idealization is the kind involved in delineating human epistemic competence; and a completed theoretical account of epistemic competence would span the whole E-spectrum, including the richly empirical portion of the spectrum.

In sum, we are recommending the construction of empirically constrained normative models that characterize human epistemic competence, as a task for an interdisciplinary form of epistemology. Such models characterize the cognitive processes that are epistemically appropriate for humans—processes that make for justified belief. The models also delimit the normative standards of rational belief-formation that are epistemically appropriate for humans—standards to which the relevant processes conform. Obviously, there will need to be a kind of idealizing selectivity here, one informed by a scientific understanding of actual and possible cognitive capacities of humans. The relevant kind of idealization is motivated by the conceptually mandated concern for managing epistemic tasks with appropriate balances of postclassical reliability, power, and speed.

5 Epistemic competence and the meliorative dimension of epistemology

One persistent theme within epistemology, both historically and in the contemporary era, has been a meliorative one—seeking out ways of *improving* the belief formation in oneself and one's peers. When first-person and/or third-person melioration are in view, it will be appropriate to distinguish actual human epistemic competence from various kinds of humanly possible epistemic competence whose inculcation is desirable. And it will be appropriate to seek out a *meliorative* theory of competence (as we will call it)—a theory that characterizes humanly possible competence of the kind one seeks to inculcate.

It will help to distinguish two goals that partially motivate a concern for melioration, and two kinds of melioration associated with these two goals respectively. First is the goal of guarding against performance errors and seeking to minimize them, in oneself and in one's peers. Let *weak* melioration be the kind that serves to further this goal, thereby helping people do better at avoiding performance errors in their belief-formation, thereby exhibiting actual epistemic competence more thoroughly and more consistently—which correlatively makes them better at avoiding cognitive processing that amounts to performance errors in relation to that form of competence.

---

inquiry situated at or near the richly empirical end being constrained by inquiry situated at or near the low-grade a priori end (and vice versa).

Second is the goal of improving belief formation, in oneself and/or one's peers, to a level that conforms not merely to actual human competence but instead to a form of humanly possible competence undergirding belief-forming processes that exhibit a yet higher degree of postclassical reliability. Let *strong* melioration be the kind that serves to further this more ambitious goal, thereby helping people achieve more exalted levels of epistemic competence.

A theory of meliorative epistemic competence would describe humanly achievable forms of competence to which humans might realistically aspire. Such a theory might well have implications for strong melioration—effective steps that might be taken in pursuit of such competence. (It also might well have implications for weak melioration, since the same or similar steps might also help people avoid performance errors relative to actual human competence.). Thus, a theory describing some form of humanly possible epistemic competence, where one wants such a theory to direct improvements upon one's own or one's peers' current actual epistemic competence, might be called a *meliorative* theory of competence. This label serves not to delineate a different class of theories other than theories of humanly possible epistemic competence, but rather to underscore melioration as an operative goal in seeking out a pertinent such theory. A theory of humanly possible competence counts as a meliorative theory to the extent one seeks to put it to meliorative use, as a means toward improved epistemic competence.[9]

What is needed in a meliorative theory of epistemic competence is an account of a cognitive system that a human might become. A meliorative theory of competence would still take the form of a selection from human cognitive dispositions. However, now the human being in question is a (more or less sophisticated) theoretical reconstruction: a possible human being who has acquired those humanly learnable dispositions that, in combination, make it as effective in pursuing epistemic goals as is humanly feasible. The resulting meliorative theory of competence would not tell people how they do manage, but rather, how they can best manage. It would consist of analyses, not of a complete human being, actual or possible, but of those epistemically productive dispositions that, in combination, would make for the most epistemically effective agent humanly possible.

A meliorative theory of competence would abstract away from human dispositions toward performance errors. As regards dispositions that constitute actual human competence, the meliorative theory presumably would draw fairly heavily upon analyses of

---

[9] The simplest and most straightforward notion of meliorative epistemic competence has to do with how one might best, or most effectively, proceed. The corresponding theory would serve to characterize the most ambitious understanding or set of standards that one might seek to implement; it might be called a theory of *optimum* meliorative competence. Of course, less ambitious notions of meliorative competence are easily recognized; one might construct standards of meliorative competence that vary in the demands they place on human agents in proportion to one's ambitions for epistemic improvement. Such accounts, while going beyond an account of agents' actual epistemic competence, are naturally viewed as *satisficing* rather than optimizing with regard to the pursuit of epistemic goals.

these dispositions—analyses to be found in the theory of actual human competence. Analyses of these actual dispositions carry important information regarding how one might learn to reason better. For, the dispositions that one can acquire are, in part, determined by the more basic dispositions one possesses, and these are described in analyses of actual systems. Epistemological standards, from the Greeks to the present, have commonly drawn on the then extant accounts of human cognitive capacities to provide an understanding of what a high-performing human epistemic agent could and should do. One of the lessons of the call for naturalized epistemology is that epistemology is not a first philosophy, but is rather a historically situated inquiry—an inquiry that should draw on one's best theoretical accounts of how humans do and can reason (where the understanding of how humans can reason is grounded at some level in models of how they do reason).

Theories of meliorative epistemic competence may be thought of as being tailored to various classes of epistemic agents: to particular individuals, to particular communities, or to human beings generally. Different kinds of, and different degrees of, humanly possible epistemic competence could get characterized by different theories of meliorative competence—and which meliorative theory would be most pertinent to one's specific meliorative purposes will depend upon which class of epistemic agents is the target of one's meliorative goals. (Some such meliorative theories might well be *partial*, of course: rather than characterizing a full-fledged, fully general, kind of humanly possible epistemic competence, they might only characterize some component of such a competence—a component whose inculcation is what one seeks to instill, by melioration, in a given class of epistemic agents.) As a result, theories of competence can be nuanced tools that can be made to address a significant range of epistemological concerns.

Weak melioration—guidance in the avoidance of performance errors, and in exhibiting actual human competence more thoroughly and more consistently—can be aided in a number of ways. The theory of actual human competence is apt to be useful as a source of such guidance. So too are cognitive-scientific accounts of the likely sources of performance errors in humans—accounts that themselves are likely to draw in part upon the theory of actual human competence. (One reason for this, inter alia, is that the theory of actual human competence provides the touchstone for ascertaining what counts as a performance error in the first place.) And, as mentioned above, meliorative theories of competence might very well be a source of insights regarding weak melioration, because facts about some form of better than actual, yet still humanly possible, epistemic competence can, in principle, provide guidance about how to avoid cognitive missteps that constitute performance errors relative to actual human epistemic competence.

Finally, it bears emphasis that good modulational-control mechanisms are always open to receiving pertinent additional new information, and are always in place to make appropriate use of such new information should it arise. It is to be hoped that the theory of meliorative epistemic competence will sometimes turn up important new results about how humans can effectively improve their own truth seeking. Such information can and should feed into people's modulational-control mechanisms, yielding belief-forming performance that further outdoes the merely baseline standards of actual epistemic competence.

6 Epistemic competence and the E-spectrum

As already emphasized, the form of naturalized epistemology we recommend incorporates a broad spectrum of mutually complementary methods of inquiry—the E-spectrum—of which the richly empirical cognitive-scientific inquiry is but one component. At one end of the spectrum is low-grade a priori inquiry—effectively doable from the armchair, and effectively doable by philosophers without assistance from cognitive science. At the other end of the spectrum is theoretical inquiry within richly empirical cognitive science, concerning aspects of human cognitive architecture that figure in actual belief-formation—aspects that underwrite actual human epistemic competence, aspects that contribute to performance errors and to resource-based deviations from full epistemic competence, and aspects that constrain the range of humanly possible epistemic competence. Theorizing at any given point along the spectrum typically exerts constraining influence throughout the spectrum. For instance, low-grade a priori reflection on the workings of the concept of epistemic justification constrains the way the competence/performance distinction is to be drawn: nature's cognitive-architectural 'engineering design' for truth-seeking belief formation should be a design for postclassically reliable belief-forming processes. Conversely, results from richly empirical cognitive science constrain the notion of postclassical reliability itself, by partially determining what counts (in humans) as suitable modulational control.

Where along the E-spectrum should inquiry in pursuit of an account of human epistemic competence—actual competence, or actual humanly possible competence—be located? One might think that the answer given by naturalized epistemology is that such inquiry belongs almost exclusively within richly empirical cognitive science: although philosophers can do low-grade a priori conceptual analysis to determine the contours of epistemic-evaluative concepts like epistemic justification, and although such conceptual analysis informs the drawing of the epistemological competence/performance distinction, thereafter the task of producing a theoretical account of actual and ideal human epistemic competence falls entirely to richly empirical cognitive science.

But that answer is too crude. A more plausible one goes as follows. Various different components of a sought-for overall theoretical account of human epistemic competence can be arrived at by inquiry from any of various different points on the E-spectrum. To begin with, one can arrive at some pertinent normative principles for belief-formation in a low-grade a priori way (even though the principles so obtainable are apt to fall far short of a complete systematization of epistemic normativity)—for instance, Mill's methods of induction, or the laws of mathematical probability, or the principles taught in statistics classes. Secondly, one can generate serviceable principles, too, by appeal to common-sense psychology (even though these principles plus the a priori ones still do not begin to amount to a full systematization of epistemic normativity). This can be done, for example, by providing people with plausible common-sense explanations of why they might be inclined to put more credence in certain forms of testimony than is epistemically appropriate (church and Sunday school come to mind), and then formulating correlative principles (e.g. 'Don't accept what you are told in church and Sunday school solely on the basis of a preacher's or teacher's testimony'). Principles arrived at by low-grade a priori reflection might very well be retained within a fully comprehensive theory of epistemic competence, and thus would be an important component of such a theory. Similarly, serviceable common-sensical cautionary principles like those lately mentioned may be thought of as somewhat unsystematic snippets of a nascent theory of competence. Thus, even though an ideally complete theoretical account of human epistemic competence would have to emerge in large part from richly empirical cognitive science, the fact remains that non-negligible progress toward such an account is still possible via other means.

Epistemologists commonly characterize their discipline as devoted to achieving a kind of wide reflective equilibrium. Naturalized epistemology, as we have characterized it, implements this idea. The ultimate goal is to pursue all the kinds of inquiry along the spectrum, and to arrive at results that fully accommodate the mutually constraining effects that these different forms of inquiry have on one another. To realize that goal would be to arrive at an overall epistemology that exhibits wide reflective equilibrium.

Construing epistemological methodology in terms of wide reflective equilibrium highlights the fact that naturalized epistemology is always *situated* epistemology. The point is reflected also in the repudiation of aspirations for a first philosophy. Epistemology is rightly and unavoidably influenced by extant understandings of human dispositions, actual and possible. The relevant understandings have not always been the product of an inquiry that has been set apart as the special discipline of psychology or cognitive science. Such separate and developed disciplines are of fairly recent vintage. But one finds in Aristotle, for example, common-sensical understandings of human cognitive capacities already at work informing epistemological standards.[10] In effect, Aristotle is doing naturalized epistemology: he is offering a theoretical account, however partial, of human epistemic competence.

Not only are forms of inquiry conducted at different points on the E-spectrum compatible with one another, and indeed mutually complementary, but in addition they all can contribute to the development of an account of human epistemic competence. Which method (or combination of methods) is most appropriate to use, in the service of developing such an account, often will depend on the degree

---

[10] Aristotle's understanding of human capacities itself serves as an early and respectable form of explanatory analysis. His thought then serves as an example of the sort of situated 'naturalized' epistemology we advocate here. Of course, both his epistemology and his 'psychology' are subject to related limitations.

of specificity one is seeking. Although prominent resources for a theory of competence include explanatory analyses to be found in cognitive science, this should not be taken to suggest that one must have a finished and highly sophisticated cognitive science in order even to begin epistemological work on standards for epistemic competence. Not at all. Instead, one rightly begins with what one has on hand—one's best extant understanding of human cognitive capacities. Refinements in one's take on these matters will, of course, sometimes call for associated refinements in one's construal of normative epistemic competence. But, one cannot afford to wait for a 'completed cognitive science' before commencing work on an understanding of how humans ought to reason. That would be at least as misguided as waiting for a 'completed physical science' before beginning to engage in engineering.[11] Just as Rome produced its aqueducts with only limited scientific understanding, so epistemic standards informed by the various, if limited, common-sense conceptions of human cognitive capacities, have usefully informed the ongoing epistemic labors of many societies. Indeed, to wait for a 'completed cognitive science' before undertaking the development of revisable epistemic standards would be even more misguided. The very inquiry on which the development of cognitive science depends itself depends on standards for cognition. Quine (1969) was right to talk of mutual containment.

Just as one can and must engage in a kind of naturalized epistemology without having access to the 'final' cognitive science, so one can engage in useful naturalized epistemology without either knowing or drawing on all the details presently understood about human cognitive capacities. Details matter where they bear in the right way on epistemic concerns. Sometimes they will matter, presumably for corresponding details of the construal of human epistemic competence. But, often, a more general conception of human cognitive capacities is what is needed to get the general outlines of the normative standards right. One can usefully engage in naturalized epistemology, and can contribute to the understanding of epistemic competence and objective justification, at various levels of detail. There are multiple roles to play in the community business of epistemological theorizing, with different roles being situated at different points on the E-spectrum.

These observations are particularly apt in connection with the present work. We ourselves do not pretend to be fully informed of the details of recent work in cognitive science. (We each would like to know more than we do.) We are not cutting-edge cognitive scientists. Rather, we would be well described as 'looking over the shoulders' of those doing ongoing cognitive science. In the following chapters, we seek to draw some general, but far-reaching, conclusions regarding human epistemic competence from what we see at some remove. We ourselves have an intermediate focus in those

---

[11] The parallel can be extended further. Engineering applications are necessary for the pursuit of scientific advancement—as reflected in the crucial use of all manner of scientific instruments. Engineering applications must develop along with the science and cannot wait until some final science to commence. Similarly, naturalized epistemology informs the inquiry on which it draws.

chapters—at the interface between different points on the E-spectrum, but with fewer details than cognitive science will ultimately be able to contribute.

In order to preclude misunderstanding, let us reiterate three observations about how we understand the relations between epistemology per se, naturalized epistemology, and the theory of competence. First, we take the subject matter of naturalized epistemology to *coincide* with that of epistemology per se—at least, insofar as one thinks of epistemology as specifically about human cognizers. Naturalized epistemology is not a *component* of epistemology, alongside other components. Rather, it is a *conception* of the nature of epistemology per se—a conception that stresses the importance of incorporating naturalizing elements into epistemology, elements that constrain the entire E-spectrum of epistemological inquiry.

Second, although an ideally complete theoretical account of actual and ideal human epistemic competence presumably would reside within richly empirical cognitive science, this hardly means that no partial progress toward such an account can be made by armchair methods or by appeal to common-sense thinking about belief-formation. On the contrary, such methods can yield significant, albeit incomplete, insight into matters of epistemic normativity—e.g. meliorative insight, which often can be harnessed to improve people's level of epistemic competence and to help them avoid certain kinds of performance errors. And for some purposes in epistemology, e.g. meliorative purposes, this kind of insight can be more pertinent than would be more specific details about human cognition, the discovery of which would require scientific investigation.

Third, epistemology comprises more than just the theory of epistemic competence. It also includes other theoretical components that are largely or entirely independent of richly empirical cognitive science. A case in point is our account in earlier chapters of the notion of epistemic justification. Another case in point is our account of low-grade a priori reasoning itself, which was arrived at in a low-grade a priori manner and without reliance on the theory of epistemic competence.

7 Toward a theory of epistemic competence

We turn next to a somewhat more detailed discussion of the project of constructing a theory of epistemic competence. Although this project is largely to be pursued within richly empirical cognitive science, nevertheless there is room for suggestive discussion and reflection, by philosophers like us, on the nature of such a project. In effect, this will be an exercise in the application of philosophy of science. It will be a discussion *about* theorizing that will largely take place within the richly empirical end of the E-spectrum, a discussion conducted from an epistemological vantage-point more toward the middle of the spectrum.

The basic idea in developing a theory of epistemic competence is to select from those portions of descriptive theory that are particularly fitted to the central epistemic concerns emphasized above. The selected portions of empirical theory will then be made to do double duty: serving both as a descriptive account of how humans *do or could* manage certain tasks, and as a normative account of how humans *should* manage them. The selection criteria are objective—roughly, a matter of what processes are humanly implementable and have an acceptable balance of postclassical reliability, power and speed. It is important that the selection criteria be objective, so that the naturalized epistemologist can account for the normative force of the resulting theory of competence. Given what is epistemically valued, one will be able to explain why one adopts a particular set of standards and not some other; these standards will amount to a humanly implementable 'engineering design' for truth-seeking belief-forming processes.

We will describe three large-scale cognitive-scientific explanatory frameworks within which a theory of epistemic competence might be developed. These frameworks are not necessarily exclusive, and thus a particular competence theory—or a particular component of a larger competence theory—could in principle fall under several of them, perhaps even all three. On the other hand, certain potential *versions* of these three respective frameworks can indeed come into conflict with one another—as shall become clear in subsequent discussion both in this chapter and the next.

7.1 *High-church computationalism*

One foundational framework for cognitive science, a framework that has been highly influential in recent decades, is what we will here call 'high-church computationalism.' On this view, human cognition is *computation over mental representations*. That is, cognition is the deployment, manipulation, and transformation of mental representations in ways that accord with *programmable rules*. Such rules are *mandatory*: they dictate what the rule-implementing system *must* do at any stage of processing, given its total representational state at that stage. (Inference rules in logic, by contrast, are permission rules: they determine which inferential steps are *allowable*.) The rules are *representation-level*: they advert explicitly to those structural aspects (often, syntactic aspects) of the system's internal representations that encode representational content.[12] The rules are expressible purely formally, i.e. as rules for manipulating the representations on the basis of their formal structure (often, syntactic structure). Content-sensitive processing of the representations is thus accomplished by structure-sensitive processing, where the structure in question is formal/syntactic. And the rules are *exceptionless*: for any total representational state the system instantiates, they dictate specifically what it is to do next. (Such exceptionless rules can be nondeterministic, because for example they can

---

[12] Representation-level programmable rules can get implemented by rules in a lower-level programming language that governs a lower-level computational system, relative to which the original system is a 'virtual machine.' This can happen repeatedly at multiple levels: there can be a whole hierarchy of virtual machines implementing other virtual machines, with the whole hierarchy ultimately 'bottoming out' in a non-virtual machine whose program is expressed in 'machine language.' Contemporary digital computers typically deploy such implementational hierarchies of virtual machines.

dictate two-stage transitions involving first a computational 'dice throw' and then a subsequent action that depends on the outcome of the dice throw.)[13]

There are various ways one might employ computers in attempting to model human cognition, not all of which would necessarily assume that cognition literally consists of computation over mental representations. Hence our label 'high-church computationalism,' for the foundational approach that really *does* make that assumption.

If this assumption is correct, then a fully completed account of any given kind of human epistemic competence—of actual competence, of or one or another humanly possible competence—would take the form of a set of programmable rules for manipulating mental representations. Such a set of rules would thoroughly and completely systematize epistemic normativity: for any potential total representational state of a human agent, the rules would determine what the agent in that representational state should believe. This kind of competence theory would meet the most optimistic hopes of those in epistemology, early and late, who seek to discover normative epistemic principles so general in scope, and yet also so specific in content, that they would subsume any potential informational-evidential situation that a human could ever be in—dictating, for each of them, what an agent in that situation would be justified in believing. Not only that, but the rules constituting the theory of epistemic competence would systematize epistemic normativity in an *algorithmic* way: such rules could be executed by automatic, formal symbol-manipulation by the hardware in a suitably programmed digital computer, or by the 'wetware' in a human brain. Tractability would therefore be assured, given the plausible-looking assumption that the human brain, with its tens of billions of neurons and thousands of billions of synaptic connections, has the physical resource capacity to implement the programmable rules that constitute human epistemic competence.

Articulation and investigation of models of various aspects of human cognition, within the framework of high-church computationalism, has been vigorously pursued in recent decades within the interdisciplinary matrix that calls itself 'cognitive science.' We ourselves applaud such theoretical work (even though we do not engage in it ourselves). But although it surely can illuminate some aspects of human cognition, in some cases even considerably, there is reason to think that human epistemic competence—competence in forming beliefs that are likely to be true given the evidence and information available to the human cognizer—may well be too subtle and complex to operate by executing programmable rules over mental representations. Some reasons for this pessimistic assessment will emerge in Chapter 7.

---

[13] For an elaboration of the remarks made in this paragraph, see Chapter 2 of Horgan and Tienson (1996). One point stressed by Horgan and Tienson is that programmable representational rules typically have two guises. In one guise they have substantive representational content—e.g. about university classes to be taught and university classrooms to be used, in the case of rules for assigning classes to classrooms. But in another guise they are purely formal, and advert only to the formal-syntactic structure of representations—say, structure that happens to encode information about university classes, university classrooms, times of day, etc. There is isomorphism between the two guises: the system follows the substantive rules (e.g. about classes and classrooms) *by virtue of* executing the rules that advert only to formal-syntactic structure.

7.2 Functional analysis

We turn next to a more generic form of scientific theorizing about human cognition, an approach that can provide the materials from which to select and construct a theory of epistemic competence for a set of cognitive systems, such as humans. (In effect, high-church computationalism is one species of this wider genus.) As suggested already, one wants to employ empirical accounts that fairly directly address the issue of how the relevant cognitive systems—by default, humans—do or can manage their epistemic tasks. That is, one wants an account of the cognitive dispositions that humans possess—an account that also affords an understanding of cognitive dispositions humans might acquire with training. Particularly useful here are *functional analyses*: cognitive-scientific accounts of how some relatively sophisticated dispositions involve the structured implementation of dispositions of simpler sorts. The simpler dispositions then provide functional components (not necessarily distinct physical components) from which more sophisticated processes get fashioned through training. (For example, an antecedently possessed process might get selectively inhibited, triggered, or informed by getting 'hitched' to other processes.) This kind of cognitive-scientific understanding begs to be employed in exploring the realities of, and possibilities for, epistemic competence. It has been discussed by a number of philosophers of mind and psychology.

Cummins (1975, 1983) cogently argues that, in order to understand talk of functions, one needs to recognize and understand an explanatory strategy that is distinct from the causal explanation of events. This alternative explanatory strategy allows one to understand *how* a system instantiates a certain property by *analyzing* either that system into interacting components, or the property into simpler properties of that system. Such explanatory analyses are widespread.

One prominent analytical approach is to *analyze the system itself into its components*. A successful analytical explanation would then show how, given the properties of these components and their mode of interaction, the system has the relevant property. Cummins calls such analyses, *compositional explanations*. Biology is replete with examples, such as the compositional analysis of the human circulatory system. A little reflection will reveal that compositional analysis is widespread in the sciences.

The second analytical approach is to *analyze the property, as instantiated* in certain systems. Cummins calls applications of this approach *functional explanations*, when the property analyzed is dispositional. The analysis of dispositions may be pursued in conjunction with a componential analysis of the relevant systems. Physiological analysis in biology often involves both a functional analysis of a disposition or capacity of the system into a set of more modest capacities, and also a componential analysis of the system into distinct subsystems possessing the simpler capacities. But in much recent psychological work functional analysis is pursued without isolating components of the system. Psychologists commonly attempt to discover and analyze human cognitive capacities or dispositions in terms of simpler dispositions, and often attempt to do this without pinning down the neurophysical mechanisms underlying the relevant processes, and without worrying over whether such mechanisms are themselves analyzable into components mirroring the capacities mentioned in the psychological analysis.[14]

Investigators begin with a concern to understand how human beings solve, or at least deal with, certain classes of problems. By analysis, they seek to specify the relevant disposition (or capacity) more clearly, and to understand how it is realized by the implementation of simpler dispositions (or capacities). For example, a central theme in Nisbett and Ross (1980) is that a significant range of human inferential practices and dispositions can be understood in terms of a set of relatively simple inferential strategies—judgmental heuristics—which, while far from foolproof, are at least effective in making many cases tractable. By appreciating how these simpler strategies are applied in context, one understands how human beings 'manage' when confronted with prediction problems, for example, or how they arrive at causal claims.

A virtue of the analytical approach is that it allows one to explain both successful and unsuccessful problem solving. A disposition as analyzed in functional analysis may be generally beneficial for the possessing system, and thus a 'capacity,' to be selectively triggered. But it can also be a general liability, to be widely inhibited. Or it may be a mixed blessing that might aptly be selectively triggered and selectively inhibited. For example, the human capacity to construct, apply, modify, and reapply mental models may prove an analyzable capacity with significant utility for theory development (Nersessian 1992, Johnson-Laird 1983, 2005, 2006). Similarly, strategies by which to localize and then resolve anomalies confronting scientific theories may prove to be analyzable capacities with notable epistemic benefit (Glymour 1980, Darden 1992). In contrast, human beings seem disposed to committing the gambler's fallacy, which is clearly a liability. However, some investigators have argued that the disposition to the gambler's fallacy is best understood in terms of the human tendency to employ a broad heuristic: the representativeness heuristic (Kahneman and Tversky 1972, Nisbett and Ross 1980, Kahneman and Frederick 2005). (In the representativeness heuristic, relatively simple judgments regarding representativeness or 'goodness of fit' are used as a basis for judging the probability of events or states of affairs.) Some reliance on such heuristics is unavoidable for limited creatures such as ourselves, who need tractable ways of dealing with a flood of cognitive tasks; thus the *limited* reliance on such heuristics can be epistemically beneficial (Cherniak 1986). Still, the noncircumspect or unmodulated use of them, the overreliance on them, leads to systematic errors as in the case of the gambler's fallacy. Accordingly, the representativeness heuristic is generally something of a mixed blessing. It becomes a more uniformly beneficial capacity as people are trained to employ it with more than common care.

---

[14] This is not to say that psychologists are, or should be, indifferent to whether their posited psychological capacities can be neurophysiologically realized. Far from it. Rather, the point is that, in their psychological analyses, there need be no suggestion that distinct neurophysiological components are responsible for distinct psychological dispositions, nor is there a suggestion that nondisjunctive neurophysiological components realize what is analyzed as a single psychological disposition. Neurophysiologically salient 'black boxes' need not correspond to psychologically salient ones.

Obviously, all this suggests a place for modulational control, and raises the empirical question of how that control might be managed. Below we will discuss some recent work in cognitive science that speaks to this question, and is also pertinent in other ways to the pursuit of a meliorative theory of epistemic competence.

7.3 Connectionist resources

A related form of theorizing is found in connectionist cognitive science. A connectionist model manages some cognitive task (e.g. recognizing a certain class of physical objects), and thereby provides an account of how that task might be accomplished. Connectionist models account for a given capacity by describing a realizing system—a connectionist network—and a regimen of training (e.g. the widely used training algorithm called 'back propagation of error'). This might lead one to think that connectionist models are themselves rather like componential analyses of a system's capacity, and that perhaps they should be understood as one special sort of componential analysis. However, whereas individual connectionist *models* deploy specific connectionist networks with specific componential structure (really, computational simulations of such networks), nonetheless typical connectionist *theorizing* about the ability of models to perform various tasks is a different matter and proceeds at a different level. In connectionist theorizing there is typically little attention to details regarding particular nodes, particular inter-node connections, or particular weights of particular connections (although these do get specified in a given up-and-running connectionist model). Connectionist theory anticipates robust multiple realizability of system-level tendencies, with each model serving as, in effect, a sub-representational implementation of a given system and capacity; thus, the theorizing that applies to the whole range of these various implementations abstracts away from details of the specific structure of any particular network implementation.

So there is a contrast to be drawn between many capacities best dealt with using connectionist theory and the capacities that typically are the targets of functional analyses. Whereas functional analyses allow one to understand a capacity by decomposing the cognitive task performed into a set of simpler cognitive steps, connectionist networks instead often seem to realize their capacity in a cognitive single step, as the network simply settles into a pattern of activation in reaction to prompting input. (Settling often takes multiple simultaneous updatings of the individual nodes, but these are *subcognitive* 'steps.') It seems likely that one approach may be particularly useful in accounting for certain capacities (which are realized in a stepwise manner), while the other shines in accounting for different capacities (which are realized more immediately).[15] Indeed, connectionism has become a focus of intensive work in

---

[15] It should also be noted that some tasks and processes may be best understood in terms of hybrid accounts in which both approaches (functional analysis and connectionist understandings) are employed in a unified account. Anderson's work with his ACT-R production systems is suggestive (see Lovett and Anderson 2005, for an overview).

large part due to the recalcitrant difficulties that analytical, program-writing cognitive science has experienced in accounting for certain capacities associated with human memory, relevance recognition, and perceptual recognition, for example.[16] Notably, these capacities have an 'almost immediate' phenomenological quality to them.

However, such contrasts should not overshadow the fact that both functionalist analyses and connectionist modeling can help illuminate how cognitive systems manage certain tasks. Accordingly, they are both useful resources in constructing a theory of epistemic competence that will allow one to describe how humans do, and prescribe how they could, employ truth-seeking, postclassically reliable, belief-forming processes.[17]

8 Some relevant work in cognitive science

By way of concretely filling out various points we have so far made fairly abstractly, let us now provide a sampling of pertinent recent work in cognitive science. We will discuss this work in a way that explicitly connects it, as appropriate, to points we have made thus far in this chapter. The work we will now discuss falls fairly clearly under the rubric of functional analysis. It does not clearly fall, or clearly fail to fall, under either high-church computationalism or connectionism, although it is not incompatible with either of those approaches.

8.1 Judgmental heuristics

We have already mentioned (e.g. in section 5 of this chapter) the enormously influential cognitive-science literature on heuristics and biases, work that largely originated with Kahneman and Tversky (1972, 1973) and Kahneman and Tversky (1972). Let us now consider that literature in a bit more detail. In an overview discussion, Kahneman and Frederick (2005) frame matters in a useful way. They suggest that one can think (in a somewhat stylized fashion, perhaps) of two systems of processes. The heuristics (and the biases to which they give rise) may be thought of as a (first) system of fast and automatic processes. There remains a set of cognitive processes, a second system, comprising learnable processes that commonly are slower, more accurate, and more costly. As one attains better understanding of the first system and its plasticity or rigidity, one thereby attains a better understanding of the cognitive chores that it would be epistemically desirable for the second system to manage (thereby exerting inhibitory modulational control over the first system).

---

[16] For general discussions, see Dreyfus and Dreyfus (1986), Horgan and Tienson (1994, 1996). We will revisit some connectionist ideas in Chapter 7.

[17] Some further examples of how cognitive psychological analyses can inform epistemology are provided by the papers in parts I and II of Giere (1992). Examples of the use of connectionist resources can be found in Churchland (1989, 1992).

Of course, there are important and subtle questions to be faced regarding what can be managed this way—regarding what forms of modulational control might be possible in this regard.[18]

It is also an open question whether thinking of these matters in terms of two distinct systems is overly stylized; ultimately a more subtle and complicated picture may be needed.[19] But, in any case, the functional analysis of human cognitive systems will be of great epistemological significance, and the Kahneman/Frederick two-systems proposal is a nice example of such an analysis. Functionally characterized cognitive processes are organized structures employing more or less sophisticated dispositions—dispositions that might be realized variously in different cognitive systems. These different possible systems of cognitive processes would vary in their epistemological desirability along several dimensions. A process or disposition that is an epistemic liability, or a mixed blessing, may become epistemically wonderful when yoked in a system. Functional analysis allows one to explore these possibilities; Kahneman and Frederick's proposed analysis clearly has implications concerning both the nature of epistemic competence and certain liabilities for performance-errors.

---

[18] It is particularly noteworthy that heuristics work by ignoring certain information that might be available to a cognitive system, and that the processes envisioned in Kahneman and Frederick's second system commonly bring into play this richer range of information. Kahneman and Frederick provide a wonderful analogy extending Kahneman, Slovic, and Tversky's (1982) parallel with perceptual illusions (Kahneman and Frederick 2005, pp. 268–9). Notably, they suggest that epistemically objectionable error obtains when the set of processes in play fails to afford the kind of epistemically desirable composite to which humans can reasonably aspire.

[19] As noted, Kahneman and Frederick (2005) provide a 'two-system' framework. We (the authors) do worry that this framework overly stylizes, particularly in its understanding of the role and character of the two distinct systems—one is thought to be automatic, quick, and needing of refinement; the other is thought to be articulate, more cognitively costly, and providing the needed refinement. Their two-system model seems to invite certain ways of thinking about what would make for suitable modulational control (questions that we find central to understanding justificatory processes). In effect, their second system provides an important kind of modulational control. Understanding what modulational control is needed, and what is possible, requires a proper account of both systems. We suspect that although this neat picture may be a useful starting point, it encourages two errors. First, the two dimensions (automatic/articulate and modulationally controlled/controlling) are unlikely to line up so neatly. Indeed, we would argue that much modulational control can be managed by processes that have become 'automatic,' that much information can be accommodated by these automatic processes, and that this can refine processes that operate on explicit information (see the chapters to follow). Second, although relatedly, it seems likely that the various kinds of cognitive processes that figure in the second or modulating system are a sundry lot, and vary across classes of problem cases. Thus, it is controversial whether the empirical data really calls for two distinct systems, or is better treated in terms of a diversity of interacting processes that are not best thought of as constituting two distinct systems. Sloman's (1996) review discussion presents a brief for the two-system view, while Osman's (2004) review presents an opposing brief. We certainly are not committed to the two-system view (although it is admittedly heuristically useful). As noted, we find ourselves at odds with the common suggestion that the simple first system is quick and cognitively inarticulate whereas the modulational control provided by the second system turns on slow and cognitively costly processes. Important forms of modulational control deploy fast processes. Also, sophisticated reasoning often deploys much implicit information. These points are developed in the chapters to follow.

8.2 Fast and frugal decision processes

Gigerenzer and Hoffrage (1995) argue that some of the epistemic flaws in human cognitive dispositions (such as the neglect of base-rate information in statistical reasoning) are largely avoidable merely by adopting the practice of framing information in terms that are more readily used by humans (say, in terms of sampling frequencies rather than probabilities). This suggests a form of modulational control that seems relatively feasible: unless the agent is prepared to systematically deploy Bayes' Theorem, the agent should insist on sampling frequencies rather than probabilities. This in turn requires less need for oversight by processes such as those envisioned in Kahneman and Frederick's 'second system,' provided that information relevant to modulational control is supplied to the first system in congenial formats. Perhaps so. But the need for modulational control has not been eliminated. For, Gigerenzer and Hoffrage's own suggestion envisions a form of modulational control—one that modulates the input on which human cognitive systems operate. It suggests this: when a human cognitive agent is not prepared to deploy sophisticated computation involving Bayes' Theorem, information regarding the case at hand should be transformed into a format that is more readily used without bias.

Gigerenzer and Hoffrage's work, and related work by others (see Gigerenzer 2007; Gigerenzer and Selten 2002), suggest that certain *fast and frugal* processes—relatively simple and undemanding dispositions—call for less, or different forms of, modulational control than has been suggested in the vast heuristics-and-biases literature. Kahneman and Frederick (2005, p. 279) express misgivings, however, arguing that the results involving frequency-formats and the like can readily be accommodated within the heuristics and biases approach. (For a useful discussion of the dispute, see Samuels, Stich, and Bishop 2002.) The empirical resolution of these issues will provide rich materials, and many lessons, for an informed understanding of human epistemic competence.

Let us now briefly consider the work of Gigerenzer and his collaborators, in a way that focuses specifically on the matter of *suitable modulational control*, and also on the matter of different kinds of *reliability* (local, global, and transglobal). Gigerenzer (2007) has advanced a case for fast and frugal decision processes. At times, he and others (see Gigerenzer and Selten 2002) suggest that at least some of these heuristics are normatively fitting without much in the way of modulation. Two coordinate questions become important, at this dialectical juncture. First, there is the question of how the fast and frugal heuristics are themselves best described and understood. This will reveal what epistemic risks and benefits they offer. Second, there is the question of how susceptible they are to tractable modulation.

For concreteness, consider the *recognition heuristic*: an agent relies on the recognition of items as a cue for judging which have some property of interest. For example, the agent might be presented with a list of pairs of cities in the United States and asked to judge which member of each pair has the larger population. An agent using the recognition heuristic would judge that the city that is recognized by name is the larger, when recognizing just one of the cities in a given pair. But the agent using just the recognition heuristic would then have no opinion when both or neither member of a given pair is recognized. Or, in another studied application, one using the recognition heuristic tends to judge the promise of stocks in which one might invest by projecting that the recognized companies will do better than the unrecognized companies. Obviously, this fast and frugal process could work only when the agent has sufficiently little information on which to proceed that the heuristic yields verdicts—if agents recognize most of the options, the heuristic yields few verdicts, so apparently other processes would need to be employed by agents with richer sets of background information.

This fast and very frugal process can be reasonably reliable. Surprisingly, perhaps, in application to questions such as those mentioned above (relative city size, or investment prospects), the recognition heuristic commonly outperforms processes that employ much more information (Gigerenzer 2007, pp. 26–39). Yet, obviously, this recognition heuristic is reliable only regarding matters on which there is significant correlation between the subject of the conjecture (population size, economic prospects, and the like) and the prevalence of information about the items (the cities, the corporations) in the agent's social environment. In such conditions, the process has what Gigerenzer terms 'ecological rationality'—it will be reliable in that environment on that topic due to the information on which it relies and the structure or significance of such information in that environment (Gigerenzer 2008, p. 7–9, see also Kahneman and Frederick 2005, p. 270). Ecological rationality is, in effect, local reliability on a specific kind of question.[20]

So the recognition heuristic is locally reliable, *given* the circumstances just noted. Global reliability then depends on whether such local environmental circumstances obtain widely in the agent's global environment. This clearly is not so for all questions on which the recognition heuristic might (for good or bad) be employed. Rather, the global reliability of the process as applied depends on whether, and to what degree, it can be, and is, deployed selectively; specifically, the global reliability depends on whether the process is applied selectively on matters regarding which there are, in the agent's environment, a correlation between items being mentioned in social context and the property in question. Without modulational control, therefore, the recognition heuristic is not globally reliable, and would often not be locally reliable. If the recognition heuristic cannot be fittingly modulated by wider information, it will lack transglobal and global reliability—and commonly, local reliability. Under these circumstances, it should not be thought of as a part of human epistemic competence.

Can the heuristic be modulated by some informed sensibility about the likelihood of significant correlation between the subject matter and messages concerning the items in question? To illustrate the sort of sensibility one might envision, we offer a conjecture regarding a case of such informed use. Suppose that the subjects were asked

---

[20] It then involves local reliability both in our sense—with respect to a local environment—and in Goldman's earlier sense—with respect to a restricted issue (from among those on which the process in question might be put to work).

to pick out which city in the presented pairs were the smaller. We doubt that they would choose the recognized cities as the smaller. On the contrary! They then would be employing the heuristic in an *adjusted* fashion, one informed implicitly by what correlations are likely. Or suppose that one has just taken several courses on rural populations and economies—or perhaps related issues have become a political topic of moment in national political contests. One should be sensitive to such facts, and that they should inhibit one's using the fast and frugal process in question. Being subject to such inhibitory modulational control clearly enhances the global reliability of the recognition heuristic. Much the same can be said about its transglobal reliability: unless the process is modulated by transglobally reliably produced information about matters such as those just mentioned, it will not have significant transglobal reliability. If it is modulated by transglobally reliably produced information about such matters, then it is arguably postclassically reliable.

As it turns out, there is an empirical basis for thinking that the several heuristics we have been discussing *are* under significant modulational control. People do tend to rely on the recognition heuristic only in cases where there is correlation between recognition and the matter in question (Gigerenzer 2008, pp. 25–7). Gigerenzer also discusses a 'take-the-best' heuristic, in which one attends to a single indicator (the best or most strongly correlated indicator on which one has information) of some feature, even when possessing information about multiple indicators. This heuristic can perform reasonably well in comparison to alternative processes when the best indicator is significantly better than the others, and it can generalize to new cases so as to be more predictive than regression results that are clearly more cognitively costly to obtain (Gigerenzer 2008, pp. 32–42). Subjects who are given feedback regarding the success of their predictions come to rely more heavily on the take-the-best heuristic when it is ecologically rational, and rely less on it when it is not.[21]

8.3 Mental models

Johnson-Laird and collaborators (Johnson-Laird 1983, Johnson-Laird, et al. 1999, Johnson-Laird 2005) have undertaken important work on mental models and reasoning. This work suggests a related possibility for cognitive improvement: if mental models representing possibilities of interest are 'tagged with their absolute frequencies or chances' within a population, then simple mathematical manipulations become both relatively intuitive and tractable (Johnson-Laird 2005, pp. 197–8).

This line of empirical work clearly bears on the question of what modulational control is fitting, in connection with inductive reasoning. Johnson-Laird and Byrne

---

[21] For reasons that will become clearer in following chapters, we do not think that such sensitivity, such modulation, need be managed by conscious processes or explicit mental representations. Gigerenzer recognizes that this deployment of heuristics can be managed in a kind of cognitive background: 'Research suggests that people hardly ever make conscious decisions about which heuristic to use but that they quickly and unconsciously tend to adapt heuristics to changing environments, provided there is feedback' (2008, p. 38).

(2002) suggest that a range of information can modulate implicit inductive reasoning by affecting which kinds of mental models (on their account) one constructs and manipulates in such reasoning. The processes in question are said to be 'rapid and automatic.'[22] To the extent that this work is vindicated, it will provide an important resource for a theory of competence.[23]

9 Conclusion

One can think of the present book as a whole as comprising two 'methods' chapters, each followed by some implementation of the methods characterized. Chapter 2 provided an account of philosophical reflection that yields low-grade a priori justification. Chapters 3 through 5 then involved an extended case study—reflection on the concept of epistemic justification. The present chapter constitutes the second methodological moment—characterizing the naturalizing of epistemology in terms of the E-spectrum and a representative product: a rich theory of epistemic competence. The following chapters will now provide some naturalized epistemological work, situated midway on the E-spectrum, drawing on some general ideas found by looking over the shoulders of those doing cognitive science.

---

[22] See also references in Johnson-Laird (2005), pp. 199–200.
[23] Some further examples of how cognitive psychological analyses can inform epistemology are provided by the papers in parts I and II of Giere (1992). Examples of the use of connectionist resources can be found in Churchland (1989, 1992).

7

An Expanded Conception of Epistemically Relevant Cognitive Processes: the Role of Morphological Content

1 Overview

In this chapter we argue that much epistemological work has been committed to an unrealistic and implausible understanding of what sorts of cognitive processes would make for being justified in holding a belief. The concept of epistemic justification is such that an account of being so justified must be psychologically committing: it must include a conception of what human belief-fixing processes should be like. This is a matter of work up and down the E-spectrum. Thus, epistemologists cannot help but commit themselves on psychological matters when developing an understanding of what makes for objective epistemic justification. The pivotal point is this: to the extent that ought implies can (a claim elaborated in preceding chapters), an account of which processes are objectively justificatory—i.e. an account of those processes by which one ought to form beliefs—implies that human processes *can* conform to the given account. It is just here that we have misgivings regarding much epistemology. We argue that epistemologists are commonly committed to a mistaken family of conceptions of how humans can manage well their epistemic chores. We identify the relevant psychological commitments—characterizing them as variants of a psychological 'proto-theory' that we label *PT*—and we diagnose the ways in which such conceptions are unrealistic from the perspective of cognitive science.

One component of our critique has to do with holistic dimensions of belief-fixation. There are myriad, highly holistic, evidential-support relations among various intentional states of an epistemic agent—states like beliefs and sensory-perceptual seemings. Postclassically reliable belief-forming processes must be sensitive to—in some sense, must 'mirror'—such holistic relations of evidential support. We argue that processes called for by *PT* and its near kin are in principle incapable of managing such sensitivity. Yet humans can and often do manage these holistic chores, and doing so is epistemically necessary. So, any account of justification committed to *PT* or its near kin will be both normatively and descriptively wrong.

These are the main critical themes of the present chapter. However, this chapter has a more positive, constructive side in which we develop certain general points regarding what epistemically apt and justificatory processes are like. In so doing, we will focus on important apparent lessons about human cognition that have emerged from recent cognitive science. Concerning cognitive science, our principal themes will be (1) the cluster of persistent difficulties in modeling human cognition known collectively as 'the frame problem' (closely related to the holistic dimension of belief-fixation mentioned above), and (2) an important apparent moral of the frame problem, namely that human cognition—including the processing that generates and sustains beliefs—apparently accommodates enormous amounts of evidentially relevant information without explicitly representing this information. What emerges is a view of human epistemic competence, of objectively justificatory human belief-fixing processes, according to which much of the epistemic action, much of what contributes to one's systematic successes, lies below the readily accessible 'surface' of one's cognition—in ways that we seek to make clear here. These considerations lead fairly directly to a conception of epistemology as having two legitimate, and complementary, foci. One focus should be the traditional one: psychological factors that are conscious during belief formation, and/or are readily psychologically accessible after the fact, as epistemologically relevant. And the other focus should be the full set of epistemologically relevant psychological factors, many of which may be only partially, piecemeal-fashion, accessible after the fact of belief-formation. We call this conception *iceberg epistemology*; the idea is that the conscious and consciously accessible aspects of belief formation are just the tip of a larger iceberg of epistemologically relevant psychological factors.

2 Transglobal reliabilism and evidence-sensitivity: a bridge

In Chapters 3–5 we argued, in a low-grade a priori manner, in favor of transglobal reliabilism concerning epistemic justification. It is a conceptually grounded necessary truth, we claim, that in order to be epistemically justified, a belief must be the product of belief-forming processes that are postclassically reliable—i.e. transglobally reliable under suitable modulational control.

In Chapter 6 we described a spectrum comprising various complementary forms of inquiry in epistemology. At one end of the spectrum is low-grade a priori reasoning aimed at uncovering conceptually grounded necessary truths; at the other end is inquiry that is highly informed by results and hypotheses from cognitive science. Conclusions reached at different locations within this spectrum typically exert constraining influence on inquiry at other locations. And most such conclusions are defeasible—even low-grade a priori conclusions concerning claims that are put forward as conceptually grounded necessary truths.

In the remainder of this book we will take up a variety of further issues concerning epistemic justification, over and above our earlier defense of transglobal reliabilism. These issues arise quite naturally in light of transglobal reliabilism itself, and what we say about them will mesh well with transglobal reliabilism in a variety of ways. Some portions of what follows will draw heavily on reflective common sense, in an armchair-conductable manner; these aspects of the discussion will be situated well toward the low-grade a priori end of the E-spectrum.[1] Other portions, however, will draw fairly heavily on results and developments within cognitive science, some of which go well beyond what can be accomplished from the armchair just by relying on one's conceptual competence and on reflective common sense. And considerations of both kinds will exert mutual constraining influence on another, as is to be expected in light of our discussion in Chapter 6 of the E-spectrum.

Our goal in the present section is to explain how our defense of transglobal reliabilism in Chapters 3–5 leads naturally into, and makes contact with, the material to follow. Also, we seek to do so in a way that highlights how different aspects of the subsequent discussion will be situated at different locations on the E-spectrum.

One important kind of question for epistemology that arises in light of transglobal reliabilism concerns the cognitive-architecture features of belief-forming agents who have large-scale belief systems like those of humans, and (more specifically) the pertinent cognitive-architecture features of humans themselves. What sort of 'engineering design' for belief-forming cognition is tractably implementable via the kinds of physical resources that are present inside a human skull, on one hand, and on the other hand yields belief-forming processes that are postclassically reliable? We will call this the *generic architectural-engineering question*.

A partial answer to this question emerged already, directly as a product of low-grade a priori reflection: namely that an appropriate engineering design for truth-seeking needs to exhibit a significant degree of modulational control. That is, some of the specific belief-forming processes possessed by the cognitive agent need to be linked to wider control-mechanisms that can, when appropriate in context, trigger the use of these specific processes, or inhibit their use, and the like. But one can press further in one's inquiry about effective truth-seeking cognitive-architectural engineering: one can ask whether there is some generic feature that would be common to such

---

[1] The category of the low-grade a priori is somewhat vague. For certain kinds of common-sensical reasoning that can be effectively conducted from the armchair, there need not be a determinate fact of the matter about whether such reasoning counts as low-grade a priori itself, or instead counts as falling outside this category and yet still close to the low-grade a priori end of the E-spectrum. (Being vague in this way, the category is also susceptible to various contextually appropriate partial resolutions of its vagueness: sometimes one can decide to treat a given form of armchair-performable reasoning as belonging—or as not belonging—to this category, depending on one's dialectical purposes in context.)

modulational-control mechanisms in virtue of which their operation makes for enhanced transglobal reliability in the processes they modulate.

A very natural answer to this question, one that arises via reflective common-sensical reasoning conductable near the low-grade a priori end of the E-spectrum, is this. What effective modulational-control mechanisms have in common is that they are systematically sensitive to *evidence* that is available to the cognitive agent and that bears upon the contextually specific reliability of the processes to which these modulational mechanisms are coupled. Modulational-control mechanisms are sensitive to, and are responsive to, such evidence.

The generic architectural-engineering question is much like the question about what common cognitive-architectural feature makes for effective modulational control, but is yet more general in scope. What is being sought is some over-arching characteristic, built into the cognitive engineering-design of humans and human-like cognitive agents, that undergirds the systematic postclassical reliability of the agents' competence-based belief-forming processes. And once again, a very natural and overwhelmingly plausible answer presents itself, via commonsensical reasoning that can be performed in the armchair: namely that such an agent's competence-reflecting belief-forming processes are systematically *sensitive to the net evidential import* of the information the agent possesses. That is, with respect to any proposition p that is candidate for being believed, the agent's processes are sensitive to the overall extent of evidential support that accrues to p, relative to the whole body of information available to the agent. The processes work in such a way that they reliably tend to generate beliefs when, and only when, those beliefs have propositional contents that are evidentially well supported by the net information possessed by the agent.

This conclusion arises in the armchair, as we said—via a mode of reasoning that is close to the low-grade a priori end of the E-spectrum. The operative form of reasoning is abductive, and could be called 'inference to the only remotely plausible explanation.' Such an inference is defeasible: in principle, there could turn out to be some alternative cognitive-engineering design that deploys processes that generate beliefs as extensive as those of normal humans, and that somehow manages to be postclassically reliable without tracking evidential relations among items of information possessed by the agent. Likewise, in principle it could turn out that such an alternative form of cognitive engineering is instantiated in humans themselves. But meanwhile, unless and until such an alternative actually gets articulated and actually gets shown capable of doing the job, the defeasible conclusion remains undefeated, and remains overwhelmingly plausible: belief-forming processes, in order to be postclassically reliable, need to be systematically sensitive to the net evidential import of information available to the epistemic agent.[2]

---

[2] One could consider going further and making yet stronger claims, such as these: (1) it is a conceptually grounded necessary truth that systematic evidence-sensitivity in one's belief-forming processes is a constitutive requirement for doxastic justification; and (2) this constitutive requirement is conceptually more fundamental than is the constitutive requirement of postclassical reliability. Although we do not make such

So our earlier emphasis on postclassical reliability as a constitutive requirement for justified belief is not at all in tension with our emphasis, in the material below, on the epistemological importance of evidential relations and on evidence-sensitivity in belief-formation. On the contrary, the former fits hand-in-glove with the latter, because evidence-sensitivity provides the only plausible answer to 'How possibly?' questions concerning the cognitive-architectural implementation of postclassical reliability. We realize, of course, that in the recent epistemology literature, self-described advocates of 'evidentialism' about justification (e.g. Conee and Feldman 2004) have often positioned themselves in opposition to reliabilism. But the kinds of scenarios they tend to offer as challenges to reliabilism are ones that make trouble for classical and neoclassical versions but not for transglobal reliabilism. And this is no accident, because these are scenarios of two kinds: first, ones in which the belief-forming process happens to be reliable even though the evidence available to the agent suggests otherwise (as in our own cases of Ashley the Valley girl and paranoid Harry), and second, ones in which the agent forms beliefs on the basis of excellent evidence even though the operative belief-forming processes happen to be unreliable (as in our own case of brain-envatted Constance). Get your version of reliabilism right, and the requirement of evidence-sensitivity emerges directly from it (rather than being in tension with it).

Transglobal reliabilism leads naturally to a second general question, which will also figure importantly below. What kinds of cognitive-architectural structures and mechanisms can exhibit systematic evidence-sensitivity on one hand, while yet on the other hand also being tractably implementable in creatures with cognitive resource-constraints on the order of the resource-constraints that apply to humankind? Important aspects of this question, as well as potentially promising answers to it, reside at a position on the E-spectrum that is well toward the end that incorporates cognitive science. We will argue below that this question arises in a stark and dramatic way in light of a deeply recalcitrant, in-principle looking, difficulty that has persistently plagued attempts to model human cognition within the framework of computational cognitive science—the so-called 'frame problem.' We also will argue, via appeal to considerations residing at various different locations on the E-spectrum, that the frame problem reveals that a common—indeed prima facie common-sensical—psychological proto-theory, one that is arguably at work (at least implicitly) in much traditional epistemology and also in much of cognitive science, looks to be radically mistaken by virtue of its inability to tractably accommodate the kind of holistic evidence-sensitivity that is required for cognitively competent belief-formation. We will also argue that frame-problem considerations reveal the need for a form of cognitive processing that is

claims in this book, our discussion in the book is almost entirely compatible with them. The principal exception is what we say in section 3 of the present chapter, to the effect that (i) doxastic justification is conceptually more fundamental than propositional justification, and (ii) propositional justification is characterizable counterfactually in terms of doxastic justification. For some elaboration and defense of a position that embraces claims along the lines of (1) and (2) but otherwise is compatible with what we say in this book—a position we call 'transglobal evidentialism-reliabilism'—see Henderson, Horgan, and Potrč (2007).

quite different from standard computational information-manipulation, and that involves a quite different mode of information-possession ('morphological content'). We will sketch a promising-looking way that this alternative conception of holistic, holistically evidence-sensitive, cognition might be implementable, involving appeal to theoretical and mathematical ideas drawn from connectionist modeling in cognitive science.

A third general question which arises quite naturally, in light of transglobal reliabilism itself together with the two questions already mentioned in the present section, also will be addressed below. What is the overall structure of evidential-support relations among information-carrying states and structures in an epistemic agent's cognitive system, and how does this structure bear upon the justificatory status of the agent's beliefs? This general issue has loomed large in much traditional epistemology, for instance in debates among advocates of three traditional competing positions concerning the overall structure of a system of justified beliefs: foundationalism, coherentism, and structural contextualism. In the discussion to follow in Chapter 8, however, the issue of the overall structure of evidential-support relations will be addressed in a way that exhibits important differences from the dialectical contours of the traditional debate. We will advocate an approach to the global structure of evidential support that widens the range of items in the network by incorporating morphological content, and that accommodates key elements from all three of the traditional approaches—foundationalism, coherentism, and structural contextualism.

In sum, transglobal reliabilism leads very naturally to several intertwined and epistemologically important questions about evidential support, and about how evidence-sensitive belief-formation can be implemented via forms of information processing that are tractable and psychologically realistic. Such questions will be our concern in the remainder of this book.

3 Reliabilism, evidential support and the being/having distinction

A distinction commonly made in recent epistemology, which will figure importantly below, is between *having justification* for a proposition *p* (sometimes called *propositional* justification), and *being justified* in believing *p* (sometimes called *doxastic* justification). In this section we will explain how we propose to understand this distinction, given transglobal reliabilism and given our remarks in the preceding section.

On our approach there are two complementary descriptive levels from which matters of epistemic justification can be addressed. One is what we will call the *constitutive* level, at which the focus is on what is constitutively required for justification. (The key constitutive requirement we have emphasized, of course, is postclassical reliability.) The other is what we will call the *cognitive-architectural* level, at which the focus is on evidential-support relations and on belief-forming psychological processes that exhibit sensitivity to these relations. (The connection between the constitutive-level requirement of postclassical reliability on one hand, and on the other hand the cognitive-architectural-level stress on sensitivity to wide ranges of evidential support relations, was discussed in the previous section.) The having/being distinction arises with respect to both descriptive levels.

We first consider the distinction from the constitutive level. One might wonder whether the having/being distinction is just irrelevant for reliablists. After all, invoking such a distinction might encourage the thought that one can begin with an idea of the justification had, itself understood prior to, and independent of, an understanding of what it would be to *be justified*. However, for a reliabilist, justification had cannot be understood independently of what processes and input would make for being justified.

Reliabilism does give pride of place to belief-forming processes, and to being justified: a constitutive requirement for an agent's belief that p to be justified, according to reliabilism, is that the belief has been produced by a relevantly reliable belief-forming process. But this still leaves room for an intelligible and potentially useful notion of justification having, albeit one that is not conceptually independent of reliability. Having justification for a proposition p, according to reliabilism, is to be understood *counterfactually* in terms of reliable processes: it is a matter of possessing information I and a reliable belief-forming process Π such that (i) if Π were to be applied to I, then the result would be a belief that p, and (ii) its not being the case that one possesses further information $I^\star$ and a reliable belief-forming process Ω (perhaps Π itself) such that, if Ω were to be applied to $I+I^\star$, then Ω either would produce a belief that not-p or would produce a state of suspended judgment about p.[3] (See also, Henderson, Horgan, and Potrč 2008.) Alvin Goldman (1986) calls this 'ex ante' justification, whereas an actually-held belief that is doxastically justified has 'ex post' justification.) Reliability of belief-forming processes is treated as fundamental within the reliabilist perspective, and as the key constitutive requirement for being justified—whereas having justification is treated as a derivative attribute that is characterizable counterfactually in terms of process reliability.[4]

---

[3] The notion of *possession* here invoked is plausibly somewhat context-sensitive, especially with respect to possessed processes. Depending upon one's specific purposes in engaging in normative-epistemic evaluation, one might be relatively liberal or relatively conservative in what one counts as an agent's 'possessing' a process-type (or an item of information) when one is assessing one of the agent's beliefs for its justification-status. Pertinent to this matter are the different dimensions of idealization that can figure in the notion of epistemic competence, discussed in sections 3 and 4 of Chapter 6.

[4] On the other hand, within the perspective of transglobal evidentialism-reliabilism (cf. note 2), justification-having (i.e. propositional justification) is treated as conceptually prior to being justified (i.e. doxastic justification). Nonetheless, transglobal evidentialism-reliabilism embraces all the same claims about conceptually-grounded necessary truths as does transglobal reliabilism—e.g. the claims (a) that it is a conceptually grounded necessary truth that a belief is doxastically justified only if it is produced by a postclassically reliable process, and (b) that it is a conceptually grounded necessary truth that a potential belief-content p is propositionally justified (for an agent A) only if it meets the conditions specified in the paragraph to which the present footnote is appended.

It is commonly held that having justification for p is a necessary condition for being justified in believing p but not a sufficient condition, and also that another necessary condition is that one believes p *because of* the justification one has for p. Both claims get honored by the counterfactual construal of justification-having, at least for versions of reliabilism that incorporate the requirement of suitable modulational control. The first claim is honored because the belief that p cannot be the *actual* product of a process that is reliable under modulational control unless the counterfactual requirements are met that are constitutive of having justification for p. (If condition (ii) for justification-having fails to obtain, then one's modulational-control mechanisms should inhibit the process Π from operating on the information I to produce a belief that p.) The second claim is honored too, because a constitutive requirement for being justified is that one's belief that p was actually generated by a process Π that has operated on information I, where Π and I meet the conditions definitive for one's having justification for p. (One's belief that p came about via process-type Π operating on information I, and not in some other way—which is a natural construal of the claim that the belief was formed *because* of the justification-had for p.)

We turn now to the cognitive-architectural level of description, with its focus on matters of evidence and evidence-sensitive cognition. Here the central issue is how having justification and being justified, respectively, are *implemented* cognitive-architecturally, rather than on their constitutive natures. From this perspective, having justification for p is plausibly viewed as comprising these conditions: (i) possessing a body of information I whose net evidential import is strongly in support of p, (ii) having the cognitive-architectural capacity to appreciate that the net evidential import of I is strongly in support of p, and (iii) not possessing further information $I^\star$ such that (iii.a) the net evidential import of $I+I^\star$ is not strongly in support of p, and (iii.b) one has the cognitive-architectural capacity to appreciate that the net evidential import of $I+I^\star$ is not strongly in support of p.[5]

This formulation is deliberately couched in a way that takes into account the cognitive-architectural capacities of the agent. Thus, if an epistemic agent happens to possess information that on one hand evidentially supports some proposition, but on the other hand is such that this evidential-support relation is not one that can be appreciated by members of the pertinent class of agents to which the given agent belongs, then this support-relation does not count as evidence *for the agent*—and thus does not figure into the proposed cognitive-architectural-level characterization of justification-having.

The cognitive-architectural implementation of being justified, as one would expect, bears a relation to the implementation of having-justification that is much like the relation between being and having that obtains at the constitutive level of description. Being justified is a matter of having a body of information I that meets the lately

---

[5] The remarks in note 3 apply again here, mutatis mutandis.

mentioned conditions (i)–(iii) vis-à-vis the proposition p (so that one has justification for p), plus believing p because of one's appreciation of the strong evidential support that I confers upon p.

Our principal focus in the remainder of this book will be on matters of evidential support and evidence-sensitive belief-formation. Thus, when we invoke the having/being distinction, it will be mainly at the cognitive-architectural level of description, with an eye on matters of cognitive-architectural implementation. But it should be borne in mind that having justification and being justified both are also characterizable, at the constitutive level of description, in reliabilist terms—and more specifically in terms of the notion of postclassical reliability. Because the issues to be addressed in the remainder of this book will primarily involve the implementation level, however, postclassical reliability will reside largely behind the scenes in the discussion to follow.

Being justified in believing a proposition p involves two factors: first, having adequate evidence for one's belief that p, and second, believing that p because of the evidence one has for p. This is a causal/explanatory 'because': in some suitable way, the pertinent information and the pertinent evidential-support relations need to be causally operative in the actual generation of the belief—causally operative in a manner that somehow 'mirrors' the evidential-support relations. Having justification for a belief one holds does not by itself render the agent justified in holding that belief, because the agent might hold the belief for epistemically objectionable reasons (rather than holding it because of the evidence for it that the agent happens to possess).

Our focal question in the present chapter is this: What constitutes the appropriate kind of causal etiology of a belief, in order for the agent to be justified in holding it? Accounts of what it is to be justified in believing cannot evade this question, and must be informative regarding the cognitive processes which would make for the appropriate etiology of a belief, as this is just what distinguishes being justified from merely having justification. Saying something about what can count as being caused 'in the right way' is central to the business of this chapter.

Hereafter in the book, as before, when we speak of epistemic justification we will mean *objective* justification rather than the subjective kind. And, in accordance with common recent usage, we will sometimes refer to justification-had for a given proposition p as *propositional* justification, and to being justified in holding a given belief as *doxastic* justification—although we will often deploy the terminology of 'having' and 'being' instead.

4 A proto-theory of human belief-generating and belief-sustaining processes

Unfortunately, the psychological implications of accounts of doxastic justification remain largely unmentioned in the work of many epistemologists. As a result, the psychological plausibility of those same accounts remains likewise ill-attended-to.

While one can tentatively tease out the apparent psychological implications of various discussions, it must be acknowledged that epistemological inquiry would be more straightforward, were the implications more forthrightly addressed by various authors. What, for example, is 'the mirroring relation' that must obtain between the evidential relations articulated in an epistemological account of propositional justification, and the psychological processes that figure in the correlative epistemological account of doxastic justification? Because such questions typically are not explicitly addressed, the psychological plausibility of various epistemological accounts is unclear. But because that relationship is important, these accounts are problematic. At best, they are incomplete. At worst, inappropriate or unworkable psychological implications are being swept under the rug.

The failure of epistemologists to address the psychological commitments of their theories is only a small part of the problem. If epistemologists were to do this, they would find that much epistemology tends toward one substantive general picture, or 'proto-theory,' of what the relevant psychological processing is like (or to a set of closely related pictures). The proto-theory is more or less implicitly taken for granted in much of the discussion of the competing epistemological positions such as foundationalism and coherentism. Its assumptions seem to us to have engendered several problematic limitations. Our task in this section is to articulate the proto-theory, in order to challenge it in later sections.

The proto-theory can be formulated as follows:

PT

PT(1). The psychological states that are relevant to doxastic justification—and thus, the psychological states that must be causally operative in the processes that make for being justified—are accessible to the agent. This is roughly to say that the relevant information possessed by the agent could be accessed in a fashion adequate for a reconstructive articulation of the agent's propositional justification.

PT(2). In cases where an agent is justified in holding a given belief, the causal structure of the belief-fixing processes (the generating and sustaining processes) are *occurrently isomorphic* to the evidential structure featured in the agent's propositional justification. This is to say, the relevant psychological states are *occurrent*, and they generate or sustain the belief in a way that mirrors the way in which they evidentially support the belief.

PT is intended to encapsulate a central tendency to which epistemologists have been drawn. We will soon wish to distinguish some prominent variations of it.

PT requires that the epistemically relevant psychological states—those whose appropriate causal involvement is required for justification—be accessible. This does not of itself entail that the justificatory relation between these states and the agent's belief be accessible itself (or even that it supervenes only on what is accessible)— although some epistemologists might well have committed themselves to this stronger claim too. Also, *PT* does not entail that the epistemic agent has conscious access to evidential-support relations among the epistemically relevant psychological states (even though the states themselves must be consciously accessible); nor, therefore, does *PT* entail that the agent is able to actually articulate the propositional justification that the agent possesses. (Again, however, some epistemologists might be committed, at least implicitly, to one or both of these claims.)

PT has considerable prima facie plausibility. After all, it is initially very plausible that the evidence one possesses in support of a current, occurrent, belief must itself be either conscious or at least consciously accessible—as asserted in *PT*(1). And initially it is very hard to see *how else* one could make adequate sense of the idea of holding a belief 'because of' the evidence one possesses, *except* by construing this 'because'-relation in terms of occurrent isomorphism between the causal generation of the belief on one hand, and the propositional justification for it on the other hand—as asserted in *PT*(2). So one would expect that *PT* is widely held.[6]

5 Examples of commitment to PT

While we can point to examples where *PT* seems to be at work, we will not attempt to document in a decisive and fully representative fashion its ubiquity in epistemology. After all, the suggestion here is that *PT* is a *pervasive assumption* that is honored in a range of epistemologies. Documenting its working in any one case requires careful attention to nuances of what is said and not said in the relevant texts. Such fine-grained textual analysis, for a thoroughly representative sample of authors, is beyond what can be undertaken here. In place of such demonstration we rely mainly (a) on setting out *PT*, expecting that it will seem familiar to those accustomed to thinking along lines that are standard in contemporary epistemology, and (b) mentioning (below) several examples where *PT* seems operative. These examples provide some indication of (but are not intended as decisive evidence of) the pervasiveness of *PT*. The examples, once set forth, will also bring with them some immediately evident reasons to think that *PT* is psychologically unrealistic—a theme that will surface several times in the present section and will be developed at some length below.

5.1 *Moser*

Paul Moser (1989) provides a fairly clear example of *PT*. Much of Moser's discussion has to do with the concept of propositional justification—with the evidence one has for a proposition, where items of evidence are construed as the 'truth-indicators' one has (1989, p. 35). As Moser recognizes, a different notion of justification is in play when one talks of someone 'being justified in believing' a given proposition, and it is this

---

[6] A related temptation to accept *PT* derives from using what can readily be elicited in the context of giving justification for a belief as a model for both propositional justification and justificatory processes. This is not to deny that such contexts can provide important data for epistemological reflection, but this resource can be used in an overly mechanical way. (See also Henderson 1994a, 1994b and Henderson and Horgan 2000b.)

second matter that is directly required for a belief's being a bit of knowledge (pp. 45, 151–8). (This second notion of justification—doxastic justification—is our central concern here.) To begin with, to be justified in believing a given proposition, one is required to have justification-as-evidence for that proposition. And Moser's analysis of justification-as-evidence is characterized by a particularly robust internalism—one that requires that the states that make for justification be more than simply accessible. On Moser's analysis, if one has justification for *P* at t, the justifying states must either be occurrent states of awareness at t, or dispositions resulting from the earlier operation of such occurrent states. His analysis of what it is to be justified in believing something then comes to inherit this robust internalism. This much is clearly stronger than, and implies, *PT*(1). It suggests something of the 'occurrent isomorphism' of *PT*(2)—a suggestion that is borne out by Moser's insistence that the causal aspects of doxastic justification involve a 'causal significance' of an *awareness* of an 'association relation' between the proposition believed and its 'justifying evidence' (pp. 156–7), where that association relation is itself established by a causal interaction of awareness-states (pp. 141–2). Doxastic justification thus requires a causal interaction of *awareness* states—paradigmatic occurrent states—a causal interaction that is isomorphic to the evidential-support relations that make for propositional justification. (To this, Moser has added the flourish that the causal relations are themselves mediated by further occurrent, conscious, intentional states—awarenesses of the evidential relations between the agent's belief and the evidence possessed. Here, it seems, Moser views cognitive processing down to the most detailed level relevant to epistemic justification as a structure of occurrent contentful states; and again, it is required to be isomorphic to the normative structure of having justification.) In all this, the central model informing Moser's analysis seems to be that of occurrent states interacting causally in a manner mirroring the evidential relations described in his analysis of justification-as-evidence. This amounts to a particularly clear example of *PT*(2).

5.2 Audi

The discussion of epistemic justification by Robert Audi (1993) is characterized by a laudable concern for a psychologically realistic epistemology, with the result that psychological presumptions are commonly relatively close to the surface in his discussions. As a foundationalist, Audi focuses largely on the generation of perceptually induced beliefs, and it is here that his discussion seems most psychologically committal. His 'modest foundationalism' posits the following sort of sequence (a sort that is fairly typical of what foundationalists commonly take as epistemically relevant processing). First a *perceptual state* occurs; using an example of Audi's (p. 130): working in my study in the evening, I 'see a headlight beam cross my window.' This immediately induces in me a *perceptual belief* 'that a car's light is moving out there.' This perceptually induced belief is taken to be epistemologically basic and to arise 'directly' out of the perceptual state. This is to say that, from the point of view of epistemologically relevant psychological processes, the link between the perceptual states and the perceptual belief is a direct causal one. Finally, on the basis of this belief and other beliefs that I antecedently possess, I may inferentially generate yet further beliefs—ones that are *non-direct and non-basic*. For example, 'that someone has entered my driveway.' The generation of these further beliefs need not be simple—they can be the joint result of the interaction of many informational states (including beliefs) in addition to the perceptual beliefs.

To relate another example, I perceive a 'distinctive patter outside my open window,' immediately generating the perceptual belief 'that it is raining,' which may inferentially spawn the belief that the seats on my convertible Maserati are getting wet. The force of what is and is not mentioned in such examples is to delimit what are the epistemically relevant states and cognitive processing to perceptual states, occurrent beliefs, and their causal interactions. (Nonoccurrent beliefs are apparently justified insofar as they are the stored results of, or the sustained results of, processing involving such elements.) The force of calling the perceptual belief 'direct' is not simply to insist that other beliefs do not feature in its generation, but also to insist that, with respect to what is epistemically important, it comes immediately from the perception (without epistemically relevant mediating states).

The point is that, on Audi's account, these transitions from perceptual experiences to perceptual beliefs are direct and simple from the epistemic point of view, not mediated by informational states and not evidentially dependent on them. The point receives further support when reflecting on Audi's discussion of the 'epistemic dependence' of beliefs on other beliefs (or other states). He relies on a distinction between positive and negative dependence—x is positively dependent on y only if x is the result of the presence of y; x's being negatively dependent on y is a matter of the realization of x turning on the absence of y. Audi seems to see epistemic justification as having dependency patterns that reflect both positive and negative psychological dependencies between states. Thus, he insists that a perceptual belief has a measure of (defeasible) epistemic justification derived from the perceptual experience from which it directly springs (and apparently only from that experience). This positive epistemic dependency (of justification) results from the belief's being positively psychologically dependent on the perceptual experience. This justification can be defeated by incoherence with other beliefs, but, Audi insists, this makes the justification negatively dependent on incoherence—it turns on the absence of incoherence. Importantly, here, beliefs and other information-carrying psychological states are dropped out of the epistemic picture when considering *the generation of* perceptual-experience states and perceptual beliefs. Perceptual beliefs are said not to be positively dependent on such states. At least at the level relevant to epistemology, perceptual beliefs arise directly out of perceptual states alone, which, from an epistemic point of view, are the beginning of the story (they just happen, and just directly cause the perceptual beliefs).

For our larger purposes in this chapter, namely calling *PT* into question, it is important to note how the epistemological action at the junctures that most concern Audi has been limited to states that are paradigmatically occurrent—namely perceptual experiences and occurrent beliefs. Yet when one reflects on these examples, one readily recognizes the role for background information that the cognitive system possesses, information that has been learned and somehow brought to bear. (We will later say more about how such information is involved and why it is causally relevant.) Depending on what exactly one takes to be the perceptual state, there will be a great deal of information somehow employed by the agent in either getting to the perceptual state itself or in getting from it to the perceptual belief. When the perceptual state is taken somewhat sparsely—say, as 'a distinctive patter'—one is less likely to notice information antecedently possessed by the system having a role in getting to the perceptual state. Thus, consider, does 'distinctive' (in 'I perceive a distinctive sound') simply mean discriminable (as in a noticeably distinct or discriminable tone) or does it mean distinctive or characteristic of a phenomenon (as in being characteristic raindrop-impacts)? The former is a 'sparse' perceptual state; the latter is not. Let us consider these alternatives. When the relevant perceptual state is taken as the more informative, less sparse state (as perceiving a sound characteristic of raindrop-impact-sounds, or as perceiving 'a headlight beam across my window') one readily notices the role of information antecedently possessed by the system and employed in the generation of the perceptual state. One's epistemology should not leave this information and its role out of the account. On the other hand, while there may not be such an obvious role for antecedent information in the generation of some sparse perceptual state (such as perceiving only some discriminable sound or other), it seems implausible that there is not an important role for antecedent information informing both the generation of the less sparse perceptual recognition of the sound as characteristic of raindrops, and in moving beyond that state to the generation of perceptual beliefs. There seems an important role of antecedent information influencing the transition from a sparse perceptual state such as the perception of a discriminable sound to the belief that there is rain falling, or in the transition from the perception of a momentary light patch on a surface to the belief that there is a moving auto in the vicinity. Cognitive systems only manage such transitions when they employ quite a bit of learned information. (That is why we humans manage it, our dogs may manage it, but infants do not.) What is important is that the role of such information gets conveniently left out of the story Audi provides. Such antecedently learned information does not feature in the sort of foundationalist reconstruction of evidential support relations that Audi is ready to provide; it gets omitted from the psychological story being told. What one then gets is a story in which the psychological goings-on are occurrently isomorphic with the normative account of relations between accessible (or, indeed, accessed) cognitive states.

5.3 BonJour

Laurence BonJour's coherentism (1985) provides an interestingly different example of the way *PT* has informed epistemology. While internalism is distinguishable from *PT* (1), BonJour's internalism certainly commits him to *PT*(1). What is more difficult to see, and more interesting when seen, is how BonJour honors *PT*(2). BonJour is clearly committed to a kind of normative psychology—to a normative account of the sorts of cognitive processes that would make for justification. On the basis of this normative psychology he is led to despair of human believers ever being actually justified, as opposed to their being merely potentially justified—in effect, he despairs of humans actualizing, or instantiating, the sort of processing called for. It is important to see that something like *PT*(2) is implicated in BonJour's very demanding normative psychology.

Reflecting on the various sorts of considerations that can come up in the context of justification, BonJour (1985) is led to his holistic-coherentistic understanding of epistemic support relations. On his view, the justification of any one belief depends upon other beliefs to such a degree that, ultimately, the justification of one's entire belief set is primary, while local justifications for individual beliefs are secondary and derivative. Now, what sort of cognitive processing is required for an agent's cognitive processing to appropriately parallel or mirror the holistic structure of coherentist evidential-support relations? BonJour rightly insists that merely having a globally coherent belief set is not enough for an agent's being justified. Somehow, the agent's cognitive processing must produce or maintain beliefs in a way that is affected by coherence relations, in a way that takes account of those relations. One might say, the agent's processing must 'take account of' global coherence. But just what do such requirements amount to, for BonJour? One very natural assumption within the context of recent epistemology is that already witnessed in Moser and Audi: that cognitive processing would need to mirror the structure of epistemic evidential-support relations by way of a causally interactive structure of occurrent states, states that jointly exhaust whatever information contributes to justification. BonJour (1985) adheres to this common line. Since the coherentist evidential structure involves one's global belief-set, BonJour presumes that an epistemic agent would need to have cognitive processes that somehow *survey*, that is, *explicitly look over*, his or her own full belief-set, noting coherence or the lack thereof, and then update the agent's beliefs appropriately. In his words, he supposes that for cognitive processes to mirror global-coherentist evidential relations in a fully appropriate, 'actual justification'-conferring way, they must work by making 'fully explicit' the agent's 'entire belief system' and its coherence relations (1985, pp. 151–3). This demand clearly reflects *PT*(2), as it requires that the full-belief set (being normatively relevant) becomes, in some appropriately encompassing fashion, occurrent and thereby causally operative. It is then upon recognizing that actual believers cannot so survey their entire belief-set that BonJour is led to conclude that actual believers are, at best, only potentially rather than actually justified in their beliefs. That is, while one's beliefs might happen to be so content-wise interrelated as to conform to the coherentist standards BonJour codifies, because agents cannot make all their beliefs explicit (and thus occurrent) as a whole—let alone occurently represent global-coherence facts concerning all those beliefs—the agent's processing cannot access this fact of coherence and thereby causally induce the agent to continue to so believe as a result. One might be potentially justified, in that, were such processing possible, one would be justified by one's fine belief-set. But, for BonJour (1985), one cannot be actually justified thereby.

BonJour (1985) thus honors *PT* in his normative psychological commitments, since he holds that justificatory processing would need to be occurrently isomorphic to the coherent structure of content relations featured in the agent's having justification (on his account). However, unlike Moser and Audi, who are committed to the non-skeptical claim that human epistemic agents can be, and sometimes actually are, justified in believing as they do, BonJour has such cognitively demanding standards that he is led to despair of their tractability. At this stage in his work, he confronts what seems the very real possibility of a virulent form of skepticism. While such a position avoids attributing implausible capacities to humans at the level of descriptive psychology it requires just such capacities, at the level of normative psychology—thus honoring *PT* at the level of what justificatory processing would be like.

6 Variants on PT

Below we will set out reasons for thinking that *PT* is problematic and that repudiating it will advance epistemology. But first, in order to get a fair understanding of the situation in contemporary epistemology, it will be useful to describe several close relatives of *PT*. Recall that *PT* characterizes a central tendency informing epistemological theorizing. However, different philosophers will tend to hold on to different components of *PT* to different degrees. In particular, some epistemologists may think that the first clause of *PT* should be a strong constraint on their thought, while not feeling a similar pull for *PT*(2). Others may embrace the second clause, while entertaining alternatives to the first. So, it will be worthwhile to explore plausible weaker versions of PT common to mainstream epistemological thinking, versions that arise in the ways just indicated.

6.1 PT-oi

A wary proponent of something like *PT* might wonder whether important states have been missed—states that are not necessarily consciously accessible, but otherwise operate causally in the way envisioned by *PT*. That is, without the assumption that all the epistemically relevant states are consciously accessible, one might still hold to *PT*(2). An epistemologist doing so would be holding to the same basic view about what it is for an agent's causal psychological processing to appropriately 'mirror the normative structure of support relations'—mirroring is still a matter of occurrent isomorphism, on this line. Call this variant *PT-occurrent isomorphism*, or *PT*-oi. Like *PT* itself, *PT*-oi insists that the epistemically relevant psychological states play their causal role as occurrent states. However, whereas with *PT* itself one looks for an isomorphism between *consciously accessible* (and hence articulable) psychological processing and epistemic support-relations, with *PT*-oi one allows for the possibility that there may be epistemically relevant processing going on that is occurrent but not consciously accessible.

Here the comparison with classical artificial intelligence seems apt. In classical AI accounts, such as the account of visual processing in Marr (1982), much information processing operates on representations that the agent is not conscious of and could not raise to consciousness. (In Marr's account, this is true for much of what happens in the early stages of vision.)[7] It is plausible that such information can, and often does, constitute part of the evidential basis for certain beliefs—e.g. visually induced perceptual beliefs.[8] But although the information can be unconscious, according to classical AI, still such representations can only have a causal role insofar as they are tokened, and thus occurrent, in the relevant processor. So AI work like Marr's suggests a model that extends the picture of occurrent, tokened, interacting states to unconscious and inarticulable epistemologically relevant processing. The further occurrent states are 'more of the same' in how they affect belief-generation and belief maintenance, except for being sometimes unconscious and not articulable.

6.2 PT-p

The sorts of concerns for accessibility reflected in the first clause of *PT* are clearly widespread. Many epistemologists might wish to adhere to these while thinking that the second clause is overly constraining. Such epistemologists might find inspiration for developing a particularly natural variant on *PT* in the psychological notion of 'procedural knowledge.' The basic psychological story here is as follows. In many contexts, how one approaches a cognitive task evolves as one acquires expertise. Initially, one might deal with a cognitive task by consciously representing all pertinent, task-specific information and employing this information in accordance with fairly general-purpose rules or procedures. In the psychological literature, information that is thus occurrently and consciously represented is often called 'declarative'; thus, the idea is that novices often attack cognitive tasks by means of general-purpose rules or procedures that operate on declarative representations of task-specific information. However, with experience dealing with a particular class of common cases falling within the

---

[7] Marr's computational theory of vision treats the human visual system as a device that receives pairs of retinal images as inputs, and produces as output a visual representation of the three-dimensional distal environment. The process breaks up into several sequential stages. Initially the system constructs a representation of certain changes and structures in the retinal image. Then the system uses this representation to construct a 'primal sketch' of the surface outside the viewer. Next, on the basis of the primal sketch, the system constructs a '2.5D sketch' of the viewed surface, explicitly representing information about contour and rough depth in a viewer-centered coordinate frame. Finally, on the basis of the 2.5D sketch the system constructs a '3D model representation' of shapes and their three-dimensional spatial orientations, relative to an object-centered coordinate frame. Stages in this process need not be accessible to conscious awareness, and some stages—the primal sketch, for instance—most probably are not. (Here and below, we draw upon the nice summary of Marr's theory in Segal 1989.)

[8] The passage from each stage to the next is regarded as an inference, yielding an overall inference comprising a chain of component inferences. Marr writes, 'the true heart of visual perception is the inference from the structure of an image about the structure of the real world outside' (p. 68). In terms of content, each successive representation in the sequence is indeed evidentially supported by the representations preceding it.

application of a general procedure, one might develop a special-purpose procedure for treating these cases, with some of the information appropriate to the special class of cases accommodated within the procedure itself. In employing such a procedure, some of the computational tasks involved in the general procedure come already done when the procedure is implemented. As a result, these subtasks do not need to be redone as the special-purpose procedure is put into play. Accordingly, not all the information on which the general-purpose procedure operated needs to be explicitly, occurrently represented; i.e. it need not all be declarative information. Instead, some of it can be *implicitly* taken into account by executing the special-purpose procedure. In the psychological literature, information that is thus implicitly accommodated is often called 'procedural,' in contrast to declarative information.

Thinking in terms of such proceduralization could lead one to loosen up in connection with $PT(2)$ as follows. As a thought experiment, suppose that one starts with an epistemic system that conforms to epistemic standards fully in keeping with PT. With respect to $PT(2)$ in particular, one would then have a system that employs explicit, occurrent, representations of all information that is epistemically relevant. The epistemic system manages to operate on those representational states in content-appropriate ways 'without skipping a beat.' So far, thinking along the lines of PT, one should be very happy with this system. However, the question now arises whether something less than, but related to, this full conformity with PT would also be unexceptionable. In particular, it seems reasonable (indeed, epistemically desirable) for the system to compact its epistemic computational tasks via proceduralization, where feasible. This might be a matter of innate cognitive architecture, or it might be a matter of acquiring an epistemic expertise in a class of cases. Either way, the system thereby ceases to conform strictly to $PT(2)$—the states on which it operates and the transitions on those states no longer will be fully occurrently isomorphic to the normatively appropriate content relations. In its present causal transformations involving occurrent states, the system is now taking shortcuts. Still, the results seem in keeping with the spirit, if not the letter, of $PT(2)$. What is important is that this system, which has come to deal so compactly with certain classes of cases, *could* have performed these epistemic tasks 'longhand' in full conformity with PT had this been called for somehow, and that the information relied on in its processing is accessible.[9]

We can then christen a slightly weakened variant on PT—call it *PT-proceduralization* (or PT-p) which insists on $PT(1)$, and insists that the system could have fully complied with $PT(2)$, while allowing for proceduralization so that in a given episode the

---

[9] Information that is procedural rather than occurrent during processing is not conscious during processing, since all conscious mental states are occurrent states. Nonetheless, procedural information can be consciously accessible anyway. Roughly, such information is consciously accessible just in case it reliably can be recovered in conscious, occurrent form under the relevant kinds of post-hoc elicitation circumstances—for instance, in contexts where one is seeking to articulate one's justification for a given belief.

processing in a system need not be fully occurrently isomorphic with the content relations specified in a set of epistemic ideals.[10]

6.3 PT-oi/p

PT-p is more thoroughly in keeping with the spirit of *PT* than is *PT*-oi. For, *PT*-p retains the accessibility requirement *PT*(1), while backing away from the full-fledged occurrent isomorphism requirement *PT*(2) in a way that still respects the general spirit, though not the letter, of occurrent isomorphism. But *PT*-oi, in eschewing the accessibility requirement, thereby acknowledges that consciously accessible states may well be just the tip of a larger iceberg of epistemically related psychological states—a theme that will loom very large in Chapter 8. In short, the requirements imposed by *PT*-p constitute only a modest weakening of those imposed by *PT*, whereas the requirements imposed by *PT*-oi constitute a more substantial weakening.

This being so, anyone who is prepared to fall back from *PT* to *PT*-oi should also be prepared to fall back still further, to a proto-theory that allows proceduralized shortcut-alternatives for processing that the system can perform in a way that is fully occurrently isomorphic to the content relations specified in a set of epistemic ideals. Call this view *PT-occurrent isomorphism/proceduralization* (or *PT*-oi/p). Just as *PT*-p cleaves to the spirit, though not the letter, of *PT* itself, so likewise *PT*-oi/p cleaves to the spirit, though not the letter, of *PT*-oi.[11]

---

[10] The notion of procedural information can be understood in various ways, some broader in scope than others. In the narrowest sense, procedural information is information that formerly was employed in declarative form within the given cognitive system, and now is accommodated implicitly in the system by virtue of proceduralization that occurred during learning; a 'longhand' procedure has been replaced by a corresponding 'shorthand' procedure. In a somewhat broader sense, procedural information is information that is accommodated implicitly and could instead have been accommodated explicitly in a corresponding longhand procedure—*whether or not* the cognitive system has ever actually employed the longhand procedure itself. This broader construal is the one we have built into our characterization of *PT*-p.

One can envision an even broader usage, illustratable by a variation on Moser's views. As noted above, Moser seems to hold *PT*. However, it is easy enough to envision a way of getting something like *PT*-p out of his view with a somewhat legislative reading. Recall that Moser's account of justification-as-evidence employs the notion of a disposition in a central fashion (as much of our evidence will typically be things like beliefs, which are understood as dispositional states resulting from episodes of assenting to a proposition). If epistemically relevant dispositions are limited to such evidential states, and this is certainly the paradigmatic fashion in which they feature in Moser's discussion, then Moser seems to hold to *PT*. The reason is that such dispositions function as stored bits of declarative knowledge. The notion of proceduralization involves a distinction between procedural and declarative knowledge—since proceduralization involves a modification in procedural knowledge that lessens the role of declarative knowledge in treating classes of cases. If, however, Moser were to allow for acquired dispositions that involve not simply the declarative knowledge he focuses on, but also procedural knowledge, then Moser could be seen as embracing the more moderate *PT*-p. One can point to aspects of Moser's (1989) that suggest an openness to such a position, but whether he would allow for *PT*-p in place of *PT* is probably indeterminate from that text.

[11] Furthermore, it also would be in the spirit of *PT*-oi to allow proceduralized shortcut-alternatives even under a more liberal construal of the notion of 'procedural information' than we have adopted in the text. This construal would allow the possibility, for instance, that (i) some epistemically relevant information is accommodated implicitly, rather than being explicitly represented during processing, (ii) an algorithm that procedurally employs this information is hardwired into the system, and (iii) the system lacks the capacity to run a corresponding longhand algorithm employing an explicit representation of the relevant information.

While *PT* seems to be the proto-theory of choice, or at least of ready assumption, among contemporary epistemologists, *PT*-oi, *PT*-p, and *PT*-oi/p provide weaker variants that might be attractive to the wary once psychological commitments begin to be articulated as done here.[12] However, our subsequent objections to *PT* will also be telling against these kindred alternatives. Our misgivings are described in the next section.

7 The frame problem and its morals for human belief-fixation

Certain problems and developments in cognitive science provide reason to believe that the human cognitive processes that typically produce and sustain beliefs diverge in important ways from *PT* and its kin.[13] Perhaps more to the point, there is reason to believe that human belief generation *must*, and *epistemically ought* to, proceed in this alternative manner—in violation of *PT* and its kin. The alternative understanding emerges in the wake of a family of recurrent, recalcitrant difficulties within the classical, computational conception of mind in cognitive science—difficulties often classified under the rubric 'the frame problem.' In this section we first describe those difficulties, drawing upon an influential discussion by Fodor (1983), and we describe the alternative conception of mind suggested by those difficulties. We then sketch one way of elaborating this conception, inspired by connectionism and by the form of mathematics that

---

Marr's theory of early vision suggests just such a possibility. Marr emphasizes that the visual system's inferences from its retinal stimulations to the nature of the distal causes of those stimulations depend on certain assumptions. One such assumption is that 'the visible world can be regarded as being composed of smooth surfaces whose spatial structure may be elaborate' (Marr, p. 44); another is that 'the items generated on a given scale tend to be more similar to one another in their size, local contrast, colour, and spatial organization than to other items on that surface' (Marr, p. 46). Given Marr's general account of the input-output function computed during early vision, it is entirely possible—even likely, for reasons of speed and resource efficiency—that the algorithm that computes this function accommodates such assumptions implicitly; it is also very likely that the algorithm is hardwired. So presumably this procedural algorithm constitutes the *only* way that the visual system can compute the input-output function; the system does not, and cannot, computationally generate a 3D visual representation by executing an alternative algorithm that employs explicit, occurrent representations of the relevant background assumptions.

In order to simplify subsequent discussion, in the body of this chapter we will largely ignore the liberalized construal of 'procedural information,' and the corresponding liberalized version of *PT*-oi/p, described in the present note; but the reader should keep them in mind. See also note 16 below.

[12] The most straightforward understanding of Pollock's (1986) sees him as embracing *PT*-oi, and some of Pollock's discussion suggests elements of *PT*-p, as he makes much of the notion of the internalization of procedural knowledge (pp. 129–32). However, the importance of *PT*-p elements within Pollock's position is rather difficult to gauge, as he seems sometimes to suggest an individuation of norms—and thus cognitive process types—that is too coarse-grained to allow a precise fix on his position regarding these matters. In any case, the *PT*-oi elements in this thought, and his appreciation for proceduralization, might lead one to read him as an adherent of *PT*-oi/p.

[13] The discussion in this section and the next draws freely on material in Horgan and Tienson (1994, 1996) and Horgan (1997a). Some points we will make about psychological processing, and their potential import for epistemology, are discussed by Herman Stark (1993, 1994, 1995).

goes naturally with it, dynamical systems theory. Finally, we underscore the ways that this alternative approach calls into question *PT* and its kin.

7.1 *The frame problem*

In the closing pages of Fodor's *The Modularity of Mind* (1983), it is argued that certain problems in classical cognitive science look to be in-principle problems, and hence that the prospects for understanding processes like belief fixation within the framework of classical cognitive science are very bleak. These problems continue to plague the computational approach to the mind, and suggest the need for a radically different approach.

The main claim of Fodor's influential book is that the human cognitive system possesses a number of important subsystems that are *modular*: domain specific, mandatory, limited in their access to other parts of the larger cognitive system, fast, and informationally encapsulated. There is good evidence, Fodor argues, that human input systems exhibit modularity. Where the classical computational approach has gotten somewhere, he says, is in understanding such modular subsystems, which by their nature delimit the class of relevant information.

Classical computationalism has made very little progress in understanding *central* processes, however. Belief fixation—the generation of new beliefs (and revising of preexisting beliefs) on the basis of current input together with other beliefs—is a paradigmatic example. Fodor argues convincingly that these processes are non-modular: they need to have access to a wide range of cognitive subsystems, and to information on an indefinitely wide range of topics. And the very considerations that point to non-modularity, he maintains, also constitute grounds for extreme pessimism about the prospects of explaining central processes within the framework of classical computational cognitive science.

Fodor articulates these considerations in terms of the analogy between belief fixation in human cognition and scientific confirmation. Concerning central cognitive processes like belief fixation, he says, 'it seems reasonable enough that something can be inferred about them from what we know about *explicit* processes of nondemonstrative inference—viz., from what we know about empirical inference in science' (p. 104). Scientific confirmation, 'the nondemonstrative fixation of belief in science,' has two crucial features. It is (in Fodor's terminology) *isotropic* and *Quineian*:

By saying that confirmation is isotropic, I mean that the facts relevant to the confirmation of a scientific hypothesis may be drawn from anywhere in the field of previously established empirical (or, of course, demonstrative) truths. Crudely: everything that the scientist knows is, in principle, relevant to determining what else he ought to believe (1983, p. 105).

By saying that scientific confirmation is Quineian, I mean that the degree of confirmation assigned to any given hypothesis is sensitive to properties of the entire belief system; as it were, the shape of our whole science bears on the epistemic status of each scientific hypothesis (1983, p. 107).

Isotropy brings in the whole of current theory: any bit of actual or potential information from any portion of the belief system might, in some circumstances, be evidentially relevant to any other. Being Quineian makes confirmation holistic in a deeper way: confirmation depends upon 'such considerations as simplicity, plausibility, and conservatism' (Fodor 1983, p. 108), which are determined by the global *structure* of the whole of the current belief system and of potential successor systems.

Since belief fixation in human cognition is commonly a matter of inductive inference from the information provided by input systems and the information in memory, evidently it too must be isotropic and Quineian. Fodor concludes that it must be non-modular. He also stresses that these global aspects of belief fixation look to be at the very heart of the problems that classical computational cognitive science has encountered in attempting to understand such central processes:

> The difficulties we encounter when we try to construct theories of central processes are just the sort we would expect to encounter if such processes are, in essential respects, Quineian/isotropic.... The crux in the construction of such theories is that there seems to be no way to delimit the sorts of informational resources which may affect, or be affected by, central processes of problem-solving. We can't, that is to say, plausibly view the fixation of belief as effected by computations over bounded, local information structures. A graphic example of this sort of difficulty arises in AI, where it has come to be known as the 'frame problem' (i.e., the problem of putting a 'frame' around the set of beliefs that may need to be revised in light of specified newly available information) (Fodor 1983, pp. 112–3).

When one considers the sorry history of attempts in philosophy of science to construct a theory of confirmation, the prospects for understanding central processing within the classical computational paradigm look very discouraging indeed:

> Consider... the situation in the philosophy of science, where we can see the issues about fixation of belief writ large. Here an interesting contrast is between deductive logic—the history of which is, surely, one of the great success stories of human history—and confirmation theory which, by fairly general consensus, is a field that mostly does not exist. My point is that this asymmetry, too, is likely no accident. Deductive logic is the theory of validity, and validity is a *local* property of sentences.... In this respect,... validity contrasts starkly with the level of confirmation, since the latter... is highly sensitive to global properties of belief systems.... The problem in both cases is to get the structure of the entire belief system to bear on individual occasions of belief fixation. We have, to put it bluntly, no computational formalisms that show us how to do this, and we have no idea how such formalisms might be developed (Fodor 1983, pp. 128–9).

These are wise words. Let us underscore their wisdom by dwelling just a bit on the depth of, and the apparently in-principle nature of, the difficulties encountered by attempts to model global cognitive processes computationally. Take the Quineian aspect of belief systems first. Simplicity and conservatism are properties of (or relations between) belief systems that depend upon the formal, semantic, and evidential relations among *all* of the beliefs in the system(s). Computational processing would have to somehow survey the entire stock of beliefs, in a manner that tracks all the multifarious interconnections among the beliefs, and somehow derive a *measure* of net overall simplicity and net overall conservatism from these local features. As Fodor said, 'We have... no computational formalisms that show us how to do this, and... no idea how such formalisms might be developed...' (Recall BonJour's problems, discussed above.)

In addition, when new information comes in from the input modules, central processing would have to find, from among the vastly many competing, incompatible ways of revising the whole belief system to accommodate this new information, a mode of revision that maintains overall simplicity and conservatism better than most of the others. All this would have to be done via *tractable* computation, executable quite rapidly. Not only do we have no computational formalisms that show us how to do this; it's a highly credible hypothesis that a (tractable) computational system with these features is just impossible, for belief systems on the scale possessed by human beings.

Now consider isotropy—the potential relevance of anything to anything. Fodor's *definition* of isotropy suggests that the problem is that there is *too much* that may need to be considered, and that there is no known manageable way to bring what is needed into consideration. This is typical of the way frame-type problems are perceived. But there is actually an even deeper problem concerning relevance, a problem suggested by Fodor's talk of local versus global properties and by his comparison with the historical failure of confirmation theory: namely that *relevance itself is a Quineian as well as an isotropic property*. How is (e.g. confirmatory) relevance to be determined computationally? Certainly, some observations are necessary to establish general beliefs like the belief that almost all crows are black. But the belief that many black crows have been observed and that no non-black ones have been observed does not, by itself, support an inference concerning crows in general or concerning any particular crow. For a cognitive system to make such an inference, the predicate 'black' must be *projectable* for the system relative to the predicate 'crow.' But projectability of predicates is a global feature of a cognitive system. The projectability of one predicate relative to another for a cognitive system depends upon features of a great many other relevantly (!) similar predicates within the cognitive system. Thus, belief fixation depends upon projectability, and in the real world, projectability of any single predicate for a cognitive system depends upon relations among large numbers of cognitive states of that system.

Fodor, in the passages bemoaning the lack of an available computational formalism, is telling us that human central processing evidently does not operate via any kinds of computation we currently know about or can even contemplate. Something else is needed. What might it be?

7.2 Belief fixation as essentially morphological

Frame-type problems arise largely because of the apparent computational intractability of managing all relevant information, insofar as that information gets *explicitly represented* in the course of cognitive processing. What this suggests is that belief fixation and related cognitive processes operate in a way that accommodates much relevant information *automatically* and *implicitly*. The suggestion is that the holistic aspects of belief fixation involve not the finding and fetching of relevant representations from memory-banks where they are stored in explicit form (a method that runs afoul of isotropy), and not the overt representation and comparative evaluation of large-scale alternative belief-systems (a method that runs afoul of the Quineian dimension). Rather, these holistic aspects are somehow implicit in the structure of the cognitive system, in such a way that temporal transitions from one occurrent cognitive state to another accommodate the holistic aspects automatically. In the terminology of Horgan and Tienson (1995, 1996), the holistic informational content is *morphological*, rather than occurrent.

Morphological content is information that:

(1) is implicit in the standing structure of the cognitive system (rather than explicitly represented in the system's occurrent cognitive states or explicitly stored in memory), and
(2) gets accommodated in cognitive processing without getting explicitly represented in occurrent cognitive states, either conscious or unconscious.

The apparent moral of the frame problem is that, in general, human belief fixation *must* operate in a way that draws heavily upon morphological content, in order to avoid computational intractability. As we will put it, these processes are *essentially* morphological.[14] Belief fixation is not accomplished by computationally manipulating explicit, occurrent, representations of all relevant information.

Nor is it accomplished by 'proceduralized' computational processes that are mere shorthand algorithms for computations that could instead have been carried out in a way that renders all relevant information explicitly. The argument for this negative conclusion goes as follows. In order for computational processes employing special-purpose rules to be implementable in human neurobiological 'wetware,' the number of special-purpose rules executed by the computational system cannot be intractably huge. (For instance, if each 'rule' is just a totally specific entry $[S_i(t) \rightarrow S_i(t')]$ in a lookup table, an entry stipulating exactly what state-transition should transpire at the next moment t' when the specific, explicit, representation S_i is instantiated at t—then the number of special-purpose rules would grossly outrun neurobiological implementability.) Hence, tractably executable special-purpose rules must still retain a significant aspect of *generality*, even though some of the background information that is

---

[14] There is a second moral of the frame problem, complementary to first one about the need for essentially morphological processing: namely that cognitive processing that exhibits the Quineian and isotropic features, and does so with respect to a range of potential total cognitive states as rich as the range of such states instantiable by humans, is too complex and subtle to conform to *programmable rules* over mental representations. Another way to put this is that Quineian/isotropic human cognition *is not computation*; computation is too brittle, too frame-problem susceptible, to accommodate the Quineian and isotropic aspects of non-demonstrative belief-fixation. For an extended discussion of the two morals, together with a sketch of a non-classical framework for cognitive science that is non-computational and that heavily emphasizes morphological content, see Horgan and Tienson (1996).

accommodated via the execution of such rules is implicitly embodied in the rules themselves rather than being explicitly represented during processing. That is, such a rule must apply to a reasonably wide range of explicit representations that can potentially occur in the cognitive system, thus generating a reasonably wide range of specific cognitive state-transitions. But such a special-purpose rule will be a rule that implicitly accommodates some *specific* body of background information; it will effect transitions from one explicit representation to another that are appropriate to the content of *that* implicit information. Change the background information, and you need a new special-purpose rule that is appropriate to the new background information rather than to the original background information. Thus, suitably general special-purpose rules will have to be *framed* rules (as one might put it), in order for the number of such rules to remain small enough for them to be tractably executable by a physical device with roughly the physical resources of a human brain; i.e. for any such rule there will have to be a specific, delimited, body of background information that the rule implicitly accommodates. But the moral of the frame problem, remember, is this: because of the holistic Quineian/isotropic ways that background information is relevant to belief fixation, one *cannot* delimit ('put a frame around') the background information that *might become relevant when some new explicit representation arises in the system*. Thus, the frame problem arises all over again, for shorthand rules. Tractably implementable special-purpose rules must be framed rules, but those can't accommodate the Quineian/isotropic aspects of belief fixation.

So, essentially morphological processing is a fundamentally different way of accommodating the holistic aspects of belief fixation. It is very different from the computational manipulation, via programmable rules, of *explicit* representations of all epistemically relevant information possessed by the cognitive system. It is also very different from the computational execution of programmable rules that are framed so as to implicitly accommodate some of the epistemically relevant information.

Some readers may be puzzled by the direction we seem to be headed here. We write of human cognitive systems possessing much morphological content. Thus, in addition to paradigmatic beliefs that the agent has, the suggestion seems to be that there is yet a richer set of information to be accommodated. But, it may be wondered, do not the problems just broached suggest that there is simply too much information to be accommodated in the first place? How can adding yet richer ranges of information help?

In response, it is important to notice that Fodor's point is not that there cannot be Quineian or isotropic elements to belief-fixation; on the contrary. Fodor's point, rather, is that one cannot understand how these elements are possible *when restricted to classical computational models*. And our point is that one cannot understand how these elements can and should be managed when restricted to conceptions of belief fixation suggested by *PT* and its kin. This emphasis on the epistemic role of morphological content, and on essentially morphological processing, must be understood as pointing to the need for cognitive-scientific models that fall outside the classical computational paradigm—a theme we pursue in sections 8–10 below. The new wine of morphological content cannot be poured into the old bottles of *PT* or classical computation. It would then make a mess—for there was already too much information to fit into those bottles.

7.3 A closer look at isotropy: underscoring the morphological nature of belief-fixation

The distinction between being justified versus merely having justification—i.e. between doxastic justification and mere propositional justification—turns on the idea that, when one is justified in one's belief, the justification that one has for that belief is not causally inert, but rather 'comes into play' or is 'appropriately operative' in generating or sustaining that belief. Whatever information one might possess, if one does not systematically use it, and use it in an appropriate way, then, even if one somehow arrives at true beliefs, one does so by accident, and not by justificatory processes. For such distinctions to make sense, it must be possible for one to have justifications for a belief which do not, and did not, 'come into play' in the fixation of that belief. In such cases, something else must then be relevantly operative in belief-fixation. Perhaps one has 'other justifications' for the belief in question, and these might be operative in the relevant belief-fixation (in which case one may yet be justified in one's beliefs). Or perhaps what is in play in fixing the belief in question is not the justificatory information one has, but something else (in this case one has justification, but is not justified). This diversity of possible cases is presupposed by the distinction between being justified in believing and merely having justification for a belief. The distinction requires the *selective efficacy* of beliefs and information states representing the justification that the agent has.

One might think that holism is incompatible with such distinctions. But, a closer look at the holistic dimension that Fodor terms 'isotropy' should serve to dispel this suggestion, and to provide a richer picture that will need to be kept in mind in this chapter.

When Fodor writes of confirmation as isotropic he insists that 'the facts relevant to the confirmation of a scientific hypothesis *may* be drawn from anywhere in the field of previously established empirical (or, of course, demonstrative) truths. Crudely: everything that the scientist knows is, in principle, relevant to determining what else he ought to believe' (p. 105, emphasis added). Fodor's first formulation reflects a point that is lost in the crude reformulation. Isotropy is the *potential* relevance of everything (all the beliefs and information one has) to everything else one believes—but this is not to say flatly that everything one believes is *actually* relevant to everything else one believes. One must be careful in conceiving of relevance here, and it will be helpful to distinguish a strict sense, *actual relevance*, and an extended sense that might best be thought of as *potential* relevance. In the extended and attenuated sense it is correct that everything that one believes (and more generally, all the information that one in some sense possesses) is relevant to any episode of belief fixation. Take any two beliefs that are mutually irrelevant on their face—that is, when considered of themselves, without taking into account what further information one might possess. Then notice that, with various sets of possible auxiliary information or beliefs serving as intermediaries, the beliefs that were of themselves irrelevant would become mutually relevant. *Actual* relevance depends then on what else one *actually* happens to believe—or on what other information one actually has (and how it 'adds up'). To then be sensitive to what is relevant to what—actually relevant—one must be sensitive to the intermediating role of background information. Much actual relevance is like this, so the point is important.

Summarizing all this, one finds that isotropy, or the potential relevance of everything to everything, poses a daunting cognitive challenge for any cognitive agent, if that agent is to have *actually relevant beliefs come selectively into play* in a fashion that would make for justified believing. What is required is a sensitivity to the full range of one's beliefs (and other information), as it is all relevant to relevance—a sensitivity that somehow puts the actually relevant beliefs and information into play. If one were to ask how this could be managed in the computational fashion of traditional AI, one quickly confronts intractability: one would have to pick up all sets of information and beliefs and see how they might mediate between other beliefs and information one possesses. To avoid such intractability, belief fixation and related cognitive processes must operate in a way that accommodates much relevant information automatically and implicitly.[15] As suggested already, the isotropic-holistic aspects of belief fixation must be somehow implicit in the structure of the cognitive system, in such a way that temporal transitions from one occurrent cognitive state to another accommodate the holistic aspects automatically. For this to obtain, the actually relevant information that the system possesses must selectively come into play by virtue of the structure of the cognitive system itself. The sensitivity to mediated relevance, and much of the relevant information as it is called into play, must be managed as morphological content.

8 PT rejected

As we argued in section 7.1, the apparent moral of frame-type problems in computational cognitive science is that the holistic, Quineian/isotropic, aspects of cognitive processing are not subserved by processes that update beliefs (and other informational states) in a manner that is occurrently isomorphic to holistic normative-justificatory relations among these items. This kind of occurrent isomorphism between normative-justificatory relations and psychological processing is just not possible. Rather, the holistic aspects of cognitive tasks like belief fixation are primarily subserved morphologically: cognitive transitions are automatically appropriate to large amounts of implicit information and to holistic normative-justificatory relations involving that information. The

---

[15] These processes also must operate in a way that does not constitute computation over representations of pertinent information—i.e. manipulation of such representations in accordance with programmable rules. See the preceding note.

holistic aspects of cognitive processing *must* be subserved morphologically; this is an essential aspect of Nature's 'design solution' to the problem of avoiding frame-like breakdowns in human cognition, and to the closely related problem of managing significant inductive reasoning without intractability.

This picture of cognitive processing—which will receive one kind of potential elaboration in section 9—is importantly different from the picture provided by *PT*. *PT* requires, as a condition of a belief's being justified, that it be causally generated and sustained by processes that are occurrently isomorphic to the normative-justificatory support relations that this belief bears to other intentional states of the cognitive system, and that these processes be consciously accessible. But according to the alternative picture, certain crucially important, holistic, normative-justificatory relations among the cognitive system's intentional states are not—and cannot be—subserved by occurrently isomorphic psychological processes; instead, they are, and must be, subserved by processes in which much of the epistemically relevant information is accommodated morphologically. Thus *PT*(2) is violated.

This kind of cognitive processing is also at odds with the psychological picture provided by each of the fallback variants of *PT*, namely *PT*-oi, *PT*-p, and *PT*-oi/p. Since *PT*-oi retains condition *PT*(2), the remarks in the preceding paragraph apply directly, mutatis mutandis. *PT*-p and *PT*-oi/p both impose the following requirement as a condition for a belief's being justified: if the cognitive processing that generates or sustains the belief relies upon morphological content, then this processing must be a proceduralized shortcut version of a form of processing that (1) could have occurred in the cognitive system, and (2) would be occurrently isomorphic to normative-justificatory support relations. This condition too is violated, if indeed holistic evidential factors can only be accommodated morphologically, not occurrently.[16]

What about conscious accessibility of epistemically relevant information and of evidential support-relations, as required by *PT* and by *PT*-p (although not by *PT*-oi

---

[16] This condition is also violated, it should be noted, by a form of processing that is allowed for under the liberalized construal of *PT*-oi/p that we mentioned in note 11—namely processing in which certain epistemically-involved information is accommodated implicitly in a hardwired 'shortcut' algorithm, and the system cannot execute a corresponding 'longhand' algorithm employing that information in explicit, occurrent form. However, in cases where a cognitive capacity has been produced by the evolutionary installation of a hardwired *shorthand* algorithm for computing a given tractably-computable cognitive transition-function, that same capacity presumably could have been produced instead by the evolutionary installation of a corresponding *longhand* algorithm for computing the same function. A cognitive system employing the longhand algorithm would be, as one might say, a *biologically feasible variant* of the actual cognitive system. So all the members of the *PT* family of prototheories, including the liberalized construal of *PT*-oi/p, impose the following requirement as a condition for a belief's being justified: if the cognitive processing that generates or sustains the belief relies upon morphological content, then this processing must be a proceduralized shortcut version of a form of processing that (1) could have occurred in the cognitive system *or in a biologically feasible variant of it*, and (2) would be occurrently isomorphic to normative-justificatory support relations. This weakened condition too is violated by the picture of cognitive processing we have described in this section, because for *any* biologically feasible cognitive system with a large-scale set of beliefs, holistic evidential factors can only be accommodated morphologically, not occurrently.

or *PT*-oi/p)? In characterizing *PT*-p, we pointed out that even information that is accommodated procedurally during belief-fixation sometimes can be accessible anyway: sometimes the agent has the capacity to represent the information occurrently and consciously after the fact, in subsequent cognitive processing aimed at explicitly articulating the justification for the belief. The same point applies to information that is accommodated morphologically during belief-fixation: in principle, some such information can be accessible for purposes of subsequent justification-giving.[17] However, states of conscious awareness are all *occurrent* mental states; hence, any information that is accessible to consciousness must be information that can be explicitly represented in occurrent cognitive states. But on the psychological picture we have been describing, the holistic, Quineian/isotropic, evidential relations involved in belief-fixation can only be accommodated morphologically, rather than being explicitly represented in occurrent cognitive states. For the most part, then, such evidential relations are inaccessible to consciousness; facts that cannot be explicitly represented at all cannot be explicitly represented *consciously*.[18] In short, the reasons why this alternative picture of belief-fixation violates the conditions on being-justified imposed by *PT*(2) are also reasons why the picture violates the conditions imposed by *PT*(1).[19]

9 Dynamical cognition and morphological content

How might the daunting task of essentially morphological processing get accomplished, in human cognition? To our knowledge, there are no models in cognitive science that come close to processing such complex cognitive tasks as those handled in real human thought. Nor is there any good reason, as far as we know, to think that any extant models are likely to 'scale up' in a smooth and direct way, so that an adequate account of real human cognition would turn out to be just a straightforward extension of the given model. This is no less true for connectionist models than it is for classical computational models.

Nonetheless, a general conception of human cognition has begun to emerge within cognitive science that is potentially more powerful than the classical computational

---

[17] This is to be expected, since procedural information is just a special case of morphological information.
[18] To be sure, holistic evidential factors often can be occurrently, consciously represented in a sketchy way. Often one can articulate specific facts that bear on the cogency of a given inductive inference, and often one can say something too about the all-things-considered plausibility of the inference. But normally, what is articulable in this way falls far short of a full-fledged reconstruction of the complete evidential basis for the inference, with all the Quineian/isotropic factors fully spelled out. What is consciously accessible is just the tip of the evidential iceberg.
[19] Polanyi (1958) already argued that unconscious psychological processes figure in the fixation of beliefs, including justified beliefs. It is an interesting question, which we will not pursue here, to what extent Polanyi's arguments point toward a conception of belief fixation like the one we have set forth here, which conflicts radically with *PT*(2) in addition to conflicting with *PT*(1). Prima facie, Polanyi's notion of tacit knowledge has affinities with morphological content.

conception of mind, and that provides the broad outlines of an answer to the question, 'How is essentially morphological processing possible?' This alternative conception draws cautiously upon connectionist modeling, in a way that eschews unduly optimistic assumptions about the scale-up potential of extant models. It also draws upon a form of mathematics that is natural for describing connectionist models—dynamical systems theory. This non-classical framework for cognitive science is described at length in Horgan and Tienson's *Connectionism and the Philosophy of Psychology*. Here we offer a very brief sketch of connectionism, dynamical systems theory, and the non-classical framework—with emphasis on features that are especially germane to morphological content.

In a connectionist system, information is actively represented as a pattern of activation. When the information is not in use, that pattern is nowhere present in the system; it is not stored as a data structure. The only representations ever present are the active ones. On the other hand, information can be said to be *implicitly* present in a connectionist system—or 'in the weights'—if the weighted connections subserve *representation-level dispositions* that are appropriate to that information. Such information constitutes morphological content in the system, rather than explicitly-represented content. Among the apparent advantages of connectionist systems, by contrast with classical computational systems, is that morphological information 'in the weights' gets accommodated automatically during processing, without any need for a central processing unit to find and fetch task-relevant information from some separate memory banks where it gets stored in explicit form while not in use.

Learning is conceived quite differently within connectionism than it is within the classical approach, since connectionist systems do not store representations. Learning is the acquisition, 'in the weights,' of new morphological content.

The branch of mathematics called dynamical systems theory is often applied to connectionist models. To describe some physical system (e.g. a planetary system, or a connectionist network) mathematically as a dynamical system is to specify in a certain way its temporal evolution, both actual and potential. The set of all possible states of the physical system—so characterized—is the mathematical system's abstract, high-dimensional *state-space*. Each magnitude or parameter of the physical system is assigned a separate dimension of this mathematical space, and each possible state of the physical system, as determined by the values of these magnitudes, corresponds to a point in state-space. A dynamical system, as such, is essentially a complete mathematical description of how the physical system would evolve temporally from any possible initial state; it is a collection of trajectories through state-space, with a trajectory emanating from each point in state-space. A useful geometrical metaphor for dynamical systems is the notion of a *landscape*. A dynamical system describing a physical system involving n distinct magnitudes is the n-dimensional analog of a two-dimensional, non-Euclidean, contoured surface: i.e. a topological molding of the n-dimensional state-space such that, were this surface oriented 'horizontally' in an (n+1)-dimensional space, a ball would 'roll along the landscape,' from any initial point p, in a way that corresponds to the way the physical system would evolve from the physical state corresponding to p.

Connectionist systems are naturally describable, mathematically, as dynamical systems. The state-space of a network is its 'activation space' (which has as many dimensions as the network has nodes), and the dynamical system associated with the network is its 'activation landscape.' In connectionist models, cognitive processing is typically construed as evolution along the activation landscape from one point in activation space to another—where at least the beginning and end points are interpreted as realizing intentional states.

So in terms of the mathematics of dynamics, occurrent cognitive states are realized mathematically as *points on the activation landscape*, which are then realized physically as distributed patterns of activation in the nodes of the network. Morphological content—the information implicit 'in the weights'—is embodied in the *topographical contours* of the network's high-dimensional activation landscape. Thus, the various superimposed slopes on the activation landscape subserve trajectories from one occurrent cognitive state to another that automatically accommodate the morphological content.

From this mathematical perspective, training a network is a matter of (i) *molding* the activation landscape, thereby inducing new topological contours embodying new morphological content, while simultaneously (ii) *refining* the cognitive/mathematical realization relation whereby intentional states get realized mathematically as points on the landscape. (The weight-change training procedures employed in connectionist modeling bring about a co-evolution of these two factors.) Once 'trained up,' the system's temporal trajectories from one occurrent intentional state to another will automatically accommodate the relevant morphological content.

Horgan and Tienson (1994, 1996) describe a non-classical framework for cognitive science that they call the *dynamical cognition* framework (the DC framework). This alternative approach offers an answer, in principle, to the question, 'How could the holistic, Quineian/isotropic, aspects of cognitive processes be accommodated automatically and morphologically?' The answer is this:

In principle, Quineian/isotropic information could be embodied morphologically in the complex and subtle topography of a high-dimensional activation landscape subserved by the human central nervous system. Given a sufficiently nuanced realization relation from cognitive states to points on this landscape, the landscape's multifarious, superimposed, topographical contours guarantee that the cognitive system's transitions from one occurrent cognitive state to another are automatically appropriate not only to the explicit content of these occurrent states themselves, but also to very large amounts of implicit Quineian/isotropic information.

As we remarked above, we know of no extant connectionist models that come anywhere close to dealing with frame-type problems of the kind routinely encountered in real human cognition, and we know of no good reason to think that current models are likely to 'scale up' in any straightforward way. Nevertheless, the DC framework offers a general, and not implausible, answer to the extremely daunting question of how the holistic aspects of belief fixation could be handled in an essentially morphological way. The classical computational approach is no longer 'the only game in town' in cognitive science; and, whereas frame-type problems look quite intractable from within the classical framework, the DC framework suggests the outlines of a solution.[20]

Before turning to the implications of all this, let us comment on the dialectical structure of our argument thus far. First, the claim that Quineian/isotropic belief fixation is 'essentially morphological' is the assertion that for creatures like ourselves, Quineian/isotropic belief fixation *must*—and therefore, *does*—operate in a way that draws heavily upon morphological content; and morphological content, recall, is information that (i) is implicit in the standing structure of the cognitive system (rather than explicitly represented in the system's occurrent cognitive states or explicitly stored in memory), and (ii) gets accommodated in cognitive processing without getting explicitly represented in occurrent cognitive states, either conscious or unconscious. So the notion of morphological content, and the claim about belief fixation, are conceptually independent of the DC framework.

Second, although we maintain that the claim about belief fixation is further reinforced by the in-principle account of such essentially morphological processing that is provided by the DC framework, it should be noted that the appeal to the DC framework is not essential here. Even if one were thoroughly dubious about connectionism and about the usefulness of dynamical-systems ideas in cognitive science, one still could accept the argument from frame-type problems to the conclusion that processes like belief-fixation must *somehow* be essentially morphological.

Third, even if one has doubts about the argument from frame-type problems to the claim that belief fixation is essentially morphological, one still should take seriously the implications of this claim for epistemology. For at the very least, the considerations we have canvassed in this section do show that the truth of the claim is a viable *empirical possibility*. This already is reason enough to make the claim relevant to epistemology.

We ourselves believe that belief fixation is actually essentially morphological—that this is more than an empirical possibility. Humans do manage to form beliefs in ways that accommodate wide swatches of information—in practice solving the frame

---

[20] What about the well known argument in Fodor and Pylyshyn (1988), to the effect that connectionist systems must either (i) exhibit the fatal inadequacies of traditional associationism (by eschewing language-like mental representations that are subjected to structure-sensitive processing), or (ii) merely constitute an implementation of the classical computational approach? The DC framework, as described by Horgan and Tienson, avoids both horns of this dilemma. On one hand, the DC framework endorses a (non-classical) 'language of thought,' with structure-sensitive processing of language-like mental representations. But on the other hand, it deviates from classicism by denying that cognitive processing conforms to *programmable rules* for manipulating these representations on the basis of their syntactic structure. Cognitive state-transitions can fail to conform to such representation-level programmable rules even if they are realized by state-transitions that do conform to programmable rules at sub-cognitive, implementational, levels of description (as do the sub-cognitive state-transitions of the connectionist systems that are simulated on standard computers). Basically, this is because the realization relation from cognitive to mathematical states can be so complex and subtle that the property of tractable computability, for state transitions, fails to 'transfer upward' from sub-cognitive levels to the cognitive level of description. For further discussion of these matters, see Horgan and Tienson (1996, pp. 63–7) and Horgan (1997b).

problem. This requires essentially morphological processes. Accordingly, the morphological content to which one automatically responds does not make for too much information, but rather for information that is used in a manner that is crucial to the power and speed of human cognitive processes. (One should not deny the phenomena simply because one lacks a fully formed and adequate account of how they occur. The pertinent science is clearly developing.)

10 The causal role of morphological content: epistemically appropriate mirroring

As now repeatedly noted, *being* justified involves two factors: first, *having* justification for one's belief that *p*, and second, believing that *p because* of the justification that one has for *p*. This is a *causal/explanatory* 'because': in some suitable way, the pertinent information and the pertinent evidential-support relations need to be causally operative in the actual generation of *p*—causally operative in a way that suitably 'reflects' the evidential-support relations. Having justification for a proposition *p*—i.e. propositional justification—does not by itself render one doxastically justified in believing that *p*, because one might hold the belief for epistemically objectionable reasons (rather than holding it because of the propositional justification that happens to be available). When a cognitive agent forms a belief for an epistemically bad reason, rather than forming it for an epistemically good reason that the agent happens to possess, then this fact prevents the agent from being justified in holding that belief—possession of the good reason notwithstanding.

The crucial question is: What *constitutes* the appropriate kind of causal etiology of the belief, given that in general, belief fixation that is appropriately sensitive to the Quinean and isotropic elements of evidential support is, and must be, essentially morphological?

It is clearly not going to be a matter of explicitly representing all relevant information, say, and also explicitly representing appropriate and suitably specific normative standards whereby a proposition counts as evidentially well-supported relative to a body of information, and then explicitly applying the explicitly represented normative standards to the explicitly represented information. That is hopelessly intractable—intractable to do *at all*, and not just at the level of conscious processing. Thus it is clear that it is not going to be a matter of occurrent isomorphism—as would be demanded by *PT*.

We will here sketch an alternative account of the causal etiology of belief, in cases where essentially morphological processing is involved. After we describe the idea in a generic and somewhat abstract way (sections 10.1 and 10.2), we will then put some flesh on the bones of the abstract account by elaborating it in a way that incorporates key ideas from the DC framework (section 10.3)—although in principle, the fundamental story might be fleshed out in other ways too. We will then conclude (in section 10.4) by considering a likely objection.

10.1 Dispositions, capacities, and causal-explanatory 'because'-claims

We begin with general observations that we will draw upon in section 10.2 in framing an account of the kinds of dependencies in causal processing that appropriately mirror evidential dependencies and thus make for being justified.

First, dispositions, and disposition-involving properties like capacities, often figure in correct 'because'-claims of the causal-explanatory kind. The recreational vehicle rolled over in the turn, although the other vehicles taking the turn at the same speed did not, *because* the RV was vertically unstable (or, in the terminology of the National Health and Transportation Safety Administration, 'prone to rollover'). Why did Bubba succeed in ordering what he wanted for dinner in the restaurant in Tokyo but Frederick not? *Because* Bubba speaks Japanese (and Frederick does not).

Second, typically when it is correct to cite a disposition or capacity in such a causal-explanatory 'because'-claim, there is an underlying causal account of the phenomenon being explained that adverts to a *basis* of the disposition in the system whose behavior is being explained. In the case of the RV's vertical instability, for example, presumably the pertinent basis involves intrinsic features of the vehicle—features that also constitute a 'categorical' basis for the disposition of vertical instability. (The case of Bubba's capacity to speak Japanese is probably not so simple, since it is a subtle and complex psychological capacity—and so is still dispositional itself. However, what we say here about human belief-fixation is likely to apply, mutatis mutandis, to this capacity too.)

Third, it is important to appreciate that even when a system possesses a certain disposition or capacity, and even when it behaves in a way that happens to accord with the disposition or capacity, this need not be *because* it possesses the disposition or capacity in question. For, it can sometimes happen that the basis-features of the disposition or capacity do not have efficacy in the particular case and so the effect is to be causally explained in some other way. (The RV tipped over because the edge of the roadway collapsed under it; Bubba succeeded in ordering dinner in a Tokyo restaurant because he assiduously imitated the sounds his Japanese companion had used in ordering dinner, in an effort to mimic his companion's pronunciation.) In such a case, the disposition or capacity is not *exercised* during the production of the phenomenon to be explained, even though the phenomenon happens to *accord* with that disposition or capacity.

Fourth, often there will be certain counterfactual conditionals whose truth value is pertinent to the truth or falsity of a given 'because'-statement that cites a disposition or capacity. (This will be so even though 'because'-statements probably cannot be *analyzed* via counterfactuals, because of cases of overdetermination, preempted potential causes, and the like.) Had the RV weighed the same without being vertically unstable, then it would have tipped over anyway (because the edge of the roadway would have collapsed under it anyway). Had Bubba not possessed the capacity to speak Japanese, he would have successfully ordered dinner anyway (because he is so good at imitating spoken speech, even in languages he does not understand).

Fifth, the preceding two points are intimately connected, of course. When a phenomenon occurs *because* of the exercise of a disposition or capacity, the features that are the basis of the disposition or capacity also figure importantly in a more complete causal explanation of the phenomenon. This fact underwrites the relevant counterfactual: had the capacity not been exercised on the given occasion, then the relevant phenomenon would not have occurred. On the other hand, when a phenomenon occurs that happens to conform to a given disposition or capacity, but does not occur *because* of the exercise of that disposition or capacity, the features that are the basis for the disposition or capacity would *not* figure importantly in a more complete causal explanation of the phenomenon. Once again, this fact underwrites the relevant counterfactual: had the disposition or capacity been lacking, the phenomenon would have occurred anyway.

Finally, some dispositions and capacities can have a basis that involves the high-dimensional topographical features of the mathematical dynamical system that characterizes a given physical system—where what is so characterized is the overall *physical potentiality profile* of the physical system, i.e. the full set of its potential temporal trajectories through its state-space (with such a trajectory emanating from any initial point in state-space). This physical potentiality-profile will itself have a further basis, of course: namely a *categorical* basis, involving the intrinsic physical structure of the physical system. In such cases, the *dynamical-system basis* of the original disposition or capacity is intermediate between the high-level disposition or capacity itself on the one hand, and the intrinsic *categorical* basis on the other hand; the categorical basis underlies both the physical potentiality profile, and also the topographical features of the potentiality profile that themselves constitute the dynamical-system basis of the original disposition or capacity.

It will be useful to illustrate this last point with an example. A very widely used technique for 'training up' connectionist networks to perform various problem-solving tasks is so-called 'propagation of error.' The mathematical basis of the technique involves dynamical-system features in a central way: the high-dimensional 'weight space' of a neural network (with one dimension for each inter-node weighted connection), and dynamical evolution through weight space during training. The core idea of error propagation is this: construe the n-dimensional weight space as a contoured surface in an (n+1)-dimensional space, with lower points on this surface corresponding to weight-settings for which the network performs better on a given input-output task than it does at higher points on the surface; then gradually alter the weights during training in a way that progressively moves the network downhill on this 'error surface,' until a weight-setting is reached that is lower than any nearby points on the surface.[21] Thus, the dynamical-system basis for the network's disposition to learn

---

[21] To quote the seminal paper:

The problem... is that whereas there is a very simple guaranteed learning rule for all problems that can be solved without hidden units, namely... the delta rule..., there is no equally powerful rule for learning in

an input-output mapping via such training is this: the network's error surface is contoured in such a way that for a large proportion of this surface, 'gradient descent' from an initial point in weight space leads to a minimum point that is sufficiently close to the global minimum that the network now generates the target output patterns in response to its input patterns.

For any specific network, of course, the categorical basis of the error surface is the network's intrinsic structure, involving intrinsic features such as the number of nodes and the specific inter-node connections.[22] Thus, these intrinsic features are also the categorical basis for the specific network's capacity to be 'trained up' via successive applications of error propagation. But if one wants to know why a *large class* of networks will tend to learn a desired input/output pattern via iterative application of the weight-alteration procedure—why this is so regardless of the specific intrinsic features of the particular network that happens to be employed—then the appropriate answer appeals not to any specific categorical basis for this capacity (since the categorical basis will vary from one particular network to another), but rather to the dynamical-system basis mentioned in the previous paragraph, namely *being so contoured that comparatively few steepest-descent downhill trajectories lead to 'shallow' local minima*. This dynamical-system basis-property is possessed in common by the error surfaces of the trainable networks generally, despite the fact that different individual networks have otherwise different error surfaces in virtue of different categorical basis-features.

---

networks with hidden units.... In this chapter we present... a clear generalization of the delta rule. We call this the *generalized delta rule*.... The learning procedure we propose involves the presentation of a set of pairs of input and output patterns. The system first uses the input vector to produce its own output vector and then compares this with the *desired output*, or *target vector*. If there is no difference, no learning takes place. Otherwise the weights are changed to reduce the difference.... With no hidden units, this generates the standard delta rule.... The weight change dictated by the delta rule... corresponds to performing steepest descent on a surface in weight space whose height at any point in weight space is equal to the error measure..... Without hidden units, the error surface is shaped like a bowl with only one minimum, so gradient descent is guaranteed to find the best weights. With hidden units, however, it is not so obvious how to compute the derivatives, and the error surface is concave upwards, so there is the danger of getting stuck in local minima. The main theoretical contribution of this chapter is to show that there is an efficient way of computing the derivatives [thereby implementing gradient descent on the error surface in weight space]. The main empirical contribution is to show that the apparently fatal problem of local minima is irrelevant to a wide variety of learning tasks. (Rumelhart, Hinton, and Williams 1986, pp. 321–24.)

[22] A network must also have certain intrinsic features in order be to be susceptible to updating of its weights by means of the generalized delta rule. In particular, the activation function for the individual units must be such that the output of a unit is a differentiable function of the net total input. Linear threshold units do not satisfy this requirement because their derivative is infinite at the threshold and zero elsewhere. (See Rumelhart, Hinton, and Williams 1986, pp. 324–35.) Notice that this intrinsic feature, common to a wide variety of networks with different specific activation functions, itself corresponds to an important dynamical-systems property of a network's *activation landscape* (for any given setting of the network's weights): roughly, being fully differentiable at every point on the landscape (although the network might well update itself in discrete time-steps). This feature allows the activation landscape to be progressively 'molded,' via gradient descent in weight space by means of successive applications of the generalized delta rule, in such a way that trajectories along the activation landscape come increasingly close to implementing the input-output function that the system is being trained to learn.

10.2 Being justified and essentially morphological belief fixation

Human beings possess a subtle and sophisticated belief-forming competence, one which involves a general capacity to generate beliefs that are well warranted relative to a very large body of background information. As argued above, in cases of beliefs in which the epistemic warrant involves substantial isotropic and Quineian aspects, the process of belief fixation is essentially morphological. That is, such processes must accommodate the evidentially relevant background information, and also must accommodate the applicable epistemic norms in virtue of which this information confers objective warrant upon the given belief, in such a way that much of the relevant information, and also the applicable normative standards, are not explicitly represented during the generation of the belief. So, for beliefs whose justificatory support is Quineian/isotropic, epistemic competence involves a more specific kind of warranted-belief forming capacity, namely the capacity for norm-implicit, and highly content-implicit, warranted-belief generation. Call this the capacity for *essentially morphological* warranted-belief generation.

We are ready now to tackle our main question. For the kinds of beliefs whose epistemic support is highly holistic in virtue of substantial isotropic and Quineian elements, what is it to form a belief *because* of the justification one has for that belief? The basic answer (to be elaborated somewhat below) is this: forming the belief *by exercising one's capacity for essentially morphological warranted-belief generation*. This means that the features of the cognitive agent that constitute the basis of this capacity would figure importantly in a sufficiently detailed causal-explanatory account of the belief's etiology. The very features in virtue of which the agent is able to generate warranted beliefs when the warranting factors are Quineian/isotropic are features that causally explain the belief in question.

As stressed already, when an entity behaves in a way that it is disposed to behave, this need not necessarily be because the entity is exercising the relevant disposition or capacity; rather, the causally efficacious features, on the given occasion, might be features other than ones that constitute a basis of the disposition. The point applies here. Suppose that Frederick has justification for the claim that Jonathan stole his poodle; but suppose he adopts this belief not because of the justification he has, but rather because his untrustworthy cousin Lucinda, whom he knows is a flagrant liar—told him so. Then his belief-forming process is not a matter of exercising his capacity for warranted-belief generation. The features that are the basis for his epistemic competence are not here causally operative in the belief-forming process. (Adopting the belief on the basis of Lucinda's testimony is a serious lapse in competence—a performance error.)

This ties in with relevant counterfactuals, since these often bear on questions of causal relevance. Had Frederick's cousin Lucinda not asserted that Jonathan stole the poodle, Frederick would not have believed it. And, had he not possessed good evidence, he would have believed it anyway, on the basis of Lucinda's testimony.

Even if one fixes on the reasons that are part of the justification one has for a given belief, one still might not form the belief because of the justification one has. For, one still might not be exercising one's epistemic competence, and thus one still might not be forming the belief because of these reasons *qua good reasons*. Suppose, for instance, that Frederick asks the Gypsy Fortune Teller who stole his poodle. She tells him that Jonathan did, and she cites some factors that she says are good evidence for this claim. Frederick uncritically accepts everything she says, even though he does not himself appreciate the evidential force of the factors she cites as reasons. Once again, his belief is not produced by the exercise of epistemic competence, and hence he does not form the belief because of the justification he has for it.

This too ties in with suitable counterfactuals. Had Frederick considered by himself the factors cited by the fortuneteller, and had she not claimed that these factors were evidence that Jonathan stole the poodle, then Frederick would not have taken them as implicating Jonathan.

When one exercises one's belief-forming competence, one does so with respect to specific reasons that one has for a given belief. Rather sophisticated distinctions arise concerning the causal roles that reasons can play or fail to play. These distinctions can be smoothly accommodated within the construal of belief-forming competence we are proposing here. For example, there can be cases where one has several justifications for a given belief, each sufficient in its own right—and where one forms the belief because of one of these justifications, but not the other. So what is needed is the idea of forming the belief by exercising one's belief-forming competence *in a way that involves the particular justification*. Basically, what this means is that in the given case, two kinds of factors are jointly implicated causally: (i) factors that constitute, or partly constitute, the basis of the belief-forming competence, and (ii) factors that constitute, or partly constitute, the embodiment (perhaps morphological rather than occurrent) of certain specific items of information (namely items because of which one is forming the belief).

Once again, counterfactuals are relevant (barring cases like ones where nonoperative features of type (iii) are 'waiting in the wings' as preempted potential causes). In a case where an agent has two justifications A and B for p, but believes p because of A and not because of B, typically this is true: Had the agent possessed A without possessing B, then the agent would have believed p anyway. Likewise, typically this is true too: had the agent possessed B without possessing A, then the agent would not have believed p.

That is the basic picture of what constitutes being justified in believing that p—of what constitutes believing that p because of a justification one has for p. In cases where the justification one has is significantly Quineian/isotropic, the exercise of one's belief-forming competence involves exercising the capacity for essentially morphological warranted-belief formation—and more specifically, exercising this capacity in a way that involves the particular justification. Let us say that the information that is accommodated morphologically in these episodes of belief-accommodation is *morphologically internalized* information, and that the objective normative standards in virtue of which the information evidentially supports the given belief are *morphologically internalized* normative standards. When a cognitive agent forms a belief by exercising the capacity for essentially morphological warranted-belief formation, and thereby forms the belief because of the justification the agent has for the belief, the morphologically internalized reasons and the morphologically internalized normative standards thereby are causally implicated in the etiology of the belief.[23] Such is the causal-explanatory role of morphological content, in cases where the agent forms a belief because of a Quineian/isotropic justification that the agent has for the belief.

10.3 Being justified and the DC framework

Within the DC framework, the picture just sketched can be filled out in somewhat greater detail. At the dynamical-system level of description, the basis of a cognitive agent's capacity for essentially morphological warranted-belief formation will be certain topographical features of the high-dimensional activation landscape for the creature's neural network—certain slopes on the activation landscape. Since these are topographical features of the network's physical potentiality profile, rather than intrinsic physical features of the network itself, they are not a *categorical* basis for the agent's capacity for essentially morphological belief formation. Nevertheless, these high-dimensional topographical features are the ones that most perspicuously explain why and how the belief-forming capacity is implemented by the network; what matters about the network's intrinsic structure is precisely that this structure subserves an appropriately contoured activation-landscape—a landscape whose structure is the key to how the cognitive agent exercises its belief-forming competence.

So, thinking in terms of the topography of the high-dimensional activation landscape for a cognitive agent's neural network, here is a way of developing the points made in section 10.2. (In principle, the approach we will now describe could be refined or further elaborated by invoking dynamical-systems ideas in various additional ways beyond what we will say here.) We are considering a cognitive agent who engages in lots of essentially morphological belief formation, relative to an overall body of background information. Insofar as the actual cognitive agent is susceptible to performance errors of one sort or another, the agent's actual activation landscape differs from an activation landscape that would be the basis for an *ideal* belief-forming competence, under objectively appropriate epistemic standards, relative to the background information. Nevertheless, the agent's activation landscape approximates an ideal landscape reasonably well, albeit not perfectly. Call this the *associated ideal-competence landscape* for the agent.[24]

---

[23] Should one also say the internalized reasons and normative standards are *causally efficacious* in the etiology of the belief? There are different positions one might take on this issue, depending (inter alia) on whether one holds that dynamical-system basis-features for a disposition can be causal properties, or whether one instead holds that only *categorical* basis properties can be full-fledged causal properties. For present purposes, we will remain neutral on this issue. Either way, dynamical-system basis properties often play a crucial role in the causal explanation of a phenomenon, and thereby are 'causally implicated' in its etiology.

[24] The ideal-competence landscape, as construed here, is supposed to be closely tied to the individual agent's psychological makeup (and not just to the total available information). Thus, even if two different cognitive agents have the same total available background information and undergo the same informational inputs, their ideal-competence landscapes might sometimes lead to different beliefs because of differences in

In various specific instances of belief formation, any of a variety of things might happen. First, the agent might form a belief that p because of justification the agent has for p—thereby being justified in believing p. Here, the agent's cognitive trajectory is determined by local sloping on the activation landscape (in the vicinity of the point in activation space from which the belief-forming process commences) that coincides closely with the local sloping on the corresponding ideal-competence landscape.

Second, the agent might fail to form a belief that p even though the agent has justification for p. Here, the agent's cognitive trajectory is predominantly determined by local sloping on the activation landscape that does *not* coincide closely with the local sloping on the corresponding ideal-competence landscape. The trajectory is significantly deflected, so much so that it does not lead to a belief that p.

Third, it might happen that the agent has justification for p, and forms a belief that p, and yet does not form this belief because of the justification the agent possesses. Here too, as with the preceding case, the agent's cognitive trajectory is predominantly determined by local sloping on the activation landscape that does not coincide closely with the local sloping on the corresponding ideal-competence landscape. Nevertheless, other aspects of the local topography happen to determine a trajectory that results in the agent's forming the belief that p.

Fourth, it might happen that the agent has more than one sufficient justification for p, and the agent forms the belief that p because of one of these justifications, and yet the agent does *not* form the belief that p because of the other justifications. In this case, the local topography of the corresponding ideal-competence landscape has two separate sets of slope-features (possibly superimposed) either of which would suffice to determine a cognitive trajectory leading to a belief that p, and that jointly overdetermine such a trajectory. But the agent's actual activation landscape is such that in the local vicinity of the point on the landscape from which the belief-forming process commences, only one of these two sets of slope-features is present; and this set of features determines a cognitive trajectory leading to a belief that p.

The four possibilities just described all involve essentially morphological belief-formation *relative to a body of information*—the idea being that this relativization parameter includes all the information available to a cognitive agent at a given moment in time. A more complete picture of competent belief-formation would have to allow for diachronic updating of the background information itself—which surely would include progressive molding of the activation landscape through learning, to incorporate new morphological information. Within the DC framework, this diachronic dimension of cognition would involve incorporating the idea of learning as the internal alteration of the factors that determine the cognitive

---

certain correlative cognitive capacities—for instance, differences in pertinent kinds of intelligence. Furthermore (and apart from any such differences in correlative cognitive capacities), the two agents' respective ideal-competence landscapes might sometimes lead to different beliefs anyway; for, sometimes two reasonable people who have the same information can just disagree.

system's synchronic activation landscape at any moment in time (internal processes corresponding roughly to the progressive application of weight-change rules when a connectionist network is being trained up). This involves thinking of the overall cognitive system as a higher-dimensional dynamical system in which these successive, progressively refined, synchronic activation-landscapes are embedded as lower-dimensional subsystems. But we will not pursue such matters here. Enough has been said to explain how the key ideas in section 10.2 can be fleshed out within the DC framework.

10.4 Objection: belief-forming competence and planetary motion

Let us briefly consider an objection to our proposed treatment of doxastic justification. The objection focuses on our claims (i) that objectively appropriate normative standards for belief formation have been morphologically internalized by an epistemically competent cognitive agent, and (ii) these internalized standards are causally implicated (along with specific items of morphologically embodied information) in epistemically competent belief formation. The objection is this:

Consider a planetary system. The system is disposed to evolve temporally in ways that conform to the laws of celestial mechanics. So, by your account, the system thereby has 'internalized' the laws of celestial mechanics. Moreover, on your account the planetary system behaves as it does *because* it has 'internalized' these laws: had it not 'internalized' them, then the laws of celestial mechanics would not have obtained vis-à-vis the system, and thus the system would have behaved differently. But it is absurd to say such things about a planetary system. Thus, your position is absurd. It does not deliver any interesting and non-trivial sense in which epistemic normative standards are 'internalized' in a cognitive system, or any interesting and non-trivial sense in which such putatively internalized standards could be causally implicated in the belief-forming process.

Reply: The story we are telling is intended to apply to a system that has a suitably complex *competence*, and involves morphological features of the system whereby that competence is implemented. Only insofar as the notion of competence makes sense and is applicable will it be appropriate or make good sense to talk about morphologically internalized information or standards—or of morphologically internalized information and standards being causally implicated. In the case of a planetary system, however, there is no purchase on talk of competence. Planetary systems always and everywhere behave in conformity to the laws of physics; there is no other physically possible way they could behave. By contrast, take some congeries of interconnected neurons, on the order of 10 to 100 billion (as in a human brain). Stick it into a human body, and in such a way that all the usual sensory-input neurons feed into the congeries and all the usual motor-neurons feed out of the congeries to the body's muscles. There are *innumerable* neuron-congeries that would not implement the relevant kind of cognitive competence, and that would not be an implementation of any sort of appropriate 'control system' for the body. Any such congeries would obey the laws of physics, of course, but that hardly means that the congeries would possess the subtle and complex dispositions that constitute the morphological internalization of epistemic normative standards, and of specific items of information—dispositions that one's own central nervous system possesses by dint of evolution and learning. So the essentially morphological belief-forming capacities we are discussing here are integral aspects of a complex and subtle kind of cognitive competence. It is because of that, and only because of that, that it is intelligible and appropriate to talk about normative standards and items of information being morphologically internalized in the system—and about the system forming beliefs because of its epistemic competence.

11 Traditional epistemology, informational demands, and real cognitive competence

The appreciation of the holistic elements of belief-fixation is not, at least not primarily, a product of cognitive science. Rather, this arises out of fairly traditional, low-grade a priori, epistemological reflection—for example, out of reflection on the role of ancillary hypotheses and webs of belief that can be found in writings of philosophers such as Hempel and Quine, and many others. While Quine may have come to a pioneering advocacy of a kind of naturalized epistemology, his reflections on holism really do not make central use of empirical psychology. Rather, here one encounters, and learns from, a fairly traditional form of philosophical reflection. A recognition of the holistic dimensions of belief-fixation is available 'from one's armchair.' Such armchair inquiry serves to highlight the information to which a successful epistemic agent must be sensitive—it characterizes the informational tasks facing an epistemic agent. (In light of such earlier philosophical reflections, and looking back in time from the present moment, it is really no surprise at all that the frame problem subsequently arose in the branch of inquiry that came to be called cognitive science.)

Our concern has been to explain how one can make use of one's relevant information, given the potential relevance of everything to everything. The frame problem—at least in the form presented here—arises when one considers that such informational tasks apparently cannot be managed within the resources provided by classic computational approaches to the mind. Because it is an empirical fact that human epistemic agents have a non-negligible competence for managing the informational tasks in question, one arrives at an empirical result of importance to both epistemology and cognitive science: to echo a recent title (Fodor 2001) 'the mind does not work that way.' That is, apparently the mind does not manage such tasks by computation. Rather, the mind must, in central processes of belief fixation, work by employing a lot of morphological content—and by doing so in ways too subtle and nuanced to conform to programmable rules.

Perhaps the best overall understanding of the dialectical situation begins with the recognition that it has been common for investigators to tentatively identify a phenomenon that ultimately needs to be accounted for. Of course, when the theory on hand in the relevant disciplines does not allow them to account for the observed regularities, investigators then have a problem. For example, when the reasonably well-documented regularity exhibited in blackbody radiation proved inexplicable within the resources of classical Newtonian physics and statistical mechanics, investigators were forced to cast about for theoretical innovations. (Historically the problem of blackbody spectra led Plank to initiate theoretical innovations that would ultimately eventuate in quantum mechanics.)

The frame problem seems analogous. While facing a problem occasioned by unexplained apparent phenomena, one can have reasonable (if defeasible) confidence regarding the reality of the phenomena for which an account needs ultimately to be given. (Again, Plank had ample experimental results characterizing the phenomenon of blackbody radiation, for which an explanatory theory was wanting.) Similarly, the philosophical reflections highlighting the holistic dimensions of belief fixation provide a reasonable (if somewhat provisional) understanding of the informational tasks facing cognitive systems as successful epistemic agents—these informational tasks represent an observed aspect of belief fixation in competent cognitive agents. The frame problem then reflects the inability of computational cognitive science to account for how humans can and do manage these tasks (to the extent that they succeed). What is clearly indicated by the phenomena—by the informational tasks to be managed, and by the limited but non-negligible human capacity for managing them—is the need for morphological content.

The discussion in sections 9 and 10 represents a suggestion regarding how those holistic informational tasks might be managed by morphological content, a suggestion inspired by some connectionist cognitive science. Were this suggestion ultimately to prove unsatisfactory, one would still need an explanation of the phenomenological regularities: the successful management of holistic elements of belief fixation by morphological content. Put simply: although they are clearly related, the case for there being something like morphological content at work in central processes of belief fixation does not stand or fall with the connectionist-inspired suggestion advanced in section 9. While those remarks are intended to extend and buttress the present points, the need for something like morphological content stands independently.

12 Summary

There is a profitable way of understanding much fairly mainline epistemology: epistemologists have commonly expressed important truths about the informational demands on successful and desirable cognitive systems. In so doing, they may be said to have begun to characterize important elements of human epistemic competence. The informational demands or tasks that they characterize represent a cognitive competence that successful epistemic agents—human beings—possess. To the extent that this holds, such informational demands are aptly thought of as corresponding to regularities characteristic of competent human epistemic agents—as roughly representing important characteristics of epistemically significant cognitive processes, processes that ultimately want a theoretical accounting within cognitive science. Traditional epistemologists commonly also have relied, often implicitly, on unexamined and unrealistic conceptions of what it would take to conform to the informational demands they identify. This is the burden of our critical focus on *PT* and its near kin.

In effect, much epistemology can be understood as engaging with two tasks. First is thematizing the informational demands that are accommodated by competent human epistemic agents—the epistemology of informational demands. Second is describing the kinds of cognitive processes by which these informational demands can and should be met—the epistemology of doxastic justification. As distilled out of influential epistemological work (in sections 5–6), *PT* and its near kin represent our reading of the common answers advanced regarding the second matter, the epistemology of justificatory cognition. In this chapter we have argued that these answers are deeply mistaken. Epistemological reflection on the epistemology of informational demands has been more promising—and it strongly suggests that central processes of belief formation are Quineian/isotropic. This then confronts the standard *PT* family of positions regarding the epistemology of justificatory cognition with a fatal problem: a variant of the frame problem (discussed in section 7). To avoid this problem, one must recognize that much of human competence involves managing informational demands by way of processes that are essentially morphological—processes in which much information implicit in the standing structure of the cognitive system gets automatically accommodated without being explicitly represented in occurrent cognitive states, either conscious or unconscious (section 7.2). One must then abandon *PT* and its near kin (section 8). In section 9, we suggested a helpful way of thinking about essentially morphological processes, drawing on what Horgan and Tienson call the dynamical cognition framework. In section 10, we explored how the recognition of the epistemic importance of morphological content allows one to make sense of the distinction between having justification and being justified—allowing retention of the idea that the agent's belief-forming processes appropriately mirror the propositional justification, and doing so without supposing *PT* or its variants.

Thinking about the epistemic significance of morphological content and essentially morphological processes opens up new possibilities in epistemology. Some venerable epistemological positions, commonly posed as competitors, now are apt to be seen as plausibly complementary partial perspectives when recast in these terms. We next turn to elaborating some of these epistemological payoffs.

8

Iceberg Epistemology: Vindicating and Transforming Some Traditional Accounts of Justification

1 Two complementary foci in epistemology

The fact that much competent belief formation is essentially morphological has an important general consequence for epistemology: namely that much that is epistemologically relevant in the psychological etiology of beliefs is *unconscious* during belief formation (since information and normative standards that are not present in the form of occurrent states or events during belief formation presumably are not something one is consciously aware of during processing). Furthermore, typically when the justification one has for a given belief has significantly Quineian/isotropic aspects, then in general it will not be possible to consciously represent the entire justification consciously and explicitly at all—not even after the fact. (Apparently, much the same can be said regarding the information that is automatically accommodated within the competent generation of perceptual beliefs.)

These considerations lead fairly directly to a conception of epistemology that allows for two legitimate, and complementary, foci. The first is the traditional one: epistemologically relevant psychological factors that are conscious during belief formation, and/or are readily psychologically accessible after the fact as evidentially relevant. (Among the considerations favoring retention of this traditional focus are epistemological interests in self-regulation and in assessing one's epistemic partners.) But the second focus should be the full set of epistemologically relevant psychological factors, many of which are morphologically internalized and may be only partially, piecemeal-fashion, accessible after the fact of belief-formation.

We call this dual-focus conception *iceberg epistemology*. The idea is that the conscious and consciously accessible aspects of belief formation are just the tip of a larger iceberg of epistemologically relevant psychological factors. To appreciate how humans can ultimately manage their epistemic chores employing processes with a satisfactory balance of postclassical reliability, power, and speed—i.e. to appreciate how human processes can have the kind of holistic integration that yields satisfactory postclassical reliability—one needs to recognize the epistemic importance of processes that rely heavily upon essentially morphological content.

Numerous important issues arise within the general purview of iceberg epistemology. Some of these issues involve the potential of iceberg epistemology to address in new ways, and to systematically transform, issues in more traditional epistemology. In this chapter we pursue one of these, namely the traditional issue of the overall justificatory structure of knowledge and justified belief—a debate in which the three standard, erstwhile competing, positions are foundationalism, coherentism, and structural contextualism. We argue that these three positions each can be given partial vindication within iceberg epistemology—and in a way that largely overcomes their apparent incompatibility with one another. On one hand, when focusing on what we will call *exposed* processes, certain foundationalist and structural-contextualist themes turn out to be very nearly apt. On the other hand, when focusing on the more inclusive set of processes that constitute full epistemic competence, certain coherentist themes can be partially vindicated.

Many foundationalists, coherentists, and contextualists have been committed (at least implicitly) to *PT*, and it is instructive to consider what comes of such positions when each is divested of this commitment. The traditional versions of these epistemological positions, which are committed to *PT*, are undermined by the arguments of the previous chapter. Still, each position has been motivated by forceful ideas about the structure of propositional justification and about the need for such structure to get suitably mirrored in belief-forming processes, and these ideas may yet be independent of the mistaken commitment to *PT* and its kin. When one reconsiders these traditional epistemological positions in light of the importance of morphological content, one finds that each position can be vindicated, in part, and that in the bargain, they cease to be competitors.

2 Traditional accounts of the structure of justification

We begin by setting out how we understand these traditional positions—since only against this background can one appreciate how central doctrines from each can be accommodated, while certain central themes associated with those approaches must be abandoned or revised in important ways.

Advocates of the three positions, although often committed to *PT* at least implicitly, typically have put primary emphasis on the having of justification for a potential belief (i.e. propositional justification)—with little explicit attention to being justified in holding a belief (i.e. doxastic justification) or to the propositional/doxastic distinction itself. Also, discussions of the large-scale structure of justification typically focus on a set of beliefs *actually possessed* by a cognitive agent (an actual agent or a hypothetical one), as opposed to potential beliefs that *would* be propositionally justified for the agent were the agent to have them.

We will follow this common practice here, as we summarize the three traditional accounts of the structure of propositional justification. That is, we will focus on the question of what structural features, exhibited by a set of beliefs actually possessed by an (actual or hypothetical) agent, make it the case that each member of that set is a belief for which the agent *has* justification—i.e. is a belief that is propositionally justified, for the agent. (The agent might, of course, have further beliefs that fall outside the set, and are not propositionally justified.)

As regards the matter of *being* justified in one's beliefs (i.e. doxastic justification), the reader should keep in mind our discussion in Chapter 7, where we argued that *PT* and its kin should be repudiated, and should be replaced by a more liberal conception of how cognitive belief-fixing processes can suitably 'mirror' propositionally-justificatory relations among beliefs. That alternative conception places heavy weight on morphological content, and on the cognitive accommodation of the holistic, Quineian/isotropic, aspects of propositional justification via processes that automatically and implicitly respect large amounts of background morphological content. The relevance of this non-traditional conception of the relation between propositional justification and doxastic justification will become prominent in section 3, where we address its revisionary import vis-à-vis the traditional debate about the evidential structure of justified belief.

2.1 Preliminaries

Although we are largely bracketing the issue of doxastic justification in the present section, focusing instead on what the three traditional views say about the structure exhibited by a set of beliefs when all those beliefs are propositionally justified, it will turn out that each of the three positions still carries certain commitments concerning matters psychological—even apart from the question of doxastic justification. For, each position has something to say about the kinds of psychological states and psychological features that can figure as bearers, and/or conferrers, and/or transmitters, of propositional justification. We will call the set of such psychological states and features, for a given cognitive agent, the agent's *epistemic psychological system*. What we will call the *component question* is this: What kinds of psychological states or features figure as components of a cognitive agent's epistemic psychological system?

Needless to say, *beliefs* are among the components of an epistemic psychological system. All three positions agree on that. Also, advocates of each position commonly distinguish two kinds of belief, and admit both as components: *occurrent* beliefs, and *dispositional* beliefs. An occurrent belief that p is an episode of explicitly holding the propositional content p before one's mind and mentally affirming that content. A dispositional belief that p is a state of being affirmatorily committed with respect to the content p—a state that disposes one to occurrently affirm p, mentally, immediately upon coming to occurrently hold that content before one's mind. But other kinds of mental states or features are potentially eligible too as components of an epistemic psychological system, and on this further issue there is some divergence—divergence among the three traditional positions, and also sometimes divergence among different variants of a given position. Our discussion in the remainder of the present section will pay due attention to the component question.

Before proceeding, let us make some distinctions that will prove useful below. First, we will distinguish between two kinds of intentional psychological states—i.e. two kinds of states with representational content. We will call these, respectively, *explicitly representational* states and *morphologically intentional* states.

Explicitly representational states are the more familiar kind. Any explicitly representational state with intentional content p can be instantiated occurrently, and some also can be instantiated merely dispositionally. An occurrent instantiation includes an explicit representation that has content p, and also includes an occurrent mental attitude or stance or relation vis-à-vis that explicitly represented content (e.g. believing that p, being visually appeared to as though p, etc.). A merely dispositional instantiation of the state is a matter of having the relevant attitude vis-à-vis the relevant content even when one is not currently entertaining that content and no explicit mental representation with that content is currently tokened; such a state involves a disposition to go into an occurrent instantiation of the state, merely upon coming to entertain the content p. Although at least some explicitly representational states can be instantiated merely dispositionally, any such state can only be causally efficacious insofar as it is being occurrently instantiated.

Beliefs, as traditionally conceived in epistemology, are a prototypical species of explicitly representational state, and can be instantiated either occurrently or merely dispositionally. We will refer to such states as *prototypical* beliefs, in order to leave open the possibility that not all beliefs are explicitly representational states.

It may be that some kinds of explicitly representational states do not, and maybe cannot, be instantiated merely dispositionally. For instance, if there are sensory-perceptual appearance-states with intentional content, then perhaps such states can only be instantiated occurrently. The thought is this: one cannot, for example, currently have an intentional attitude of the kind *being visually appeared to as though p* unless an explicit representation with the content p is presently tokened mentally.

In contrast to explicitly representational states are morphologically intentional states. These are persisting states of the whole cognitive system that obtain in virtue of the system's standing structure—its morphology. Such states have the features described in Chapter 7 under the rubric 'morphological content.' A morphologically intentional state with content p does not involve an explicit representation with that content; instead, the content is *implicit* in the cognitive system's morphological structure. Such implicitness is a matter of the system's dispositions to undergo transitions, from one occurrent total cognitive state to another, in ways that are appropriate to the content p—and to do so without deploying any explicit p-representations in the course of such processing. (The pertinent dispositions might well include the disposition to generate, in certain circumstances, an occurrent belief that p; but, unlike a merely-dispositional belief that p, a state with morphological content *p* undergirds the capacity for cognitive processes that can accommodate the content *p* without first generating an explicit, occurrent, representation with that content.)

The question arises whether some morphologically intentional states qualify as *beliefs*. We ourselves are inclined to say yes to that question, but nothing will turn on it in the remainder of this chapter. The important point to bear in mind is that no morphologically intentional states are *prototypical* beliefs, as we are using this phrase here. (Prototypical beliefs are the only kind that are discussed in traditional epistemology.)

Let us now introduce a three-way distinction among several alternative conceptions of an epistemic psychological system, a distinction drawn in terms of how one answers the component question. We will call these positions *minimalism, conservatism,* and *liberalism,* respectively. Minimalism asserts that the only components of an epistemic psychological system are prototypical beliefs—i.e. beliefs that are explicitly representational states, either occurrent or merely dispositional.

Conservatism recognizes, as eligible components of an epistemic psychological system, not only prototypical beliefs but also certain other explicitly representational mental states too. A version of conservatism might, for instance, allow into the system certain belief-like states like hunches, conjectures, working hypotheses, and the like. (These, along with prototypical beliefs can usefully be called *prototypical doxastic states*—with 'prototypical' again indicating that the states in question are all explicitly representational, and 'doxastic' being used deliberately vaguely to mean 'belief-like.') Another version of conservatism might allow in certain non-doxastic states—for instance, sensory-perceptual experiential states, insofar as these are explicitly representational and have truth-evaluable intentional content. (For example, the sensory-perceptual content of one's visual experience when one is looking at a Müller-Lyer display is as-of two horizontal lines one of which is longer than the other, even if one confidently believes they are the same length. Likewise, the sensory-perceptual content of one's visual experience when looking at a partially immersed stick is as-of a stick that is bent at the water-line, even if one confidently believes that the stick is straight.)

Liberalism allows epistemic psychological systems to include, in addition to prototypical beliefs, a kind of component not allowed in by either minimalism or conservatism (and traditionally not even recognized as a distinctive kind of psychological state at all)—namely morphologically intentional states. Liberalism could potentially come in a variety of different versions, depending inter alia on which kinds of morphologically intentional state are allowed in, and/or which explicitly representational states other than prototypical beliefs are allowed in (e.g. doxastic states like hunches and conjectures, and/or non-doxastic states like perceptual seemings).

Armed with the distinctions lately introduced, we are ready now to describe the key tenets of the three traditional accounts in epistemology regarding the structure of empirical justification: foundationalism, coherentism, and structural contextualism.

2.2 Foundationalism

Foundationalists begin with an *inferential model* according to which much justification-having can be understood as a matter of there being an argument based in antecedently justified beliefs from which the justified or supported belief could itself be inferred. Foundationalists then insist that some beliefs—basic beliefs—must have justification of some other kind. They insist that, for a belief of one of the select sorts, an agent can have justification that is not dependent on other beliefs (much less other antecedently justified beliefs). Foundationalists tend to offer one of two alternative general conceptions of the select set of beliefs.

First, some think of these basic beliefs as having non-doxastic sources of justification—and this is particularly attractive when thinking of perceptual beliefs as basic beliefs. Commonly, sensory experiences are thought to provide justificatory reasons for holding perceptual beliefs. (Sensory experiences are typically regarded as intentional—as in the Müller-Lyer case—and often are regarded as having content that is also the content of the basic beliefs they justify.) On this approach, the component question gets answered in a non-minimalist way that incorporates sensory experiences into an epistemic psychological system. These non-doxastic components play a pivotal role, by conferring justification upon perceptual beliefs; and perceptual beliefs, in turn, are foundational beliefs within an epistemic psychological system. (Sometimes, especially when the focus is on a priori justification, certain non-sensory experiences are taken to play an analogous role with respect to certain non-perceptual basic beliefs—e.g. *intellectual seemings*, like it's seeming to be the case that, necessarily, $2 + 2 = 4$. The idea is that such a non-doxastic seeming-experience confers justification upon a belief whose representational content is the same as that of the seeming-state itself; and such beliefs, in turn, are also foundational within the a priori segment of an epistemic psychological system.)

Second, others think of the basic beliefs as somehow each providing reason for thinking that it itself must be true—as in the awkward suggestion that basic beliefs are 'self-justifiers' or that one just sees that a basic belief must be true when contemplating it. This approach has seemed attractive to some when thinking of relatively simple, putatively a priori beliefs (although the appeal to intellectual seemings is another foundationalist alternative). To the extent that one appeals to self-justifying beliefs, one answers the component question in a way that does not incorporate non-doxastic components into an epistemic psychological system. (The two approaches are not exclusive, of course. A foundationalist could, for example, take the first approach with respect to perceptual basic beliefs, and the second approach with respect to non-perceptual basic beliefs—thereby incorporating sensory experiences as components of a psychological epistemic system, but not intellectual seemings.)

Part of the art in foundationalist accounts of having justification is in providing an account of how sensory experiences can provide a reason for a perceptual belief, or of how reflection on a proposition might by itself provide some reason for believing it (without invoking other beliefs). More precisely, the art in foundationalist accounts of propositional justification turns on providing an account according to which (a) an agent's reasons for non-basic beliefs must have the structure of appreciable inferential dependencies on already justified beliefs, and (b) the structured series of inferential dependencies originates from basic beliefs which themselves have justification in some other way—either by individually being their own justification (whatever that might mean) or by getting justification from some non-doxastic state or event such as a sensory experience or an intellectual seeming.

Traditionally, foundationalists who have thought that basic beliefs derive justification from non-doxastic states have been committed to the claim that this justificatory route is 'simple' or 'direct.' This is to say at least this much: the justificatory reason provided by the non-doxastic state for the 'basic belief' does not go through some further beliefs. For example, such justification cannot include an argument (from other beliefs) to the conclusion that when one is in a certain non-doxastic state, the spawned belief is likely true.

Summing up, traditional foundationalist accounts of having justification may be thought of as having three components:

(F1) Much having of justification is a matter of a belief's being inferentially supported by other beliefs which themselves are justified (the inferential model of justificatory structure).[1]

(F2) Inferential justificatory support originates with basic beliefs that possess justification independently of other beliefs—and which jointly serve as the foundation for the full justificatory structure (the foundations model of the structure).

(F3) Insofar as the justification of basic beliefs turns on non-doxastic states—such as perceptual-experience states—it does so by virtue of some relation to such states that is local, and does not 'go through' a ramified inferential route (the directness model of the foundations).

While these three claims provide a good start at formulating foundationalism, it is safe to say that traditional foundationalists have been committed to one further central claim regarding what it is to have justification:

(F4) The basic beliefs constitute a homogeneous set or a few homogeneous sets (homogeneous regress-stoppers).

Here the idea is that the basic beliefs fall into a few kinds, each of which is such that beliefs of that sort have a distinct and clear entitlement to serve as regress-stoppers.

---

[1] Inferential support, in the operative sense, is not a matter of being the product of a *process* of inference; rather, it is a relation of evidential support (either deductive or non-deductive). This kind of inferential support pertains to propositional justification rather than doxastic justification—which means that a potential belief might be inferentially supported even if the agent does not possess that belief at all (let alone possessing it by virtue of an inferential process).

Simple high-grade a priori beliefs are commonly taken as one plausible set of basic beliefs, wearing their epistemic credentials on their sleeves. Simple perceptual beliefs, induced by directly supporting perceptual experiences, are taken to be another case in which one can uniformly rest epistemically assured. Occurrences of such perceptual beliefs are thought to come with much the same epistemic credentials—given their initiating perceptual experiences, they are thought all to come with some significant measure of justification (although this might subsequently be undermined in special situations by collateral information).[2]

Historically, it was common for foundationalists to think of basic beliefs as an absolutely secure foundation—as indubitable, irrevisable, and foundational bits of knowledge. Empiricist foundationalists might look to sense data as such a foundation. But it has since become more common to adopt a more moderate foundationalist stance, and this is what we have sought to characterize above. On the moderate foundationalist view, the basic beliefs need only have some significant measure of justification independent of other beliefs—enough justification to count as bits of knowledge, when true. For example, perceptual beliefs, induced by supporting experience, have significant justification thereby. In many cases, this justification would be sufficient to qualify a veridical perceptual belief as knowledge. Still, says the moderate foundationalist, in some such cases, one's experiential justification can be undermined by one's wider set of beliefs—one's experience need not be all the evidence bearing on one's perceptual belief—so some measure of their justification may depend on other beliefs. Below we will take a closer look at this moderate foundationalism (represented by Audi, 1993).

The foundationalist ideas we have been summarizing are naturally construed as being about propositional justification, first and foremost. However, prominent versions of foundationalism certainly do stress that certain psychological factors need to be actually present in an agent's epistemic psychological system, in order for the agent to have justification for any beliefs. One kind of traditional foundationalism is minimalist about the component question: it recognizes only beliefs as components, and claims that the foundational ones are 'self-justifying.' Another kind is conservative but non-minimalist: it recognizes certain non-doxastic states as components—e.g. sensory-perceptual seemings. Such non-minimalist versions also carry a specific commitment concerning requisite causal linkages among such psychological factors—namely that the non-doxastic mental states (e.g. perceptual experiences) that evidentially 'ground' those basic beliefs must causally generate them without any supplemental counterfactual dependency upon, or

---

[2] How exactly the foundationalist should understand the general justificatory status supposedly enjoyed by basic beliefs (in those cases where it is not undermined) is a delicate matter. Plausibly, something along the lines of the default *entitlement* that Burge (1993) posits in connection with perceptual, remembered, and testimonial beliefs might serve. Henderson (2008) argues that such a default entitlement structure cannot be well understood without positing background processes that manage certain holistic chores—a point that feeds into the view of quasi-foundationalism that will emerge in the present chapter.

modulation by, the agent's other informational resources.[3] Nonetheless, the superstructure of justification that rests on such foundations is, first and foremost, a structure of justification-had for the nonbasic beliefs—i.e. a structure of propositional justification.

Although some traditional versions of foundationalism are minimalist about the component question whereas others are not, none recognize morphologically intentional mental states as components of an epistemic psychological system. (The idea that there might be morphologically intentional mental states typically is not even considered.) Thus, the non-minimalist versions of traditional foundationalism embrace conservatism about the component question, not liberalism. It is small wonder, then, that traditional foundationalism almost inevitably ends up committed to *PT* concerning *doxastic* justification, at least implicitly; for, unless and until one countenances implicitly morphological states as an element of human psychology, it is very hard to see what account could be given, other than *PT*, of what constitutes believing a proposition *because of* the justification one has for that proposition.

2.3 Coherentism

Coherentism takes as its starting point the recognition that there commonly are important holistic elements involved in propositional justification. Isotropic and Quineian factors figure importantly in the holistic support relations between beliefs that coherentists take as central to, or constitutive of, propositional justification. Consider any two beliefs that are unrelated when considered just by themselves, that is, when considered as a pair in isolation from other beliefs one might hold. Any two such beliefs can become highly relevant to each other when one takes into account other beliefs one holds or might hold. This is isotropy. The relevance of one belief to another may be mediated through untold possible additional sets of beliefs. The beliefs that are relevant to and support a given belief can be highly ramified. As a result, what beliefs are relevant to some given belief is dependent on what other beliefs one holds. Thus, isotropy: the potential relevance of any belief to any other belief, and the relevance of all one's beliefs to what beliefs are relevant to what others. On a coherentist account, at least one which accommodates such isotropy, the extent to which an agent has justification for a given belief can be a function of the ways in which disparate beliefs within the agent's global set of beliefs conspire together to make for mediated support relations.

---

[3] It is a tricky matter formulating this in a way that allows for the defeasibility of basic beliefs—something which many contemporary foundationalists would want to provide. One would want to insist that the processes involved in the generation of a perceptual belief, B, be such that the agent would not hold B were that agent not to have undergone the supporting experiences. However, 'moderate foundationalists' must struggle to allow for cases in which coherence with wider theory (for example) can provide additional reasons for holding a belief, and processes sensitive to this can add to the agent's justification for so believing. Perhaps counterfactual dependency involving strength of belief, or confidence, is what is needed. Other complications would be needed to treat cases in which the belief is undermined somewhat by countervailing considerations. Generally, it would seem helpful to distinguish something like primary processes of the direct sort the foundationalists envision and secondary, more coherence-sensitive, processes. Audi (1993) provides a careful attempt at developing such moderate foundationalism.

Yet more striking from a coherentist perspective would be various Quineian aspects of support relations: the justification one has for one's belief can be dependent on global features of one's system of beliefs, of which the justified belief is a part. The individual belief then seems to have justification derivatively, as a component of a whole system of beliefs which itself has a more fundamental kind of justification. One encounters various accounts of the global features of belief systems that give rise to an agent's having holistic justification. Coherentists commonly mention simplicity and consistency, of course, but the global coherence which they prize as featuring in epistemic justification is thought to involve more than such virtues. Thus BonJour writes of 'explanatory coherence.'[4]

Enough has been said to allow us to distill out and express the first core coherentist theme:

(C1) Numerous epistemic support relations are holistic—involving isotropic or Quineian features of systems of beliefs—and this sort of justification that a belief-system may have is antecedent to, or more fundamental than, the justification of component beliefs (*the fundamentality of holistic support relations*).

This is nicely captured in BonJour's (1985, p. 92) model for the justification of individual empirical beliefs, which requires holistic justification to provide a more fundamental and central piece of the epistemic action. The justification had by individual beliefs is then understood as derivative upon the justification had by the coherent system.

Of course, many foundationalists would allow that systems of nonbasic beliefs can have global features—forms of coherence—that bestow some measure of justification on those beliefs, and that can augment or diminish the justification of particular basic beliefs. However, foundationalists would want to add that this obtains only when those systems themselves cohere with basic beliefs that have a substantial measure of justification independent of other beliefs. To speak poetically, perhaps, the foundationalist thinks of systematic coherence as rather like well-placed mirrors in a candlelit dining room: the illumination provided by the candles can be helpfully spread about to objects that lack their intrinsic measure of light, and some of that illumination may fall on another candle. To the foundationalists, the justificatory 'juice' derives from the basic beliefs, paralleling the way in which the light derives from the candles. To avoid having their position subsumed as a mere variation on foundationalism, coherentists must insist that there are no basic beliefs.[5] Thus, in addition to (C1), the centrality of holistic support relations, the coherentist must also be committed to:

---

[4] One might here seek to draw on Kitcher's (1981, 1993) idea of 'explanatory unification' to flesh out one's understanding of at least part of what this might amount to.

[5] Or, at least, that there are no basic empirical beliefs. As reflected in BonJour's coherentist thought, it is common to think of these matters with attention focused on the justification that one has for empirical belief—allowing coherentists to help themselves to putative a priori truths which they may think of as high-grade a priori and basic. In keeping with this tradition, we will here focus on coherentism with respect to the justification had by empirical beliefs.

(C2) Holistic support relations are the basis for the justification of all beliefs (*the pervasiveness of holistic support relations*).

Thus, on BonJour's account, the propositional justification of individual beliefs, including perceptual beliefs, is always a derivative matter; hence, there are no foundationally basic beliefs.

The importance of providing for the epistemic role of observation—or perceptual beliefs—is reflected in the structure of BonJour (1985); a central theme running through that book is that an adequate coherentist account of observation would provide the coherentist with important resources for meeting a set of familiar, and threatening, objections (pp. 106–110). One such objection is this: without empirical discipline, there would seem to be *many alternative coherent systems*. This possibility of underdetermination seems at least partially to result from the fact that the core coherentist model as yet fails to provide an account of what is distinctive of empirical knowledge—namely that it is disciplined by some sort of 'input from the world.' This is troubling because it leaves the coherentist open to a second crucial objection, the *truth objection*—namely that coherentists have not met (perhaps cannot meet) the central meta-epistemic task confronting any advocate of a set of epistemic standards: the task of showing that the standards are conducive to the production of true beliefs. BonJour proposed to deflect these objections by providing a coherentist basis for observationally constraining empirical belief systems. With such constraint in play, he argued, 'adhering to coherentist standards over the long run is very likely to yield beliefs that correspond to reality' (p. 169).

So, much depends upon whether or not the coherentist model can be elaborated to provide an account of empirical input—one in which perceptual-experience-generated beliefs serve as *non-optional* anchors for empirical belief-systems and yet are derivative in the justification they possess. BonJour outlines a reasonable coherentist response. The basic idea is that, while there are beliefs that arise noninferentially, these must still have what justification they possess by virtue of holistic, coherence-involving relations of evidential support. These (characteristically rich and 'forceful') beliefs are termed 'cognitively spontaneous beliefs' by BonJour. Although a belief might arise spontaneously (or noninferentially), the agent only has justification for it if the agent also has a system of (globally justified) beliefs from which it could be inferred. The rudimentary model for the propositional justification of a cognitively spontaneous belief, spelled out in the format of an explicit argument-form, would be the following (BonJour 1985, p. 123):

(1) I have a cognitively spontaneous belief that P which is of kind K.
(2) Conditions C obtain.
(3) Cognitively spontaneous beliefs of kind K in conditions C are very likely to be true.

Therefore, my belief that P is very likely to be true.
Therefore, (probably) P.

Something very much along these lines seems indicated when one attempts to honor the above-mentioned coherentist principles (C1) and (C2).

In addition to these two principles there is a third element in traditional coherentist accounts of what it is to have propositional justification—an element that ultimately provides traditional coherentists one motivation for accepting (C1) and (C2) in the first place. The central line of thought unfolds as follows. One can reflectively appreciate that holistic support relations are crucial in the justification one can have for many beliefs (C1). Now, many foundationalists would be happy to grant this much—allowing that, once one moves beyond basic beliefs, explanatory coherence becomes epistemically significant. Moderate foundationalists might even grant that such support relations might augment the justification had by basic beliefs, or that a lack of coherence might detract from the justification had by basic beliefs. However, they would insist that, in the case of the basic beliefs, one can and must have a kind of justification for belief that does not depend on other beliefs, and that such justification can be decisive.

In contrast, coherentists insist that holistic support relations are required to have significant propositional justification even for those beliefs that foundationalists take to be 'basic.' Their reason for taking issue with foundationalism at this point is a systematic and general problem facing foundationalist accounts of propositional justification for basic empirical beliefs in particular. At least when propositional justification for a belief is understood as having a reason to think that belief true (and the matter is commonly understood in just such terms), one can pose a general objection to foundationalism regarding empirical beliefs. First, consider those foundationalist accounts that do not begin with the somewhat mysterious and paradoxical idea that certain empirical beliefs are self-justifying. This sort of foundationalist approach takes sensory experiences, non-doxastic perceptual-experiential *states*, as providing the justification for the basic empirical beliefs, the perceptual *beliefs*. But, then, one must face an objection expressed by BonJour:

Remember that the issue we are presently concerned with is whether sensory experience can *justify* beliefs. But if sensory experience is... nonconceptual, and given that beliefs are obviously formulated in propositional and conceptual terms, it becomes hard to see how there can be an intelligible justificatory relation between the two. How can something that is not even formulated in conceptual terms be a reason for thinking that something that is thus formulated is true? (2002, p. 200).

The problem is reflected in Davidson's remarks:

The relation between a sensation and a belief cannot be logical, since sensations are not beliefs or other propositional attitudes. What then is the relation? The answer is, I think, obvious: the relation is causal. Sensations cause some beliefs and in *this* sense are the basis or ground of those beliefs. But a causal explanation of a belief does not show how or why the belief is justified (1983, p. 428).

BonJour elaborates:

The basic idea of givenness, after all, is to distinguish two aspects of ordinary cognitive states, their capacity to justify other cognitive states and their own need for justification, and then to try to find a kind of state which possesses only the former aspect and not the latter—a state of immediate apprehension or intuition. But we can now see plainly that any such attempt is fundamentally misguided and intrinsically hopeless. For it is clear on reflection that it is one and the same feature of a cognitive state, namely, its assertive or at least representational content, which both enables it to confer justification on other states and also creates the need for it to be itself justified—thus making it impossible in principle to separate these two aspects (1985, p. 78; see also 1985, Chapter 4).

All this boils down to a strongly held coherentist judgment that only another 'cognitive' state—i.e. only another state that represents things as being a certain specific way, and is assessable for being correct or incorrect in how it represents things—can serve as the justification had for a belief. Beliefs are paradigmatic cognitive states, in this sense of 'cognitive,' and there are various potential views about which further kinds of mental states can be cognitive in the relevant sense. Since traditional coherentist writings do not entertain the idea of morphological content or the correlative notion of a morphologically intentional state, we take it that the operative sense of 'cognitive state' comes to the same thing as what we ourselves are calling an *explicitly representational* state. We can then formulate a third traditional coherentist theme:

(C3) Only an explicitly representational state (either occurrent or dispositional) can contribute to the justification one has for a belief.

We will take (C1)–(C3) to characterize the central themes of traditional coherentist accounts of propositional justification.

What does traditional coherentism say about the component question? There are two potential routes one could take here, corresponding to two potential variants of the view. One alternative is to be minimalist: say that only *beliefs* are components of an epistemic psychological system. This is the tack that has in fact been taken by influential recent advocates of coherentism, such as BonJour and Davidson; witness the lately quoted passages, which effectively treat sensory-experiential states as non-cognitive (i.e. as lacking truth-assessable representational content), and effectively treat prototypical beliefs as the only constituents of an epistemic psychological system.

Another potential variant of traditional coherentism is worth noting, however. This alternative version would answer the component question in a non-minimalist way, thereby admitting into an agent's epistemic psychological system certain cognitive states other than beliefs. In particular, it might admit various sensory-perceptual experiences, which after all are very plausibly regarded as 'cognitive' in the pertinent sense: they represent things as being a certain specific way (whether or not the experiencer thereby comes to *believe* that things are that way), and are themselves assessable for accuracy. (Think again of familiar examples like the visual experience of a partly submerged stick that looks bent even if one believes it is straight, or the horizontal lines in the Müller-Lyer illusion that look different in length even if one believes they are not. Think of ordinary visual experience, which is no buzzing, blooming, confusion but rather presents to the experiencer an apparent scene involving numerous apparent objects apparently instantiating numerous properties and relations.) These non-doxastic states, being truth-assessable, are themselves capable of being components of an overall system of intentional psychological states that is holistically assessable for global coherence. And a coherentist can claim that the coherence-wise 'fit' (or lack of 'fit') possessed by such a state is—just as in the case of beliefs—a feature that is derivative from the overall coherence of the agent's epistemic psychological system.[6]

But although some traditional versions of coherentism are minimalist about the component question whereas others are not, none recognize morphologically intentional mental states as components of an epistemic psychological system. (As with traditional foundationalist writings, the idea that there might be morphologically intentional mental states typically is not even considered.) Thus, the non-minimalist versions of traditional coherentism embrace conservatism about the component question, not liberalism. It is small wonder, then, that traditional coherentism almost inevitably ends up committed to *PT* concerning *doxastic* justification, at least implicitly; for, without recourse to implicitly morphological states, it is very hard to see what alternative account could be given of what constitutes believing a proposition because of the justification one has for that proposition.

2.4 Structural Contextualism

Let us begin with a remark about the term 'contextualism' and its cognates. The term was employed at least as early as 1978 by David Annis to refer to an account of the normative structure of articulable justification. Annis's proposals were inspired by ideas in the later Wittgenstein, and were intended to serve as an alternative to foundationalist and coherentist accounts of such things. More recently, the term 'contextualism' has come to be associated with accounts of the workings of concepts according to which what it takes to satisfy the concept in question varies with contexts (commonly conversational contexts). These contexts determine how much is required along certain dimensions to satisfy the concept in question. Call this *parameter contextualism*; the idea is that the concept is semantically governed, perhaps implicitly, by contextually variable parameters. For example, the most prominent epistemological applica-

---

[6] Does this mean that such states are themselves susceptible to epistemic *justification*? Not necessarily. There may well be good reasons for restricting the applicability of the notion of justification to doxastic states, even while allowing that certain non-doxastic states with intentional content can contribute to the justification of doxastic states. In the case of sensory-perceptual experiences, for instance, such a justificatory contribution could be a matter of fitting well into a holistically coherent epistemic psychological system—rather than, say, generating beliefs that count as epistemically 'basic' in a foundationalist way.

tion of parameter contextualist ideas has been in accounts of the concept of knowledge (Lewis 1979, 1996; Cohen 1987; DeRose 1995). Thus, it has been said that the concept of knowledge has to do with whether the agent's evidence and belief-forming processes would track the truth regarding the proposition in question across the relevant range of alternative scenarios or possible worlds. The class of relevant alternatives is thought to vary with context—which makes that class a contextually variable parameter governing the concept knowledge. In everyday contexts, the relevant alternatives extend only to the nearest possible world in which the proposition under consideration would happen to be false. In skeptical contexts where some scenario such as demonic deception has come to folks' attention, the relevant alternatives extend farther, to possible worlds in which there are such pitfalls. Most of us qualify as knowing that we have hands in the everyday context, and all fail to know that much in the skeptical context. The common view is that conversations give rise to the contexts—conversational contexts, with contextually determined parameter settings (the set of contextually relevant alternatives).

Parameter contextualism is distinct from the sort of contextualism that we want to focus on here. To mark the difference, we will write of *structural contextualism,* at least where confusion threatens. (In this section and chapter we will usually write flatly of contextualism without fear of confusion, since parameter contextualism is not directly pertinent to our present concern, namely the structure of empirical justification.)[7]

Structural contextualist epistemologies retain elements of both foundationalist and coherentist epistemologies, but each is significantly altered. Contextualists can and do allow that the sort of relations of mutual support featured in coherentist accounts play a central role in epistemic justification. (Here they hold to something like (C1).) However, contextualists insist that such coherentist considerations are never, and could never really be, applied to one's belief system globally. (They deny (C2).) A strictly global application (to the whole of one's belief set)—the central coherentist ideal—is simply not an ideal for structural contextualists. Such global coherentist ideals are repudiated for at least two sorts of reasons. First, global coherence allegedly is not an appropriate standard for any finite cognitive system, and particularly not for systems with capacities in the range characteristic of human cognizers. Second, epistemic standards are themselves influenced by one's beliefs. As a result, putting the whole of one's belief system 'up for grabs' at once would allegedly undercut all epistemology; it would allegedly leave the agent with no epistemological standards by which to judge alternative global systems of belief. The fully global application of coherentist thought would allegedly undermine coherentism, and thus be self-defeating.[8]

Similarly, central elements of foundationalism are appropriated and transformed in structural contextualist epistemology. In particular, along with the foundationalists,

---

[7] Various common contextualist themes are carefully distinguished in Timmons (1993, 1996).
[8] This second objection is most forcefully formulated in Michael Williams (1977, 1980). However, it may also be reflected in Dudley Shapere (1987, pp. 1–39) and Kitcher (1992, 1993).

contextualists recognize that, as an ideal as well as in practice, linear episodes of justification-giving can properly terminate in beliefs that really are not susceptible to, or helped by, further (presumably coherence-theoretic) justification. (They hold to something like (F1), while also claiming that epistemic justification is regarded as tied to contextually appropriate requests that one *articulate* a justification for one's belief.) However, contextualists contend that these regress-stopping beliefs do not constitute an epistemically homogeneous class with a distinct characteristic that gives them a measure of justification (Here they repudiate (F4).) Contextualists insist that one belief may stand in need of no futher justification, and serve as a regress-stopper, while a second belief, characterizable in just the same way as the first, may stand in need of justification.

To foundationalists and coherentists, this proposal will appear inconsistent. The foundationalist will insist that, if a belief of a (fully characterized) epistemic kind can serve as a regress-stopper anywhere, beliefs of that sort must always and everywhere possess some measure of justification on their own. Structural contextualists, however, are apt to respond that such reactions on the part of foundationalists and coherentists rest on a mistake—namely the mistaken assumption that one's belief system as a whole requires, and is somehow capable of, justificatory support. Contextualists, with an eye on the kinds of demands for epistemic justification that arise and are considered legitimate in typical real-life situations, and with an eye also on the kinds of responses to such demands that are typically regarded as legitimate, insist that real epistemic justification is inevitably a *local* affair, in which substantial amounts of background information are taken for granted in context. There is no such thing as global justification for one's belief system, says the contextualist. Foundationalists and coherentists both mistakenly assume otherwise, and then offer competing answers to a question that should not have been asked in the first place, namely the misguided question: 'What is the global structure of a system of epistemically justified beliefs?'

The contextualist position as explained up to this point may be represented in two claims:

(X1) Holistic virtues such as explanatory coherence play some role in one's having justification for what one believes, but such desiderata never apply strictly globally—as if the whole of one's belief system could be called into question and be up for grabs all at once.

(X2) Justificatory chains of support relations commonly have a linear structure and terminate in regress-stopping, epistemically justified, beliefs that are not susceptible to, or 'helped by,' further justificatory support. That is, linear justification commonly terminates in beliefs that the agent holds without having further beliefs that might significantly enhance their justification.

In much of the contextualist literature, there is this further suggestion: when and where a belief-token can serve as a regress-stopper is ultimately a (perhaps negotiated) social matter. This theme is commonly associated with the Wittgensteinian heritage of some contextualist thought. We ourselves, however, are not convinced of the force or exact nature of these claims, and we leave them aside for our purposes here. Let us simply note that this might provide some help in fashioning a full understanding of the context. In any case, any socially determined aspects of context will have to be accommodated psychologically by individual epistemic agents—typically implicitly, as part of what the agent takes for granted.

There is a tendency among advocates of coherentism and foundationalism to conceive of contextualism as something of a poor-kin approximation to the more mainline positions, particularly coherentism.[9] The thought is this: what contextualists seem to envision roughly accords with what one would get if one were approximating coherence-theoretic justifications to the extent that they could reasonably be implemented by finite agents who are subject to varying pressures to settle on beliefs and act accordingly. However, traditional coherentism is committed to it being true of all beliefs that they are subject to holistic support from other beliefs ((C2) and (C3)), while contextualism denies this (X2). Thinking of contextualism as a scaled-back approximation to coherentism reflects the idea that there is a traditional coherentist justification in the offing, accessible and available if only one had more leisure and energy. Contextualists will deny this, and will insist again that overall belief systems neither have, nor need, global epistemic justification.

The term 'contextualism' was adopted by Annis and other writers, such as Williams, to serve as a label for positions that conform to the general lines set out here. (The reason for the modifier—'structural'—was explained earlier: to avoid confusion with those recent positions commonly also called 'contextualism,' which we term 'parameter contextualism.') There are good reasons for describing the position we have in mind as (structural) contextualism. It is central to this sort of account that epistemic justification is always circumscribed by a presupposed background that is properly taken for granted, not because it has already received justification itself, but because there is no epistemic basis for, nor desirability to, proceeding further in the particular case. There is rhyme and reason, insists the contextualist, to what seem to foundationalists and coherentists to be mere arbitrary irregularities in the structure of justificatory reasons one has. The real-life context determines what counts as an appropriate demand for epistemic justification for a given belief, and what counts as an adequate response to such a demand. Thus, context determines whether one can fittingly stop with a given perceptual belief, for example, or must go on. The context allows one to rest with a stretch of holistic justification, never demanding that one puts all one's beliefs up for epistemic grabs at once. This contextualist background determines what

---

[9] For example, BonJour classifies Williams' avowedly contextualist (1980) account as a kind of unambitious coherentism (an understanding that is fostered by Williams' initial discussion of his view using the label 'coherentism' which he later dropped). Admittedly, coherence-theoretic aspects of contextualist views have occasionally led those sympathetic to contextualist epistemology to conceive of it as a mere approximation to other ideals. This is not true of Williams' own contextualism, for he argues that our most basic epistemic standards are incompatible with thoroughgoing coherentist ideals (which would be global in their application).

counts as having justification (propositional justification) and being justified (doxastic justification) without itself being subject to demands for justification. (One recalls Wittgenstein's writing of things that just stand fast for him.)[10] We can thus add a third hallmark claim to our formulation of structural contextualism:

(X3) The structure of support relations between beliefs (described in (X1) and (X2)) is ultimately determined by a context which (at least partly) takes the form of a body of information that often is implicitly accommodated psychologically, often is not fully articulable, and is taken for granted.

We take (X1)–(X3) to characterize structural contextualism as an account of the justificatory support relations featuring in one's having justification for a belief (i.e. in one's propositional justification). To be a little less abstract, focus on the stopping places in the articulable justification of empirical beliefs. *Commonly* one can stop with perceptual beliefs. As contextualists say, (linear) justification comes to an end in a class of beliefs that, in context, are not subject to, are not in need of, and are not epistemically improved by, appeal to further doxastic states. Nor are they 'self-justified.' (They are not *un-justified either; rather, the question of justificatory status just does not arise for them.*) In a plausible account of perceptual competence, simple perceptual beliefs *can commonly* serve this role. But, this is not to say that all such simple perceptual beliefs do or can. Much depends on the particular case. In the last chapter, we said enough to suggest how the generation of such beliefs can rely on much important information that is not explicitly represented in the system, and may not be articulable by the system. But, it can yet be information possessed by the cognitive system (in the form of morphological content) and contributing to the system's epistemic success and well-working. In such cases, then, such simple perceptual beliefs commonly serve as contextually appropriate stopping places, neither needing, nor susceptible to, epistemic improvement. In other cases, the perceptual belief may arise already tagged with concerns that 'bubble up' to the level of articulable processing from the rich information that informs the agent's perceptual sensitivities. In such cases, the perceptual belief does not constitute a fitting regress-stopper.

Contextualists insist that the proper resting places for justification are a diverse lot. When one thinks of epistemological justification being pursued ideally far, to the ideal exhaustion of legitimate demands for epistemic justification in any given context, the contextualist believes that agents arrive, in typical contexts, at some *nonhomogeneous* set of beliefs that neither need to be, nor can be, justified. (In contrast, the foundationalist envisioned a homogeneous set of basic beliefs—homogeneous with respect to some intrinsic characteristic which makes them already justified, and makes them regress-

---

[10] As emphasized in the previous chapter, perceptual competence often seems informed by much information that, in many common cases, cannot be articulated. In such 'run of the mill' cases, there is obviously no basis for challenging what cannot be articulated. Further, it seems that the cognitive 'mill' in these cases can be working ideally—i.e. in a way that accords with an ideal epistemological competence for perceptual processing. From the point of view of appropriate epistemic ideals, then, there is no blemish in the unexamined, and unexaminable, reliance on this information.

stoppers within a *global* structure of epistemic justification. On the other hand, the coherentist too thinks of epistemic justification as a global feature of a belief system, encompassing the subject's entire set of beliefs considered in a decidedly nonlinear fashion.)

To illustrate the kind of nonhomogeneity that could be at issue here, think of the quick perception of a traffic accident. Perhaps one comes to have a perceptual belief that the accident involved a blue vehicle changing lanes—something one seemed to see as one's attention was momentarily diverted in the direction of some squealing tires. In one case, the perceptual belief that a blue vehicle changed lanes might serve as a stopping place, subject to no further justification. In another case, a token of the same belief type might be held justificatory hostage until supporting beliefs are obtained. Perceptual beliefs are sometimes stoppers, sometimes not. Sometimes the articulable basis for judgment will end with a given perceptual belief, in other cases, one's perceptual system will throw up reservations—further justificatory problems that must be addressed. 'The car looks to be blue,' one may think, 'but the light makes it hard to tell.' A quick glance at familiar objects ready to hand may suffice to reassure oneself of one's discriminative ability in the conditions at hand. (Or it may not.) The further justificatory work may rely on a rather diverse set of beliefs—on a range of general and particular beliefs, as coherentists would point out. But it is not necessary to have in place the kind of *global justificatory* holism for belief-systems that the traditional coherentist envisions.

Structural contextualism, in its reliance on the notion of a background of information that is implicitly taken for granted in contexts where one is giving justification for one's beliefs, takes a step toward repudiating both minimalism and conservatism about the component question, in favor of liberalism. In effect, contextualists answer the component question in a more expansive way than do either traditional foundationalists or traditional coherentists: contextualists treat an epistemic psychological system as comprising not only a body of prototypical beliefs (together perhaps with other explicitly representational states such as sensory-perceptual seemings), but also a rich background of information that is taken for granted in contexts of real-life justification-giving. In attributing to the competent cognitive agent an implicit grasp of this informational background (including pertinent background facts about social factors that affect contextually appropriate demands for articulate justification, and contextually appropriate responses), structural contextualism gestures toward a conception of competent human cognition that looks naturally explicable in terms of morphological content and morphologically implicit mental states.[11]

---

[11] We say that structural contextualism *takes a step* toward liberalism, and that it *gestures* toward states with morphological content, because extant versions of the position often tend to conflate three matters: *having* justification for one's belief (i.e. propositional justification), *being* justified in one's belief (i.e. doxastic justification) and being able to meet contextually appropriate demands for *giving* an articulate justification for one's belief. This conflationary tendency makes it hard to distill from contextualist writings any clear-cut, fully self-consistent, treatment of either propositional justification or doxastic justification. Nonetheless, there

3 Iceberg epistemology and its revisionary consequences

The versions of foundationalism, coherentism, and structural contextualism canvassed in section 2 each are fairly traditional with respect to propositional justification, but are silent about doxastic justification. In order for an agent to *be* justified in holding a belief—i.e. in order for the belief to be doxastically justified—the agent not only needs to have justification for the belief, but also needs to hold the belief *because* of the justification-had. That is, the causal etiology of the belief must suitably 'mirror' its propositional justification.

The idea of propositional-justificatory relations being 'mirrored' in the operation of belief-forming cognitive processes needs to be cashed out in terms of a general conception of how such mirroring can and does get implemented—a conception that draws upon pertinent work in cognitive science. In Chapter 7 we set forth, and argued for, the conception we favor—one that is motivated in part by the frame problem and by certain aspects of connectionist modeling in cognitive science, and looks much more plausible than *PT*. The cornerstone of this proposed replacement for *PT* is the idea that cognitive processes of belief-fixation often must operate in a way that relies heavily and essentially on extensive morphological content; this is the only tractable way to accommodate the holistic, Quineian/isotropic, aspects of evidential support. Henceforth we will refer to the kind of doxastic justification that rests upon such processes as *morphologically mediated* doxastic justification.

Iceberg epistemology takes to heart the claim that processes of belief fixation are and must be, in large measure, morphologically mediated. This, in turn, gives iceberg epistemology its two complementary foci. One focus is the complete epistemic iceberg: the entire cognitive system that generates and sustains beliefs, often in ways that draw holistically upon information that gets accommodated morphologically rather than by being explicitly represented during processing. The other focus is the 'exposed' portion of the epistemic iceberg, comprising those aspects of belief-forming and belief-sustaining cognition that involve explicitly represented, consciously accessible, information.

Iceberg epistemology, with its dual foci and its emphasis on the role of essentially morphological processing, allows for a significant reconfiguring of the traditional debate among foundationalists, coherentists, and structural contextualists about the structure of propositional justification. Important ideas from each camp can be incorporated in suitably modified form—and should be. Also, the resulting revisionist picture of the structure of propositional justification is one that largely reconciles the three camps, overcoming the principal sources of incompatibility that are present in the traditional versions of these positions. Describing this revisionist picture is the business of the present section. In the first subsection we sketch the overall picture in broad brushstrokes, in order to highlight its principal contours. In the next three subsections

---

are suggestive ideas in this literature that are pertinent to propositional justification, and it is these that we have here been highlighting.

we address the three traditional positions in turn, in each case saying in more detail which ideas we propose to retain in some form, which we propose to reject, and how we propose to modify the retained ideas.

3.1 The two-tiered structure of epistemic justification

In section 2.1 we invoked the notion of an agent's *epistemic psychological system*, comprising the psychological states of the agent (occurrent, dispositional, or morphological) that figure as bearers, and/or conferers, and/or transmitters, of propositional justification. The question of the structure of epistemic justification asks what the components are of an epistemic psychological system, and how they need to be related to one another in order for the justification-susceptible components of the system (in particular, the component beliefs) to be propositionally justified. Within the framework of iceberg epistemology, this question gets subdivided into two distinct, albeit interconnected, questions. First, one can ask about the nature of justification-conferring structural relations among the components of the *entire* epistemic psychological system—the whole iceberg. (Hereafter we will abbreviate 'epistemic psychological system' as 'EPS.') But second, one also can ask, more specifically, about the nature of justification-conferring structural relations among the components of a specific *proper part* of the overall epistemic psychological system, namely the part comprising the readily accessible psychological states—the 'exposed' portion of the iceberg. (Hereafter we will refer to this as the *accessible* EPS.) Once the traditional question about the structure of epistemic justification is thus bifurcated, space opens up to incorporate aspects of all three of the erstwhile incompatible positions in epistemology concerning the structure of justification—foundationalism, coherentism, and structural contextualism.

It is important to bear in mind, of course, how these two questions about the structure of propositional justification are related to one another. Insofar as the accessible EPS is considered in itself, apart from the wider EPS in which it is embedded, the kind of propositional-justification relations possessed by its components will be, in general, *mediated* justificatory relations. Such relations within the exposed portion of the iceberg, and their exposed-portion structural interconnections, are well worthy of attention in their own right—inter alia, because of their importance with respect to what counts, in real-life contexts, as a legitimate demand for justification, or what counts as an adequate response to such a demand. But above-surface justificatory relations will not be, in general, autonomous and complete; on the contrary, typically they will be mediated by a background involving unmediated global-structural relations of propositional-justificatory support within the *entire* EPS.

We now sketch our overall conception of the two-tiered structure of propositional justification, a conception incorporating aspects of all three traditional positions. As already remarked, structural contextualists commonly insist that one's overall system of beliefs neither has, nor needs to have, holistic epistemic justification. Although individual beliefs sometimes can be appropriately challenged in certain real-life contexts, and can have (or fail to have) propositional justification in context, such local justification typically rests on a rich background of psychologically accommodated information that is legitimately taken for granted and that (in the given context) neither has, nor needs to have, its own justification.

On the revisionist approach we ourselves recommend, these structural-contextualist claims are quite mistaken if asserted with respect to an epistemic agent's entire EPS. Contrary to such claims, the whole epistemic iceberg must exhibit a very high degree of global coherence, because nothing less than that will suffice to accommodate the Quineian/isotropic nature of epistemically competent belief-formation. When one's theoretical focus is the whole iceberg, we maintain, global propositional justification is *needed* for beliefs in the EPS, and to a large extent is actually *exhibited* by the EPS's of typical human believers. Coherentism is essentially right about the whole iceberg, and structural contextualism is profoundly wrong.

On the other hand, as regards the 'exposed' states in the epistemic iceberg—i.e. the agent's *accessible* EPS, including the prototypical beliefs within it—the claims of structural contextualism are essentially correct.

Themes from traditional foundationalism also are honored, at least to some extent, within our recommended conception of the two-tiered structure of propositional justification. Within the accessible EPS, certain beliefs are legitimate justificatory 'stopping points'; they neither possess, nor require, further justificatory support within the EPS itself. This is enough to qualify the conception as 'quasi-foundationalist' (as we will put it) with respect to the accessible EPS. However, we contend that, even within this higher-tiered level of structure, one key contention of traditional foundationalism is false—namely the claim that the beliefs comprising the relevant 'stopping points' constitute an autonomous class. Moreover, the global justificatory structure of the *entire* EPS is coherentist in nature, rather than foundationalist.

That is the short version of the account of the two-tiered structure of propositional epistemic justification that looks to us most plausible, in light of all that has been said earlier in this book. We proceed now to elaborate the account itself, and the considerations that favor it.

3.2 Transforming coherentism

According to coherentism, an agent's belief that *p* has justification—i.e. is propositionally justified—only if this belief belongs to a system of psychological states, all instantiated by the agent, that exhibit the features described in (C1)–(C3). Propositional justification is a matter of coherently related, propositionally structured, truth-evaluable, representational states ('cognitive' states). Familiar versions of traditional coherentism, such as those of BonJour and Davidson, are minimalist concerning the component question: an epistemic psychological system is regarded as consisting entirely of prototypical beliefs, either occurrent or dispositional. More expansive versions of traditional coherentism can be envisioned too—e.g. conservative but non-minimalist versions that countenance as components certain other doxastic states (e.g. hunches, working hypotheses, and the like), and/or non-doxastic states like visual-perceptual seemings, and/or intellectual seemings.

Coherentism holds that justification had—i.e. propositional justification—is a matter of coherence-relations among these kinds of cognitive states—i.e. among *explicitly representational* states (as we are calling them here). One can learn much from coherentists, and it is important to hold onto the insights they emphasize regarding holistic epistemic chores. But, to do so, one will need to dissent from their (C3) limitation of the epistemically relevant cognitive action to processes at the level of explicitly representational cognitive states. Instead, one should embrace liberalism about the nature of an epistemic psychological system—which means including morphologically intentional states within the system. And one should hold that the kinds of holistic evidential support that are rightly emphasized by traditional coherentism are really exhibited by the whole epistemic psychological system, thus liberally construed—i.e. the whole iceberg.

The central insights provided by coherentism center on (C1) and (C2). Coherentists point to the need for cognition to manage certain holistic tasks, and we echoed such calls in the previous chapter. Thus, suppose that one possesses much putative information about the world—suppose that this is information generated by imperfect, but generally reliable, processes. Being imperfectly reliable, such processes have 'blind spots'; they are subject to systematic errors in certain limited ranges of environmental circumstances. It is likely that different processes are subject to different limitations, and thus can be put to work correcting for each other. By putting information together, one can then improve on the overall reliability of one's overall belief-forming system by using the results of various specific processes as checks on each other. In a suggestive phrase, one can 'triangulate' on truths about the world. A special case of such triangulation is the ubiquitous use of various sensory modalities to jointly provide a more reliable impression of how the world is than can be gotten from any one sensory modality alone. But the principle applies quite generally: one can use pieces of relevant information, gotten by various reliable lines of thought, to check up on the others. Think here of how the concern for explanatory coherence can bring together results from multiple scientific fields to constrain which theories are acceptable in each discipline. Such coherence-based triangulation also seems to enhance the reliability of one's belief-forming processes taken individually, by exerting modulational control. (Compare the earlier discussion, in the third and fourth chapters, of both the global and transglobal reliability of processes under suitable modulational control.)

The kinds of coherence that come from taking account of the range of one's relevant information, and the highly desirable epistemic payoffs of doing so, are only available to the extent that one can settle upon what information is relevant to what and bring that information to bear. Thus, one's belief-forming processes encounter the frame problem as it is posed by isotropy (as discussed in Chapter 7): the potential relevance of any information one possesses to any claim one potentially might come to believe. All information is potentially relevant to all other information—and the select set of one's information that is actually relevant to some claim under consideration commonly is a function of what other information one possesses that mediates relevance. Thus, to garner the benefits promised by bringing together one's relevant information in an episode of belief-fixation, one must somehow be sensitive to all one's information and how some of it makes for mediated relevance between far-flung pieces of information. We have argued that this can only be accomplished by reliance on morphological content, since that allows the system to automatically accommodate much information without needing to explicitly represent that information and ascertain its relevance. So, sensitivity to the kinds of coherence that comes of the full range of one's relevant information requires processes in which morphological content is crucially in play.

To honor (C1) and (C2)—which are important insights, reflecting epistemic tasks that constitute an important component of human epistemic competence—one must engage in processes that track a wider set of information than is allowed by (C3). It cannot be by processes *only* at the level of explicit mental representations that one garners the epistemic benefits of coherence. (Quineian/isotropic aspects of the information possessed by a cognitive agent figure importantly in the overall coherence of the intentional states constituting the agent's epistemic psychological system, thereby contributing to the holistic evidential support possessed by the explicitly representational states within the system, including the articulable beliefs.) But, as we argued in Chapter 7, the only way for belief-forming processes in humans (and like creatures) to accommodate the holistic, Quineian/isotropic, aspects of evidentially relevant background information is for these processes to be essentially morphological—i.e. essentially reliant on morphological content. It is for this reason that we insist that, to hold onto the insights afforded by coherentist thought, one will need to dissent from the traditional coherentist limitation on what constitutes the epistemically relevant cognitive states and processes. That is, one will need to construe the cognitive epistemic system that exhibits holistic coherence-relations as comprising a body of intentional mental states that includes as components not merely explicitly representational states, but morphologically intentional states too.

The above remarks attest to the continuing epistemological significance of (C1) in particular—the centrality of holistic support relations to many episodes of belief fixation. Now, foundationalists could grant a place for such support, and for attendant processes, in many cases of belief fixation, yet insist that these are secondary when what is at issue are what they would understand to be basic beliefs. This way of seeing the matter continues to neglect the epistemically crucial respects in which the generation of what foundationalists take to be basic beliefs is conditioned by much relevant information in ways that are congenial to the coherentist thesis (C2). For example, consider again perceptual beliefs, as a class of putatively basic beliefs. In the previous chapter we argued that a competent human perceiver has come to be trained up to make automatic use of much relevant information. In generating perceptual beliefs, one makes use of much information of the sort that is suggested in BonJour's discussion of the justification of 'cognitively spontaneous beliefs'—information about the conditions in which the belief was generated and their conduciveness to the generation of veridical judgments. In many respects, then, BonJour and various coherentists seem to have characterized informational demands to which a competent human agent would need to be sensitive—if the agent is to generate veridical perceptual judgments in a fashion that is highly robustly reliable. If this is right, then the coherentist is right to think of such demands as having application to those processes in which perceptual beliefs are generated. This is sufficient to support (C2) (and to provide further reason for rejecting (C3)).[12]

We thus advocate revising traditional coherentism, within the two-tiered framework of iceberg epistemology, in two principal ways: first, by jettisoning minimalism and conservatism about the component question, in favor of a form of liberalism that acknowledges the pervasiveness of morphologically intentional states within the overall epistemic psychological system (the EPS) of a cognitive agent; and second, by formulating coherentism as a thesis about the entire EPS rather than the accessible EPS (i.e. a thesis about the entire iceberg rather than the exposed portion of it). The revised coherentist theses, with the subscript 'w' to indicate that they pertain to the *whole* EPS, are these:

(C1$_w$) Numerous epistemic support relations are holistic—involving isotropic or Quineian features of systems of beliefs—and this sort of justification that a belief-system may have is antecedent to, or more fundamental than, the justification of component beliefs (*the fundamentality of holistic support relations within the whole EPS*).
(C2$_w$) Holistic support relations are the basis for the justification of all beliefs (*the pervasiveness of holistic support relations within the whole EPS*).
(C3$_w$) The mental states that can contribute to the justification one has for a belief include not only prototypical beliefs and other explicitly representational states (either occurrent or dispositional), but morphologically intentional states as well.

On this revised coherentism, it is an important feature of one's epistemic competence that one manages certain cognitive tasks that are very much like those that traditional coherentists urged. One must be reasonably sensitive to how the full range of one's information makes for extended relevance relations between pieces of information, and must bring the pertinent information together to inform each belief-fixing episode. Propositional justification of beliefs is fundamentally a matter of how these beliefs fit into a holistically coherent epistemic psychological system, and competent belief-fixation must somehow mirror such holistic evidential support. This is what we are preserving from coherentism.

At the same time, we are led to a revisionary stance as well. Coherentists have tended to unduly restrict the range of epistemically relevant states to explicitly representational states (as (C3) asserts), and have thought that holistic coherence pertains to such states exclusively. (Indeed, often they have been yet more restrictive, by embracing the

---

[12] But we have also argued that these demands could not be met without the system accommodating much of the relevant information automatically. Again, the traditional coherentist informational demands must be accommodated by a cognitive system that employs morphological content.

minimalist view that only prototypical beliefs can be components of an epistemic psychological system.) We maintain, however, that the central coherentist insights can only be retained when abandoning this element of traditional coherentism. In terms of our iceberg epistemology, one can say that coherentism is vindicated, but only with respect to the full EPS—a system of psychological states that includes numerous morphologically intentional states in addition to the explicitly representational ones. This is a very non-traditional, non-standard, form of coherentism that embraces liberalism about the component question rather than minimalism or conservatism. The total epistemic psychological system that is the locus of holistic coherence—the whole epistemic iceberg—includes many mental states that are morphologically intentional rather than explicitly representational.[13]

It is also worth noting a point made vivid by this transformed coherentism. One can begin with a fairly traditional understanding of what is 'the justification had' by agents (i.e. the propositional justification)—an understanding that focuses only on internalistically accessible states (or, even more narrowly, only on internalistically accessible beliefs). We have argued that coherentists aptly highlight certain holistic chores that should be managed. But, these chores must be accomplished in a fashion that avoids frame-type problems—and this requires that some of the information enter morphologically. Thus, the information possessed by the agent, the information by which the agent as cognitive system fixes belief, is wider than what might have been supposed at the start. It then seems fitting to revisit the understanding of what is the 'justification had' by the agent. Propositional justification should not be understood independently from whatever information features in suitable processes of belief fixation. The point is reflected in $(C3_w)$.

3.3 Transforming foundationalism

The above discussion is a vindication (with respect to the whole EPS) of (C1) and (C2), and this then provides ample reason to reject foundationalism, at least as the *full story* about propositional justification. But it is difficult to escape the feeling that foundationalists were onto significant truths about propositional justification, nonetheless—truths about the structure of justificatory support-relations within that portion of the whole EPS that we are calling the *accessible* EPS. Within the two-tiered iceberg that is the whole EPS, the above-surface justificatory structure is not autonomous, of course; rather, it is pervasively mediated by a rich background of morphologically intentional states, and by richly holistic coherence-relations among the components of the full EPS.

---

[13] It bears emphasis too (reiterating the theme of note 6) that although the whole EPS is the proper locus of epistemic coherence, this does not necessarily mean that every component of the EPS is a state that needs, or is susceptible to, epistemic justification. Maybe only *doxastic* states are susceptible to epistemic justification, even though non-doxastic intentional states can *contribute* to the justification of doxastic states—where such contribution is a matter of suitable global coherence of the whole EPS, including its non-doxastic components.

Nonetheless, iceberg epistemology provides the resources for understanding how foundationalists can yet prove to be correct in some of their most cherished claims. It is epistemologically feasible, and will prove rewarding, not only to study the (unmediated) justificatory structure of the full set of epistemically relevant states (including those that involve morphological content and violate traditional epistemological expectations), and also to study the more restricted range of states that traditionally have been thought to be epistemically relevant (the 'exposed states'—i.e. the accessible states of traditional internalistic epistemology).

Coherentism has turned out to provide a general account of the character of the full epistemic psychological system. Let us explore the possibility of treating foundationalism as no longer a competitor to coherentism, but instead as seeking to provide an account of epistemically significant (albeit morphologically mediated) support-relations among accessible, explicitly representational, mental states. In the terms provided by iceberg epistemology, think of foundationalism as providing an account of the structure of propositional justification at the level of exposed processes—an aspect of structure that pertains to a *proper part* of the overall epistemic psychological system. Such structure is not autonomous, but rather is thoroughly embedded within the whole system of which it is a proper part. Just as the exposed topographical structure of icebergs is worth studying even though it must be understood in light of the total structure of the whole chunk of ice, likewise the exposed propositional-justification structure of epistemic psychological systems is worth studying even though it must be understood in light of the (holistically coherence-based) propositional-justification structure of the whole epistemic psychological system.

It is to be expected too, given the dual-focus framework of iceberg epistemology, that the non-autonomous aspects of propositional justification that pertain specifically to accessible, explicitly representational, mental states will be closely connected to the *giving* of explicit justifications for one's beliefs. Demands for articulate justification are sometimes legitimate and appropriate, and certain kinds of articulate responses to such demands are also legitimate and appropriate. An explicit articulation of one's justification for a given belief will have to commence from certain initial claims or premises, however—claims or premises that must get treated, in the context of real-life justification-giving, as not in turn requiring articulated justification themselves. (Articulate justification-giving cannot go on *ad infinitum*, which means that legitimate demands for articulated justifications also cannot go on *ad infinitum*. Ought implies can.) It is of considerable interest, therefore, to investigate which kinds of claims can be legitimately invoked, in articulate justification-giving, without being subject themselves to legitimate demands for explicit justification. And it is just here that certain ideas stressed by traditional foundationalists may well become pertinent.

So, consider theses (F1)–(F4) of foundationalism, viewed now as theses that pertain specifically to internalistically accessible, explicitly representational, states like prototypical beliefs and perceptual appearing-states. We will designate these theses, as thus restricted in scope, as $(F1_a)$–$(F4_a)$, with the subscript 'a' for 'accessible.' There are two ways that one could interpret $(F1_a)$–$(F4_a)$. On one hand, one could regard them as positing *unmediated* relations of justificatory support among accessible states—i.e. relations that involve no additional intentional mental states, and nonetheless render an agent's beliefs propositionally justified. On the other hand, one could instead regard theses (F1$_a$)–(F4$_a$) as positing *mediated* justificatory-support relations, i.e. relations that involve not only the accessible, explicitly representational, states themselves but also a background of further information embodied in the cognitive system—information that need not be readily accessible itself, and that might very well be embodied as morphological content rather than in the form of explicitly representational states. We will call these two potential interpretations of (F1$_a$)–(F4$_a$) the *unmediated* and *mediated* construals, respectively. And we will designate the theses construed the first way as (F1$_{a/u}$)–(F4$_{a/u}$), and construed the second way as (F1$_{a/m}$)–(F4$_{a/m}$), with the additional subscripts 'u' and 'm' for 'unmediated' and 'mediated.' What can and should be incorporated into iceberg epistemology as a thesis about the accessible EPS, we suggest, is a view we will call *quasi-foundationalism*. This position affirms the three theses (F1$_{a/m}$)–(F3$_{a/m}$), but not the thesis (F4$_{a/m}$). It repudiates the four theses (F1$_{a/u}$)–(F4$_{a/u}$). The three theses it takes on board can be explicitly formulated this way:

(F1$_{a/m}$) Within the accessible EPS, much having of justification is a matter of a belief's being inferentially supported, mediately, by other beliefs in the accessible EPS which themselves are justified (the inferential model of accessible justificatory structure).

(F2$_{a/m}$) Within the accessible EPS, inferential justificatory support originates with basic beliefs which possess mediated justification independently of other beliefs in the accessible EPS—and which jointly serve as inferentially basic within the accessible EPS (the foundations model of the mediated structure of the accessible EPS).

(F3$_{a/m}$) Insofar as the justification of basic beliefs turns on non-doxastic states—such as perceptual-experience states—it does so by virtue of some relation to such states that is local (although perhaps mediated), and at the level of the accessible EPS does not 'go through' a ramified inferential route (the directness model of the foundations).

On this approach, accessible mental states bear justificatory relations to one another that exhibit the following features. First, numerous justified beliefs are inferentially supported—albeit often mediately, against a rich background of morphological content—by other beliefs that themselves are both justified and internally accessible (thesis (F1$_{a/m}$)); these accessible supporting-beliefs are appropriate to cite in the context of explicit justification-giving. Second, some accessible beliefs are epistemically justified—albeit often mediately, against a rich background of morphological content—in a way that does not depend upon other accessible beliefs (thesis (F2$_{a/m}$)); these beliefs are suitable 'stopping points' in terms of legitimate demands that can be made upon epistemic agents to explicitly justify certain of their beliefs, and thus are epistemically *basic* in the context of explicit justification-giving. Third, insofar as the justification of such basic beliefs involves accessible non-doxastic states such as perceptual-experiential states (perhaps in an unmediated manner, or perhaps mediately against a rich background of morphological content), it does so in a way that is cognitively spontaneous and experientially direct, rather than in a way that involves an experientially accessible, ramified, inferential route (thesis F3$_{a/m}$). However, there are no homogeneous sets of beliefs that have the status of being 'stopping points' or 'regress-stoppers' in the context of explicit justification-giving; hence, thesis (F4$_{a/m}$) is not taken on board.

Numerous beliefs of the kind that traditional foundationalists consider non-basic must be produced by processes that involve extensive morphological mediation; this is a moral of the frame problem in cognitive science, and is a claim we defended at some length in Chapter 7. So enough has been said to motivate the repudiation of thesis (F1$_{a/u}$). There is little to object to about the much more modest thesis (F1$_{a/m}$), however. After all, even in cases where one's full propositional justification depends upon a significant range of Quineian/isotropic factors, that justification will often depend at least *in part* on accessible beliefs that are themselves justified.

One might be inclined to think, however, that with respect to the kinds of beliefs that traditional foundationalism treats as basic, iceberg epistemology should adopt an approach that is closer to the spirit of traditional foundationalism than is our recommended quasi-foundationalism. Why not say, for example—even within the two-tiered, dual-focus perspective of iceberg epistemology—that certain perceptual beliefs are justified in a direct and unmediated way by perceptual-experiential states? If one did say that, then one could hold onto lots more of traditional foundationalism while still embracing iceberg epistemology. Morphological mediation would enter into the picture only with respect to the kinds of beliefs that traditional foundationalism treats as nonbasic. The basic beliefs would constitute a homogeneous set, or a few homogeneous sets (in accordance with thesis (F4$_{a/m}$)), and would serve as a global foundational basis for the entire epistemic psychological system—the whole iceberg. The basic beliefs would provide the justificatory 'juice' for the whole EPS, even though the global-coherentist connections whereby that juice is circulated to nonbasic beliefs would include major portions of the overall EPS that are embodied in the cognitive system in the form of morphologically intentional states. (To extend a suggestive metaphor introduced above, think of a room whose overall pattern of illumination is determined by the ways that the light from candles in the room is reflected around not just by mirrors in the room, but also by additional mirrors, off in the wings, that are not visible from within the room itself.)

We maintain, however, that such a version of iceberg epistemology is not plausible or attractive. Even beliefs that traditional foundationalists regard as basic, receive and require, considerable holistic epistemic support within the whole iceberg—i.e. within a cognitive agent's overall epistemic psychological system. Making a case for this claim will be the business of the remainder of the present section. The emphasis will be on the frequently important role of morphological content in the justification of cognitively spontaneous beliefs (e.g. perceptual beliefs), and on the ways the morphological content sometimes *prevents* certain beliefs or candidate-beliefs within a putative 'privileged class' (e.g. spontaneous perceptual beliefs) from being justified.

Recall the outlines of Audi's foundationalist account of empirical justification. His 'modest foundationalism' seems fairly representative of contemporary foundationalism. As he characterizes the cognitive processes giving rise to justified perceptual beliefs, perceptual states provide a beginning to the epistemically relevant action, and these directly give rise to perceptual beliefs. Here, the mention of just these two components, and Audi's insistence on an epistemically 'direct' move from the one to the other, reflect the common foundationalist focus on a limited range of states and processes. First a *perceptual state* occurs. Using Audi's example (1993, p. 130), working in his study in the evening, he 'sees a headlight beam cross my window.' This immediately induces him to form a *perceptual belief* 'that a car's light is moving out there.' This perceptually induced belief is taken to be epistemologically basic and to arise 'directly' out of the perceptual state. On such a foundationalist view of epistemologically relevant psychological processes, the link between the perceptual states and the perceptual belief is a direct causal one. In such foundationalist accounts, one finds no mention of mediating information. Finally, on the basis of this belief and other antecedently possessed beliefs, the agent may inferentially generate yet further beliefs—*nondirect and nonbasic beliefs*. For example, 'that someone has entered the driveway.' Foundationalists readily allow that the generation of these further beliefs can be the product of the interaction of many informational states (including beliefs) in addition to the perceptual beliefs featuring in their etiology.

In another example, one perceives a 'distinctive patter outside one's open window,' immediately generating the perceptual belief 'that it is raining,' which may inferentially spawn the belief that the seats on one's convertible Maserati are getting wet. (Of course, the inferential move is obviously dependent on the agent's antecedently possessed beliefs that one's car is a convertible Maserati, that one (carelessly) left its top down, and that one parked it in the driveway instead of in the garage.) In such presentations of the generation of basic beliefs of the perceptual sort, one finds the foundationalist delimiting what are the epistemically relevant states and cognitive processes. Included are: perceptual states, occurrent beliefs, and their causal interactions.

We discussed Audi's account in the previous chapter. There we noted that there was a pronounced tendency to underplay the kinds of information that *must* be involved either in the competent agent's coming to have perceptual states, or in the subsequent generation of perceptual beliefs. Whether one should understand the information as being at work in spawning the perceptual state itself, or in the subsequent transition to a perceptual belief, seems to depend on just how one understands the perceptual states in question.

Consider how one is to understand the 'perception' of 'a distinctive patter outside the window' in the above example. It might be understood to be a matter of occurrent attention to some uncharacterized but discriminable noise—comparable to attention to some color perception, without attendant classification of it as a shade of blue, green, or any other color category—or comparable to the case in which one attends to a tone without classifying it as Middle C, or any tone on a scale at all. Then the distinctive patter is 'distinctive' only in that other perceptual states might be discriminable as qualitatively different. Perhaps the cognitive agent need employ little information in coming to perceive such a discriminable patter (although more information would seem to inform the perception of it as deriving from 'outside the window'). But, if the perceptual state is understood as so 'thin' in its content, it seems that there must be much information brought to the subsequent processes in which the agent generates the belief that it is raining. If, in contrast, the perceptual state is understood as involving more categorization, as the perception of the patter as one distinctive of rain, then it seems that much information is at play in the generation of that perception itself. Either way then, much information is brought to bear in competent human cognition issuing in perceptual belief. The automatic and unconscious use of such information—plausibly in the form of morphological content—is of great epistemological moment. One would not be a competent perceptual system were one not to make use of such information. The moral is this: insofar as perceptual beliefs are concerned, the only viable versions of the foundationalist theses (F1)–(F3) are the versions embraced by quasi-foundationalism, namely $(F1_{a/m})$–$(F3_{a/m})$. These theses recognize that in general, even those perceptual beliefs that are cognitively quite spontaneous rest upon a body of evidential support that includes substantial morphological content.

Although quasi-foundationalism does embrace $(F1_{a/m})$–$(F3_{a/m})$, which are qualified variants of the traditional foundationalist theses (F1)–(F3), it does not embrace (F4) in any version. (Recall that (F4) says that basic beliefs constitute a homogeneous set or a few homogeneous sets.) Why not? In a nutshell, it is because the epistemically mediational role played by morphological content sometimes actually undermines the justificatory status of certain actual or potential beliefs that fall within one or another of the homogeneous sets in question. Let us elaborate.

The idea behind (F4) is that the basic beliefs fall into a small set of kinds, each of which are such that beliefs of that sort have a distinctive and clear entitlement to serve as regress-stoppers. Simple high-grade a priori beliefs are commonly taken as one plausible set of basic beliefs, wearing their epistemic credentials on their sleeves. Simple perceptual beliefs, induced by directly supporting perceptions, are taken to be another case in which one can uniformly rest epistemically assured, at least until one has on hand an undermining reason for thinking otherwise. The perceptual belief, perhaps together with the perceptual state that spawned it, is thought to come with epistemic credentials immediately open for reassuring inspection. We will focus on this view of perceptual basic beliefs.

In real life, epistemically appropriate belief fixation is managed in real time. A perceptually competent agent will go almost immediately from undergoing perceptual experiences to forming perceptual beliefs. Commonly, the generation of perceptual beliefs is informed by perceptual states that are here and gone, in a flux of rapid transience. Typically, memory preserves little of the richness of the perceptual states themselves, and thus memories cannot be looked to as full and faithful records of the perceptual states. One cannot readily re-inspect the perceptual state by inspecting one's memory of it.

Consider an incident like many one has doubtless lived: for a fleeting second or two, one might have a developing series of perceptual states that induce one to believe that yonder goes a rat. Perhaps the perceptual states are a series of more or less obscured glimpses of a small, somewhat furry, brownish gray creature scurrying through the grass in one's yard, at a distance of 7–10 meters. For only a portion of that period will the agent's attention (and then eyes) be focused on the creature that so soon disappears under the fence or hedge. Then, the perceptual episode is over. Its detail (such as information about the momentary illumination of the creature along its retreat through various shadows, or about the various instantaneous degrees of obstruction by vegetation) may be largely unrecoverable in memory.[14] It is reasonable to think that attempts to recover such matters of perceptual detail from memory produce convenient reconstructions in which the remembered perceptual state is as much a product of the ensuing beliefs as the reverse.

Suppose that the agent competently forms a belief that yonder went a rat. The perceptual states will themselves have been fairly rich in information, richer than could be articulated in the moment. But, by the time that these spawn the perceptual belief, they will be effectively over and gone. Some of the rich information may have had to do with matters of importance for distinguishing rats from squirrels, for example. One knows that rats and squirrels have rather different tails, and it is plausible that one's passing perceptual states contained information that was relevant to determining tail characteristics. For example, by virtue of that inarticulable information, one might be sensitive to the extent to which the creature's tail was obscured or displayed in the course of its retreat. Patterns of shadows and background could compromise the perceptions, and one might be sensitive to this. Differences in characteristic flight behavior might also be on display—and the extent to which this was exhibited might be a matter to which one was sensitive. To be sensitive to these matters, and a competent perceiver will be somewhat sensitive to them, the information must be somehow there in (or associated with) the transient perceptual states. One way that the agent could muster the desirable degree of sensitivity is by bringing to bear pertinent background information in the form of morphological content—and thus some of the epistemically operative information might never even get explicitly represented, not even fleetingly, by the system in the course of the perceptual processes. Furthermore, once the perceptions are past, having disappeared with the rat, there may be little that the agent can do to recover the full range of information—fleetingly occurrent, and/or morphological—on which it relied.

---

[14] Some of these matters of perceptual detail may be reliably partially reconstructed, depending on the case. Plausibly the degree of momentary illumination may be quickly reconstructed from observation of light levels that presumably are not changing too rapidly if one were to inquire quickly, and from memory of the creature's rough path together with further observation of patterns of shadows across that path. Other matters will not be so readily recovered and articulated after the fact. Commonly what one remembers is just seeing a creature that looked like a rat scurrying along roughly such-and-such a path, and catching what seemed a more or less decent glimpse of the creature.

How is all this supposed to show that (F4) is a distortion? Let us first flesh out the epistemological picture encapsulated in (F4); then we will look at various situations that can face an epistemic agent in view of the above remarks. It will be found, as described above, that (F4) leads one to gloss over important variations in epistemic situations. Again, the idea represented by (F4) has been that the basic beliefs fall into a small set of kinds, each of which is such that beliefs of that sort have a distinct and clear entitlement to serve as regress-stoppers. Simple perceptual beliefs, induced by directly supporting perceptions, are taken to be a prominent case of a homogeneous class of beliefs, each wearing its epistemic credentials 'on its sleeve'—beliefs on which one can uniformly rest epistemically assured, at least until one actually has on hand an undermining reason for thinking otherwise. One must look carefully at this picture of basic empirical beliefs. What exactly is assumed here?

A minimal reading is suggested by modest foundationalist views, such as Audi's. On such views, there are really two distinct stages in the epistemic action associated with perceptual beliefs: (1) their generation with justification directly from perceptual states, and (2) (at least in some cases) the subsequent enhancement or undermining of that support by virtue of something like coherence. The first stage supposedly provides the agent a belief that is justified adequately for knowledge—although this justification may be subsequently undermined. It is thought that, at least in some cases, there may be a second distinct stage in which much that one knows may be brought to bear in ways that would be congenial to coherentists. In this second stage of epistemic action, the perceptual belief may come to be yet more justified, or it may have its initial degree of justification undermined. In the first stage, the perceptual belief (perhaps together with its spawning perceptual state) is thought to come with epistemic credentials immediately open for reassuring inspection. That inspection reveals it to be justified in a way that is not 'positively' dependent on other beliefs that the agent possesses. However, the belief's justification-status is also acknowledged to be 'negatively dependent' on such beliefs, since the belief's current justification may subsequently be undermined in the second stage. On this picture, until such second-stage undermining, and in its absence, the perceptual belief—like all such perceptual beliefs—can serve as a foundational belief in the structure of justification.

We ourselves contend that (F4), understood in this modest foundationalist fashion, is distorting in at least two ways. First, commonly there is the suggestion that the perceptual state is fully there for the agent in a way that enables the agent to fully inspect the first-stage credentials of the belief. As BonJour (2002, p. 15) suggests when thinking of that very restricted set of perceptual beliefs that count for him as basic, one can always compare the perceptual state with the belief and see that the belief is well-born.[15] Second, the

---

[15] Of course, for foundationalists of BonJour's stripe, perceptual beliefs, insofar as they arise directly from perceptual states—from what is given in perception—would seem to have to do with appearances—believing that I seem to see blue, for example—rather than with things perceived. On such a view, beliefs about rats and other common middle-sized objects are not basic.

'two distinct stages' view is dubious as psychology, because various additional sources of information—over and above one's current perceptual-experiential state—often are apt to be operative right from the start.[16] (For instance, when one spontaneously forms the perceptual belief that yonder is an iPhone, considerable background information—some of it probably morphologically embodied in one's cognitive system—is brought to bear in combination with the sensory experience itself.)

The first misgiving is less fundamental than the second, but it is worth attention. The idea that one's perceptual beliefs have a kind of solid epistemic warrant that is backed by the agent's ability 'to compare the belief with the experience' certainly could encourage foundationalists to underplay the variation in the ways perceptual beliefs may arise out of perceptual states. In our example of the rat-sighting, however, we have given reason to doubt that this is so. Commonly, perceptual beliefs arise out of a brief series of perceptual states—a short episode that is here and gone as the belief is formed. Its detail and richness is not preserved in memory, so there is no robust sense in which one can make a studied comparison of the perceptual belief with the perceptual states that spawned it. It is common to suppose that one's experience is there in memory, in its richness, and that the agent can compare the belief to it. Those who think in these terms are probably thinking of a case where one can 'reproduce' the experience for further study—as when one continues to look at some object in unchanging conditions. But this is surely a special case of the generation of justified perceptual beliefs. (And on reflection, one should wonder whether it is appropriate to think of it as a matter of comparing the belief and its 'spawning experience.' It seems more correct to think of this sort of special case as one in which the agent can conveniently generate further experiences that are similar to the spawning experience.) When one recognizes the common sort of case in which an ephemeral experience gives rise to a justified belief, one must confront the fact that so much of what the epistemic agent must be sensitive to in the experience is not accessible. Along with substantial information antecedently possessed and deployed (often morphologically) by the competent perceptual agent, much of the richness in the passing experience must have been rapidly accommodated in the generation of the fitting perceptual belief. So, attention to such real-life epistemic chores and accomplishments points to the respect in which the foundationalists' attention to the perceptual state/perceptual belief-pair invites attention to a wider range of processing.

Turn now to the second, and more serious, misgiving about the two-stage conception of the etiology of perceptual beliefs. The modest foundationalist suggestion is basically that, at the level of classically accessible states, perceptual states directly spawn perceptual beliefs, and that as so based, perceptual beliefs constitute a homogeneous

---

[16] It is worth noting that even the idea that perceptual experiences causally generate perceptual beliefs may be largely mistaken. Perhaps token perceptual-experiential states themselves typically are also token beliefs—at least in cases where one has no reason to suspect that one's perceptual experiences might be misleading or non-veridical. But, for purposes of simplicity, we ignore this possibility in the text.

class with a uniform measure of first-stage warrant. Differentiation in epistemic justification must await developments (if any) within the posited second stage. We maintain that this two-stage conception not only is psychologically implausible (because collateral information often is apt to figure in the generation of perceptual beliefs right from the start), but also that thereby it artificially simplifies and artificially equates the epistemic statuses of different perceptual beliefs at their inception. Various kinds of collateral information, when operative in the spontaneous formation of perceptual beliefs, can affect in various ways the epistemic status of those beliefs. That is, perceptual beliefs may emerge with very different epistemic warrant *from inception*. Although some perceptual beliefs may emerge with a justification that is not readily put into question and conforms with the modest foundationalist conception of perceptual beliefs, there are two other ways (not exclusive of one another) that perceptual beliefs can emerge instead. First, some perceptual beliefs may emerge 'with a warning flag,' since the agent has from the start the sense that the belief, while reasonable, *needs* further checking. Second, some perceptual beliefs may depend epistemically, in part, upon a body of background information so rich that these beliefs could not plausibly be considered epistemically basic in the traditional foundationalist sense. Let us consider these latter two cases, in turn.

Warning flags: Return to our example of the glimpsed rat. One might form the belief that yonder goes a rat with a clear title or entitlement. No questions asked, and none that epistemically need be asked. But one might form a belief with just that content in a more tenuous manner that incorporates from the start an awareness of the need to investigate further (and not just about where the rat went, but also to 'get a better look.') The agent might from the start have a sense that the belief was just barely warranted, just barely reasonable, and the agent might desire more. In either case, inarticulable details of the passing experience may influence the production of the perceptual belief in pivotal ways. But background information might also be automatically accommodated in the production of the perceptual belief itself. Perhaps one has a standing belief that the neighborhood is not (or is) conducive to maintaining a rat population; perhaps one believes that there are few (or plentiful) sources of food to draw such vermin; etc. Such expectations are known to color perceptual beliefs—something that can also happen with the pertinent expectations operating morphologically.

Now, a perceptual belief that arises with cautionary flags—'warranting further checks'—is not a proper stopping place for justification of the sort that the foundationalist imagines. So, not all perceptual beliefs come with the envisioned entitlement to serve as stopping places in some regress of justification. Thus arises the epistemic nonhomogeneity of the class of perceptual beliefs. As a consequence, where one is entitled to rest in the course of explicit justificatory thought is also nonhomogeneous. Sometimes a perceptual belief will be firm as a foundation. Other times, one will need to articulate general background information supporting the perceptual belief, or undermining it. This is to reject (F4).

Rich background information: One can trace at least part of the flaw in (F4) to the associated 'two distinct stages view' of the epistemically relevant processing. For, the two-stages view seems to envision a first stage in which perceptual beliefs are pretty much created equal—after all, they are all spawned by supporting perceptual states. But, as we have already indicated, the distortion effected by (F4) and the two-stages view is that they cover over epistemic heterogeneity that can be appreciated when looking beyond what is the classic epistemic focus on accessible states. We have already remarked that the heterogeneity of perceptual beliefs—their differing entitlement to serve as regress-stoppers in the classic foundationalist fashion—is the result of their being spawned by processes that automatically accommodate much information only briefly present in the perceptual state, and much information in the form of background information antecedently held. In effect, some of what foundationalists would see as the business of the alleged second stage is already involved from the start. As a result, the two-stage understanding is bound to oversimplify things. The result is a distorting view of perceptual beliefs as a homogeneous set of beliefs with epistemic warrant appropriate to regress-stopping. Note the two claims here. First, due to the rich information commonly accommodated in the generation of perceptual beliefs, the two-stage model is distorting. Second, due to that information, perceptual beliefs at their inception may have various epistemic statuses. So, they do not all at their inception constitute a homogeneous class of regress-stopping beliefs. For instance, a spontaneous perceptual belief, concerning a briefly glimpsed object, that *that was an iPhone*, may serve as a basic belief from its inception, or it may not. Much depends on how it arises out of the myriad background information—the morphological content—to which the agent in question was sensitive in the episode—and also upon information-rich details of the original experience that are not retained in memory. It may arise with 'warning flags,' or without.

When the above considerations are acknowledged, and (F4) is abandoned as an overly crude approximation, then one arrives at what we are calling quasi-foundationalism— the view asserting that (F1$_{a/m}$)–(F3$_{a/m}$) characterize propositional justification at the level of classically accessible states. When one's concern is with classically accessible states and processes, some perceptual beliefs can serve as regress-stoppers, whereas others are from their inception in need of further propositional justification at that level. However, quasi-foundationalism denies that such regress-stopping states constitute a homogeneous class or a small set of homogeneous classes (thereby repudiating (F4)), and it claims instead that the beliefs that are regress-stoppers within the *accessible* EPS still need global-coherentistic evidential support within the *whole* EPS. Quasi-foundationalism thus also repudiates the traditional idea that the whole edifice of global epistemic justification rests upon a foundation of basic beliefs.

The upshot of the present section is that although certain ideas from traditional foundationalism can and should be incorporated into iceberg epistemology, they ought to be embraced only in significantly altered form. Although beliefs of the kind traditionally considered nonbasic often do enjoy justificatory support from other beliefs, that support is typically mediated by background information in the epistemic psychological system—much of it morphological. Likewise, although beliefs of the kind traditionally considered basic often do enjoy justificatory support from non-doxastic states such as perceptual-experiential states, this kind of justificatory support too is typically mediated by background information, including morphological content. Furthermore, although some beliefs are indeed 'basic' at the above-surface level in iceberg epistemology, in the sense that legitimate demands for the articulate giving of justification normally cannot be lodged against such beliefs, beliefs that are basic in this sense do not automatically constitute a homogeneous set, or several homogeneous sets; rather, the above-surface regress only stops when below-surface morphological features are suitably stable. Finally, the beliefs that are epistemically basic above the surface still require global-coherentistic justification within the whole epistemic iceberg, as do other beliefs. Thus, the traditional foundationalist vision, of an edifice of justified beliefs that rests holistically upon a foundation of basic beliefs that themselves need no systemic justification at all, is repudiated.

3.4 Transforming structural contextualism

So far we have argued that coherentism is essentially correct as an account of the structure of belief-justifying support-relations within the whole EPS, and that certain key themes from foundationalism are applicable to the (background-mediated) structure of belief-justifying support-relations within the accessible portion of the whole EPS. But foundationalist ideas have been accommodated only in a partial and limited way as regards the accessible, leaving ample room for structural contextualism to apply to the accessible EPS too.

Three specific aspects of our proposed partial accommodation of foundationalism are especially salient, and each points to a respect in which structural-contextualist ideas should be incorporated too. First, we have emphasized that in general, justificatory-support relations within the accessible EPS itself are *epistemically mediated* relations, i.e. they confer justificatory support upon the agent's beliefs only against a very rich background of morphological content—a background that renders the *whole* EPS globally coherent. In light of this fact, the kinds of accessible, readily articulable, evidential considerations that will suffice as legitimate answers to legitimate real-life demands for epistemic justification normally will be *local* components of one's accessible EPS—and normally will only count as justificatory given a specific context in which enormous amounts of globally-holistically coherence-related background information is taken for granted, and is cognitively accommodated automatically and implicitly. Thus, at the above-surface level of articulable justification within the overall epistemic iceberg, the relevant kinds of coherence-relations will be fairly local rather than holistic, even though they are situated in the context of a taken-for-granted background of globally coherent psychological states. At the level of reasons that can be explicitly considered, holistic virtues such as explanatory coherence can feature episodically, but only episodically, and can feature only fairly locally rather than strictly globally. So, our recommended version of iceberg epistemology accommodates the following variant of the contextualist thesis (X1), with the subscript 'a' indicating that it pertains to the level of accessible aspects of the agent's EPS:

(X1$_a$) Holistic virtues such as explanatory coherence play some role in one's having justification for what one believes, but such desiderata apply not globally within the accessible EPS, but only locally in the context of a rich background of information that is taken for granted.

Second, we have emphasized that within the accessible EPS, certain beliefs do sometimes have the status of regress-stoppers. As far as matters of articulable justification are concerned, these may legitimately be treated, in context, as the source-points for articulable justification and as not needing justification themselves. This modest kind of epistemic basicness, as expressed in the foundationalist thesis (F$_{a/m}$), comports smoothly with the following variant of the contextualist thesis (X2), which we propose to embrace too:

(X2$_a$) Justificatory chains of support relations commonly have a linear structure and terminate in regress-stopping beliefs (that the agent is justified in holding) that are not susceptible to, or 'helped by' further justificatory support.

This may now be understood to say that many justificatory-exposed processes have a linear character. Certainly this is commonly so when the articulable justification for one's belief emanates from perceptual beliefs that are themselves contextually appropriate stopping-points, for example. Often in such cases, one arrives at a belief or set of beliefs that seem unchallenged, and any reasons one might adduce to support them would be less secure than are these perceptual bases. The belief that the coffee in one's mouth is hot is commonly not helped by supporting reasons—at least not at the level of articulating what is accessible. All sorts of information may condition such perceptual beliefs in the background (below the surface of what is accessible). One can get some sense for this by thinking of cases in which one's background information might emerge into a kind of salience. One's perception of hot coffee might call for some support if one believes that one is presently embedded in a society in which coffee is prohibited, or that severe energy shortages have led to the clever use of chemicals or spices to give some drinks the mere appearance of warmth. With certain background information, further support might then be called for. What would call for this further support must be understood as a delicate matter, involving the potential relevance of anything to anything (isotropy again). Holistic chores in the background make for a certain heterogeneity at the level of the accessible.

Third, we have repudiated thesis (F4)—not only with respect to the whole EPS, but with respect to the accessible EPS too; i.e. we have denied that the beliefs that qualify (in context, and within the accessible EPS) as regress-stoppers constitute a homogeneous class or small set of homogeneous classes. Moreover, we have argued that in general, beliefs that count as regress-stoppers within the accessible portion of the EPS still require global-coherentist justificatory support within the whole epistemic iceberg. These two interrelated themes, which prompted us to call the resulting view 'quasi-foundationalist' rather than full-bloodedly foundationalist, together amount to eschewing the venerable foundationalist idea of a global edifice of justified beliefs that is ultimately supported entirely by epistemically self-secure basic beliefs. Instead, above-surface justification always depends upon a background of information that is taken for granted in context. Thus, iceberg epistemology also embraces this version of the contextualist thesis (X3):

(X3$_a$) The structure of support relations between accessible beliefs (described in (X1$_a$) and (X2$_a$)) is ultimately determined by a context which (at least partly) takes the form of a body of information that is implicitly present psychologically, is not fully articulable, and is (in effect) taken for granted.

Within iceberg epistemology, of course, background information that is taken for granted in contexts of real-life justification-giving, and is treated in such contexts as not in need of justification itself, nevertheless does figure in a holistic justificatory structure within the *whole* EPS—namely a globally coherentist structure. In contrast to standard versions of structural contextualism, which typically seek to reject altogether the idea that there is or needs to be a global structure of epistemic justification, iceberg epistemology acknowledges the need for a globally coherent EPS. Real believers need to accommodate the holistic, Quineian/isotropic aspects of evidential support. The trick is to do it in a way that is largely implicit and automatic, with heavy reliance on morphological content.

There yet might seem to be a tension between our suggested vindication of coherentism concerning the whole EPS, and certain contextualist arguments rehearsed above. Williams (1977, 1980) argues that, whatever there is to coherentism, it cannot be understood as requiring agents to 'put everything up for grabs at once,' as if all beliefs are to be momentarily suspended so that one might seek the best or most coherent system (with none of the agent's extant beliefs anchoring this process). Because epistemic standards themselves are influenced by one's understanding of the world in which one lives (recall the modulational control demanded in our discussion of global and transglobal reliabilism), 'putting everything up for grabs at once' in this sense would be incoherent. If this were the project, then arguably there would not be any sense to be made of what makes one holistic solution better than another—since all supposed virtues of belief systems would be up for grabs along with the belief systems themselves. Think of this as a contextualist constraint on an acceptable holism—since it represents a constraint on how one should understand the coherentist chores that we seek to honor within our revised coherentism. The argument and constraint seem to apply at the level of the whole chunk of ice just as well as at the level of accessible processes.

What this shows is that the processes operative below the surface should not be understood as 'bracketing' everything and putting it all up for grabs at once. Notably, this is not how we described holistic belief fixation. Rather, we represented such processing as involving vast ranges of information that must be accommodated automatically and largely morphologically, in light of the isotropic and the Quineian aspects of evidential support. There is admittedly a sense in which the information that comes into play in that processing is revisable. Insofar as it gets represented, it may itself be put into doubt. But, this is not to say that such information is simply up for grabs. Although such information is accommodated without being explicitly represented, still the sensitivities to which that information (or morphological content) contributes are subject to feedback, and thus to replacement or revision. Quine's venerable figure of a field of force seems appropriate, along with his famous invocation of Neurath's figure of the sailor making repairs at sea (1960, pp. 3–5). These remarks may be understood as further clarifying the refined form of coherentism vindicated within our iceberg epistemology.

Structural contextualists such as Annis (and Williams—or Wellman in moral epistemology), influenced by the later Wittgenstein, were always revisionary epistemologists of a sort. They sought to cautiously take up and refashion more traditional themes. Our own iceberg epistemology puts us in a similar business. We recognize much that is to be salvaged in the traditional foundationalist and coherentist epistemologies, but reflection on the character of human epistemic competence leads us also to recognize that epistemology must come to terms with the importance of morphological content in human cognitive capacities. This has led to a rethinking of the more traditional epistemologies, with the result that each has important truths to express. And because the truths apply at different levels, the positions should be understood as noncompeting (under revision). We are coherentists, of a stripe: coherentists at the level of the 'whole chunk of ice,' the full cognitive dynamic that makes for human epistemic competence. We are foundationalists, of a stripe—at least quasi-foundationalists with respect to the 'exposed' processes, those processes contributing to human epistemic competence at the level of what is largely classically accessible to the reflective agent. The qualified term 'quasi-foundationalism' signals the recognition that the beliefs that serve as regress-stoppers are not as homogeneous as traditional foundationalists would have thought, and are foundational only at the exposed surface (and modulo-implicit background information), rather than being foundational within the 'whole chunk of ice'. This heterogeneity of regress-stoppers at the accessible level reflects the effects of much information being accommodated at the background level. Thus, we are structural contextualists, of a stripe. The kind of context we emphasize is not social and interpersonal, but rather is provided by the vast range of information that a normal adult human agent will have acquired with her or his own epistemic psychological system—information that will often take the form of morphological content, and will often be accommodated automatically in the course of competent belief fixation.

In closing, let us note some ways of potentially incorporating further contextualist ideas within the ecumenical approach just sketched. Central to this approach is the idea that a context or background can be reconstructed within iceberg epistemology in ways that draw on the distinction between exposed processes and submerged processes. Treating structural contextualism as a story about the structure of exposed processes—one that appeals to a context involving informational resources which modulate those processes—one can naturally think of the context as itself understood (at least to a good first approximation) in terms of the resources and dynamic of information at the submerged level. We ourselves believe that this goes a long way toward vindicating the basic contextualist claims. However, we have set to the side the rather common contextualist idea that the context is to be understood in social terms—say, in terms of what one's interlocutors will let one get away with, or let pass without challenge. We need not resist this idea. It could prove a fruitful addition to our approach (although this raises questions about how to integrate individual-level epistemology with social epistemology). One possibility, which we think would be worth pursuing, is the idea that all competent agents have and necessarily deploy the kind of individual-level contextual sensibility that we have sketched. But, of course, such agents are embedded in a community, and this community might be thought of as cumulatively constituting a kind of distributed contextualist sensibility. Differences in the individual sensibilities might then lead the community to jointly explore considerations, misgivings, avenues of alternative inquiry, and the like, in a particularly efficient way.[17]

4 Summary

Iceberg epistemology repudiates all variants of the psychological prototheory *PT*, on the grounds that belief fixation on the model of *PT* would be utterly intractable for human cognizers. Yet iceberg epistemology also acknowledges that real-life belief fixation nonetheless does need to accommodate enormous amounts of holistic, Quineian/isotropic, information. Much of this accommodation presumably is and must be essentially morphological, involving the automatic and implicit use of information that is embodied in the standing structure of the cognitive system and does not get explicitly represented in the course of belief fixation.

On this conception of the cognitive processing involved in belief fixation, the epistemic psychological system—the system of psychological states that possess and/

---

[17] Kitcher (1993) provides some useful suggestions along these lines. See also, Goldberg (2010) and Henderson (2009). Having said this much, let us mention a potential way of incorporating themes from parameter contextualism. It is presumably in conversation, broadly understood, that members of a community would contribute to the joint contextual sensibility just suggested. So, one might imagine that conversational contexts are not the sort of free creations of moves in a language game that it sometimes seems in parameter-contextualist discussions. Rather, contextual parameters are properly set by a kind of community pumping of individual backgrounds or contextual sensibilities. (This is not to deny that the individual sensibilities are themselves influenced by training within communities.)

or confer justification upon an agent's beliefs—is to be construed in accordance with liberalism about the component question, rather than minimalism or conservatism. That is, the full EPS comprises not only prototypical beliefs both occurrent and dispositional, and not only these plus certain additional occurrent intentional states such as perceptual seemings and intellectual seemings, but also a vast range of morphologically intentional states as well.

When the EPS is conceived in this way, two kinds of questions arise concerning the structure of propositional justification exhibited by the intentional states in a cognitive agent's EPS. On one hand are questions about unmediated propositional-justification relations within the whole EPS (the full epistemic iceberg). On the other hand are questions about mediated propositional-justification relations within the consciously accessible portion of the EPS (the above-surface portion of the iceberg), with the morphologically intentional states relegated to the taken-for-granted mediating background. Propositional justification thus has a two-tiered structure.

The version of iceberg epistemology we have expounded and defended in this chapter incorporates and synthesizes key ideas from all three erstwhile competing traditional positions in epistemology concerning the structure of epistemic justification. Unmediated propositional justification within the entire EPS is a matter of global-coherence relations among all the states in the EPS, including morphologically intentional states and non-doxastic states like perceptual seemings and intellectual seemings.

On the other hand, mediated propositional justification within the accessible EPS exhibits some key features stressed by foundationalists, some stressed by structural contextualists, and some that are common to both views. Above-surface, articulable justification rests on certain beliefs that are rightly treated as regress-stoppers—as stressed by both foundationalism and contextualism. Other beliefs typically are justified in a linear inferential fashion, so that above-surface justification exhibits a foundational structure—as stressed by foundationalists. Although considerations of coherence often figure in the above-surface justification of beliefs that are not regress-stoppers, explicit justificatory appeals to matters of coherence must be fairly local rather than global—as stressed by coherentists.

Traditional theories of the structure of justification were incompatible with one another because they shared two assumptions that are jettisoned by iceberg epistemology: first, that the right answer to the component question concerning the EPS is some version of either minimalism or conservatism, and second, that the prototheory *PT* rightly describes the kind of belief-fixing cognitive processing that is needed in order for an agent's propositionally justified beliefs to qualify as doxastically justified. We have argued that both of these assumptions are profoundly mistaken. Once they are rejected, what emerges is a two-tiered account of the structure of epistemic justification that incorporates aspects of all three of the traditional positions.

Bibliography

Alston, W. 1985: 'Concepts of Epistemic Justification.' *The Monist* 68: pp. 57–89.
—— 1989: 'An Internalist Externalism,' in W. Alston, *Epistemic Justification: Essays in the Theory of Knowledge*. Ithaca, NY: Cornell University Press.
Annis, D. 1978: 'A Contextualist Theory of Epistemic Justification.' *American Philosophical Quarterly* 15: pp. 213–9.
Audi, R. 1993: The Structure of Justification. Cambridge: Cambridge University Press.
Beecher, H. 1955: 'The Powerful Placebo.' *Journal of the American Medical Association* 159: pp. 1602–6.
Berg, G. 1992: 'A Connectionist Parser with Recursive Sentence Structure and Lexical Disambiguation,' in AAAI-92: Proceedings of the Tenth National Conference on Artificial Intelligence. Cambridge, MA: AAAI Press/MIT Press.
Bishop, M. and Trout, J. 2005a: *Epistemology and the Psychology of Human Judgment*. New York, Oxford University Press.
—— 2005b: 'The Pathologies of Standard Analytic Epistemology.' *Nous* 39: pp. 696–714.
Block, N. and Stalnaker, R. Forthcoming: 'Conceptual Analysis, Dualism, and the Explanatory Gap.' *Philosophical Review*.
BonJour, L. 1985: *The Structure of Empirical Knowledge*. Cambridge, MA: Harvard University Press.
—— 1995: 'Sosa on Knowledge, Justification, and Aptness.' *Philosophical Studies* 78: pp. 207–20.
—— 1998: *In Defense of Pure Reason*. Cambridge: Cambridge University Press.
—— 2002: *Epistemology: Classic Problems and Contemporary Responses*. Oxford: Rowman and Littlefield.
Brandom, R. 1994: *Making it Explicit*. Cambridge, MA: Harvard University Press.
Brink, D. 1997: 'Kantian Rationalism: Inescapability, Authority, and Supremacy,' in G. Cullity and G. Berys (eds), *Ethics and Practical Reason*. Oxford: Clarendon Press.
Burge, T. 1993: 'Content Preservation.' *Philosophical Review* 102: pp. 457–88.
Casullo, A. 1988: 'Revisability, Reliability, and A Priori Knowledge.' *Philosophy and Phenomenological Research* 49: pp. 187–213.
—— 2003: *A Priori Justification*. New York: Oxford University Press.
Chalmers, D. 1996: *The Conscious Mind*. Oxford: Oxford University Press.
—— Forthcoming: 'The Components of Content.' *Mind*.
Chernaik, C. 1986: *Minimal Rationality*, Cambridge, MA: MIT Press.
Churchland, P. 1989: *A Neurocomputational Perspective*. Cambridge, MA: MIT Press.
—— 1992: 'A Deeper Unity: Some Feyerabendian Themes in Neurocomputational Perspective,' in R. Giere (ed.), *Cognitive Models of Science*, Minnesota Studies in the Philosophy of Science, vol. 15. Minneapolis: University of Minnesota Press, pp. 341–63.
Cohen, S. 1987: 'Knowledge, Context, and Social Standards.' *Synthese* 73: pp. 3–26.
—— 1988: 'How to be A Fallibilist.' *Philosophical Perspectives* 2: pp. 91–123.

Cohen, S. 1999: 'Contextualism, Skepticism, and the Structure of Reasons.' *Philosophical Perspectives* 13: pp. 57–89.

—— 2005: 'Knowledge, Speaker and Subject.' *Philosophical Quarterly* 66: pp. 199–212.

Conee, E. and Feldman, R. 2004: 'Evidentialism,' in E. Connee and R. Feldman (eds), *Evidentialism: Essays in Epistemology*. New York: Oxford University Press, pp. 83–100.

—— 2004: *Evidentialism: Essays in Epistemology*, New York: Oxford University Press.

Cummins, R. 1975: 'Functional Analysis.' *Journal of Philosophy* 72: pp. 741–60.

—— 1983: *The Nature of Psychological Explanation*. Cambridge, MA: MIT Press.

Darden, L. 1992: 'Strategies for Anomaly Resolution,' in R. Giere (ed.), *Cognitive Models of Science*. Minnesota Studies in the Philosophy of Science, vol. 15. Minneapolis: University of Minnesota Press, pp. 251–73.

Davidson, D. 1983: 'A Coherence Theory of Truth and Knowledge,' in D. Henrich (ed.), *Kant oder Hegel*. Stuttgart: Klett-Cotta Buchhandlung, pp. 423–38.

DeRose, K. 1992: 'Contextualism and Knowledge Attribution.' *Philosophy and Phenomenological Research* 52: pp. 913–29.

—— 1995: 'Solving the Skeptical Problem.' *Philosophical Review* 104: pp. 1–52. Reprinted in K. DeRose and T. Warfield (eds), *Skepticism: A Contemporary Reader*. Oxford: Oxford University Press (1999).

—— 2004: 'The Problem with Subject-Sensitive Invariantism.' *Philosophy and Phenomenological Research* 68: pp. 346–50.

—— 2009: *The Case for Contextualism: Knowledge, Skepticism, and Context*, vol. 1. Oxford: Oxford University Press.

—— and Warfield, T. 1999: *Skepticism: A Contemporary Reader*. Oxford: Oxford University Press.

Dreyfus, H. and Dreyfus, S. 1986: 'How to Stop Worrying about the Frame Problem Even though It's Computationally Insoluble,' in Z. Pylyshn (ed.), *The Robot's Dilemma: The Frame Problem in Artificial Intelligence*. Norwood, NJ: Ablex, pp. 95–111.

Dretske, F. 1970: 'Epistemic Operators.' *Journal of Philosophy* 67: pp. 1007–1023. Reprinted in K. DeRose and T. Warfield (eds), *Skepticism: A Contemporary Reader*. Oxford: Oxford University Press (1999).

Evans-Pritchard, E. 1937: *Witchcraft, Oracles and Magic among the Azande*. Oxford: Clarendon Press.

Fodor, J. 1983: *The Modularity of Mind: An Essay in Faculty Psychology*. Cambridge MA: MIT Press.

—— 2001: *The Mind Doesn't Work That Way: The Scope and Limits of Computational Psychology*. Cambridge, MA: MIT Press.

—— and Pylyshyn, Z. 1988: 'Connectionism and Cognitive Architecture: A Critical Analysis.' *Cognition* 35: p. 183–204.

Foley, R. 1993: *Working Without a Net: A Study of Egocentric Epistemology*. Oxford: Oxford University Press.

Giere, R. 1992: *Cognitive Models of Science*. Minnesota Studies in the Philosophy of Science, vol. 15. Minneapolis: University of Minnesota Press.

Gigerenzer, G. 2007: *Gut Feeling: The Intelligence of the Unconscious*. London: Viking Publishing.

—— 2008: *Rationality for Mortals*. Oxford: Oxford University Press.

—— and Hoffrage, U. 1995: 'How to Improve Bayesian Reasoning Without Instruction: Frequency Formats.' *Psychological Review* 102: p. 684–704.

—— and Selten, R. (eds) 2002: *Bounded Rationality: The Adaptive Toolbox*. Cambridge, MA: MIT Press.

Glymour, C. 1980: *Theory and Evidence*. Princeton, NJ: Princeton University Press.

Goldberg, S. 2010: *Relying on Others*. Oxford: Oxford University Press.

Goldman, A. 1976: 'What Is Justified Belief?' in G.S. Pappas (ed.), *Justification and Knowledge*. Dordrecht: D. Reidel.

—— 1986: *Epistemology and Cognition*. Cambridge, MA: Harvard University Press.

—— 1992a: 'Strong and Weak Justification,' in A. Goldman, *Liaisons*. Cambridge, MA: MIT Press.

—— 1992b: 'Epistemic Folkways and Scientific Epistemology,' in A. Goldman, *Liaisons*. Cambridge, MA: MIT Press.

—— 1992c: 'Psychology and Philosophical Analysis,' in A. Goldman, *Liaisons*. Cambridge, MA: MIT Press.

—— 1999: 'A Priori Warrant and Naturalistic Epistemology.' *Philosophical Perspectives* 13: pp. 1–28.

—— and Pust, J. 1998: 'Philosophical Theory and Intuitional Evidence,' in M. DePaul and P. Ramsey (eds), *The Psychology of Intuition and Its Role in Philosophical Inquiry*. Lanham, MD: Rowman and Littlefield.

Goodman, N. 1973: *Fact, Fiction, and Forecast*, 3rd edition. Indianapolis: Bobbs-Merrill.

Graham, G. and Horgan, T. 1988: 'How to be Realistic About Folk Psychology.' *Philosophical Psychology* 1: pp. 69–81.

—— 1991: 'In Defense of Southern Fundamentalism.' *Philosophical Studies* 62: pp. 107–34.

—— 1994: 'Southern Fundamentalism and the End of Philosophy.' *Philosophical Issues* 5: pp. 219–47.

Greco, J. 2000: *Putting Skeptics in Their Place*. Cambridge: Cambridge University Press.

Haack, S. 1993: *Evidence and Inquiry: Towards Reconstruction in Epistemology*. Oxford: Blackwell Publishing.

Harman, G. 1988: *Change in View*. Cambridge, MA: MIT Press.

Henderson, D. 1988: 'The Importance of Explanation in Quine's Principle of Charity.' *Philosophy of Social Science* 18: pp. 355–69.

—— 1993: *Interpretation and Explanation in the Human Sciences*. Albany: SUNY press.

—— 1994a: 'Epistemic Competence.' *Philosophical Papers* 23: pp. 139–67.

—— 1994b: 'Epistemic Competence and Contextualist Epistemology.' *Journal of Philosophy* 91: pp. 627–49.

—— 1995: 'One Naturalized Epistemological Argument Against Coherentist Accounts of Empirical Knowledge.' *Erkenntnis* 43: pp. 199–227.

—— 2008: 'Testimonial Belief and Epistemic Competence.' *Nous* 42: pp. 190–221.

—— 2009: 'Motivated Contextualism' *Philosophical Studies* 142: pp. 119–31.

—— and Horgan, T. 2000a: 'What Is A Priori And What Is It Good For?' *Southern Journal of Philosophy: The Role of the A Priori (and of the A Posteriori) in Epistemology*, Spindel Conference Supplement 38: pp. 51–86.

—— 2000b: 'Iceberg Epistemology.' *Philosophy and Phenomenological Research* 61: pp. 497–535.

—— 2001: 'Practicing Safe Epistemology.' *Philosophical Studies* 102: pp. 227–58.

Henderson, D. and Horgan, T. 2001: 'The A Priori Isn't All That It Is Cracked Up to Be, But It Is Something.' *Philosophical Topics*, pp. 219–50.

—— 2003: 'What Does It Take to Be a True Believer? Against the Opulent Ideology of Eliminative Materialism' in C. Erneling and D. Johnson (eds), *Mind as a Scientific Object: Between Brain and Culture*. Oxford: Oxford University Press.

—— 2007: 'The Ins and Outs of Transglobal Reliabilism,' in Sanford Goldberg (ed.), *Internalism and Externalism in Semantics and Epistemology*. New York: Oxford University Press, pp. 100–130.

—— 2008: 'Would You Really Rather Be Lucky Than Good? On the Normative Status of Naturalizing Epistemology,' in Chase Wrenn (ed.), *Naturalism, Reference and Ontology: Essays in Honor of Roger F. Gibson*. New York: Peter Lang Publishing, pp. 47–76.

—— and Potrč, M. 2007: 'Transglobal Evidentialism-Reliablism.' *Croatian Journal of Philosophy* 22: pp. 281–300.

—— 2008: 'Transglobal Evidentialism-Reliabilism.' *Acta Analytica* 22 (2007): pp. 281–300.

Horgan, T. 1979: '"Could," Possible Worlds, and Moral Responsibility.' *Southern Journal of Philosophy* 17: pp. 345–58.

—— 1985: 'Compatibilism and the Consequence Argument.' *Philosophical Studies* 47: pp. 339–56.

—— 1993: 'The Austere Ideology of Folk Psychology.' *Mind & Language* 8, pp. 282–97.

—— 1997a: 'Connectionism and the Philosophical Foundations of Cognitive Science.' *Metaphilosophy* 28: pp. 1–30.

—— 1997b: 'Modeling the Noncomputational Mind: Reply to Litch.' *Philosophical Psychology* 10: pp. 365–71.

—— and Tienson, J. 1994: 'A Nonclassical Framework for Cognitive Science.' *Synthese* 101: pp. 305–45.

—— 1995: 'Connectionism and the Commitments of Folk Psychology.' *Philosophical Perspectives* 9: pp. 127–52.

—— 1996: *Connectionism and the Philosophy of Psychology*. Cambridge, MA: MIT Press.

—— and Graham, G. 2004: 'Phenomenal Intentionality and the Brain in a Vat,' in R. Schantz (ed.), *The Externalist Challenge*. Berlin: Walter de Gruyter, pp. 297–317.

Horgan, T. and Timmons, M. 2000: 'Nondescriptive Cognitivism: Framework for a New Metaethic.' *Philosophical Papers* 29: pp. 121–55.

Jackson, P. 1998: *From Metaphysics to Ethics: A Defense of Conceptual Analysis*. Oxford: Clarendon Press.

Johnson-Laird, P. 1983: *Mental Models*. Cambridge, MA: Harvard University Press.

—— 2005: 'Mental Models and Thought,' in K. Holyoak and R. Morrison (eds), *The Cambridge Handbook of Thinking and Reasoning*. Cambridge: Cambridge University Press, pp. 185–208.

—— 2006: *How We Reason*. Oxford: Oxford University Press.

—— and Byrne, R. 2002: 'Conditionals: A Theory of Meaning, Pragmatics, and Inference.' *Psychological Review* 109: pp. 648–78.

—— Legrenzi, P., Girotto, V., Legrenzi, M. and Caverni, J. 1999: 'Naïve probability: A mental model theory of extensional reasoning.' *Acta Psychologica* 93: pp. 62–88.

Kahneman, D. and Frederick, S. 2005: 'A Model of Heuristic Judgment,' in K. Holyoak and R. Morrison (eds), *The Cambridge Handbook of Thinking and Reasoning*. Cambridge: Cambridge University Press, pp. 267–93.

—— Slovic, P. and Tversky, A. 1982: *Judgment Under Uncertainty: Heuristics and Biases*. Cambridge: Cambrige University Press.

—— and Tversky A. 1972: 'Subjective Probability: A Judgment of Representativeness.' *Cognitive Psychology* 3: pp. 430–54.
—— and Tversky, A. 1973: 'On the psychology of prediction.' *Psychological Review* 80: pp. 237–51.
Kim, J. 1988: 'What is "Naturalized Epistemology"?' in *Philosophical Perspectives* vol. 2: *Epistemology*, pp. 381–405.
Kitcher, P. 1981: 'Explanatory Unification.' *Philosophy of Science* 48: pp. 507–31.
—— 1983: *The Nature of Mathematical Knowledge*. New York: Oxford University Press.
—— 1992: 'The Naturalist Returns.' *Philosophical Review* 101: pp. 53–114.
—— 1993: *The Advancement of Science*. Oxford: Oxford University Press.
'Knowledge of Knowledge.' *Philosophical Quarterly* 55: pp. 213–35.
Kripke, S. 1972: *Naming and Necessity*. Cambridge, MA: Harvard University Press.
Lee, C. 2008: 'Applied Normative Psychology and the "Strong Replacement" of Epistemology by Normative Psychology.' *Philosophy of the Social Sciences* 38: pp. 55–75.
Lehrer, K. and Cohen, S. 1985: 'Reliability and Justification.' *The Monist* 68: pp. 159–74.
Lewis, D. 1970: 'How to Define Theoretical Terms.' *Journal of Philosophy* 67: pp. 427–46.
—— 1979: 'Scorekeeping in a Language Game.' *Journal of Symbolic Logic* 8: pp. 339–59.
—— 1994: 'Reduction of Mind,' in Samuel Guttenplan (ed.), *A Companion to Philosophy of Mind*. Oxford: Blackwell Publishing, pp. 412–31.
—— 1996: 'Elusive Knowledge.' *Australasian Journal of Philosophy* 74: pp. 549–67. Reprinted in K. DeRose and T. Warfield (eds), *Skepticism: A Contemporary Reader*. Oxford: Oxford University Press (1999).
Lovett, M and Anderson, J. 2005: 'Thinking as a Production System,' in K. Holyoak and R Morrison (eds) *The Cambridge Handbook of Thinking and Reasoning*. Cambridge: Cambridge University Press, pp. 401–30.
Marr, D. 1982: *Vision*. San Francisco, CA: W. H. Freeman.
Miller, R. 1995: 'The Norms of Reason.' *Philosophical Review* 104: pp. 205–45.Miscevic, Nenad (manuscript).
Moser, P. 1989: *Knowledge and Evidence*. Cambridge: Cambridge University Press.
Nersessian, N. 1992: 'How Do Scientists Think?' in R. Giere (ed.), *Cognitive Models of Science*. Minnesota Studies in the Philosophy of Science, vol. 15. Minneapolis: University of Minnesota Press, pp. 3–44.
Nisbett, R. and Ross, L. 1980: *Human Inference: Strategies and Shortcomings in Social Judgment*. Englewood Cliffs, N.J: Prentice Hall.
Nozick, R. 1981: *Philosophical Explanations*. Cambridge, MA: Harvard University Press.
Osman, M. 2004: 'An Evaluation of Dual-Process Theories of Reasoning.' *Psychonomic Bulletin and Review* 11: pp. 988–1010.
Peacocke, C. 1992: *A Study of Concepts*. Cambridge, MA: MIT Press.
—— 1993: 'How Are A Priori Truths Possible?' *European Journal of Philosophy* 1: pp. 175–199.
—— 1998: 'Implicit Conceptions, Understanding and Rationality.' *Philosophical Issues* 9: pp. 43–88.
Plantinga, A. 1993a: *Warrant: The Current Debate*. Oxford: Oxford University Press.
—— 1993b: *Warrant and Proper Function*. Oxford: Oxford University Press.
Polanyi, M. 1958: *Personal Knowledge*. New York: Harper and Row.
Pollack, J. 1990: 'Recursive Distributed Representations.' *Artificial Intelligence* 46: pp. 77–105.
—— 1986: *Contemporary Theories of Knowledge*. Lanham, MD: Rowman and Littlefield.
Potrč, M. 2000: 'Justification Having and Morphological Content.' *Acta Analytica* 24: pp. 151–73.

Pritchard, D. 2005: *Epistemic Luck.* Oxford: Oxford University Press.
—— 2010: 'Knowledge and Understanding,' Part I of D. Pritchard, A. Millar, and A Haddock, *The Nature and Value of Knowledge: Three Investigations.* Oxford: Oxford University Press.
Putnam, H. 1975a: 'The Meaning of Meaning,' in Putnam, *Mind, Language, and Reality: Philosophical Papers*, vol. 2. Cambridge: Cambridge University. Press, pp. 215–71.
—— 1991: *Representation and Reality.* Cambridge, MA: MIT Press.
Quine, W. 1953: 'Two Dogmas of Empiricism,' in W. Quine, From *a Logical Point of View.* Cambridge, MA: Harvard University Press.
—— 1960: *Word and Object.* Cambridge, MA: MIT Press.
—— 1969: 'Epistemology Naturalized,' in W. Quine, *Ontological Relativity and Other Essays.* New York: Columbia University Press.
—— 1986: 'Reply to Morton White,' in L. Hahn and P. Schilpp (eds), *The Philosophy of W. V. Quine.* La Salle, IL: Open Court.
—— 1986: *Philosophy of Logic*, 2nd edition. Cambridge, MA: Harvard University Press/Prentice Hall.
Railton, P. 1996: 'In Search of Nonsubjective Reasons,' in Schneewind, J. (ed.), *Reasons, Ethics, and Society.* Peru, IL: Open Court.
Rumelhart, D. E., Hinton, G. E. and Williams, R. J. 1986: 'Learning Internal Representations by Error Propogation,' in D. E Rumelhart and J. L. McClelland (eds), *Parallel Distributed Processing: Explorations in the Microstructure of Cognition*, vol. 1: *Foundations.* Cambridge, MA: MIT Press, pp. 318–362.
Samuels, R., Stich, S. and Bishop, M. 2002: 'Ending the Rationality Wars: How to Make Disputes about Human Rationality Disappear,' in R. Elio (ed.), *Common Sense, Reasoning, and Rationality.* New York: Oxford University Press, pp. 236–68.
Schaffer, J. 2004: 'From Contextualism to Contrastivism.' *Philosophical Studies* 119: pp. 73–103.
Segal, G. 1989: 'Seeing What Is Not There.' *Philosophical Review* 98: pp. 189–214.
Sejnowksi, T. and Rosenberg, C. 1987: 'Parallel Networks that Learn to Pronounce English Text.' *Complex Systems* 1: pp. 145–68.
Shapere, D. 1982: 'The Concept of Observation in Science and Philosophy.' *Philosophy of Science* 49: pp. 485–525.
—— 1987: 'Method in the Philosophy of Science and Epistemology,' in N. Nersessian (ed.), *The Process of Science.* Dordrecht: Kluwer, pp. 1–39.
Sloman, S. 1996: 'The Empirical Case for Two Systems of Reasoning.' *Psychological Bulletin* 119: pp. 3–22.
Smolensky, P. 1990: 'Tensor Product Variable Binding and the Representation of Symbolic Structures in Connectionist Systems.' *Artificial Intelligence* 46: pp. 159–216.
—— 1995: 'Connectionist Structure and Explanation in an Integrated Connectionist/Symbolic Cognitive Architecture,' in C. MacDonald and G. MacDonald (eds), *Connectionism: Debates on Psychological Explanation*, vol. 2. Oxford: Blackwell Publishing.
Sosa, E. 1991: *Knowledge in Perspective.* Cambridge: Cambridge University. Press.
—— 1991a: 'Reliabilism and Intellectual Virtue,' in E. Sosa, *Knowledge in Context.* Cambridge: Cambridge University Press, pp. 131–45.
—— 1999: 'How Must Knowledge Be Modally Related to What Is Known?' *Philosophical Topics* 26: pp. 373–84.
—— 2000: 'Skepticism and Contextualism.' *Philosophical Issues* 10: pp. 1–18.

—— 2001: 'Goldman's Reliabilism and Virtue Epistemology.' *Philosophical Topics*, vol. 29: pp. 383–400.
—— 2007: *A Virtue Epistemology: Apt Belief and Reflective Knowledge*, vol. 1. Oxford: Oxford University Press.
Stark, H. 1993: 'Rationality is not Algorithmic.' *Kinesis* 20: pp. 16–30.
—— 1994: 'Connectionism and the Form of Rational Norms.' *Acta Analytica* 12: pp. 39–53.
—— 1995: *Rationality Without Rules*, Doctoral Dissertation, University of Memphis.
Stich, S. 1990: *The Fragmentation of Reason*. Cambridge, MA: MIT Press.
Tienson, J. 1990: 'About Competence.' *Philosophical Papers* 14: pp. 19–36.
Timmons, M. 1993: 'Moral Justification in Context.' *The Monist* 76: pp. 360–78.
—— 1996: 'Outline of a Contextualist Moral Epistemology,' in W. Sinnott-Armstrong and Mark Timmons (eds), *Moral Knowledge*. Oxford: Oxford University Press.
Tversky, A. and Kahneman, D. 1974: 'Judgment under uncertainty: Heuristics and biases.' *Science* 185 (4157): pp. 1124–1131.
van Cleve, J. 1979: 'Foundationalism, Epistemic Principles, and the Cartesian Circle.' *Philosophical Review*, 88: pp. 55–91.
Williams, M. 1977: *Groundless Belief*, New Haven: Yale University Press.
—— 1980: 'Coherence, Justification, and Truth.' *Review of Metaphysics* 34; pp. 243–72.
Williamson, T. 2005a: 'Contextualism, Subject-Sensitive Invariantism, and Knowledge of Knowledge.' *The Philosophical Quarterly* 55 (219): pp. 213–235.
—— 2005b: 'Knowledge, Context and the Agent's Point of View,' in G. Pryer and G. Peters (eds), *Contextualism in Philosophy*. New York: Oxford University Press, pp. 91–114.
Woodward, J. 2000: 'Explanation and Invariance in the Special Sciences.' *British Journal for Philosophy of Science* 51: pp. 197–354.

Index

activation landscape *see* landscape, activation landscape
ameliorative psychology 176
Anderson, J. 188
Annis, D. 252, 255, 278
aptness 159–162
Aristotle 139, 172, 181
artificial intelligence 211, 216, 221
Ashley the Valley girl 100–3, 107, 113, 115–6, 119, 127, 130–2, 140, 141, 155, 199
Athena and Fortuna 63–5, 66–9, 70–3, 76–7, 79–81, 91–2, 94, 99–100, 103, 105–6, 115, 129–32, 155, 160
Audi, R. 206–10, 246, 247, 268, 271

Bayesian reasoning 176, 191
Beecher, H. 145
belief
  dispositional or occurrent 174, 205–7, 241–3, 251, 260, 280
  dispositional, occurrent, or morphological 259, 263
Bishop, M. 176, 191
Bonjour, L. 15, 17, 18–20, 25, 83–4, 86–8, 94, 130, 131, 160, 173, 208–10, 217, 248–51, 255, 260, 262, 271
brain-in-vat scenario 3–4, 50–3, 62, 91, 96, 106, 109–10, 112–3, 115, 117, 139, 141, 157, 199
brain lesion 83, 88–9, 130–1
Brandom, R. 30
Burge, T. 246
Byrne, R. 193

Carnap, R. 175
Casullo, A. 19
causal/explanatory 'because' 203, 227–9, 231–4
causation 17
Cherniak, C. 172, 176, 187
Chisholm, R. 169–70
Chomsky, N. 174
Churchland, P. 189, 194
clairvoyance 83–7, 94, 130–1, 152
classical computational models *see* computationalism
cognitive engineering 8, 164–7, 170, 173–4, 180, 184, 197–8
Cohen, S. 50, 95, 253
coherence
  explanatory 248, 250, 254, 261, 275–6
  holistic 175, 209, 248, 252, 253, 260, 262–5, 275, 277, 280
coherentism 1, 5, 8, 169–70, 173, 175, 200, 204, 208–9, 240, 243, 247–55, 257, 258, 259, 260–5, 267, 271, 275, 277–8, 280
competence
  conceptual *see* conceptual competence
  /performance distinction 166, 168, 180
component question 241–4, 246–7, 251–2, 257, 260, 263–4, 280
  conservatism 243, 247, 252, 257, 263–4, 280
  liberalism 243, 247, 252, 257, 261, 263–4, 280
  minimalism 243–4, 246–7, 251–2, 257, 260, 263–4, 280
computationalism 184–6, 188, 189, 199, 214–21, 223–6, 236–7
conceptual competence 6, 32–3, 34–5, 59, 154
  and Goldman 48, 57, 162
  and noise elimination 45–9
  and Peacocke 56
  and the concept of knowledge 37–8, 41, 52–3, 67, 91
  and the high-grade a priori 12, 15, 16, 21–4
  and the low-grade a priori 24–7, 55
Conee, E. 199
connectionism 188–9, 194, 200, 214, 223–6, 229, 235, 237, 258
Connie 115–7
conservatism *see* component question, conservatism
Constance 96–100, 106–7, 115, 117, 119, 124, 126–31, 151, 156, 159–60, 199
constitutive desiderata 81–3, 103, 126, 139, 147, 151, 156
  as end 82, 126–7, 131, 142–4, 150, 159
  as manner and means 82–3, 104, 108–9, 127, 130–2, 150, 159
content externalism 22–3, 96
context
  and competing judgment tendencies 50, 52, 134, 147–52
  and dispositions 137, 187
  and Goldman 48
  and idealization 174–5
  and knowledge *see* knowledge, and context
  effects 48–9
contextualism 51, 142
  parameter 50, 52–3, 252–3
  structural 200, 240, 243, 252

counterfactual
  conditionals 228–9
  dependence 246, 247
crediting 144, 147, 149–50, 161
Cummins, R. 186

Darden, L. 187
Davidson, D. 250–1, 260
DC framework *see* dynamical cognition
declarative information *see* knowledge, procedural and declarative
degenerate processes 92–3, 158, 159
delta rule, the 229–30
demon
  evil demon 50, 51, 91, 110–11, 117–20, 127–30, 138, 154, 157–8, 253
  friendly demon 116–7, 138
  Great Deceiver, the 106–7, 120, 158
  new evil demon problem, the 7, 95–100, 102, 104–6, 128, 139, 152–4, 159–60, 162
deontological epistemic appraisal 9, 143–4
DeRose, K. 50, 253
Descartes, R. 4, 18, 50, 51, 169
Diana and Elena 72–6, 79–81, 93, 99, 100, 130, 132, 160
disposition
  analysis of 186–7, 190
  and causal/explanatory 'because'-claims 228–9
  and the problem of infinities 135–9, 161
  reliability as a 68–9
  to believe *see* belief, dispositional or occurrent
  to modulate 74, 78
  to performance error 174, 178–9, 191
Dreyfus, H. 189
Dreyfus, S. 189
dynamical cognition 223–7, 233–5, 238
dynamical systems theory 215, 224–6, 229–30, 233–5

ecological rationality 192–3
egocentric rationality 10
Elena *see* Diana and Elena
empiricism and rationalism 12, 15–8, 19, 20–2, 59, 246
engineering *see* cognitive engineering
epistemic competence, meliorative 177–9, 183, 188
epistemic dependence 207
epistemic luck 39, 64, 67, 70–1, 76, 107, 126–7, 129–30, 151, 154–5
epistemic normativity 8, 139, 144, 163–71, 174–7, 180–5, 191
epistemic psychological system 241, 243–4, 246–7, 251–2, 257, 259–69, 274–7, 280
EPS *see* epistemic psychological system
erotetic model of explanation 90

E-spectrum 8–9, 126, 163, 166–9, 176–7, 180–3, 194, 195–9
evidentialism 199
experientially possible global environments 3, 7, 108–117, 120–4, 126, 128–30, 135, 138, 140–1, 158
explanatory coherence *see* coherence, explanatory
externalism, content *see* content externalism
externalism, epistemological 1, 3–4

Faith 98–100, 106, 127–9, 131, 160
fake barn scenario 2, 3, 63–7, 69, 70–3, 76–7, 79–81, 91–2, 93, 103, 130
Feldman, R. 199
first philosophy 179, 181
Fodor, J. 214–20, 226, 236
Foley, R. 10
Fortuna *see* Athena and Fortuna
foundationalism 1, 5, 8, 169–70, 200, 204, 240, 244–8, 250, 252–60, 262, 264–5, 267–9, 271–8, 280
  modest 206–8, 246, 247, 250, 268, 271–3
  quasi- 246, 260, 266–9, 271, 274, 277, 278
frame problem 5, 8, 196, 199, 214–9, 221–2, 236–8, 258, 261, 267
  and models of cognition 225–7
Frederick, S. 187, 189, 190, 191, 192
functional analysis 186–90

gambler's fallacy 98–9, 128–9, 187
gatekeeping 144, 147–50, 161, 172
generality problem, the 89–92, 158
generic architectural-engineering question *see* cognitive engineering
Gettier, E. 36–44, 51
Giere, R. 189, 194
Gigerenzer, G. 176, 191–3
Glymour, C. 187
God 18
Goldberg, S. 279
Goldman, A. 3, 48, 56, 57–8, 65, 78, 87, 152–5, 162, 163, 172, 192, 201

Harman, G. 87
Harry and Ike 103–7, 115, 119, 126–7, 129–31, 140–1, 155–6, 158, 160, 199
Hempel, C. G. 236
heuristics 47, 187, 189–93
  recognition heuristic 191–3
  representativeness heuristic 187
high-church computationalism *see* computationalism
Hinton, G. E. 230
Hoffrage, U. 176, 191
holism 74, 86, 173, 175, 195–6, 199–200, 209, 216–25, 231, 236–7, 257, 277

Hume, D. 17
Hypatia *see* Sophie and Hypatia

iceberg epistemology 5, 196, 213, 223, 239–40, 258–61, 263–7, 274–80
idealization 8, 13–4, 30, 56–7, 172–7, 180–1, 183, 201, 213, 233–4
Ike *see* Harry and Ike
internalism, epistemological 1, 3–4, 152, 206, 208, 265
isotropy 215–27, 231–3, 238, 239, 241, 247–8, 258, 260–3, 267, 276–9

Johnson-Laird, P. 187, 193, 194
justification
  conscious accessibility of 204–6, 208, 210–3, 222–3, 239, 258, 280
  doxastic and propositional 4, 61, 95, 199, 200, 201, 203–6, 220, 227, 240–1, 245–7, 256, 257, 258, 280
  ex ante and ex post 201
  objective and subjective 6, 8–9, 10, 61, 95, 99–100, 142, 144, 146, 195–6, 203

Kahneman, D. 187, 189–92
Kant, I. 17
Kim, J. 164
Kitcher, P. 248, 253, 279
knowledge
  and context 50, 52–3, 131, 150–2, 159
  and safety 70, 131–2, 150, 157–9, 162
  conceptual analysis of 26, 36–41, 44–5, 48, 50–3, 67, 131–2, 134, 163, 167, 253
  procedural and declarative 211–4, 223
  tacit 223
Kripke, S. 27

landscape 224
  activation landscape 225, 230, 233–5
Lewis, D. 50, 96, 253
liberalism *see* component question, liberalism
lottery paradox 44–5
Lovett, M. 188
luck *see* epistemic luck

Marr, D. 211, 214
Matrix, The 117, 151–2
meliorative epistemic competence *see* epistemic competence, meliorative
mental models 187, 193–4
meta-reliability 152, 154–7
Mill, J. S. 180
minimalism *see* component question, minimalism
mirroring relation 195, 203–6, 209–10, 227–8, 238, 240–1, 258, 263
Miscevic, N. 58
modularity 215–7

modulation,
  definition of 73–8
morphological content
  definition of 218
Moser, P. 205–6, 209–10, 213
Müller-Lyer illusion 85–6, 89, 243, 244, 252
multiple realizability 188

naturalized epistemology 1, 2, 3, 6–9, 77, 78, 162, 163–72, 175–6, 179–84, 194, 236
Nersessian, N. 187
Neurath, O. 54, 278
new evil demon problem *see* demon
Nisbett, R. 187
noise 45–50, 56
normativity *see* epistemic normativity

observer-expectancy effects 145
Osman, M. 190
ought implies can 171, 195, 265

parameter contextualism 50, 52–3, 146, 149, 252–3, 255, 279
Peacocke, C. 46, 56–8
performance error 30–2, 35, 40, 41, 43–5, 49, 56, 132, 152, 154, 162, 165–6, 170, 173–80, 183, 190, 231, 233
placebo 145–6, 149
Plantinga, A. 10, 88, 131
Polanyi, M. 223
Pollock, J. 214
possible world 22–4, 27, 38, 66, 114, 158, 253
Potrč, M. 199, 201
Pritchard, D. 3, 39, 70, 159
problem of infinities 135–9, 141, 161
procedural information *see* knowledge, procedural and declarative
proceduralization 212–3, 214, 218, 222
projectability of predicates 217
propagation of error 188, 229–30
Pust, J. 56
Putnam, H. 25–7, 33, 48
Pylyshyn, Z. 226

quasi-foundationalism *see* foundationalism, quasi-
Quine, W. 2, 54, 163, 164, 167, 182, 236, 278
Quineian 215–9, 221–7, 231–3, 238, 239, 241, 247–8, 258, 260, 262–3, 267, 277–8, 279

rationalism and empiricism *see* empiricism and rationalism
reciprocal equilibration 31–2, 40, 43–6, 49–50, 56
recognition heuristic *see* heuristics, recognition heuristic

reflective equilibrium 28–9, 32, 35, 43, 53, 97, 181
reliability
  judgments regarding *see* crediting; gatekeeping
  likelihood of 140–1
representativeness assumption 32, 39–43, 45, 50, 56
Ross, L. 187
Rumelhart, D. E. 230

safety
  and knowledge *see* knowledge, and safety
  experiential and de facto 107–9, 118–9, 126–7, 131, 140, 143–4, 150, 159, 161–2
  Pritchard's and Sosa's notion of 3, 70, 153, 157–9
Samuels, R. 191
Schaffer, J. 50
Segal, G. 211
self-justifiers 244, 246, 250, 256
Selten, G. 191
Sextus Pessimisicus 106–7, 119–20, 124, 127, 130–1, 155, 158, 160
Shapere, D. 122, 253
skeptical invariantism 52–3
skepticism 51, 210, 253
Sloman, S. 190
Slovic, P. 190
social epistemology 279
Sophie and Hypatia 144–50
Sosa, E. 3, 70, 95, 152–3, 157–9, 162
Stark, H. 214

Stich, S. 191
Swampman 156–7

teleological epistemic appraisal 9–10, 142–4, 147, 150, 161
testimony 50, 92, 124, 181, 231
Tienson, J. 96, 185, 189, 214, 218, 224–5, 226, 238
Timmons, M. 253
transglobal evidentialism-reliabilism 199, 201
Trevor 151–2
Trout, J. 176
Truman Show, The 103–4, 115,
truth
  conceptual analysis of 41
  objection, the 249
Tversky, A. 187, 189, 190
Twin Earth 25–6, 33, 34, 36, 58

uncertainty 121, 142–4, 149–150, 154, 161
underdetermination 249

van Cleve, J. 169

Wellman, C. 278
Williams, M. 230, 253, 255, 277, 278
Williamson, T. 50
Wittgenstein, L. 252, 254, 256, 278
Woodward, B. 90

young Earth creationism 111, 155–6